Sketches by Hootum the Owl

Sketches by Hootum the Owl

A Satirist's View of Colonial Calcutta

A translation of the original Bengali text, *Hootum Pyanchar Naksha*

Kaliprasanna Sinha

Translated, edited, and with an Introduction by CHITRALEKHA BASU

Foreword by AMIT CHAUDHURI

Illustrations by SUMITRO BASAK

Samya

Sketches by Hootum the Owl: A Satirist's View of Calcutta
was first published in 2012 by SAMYA,
an imprint of Bhatkal and Sen,
16 Southern Avenue, Kolkata 700 026.

ISBN 978-81-85604-86-2
81-85604-86-X

Rs 800.00

Design by SAMYA and Compuset International,
typesetting by Compuset International,
85 Park St, Kolkata 700 016; printed at
Roman Printers Pvt. Ltd., 37 Andul Road
Howrah 711109

Published by Mandira Sen for STREE,
An imprint of Bhatkal and Sen,
16 Southern Avenue, Kolkata 700 026.

To the next writer who
will bring Hootum's panache,
verve and insights when
she/he writes about Calcutta.

Foreword

IT'S TEMPTING, WHEN writing a foreword to a writer's work, to point out parallels between the age that the writer lived in and our own. Ted Hughes' brilliant, concise preface to his own translations of Ovid comes to mind. Yet I wasn't thinking of Hughes' piece when I was wondering what to say about Kaliprasanna Sinha; I'd been reflecting on the strange and unexpected world he inhabited, an India and especially a Calcutta awaiting the imminent arrival of the *bhadralok*, a world inchoate and fairly recently created, already about to be subsumed under the bhadralok's humane vision and his language. That subsuming, in *Hutoom Pyanchar Naksha*, still hasn't quite happened. Kaliprasanna is giving form to an anarchy and variety of life that is synonymous with the rise, from the early nineteenth century, of Calcutta as a colonial and global metropolis, a city as yet without a notion of a great modern author (although two great moderns, Kaliprasanna himself and Michael Madhusudan Dutt, and their principal literary offerings, have, by now, in 1862, just come into existence); without a fixed and recognizable notion of Bengali literature (Bankimchandra Chatterjee, who was quick to notice Kaliprasanna's idiosyncratic genius, would write 'A Popular Literature for Bengal' nine years later, lamenting its absence); or even a safe, working idea of Bengali culture, such as we take for granted today. Tagore, at this moment, is a one-year-old infant. Everything is transient, confusing, uncertain, alive. It's not a culture comprising canons, or great authors and oeuvres, but pictures, posters, bulletins, scandals, and fads (what Sinha, in *Hutoom*, calls *hujug*). It's an age given shape and diversion and colour by the *pat* and the *battala* press. *Hutoom* isn't quite yet, in the year in which it sees the light of day, part of a proper 'literature', as you and I understand that word.

In the last twenty years, we've been living—in India certainly; perhaps even globally—in a similar sort of universe. 'High' culture, even culture, has long lost its autocratic definition; it's difficult to recall in any detail today what it meant to live, and to read and think, governed by its values. Literature as a practice that is distinct and set apart from other practices is a faint memory. We abide in a perpetual present, in the grip of an astonishing range of ephemera, with no ambition towards, or awareness of, immortality. Our battala press produces a range of magazines and journals and newspapers and horoscopes, and furnishes pirated copies of Booker prize-winning bestsellers, self-help books, autobiographies of dictators and sportspeople, the stream of mysticism periodically emanating from Paulo Coelho, and, of course, it gives us Chetan Bhagat. They sit on pavements, the vendors who display these books in an unfurling fan or procession, not under the *bat* or banyan, but at a traffic light or near a restaurant on Park Street. The *bat* is globalization; its branches hang over them, and us, more palpably than any visible roof does. The language of the virtual (and virtual is more actual than the 'real' is today) market is English, as it used to be Bengali and Hindi in the unruly bazars in north Calcutta in Kaliprasanna's age. The 'real' markets, still indefatigably purveying fish and vegetables in Gariahat or at Lake Market, are part of this new, larger market of buying and selling—or they soon will be. And this world has its authors who can't be contained by that anachronistic but persistent word, 'literary': again, Chetan Bhagat comes to mind. Bhagat isn't a 'popular' writer in the sense given to us by modernity: that is, a writer who satisfies tastes and requirements that the more cultured, highbrow authors deliberately ignore. In the new battala world of post-liberalization, post-Nehruvian India, with its embrace and affirmation of the evanescent, its teeming speculative activity, its impatience with the static and enduring, such dichotomies and contrasts don't hold.

But Chetan Bhagat isn't *Hutoom*; he probably wouldn't want to be. Bhagat's concerns (from the little I've been able to deduce from lately dipping into his novels) don't have to do with the intricacies and secrets of neighbourhood, or with the Hokkusai-wave-like assault upon the senses that the city comprises —what the modern, from the nineteenth century onwards (indeed, from Samuel Johnson onwards), generally calls 'life'—but with the urgency of storytelling; of, especially, fulfilling the task that Walter Benjamin said the novel performed in that time, of giving to the reader a likeness of himself. This Bhagat seems to do with élan, given the reader now is a call centre worker, or a young management diploma holder, or a saleswoman who has recently acquired a visa to move to the United States. But Bhagat uses language as if it were a transparent, non-resistant medium, as if it were giving him no trouble at all as he tells his tales. In his newspaper pieces, especially, where he writes about politics and society, his language, like his views, lacks individuality and pressure, and is almost—respectable.

What if we go back to three decades ago, to Salman Rushdie's *Midnight's Children*? Here is a new voice and a new language, in a book published eight years before the fall of the Berlin Wall, ten years before economic liberalization in India, and prescient, in its way, of the energies to be unleashed. Yet its career, compared to *Hutoom*'s, is decidedly literary. Published in 1981, it is hardly noticed, and then, in one of those Arnoldian, disinterested acts of critical judgement, such as is hardly known in India today, and was known little in Kaliprasanna's time, is called in by judges such as Malcolm Bradbury and Germaine Greer for consideration for the Booker Prize for Fiction. The Booker Prize itself, then, was still adjudicated on the lower slopes of Parnassus, and not yet arbitrated by comics, chefs, and former Tory cabinet ministers. What Kaliprasanna or Dickens would have made of the Booker Prize today is something we can only daydream about—I presume they would have portrayed its goings-on with alacrity. It's a cliché to say that globalization turns the world into a village, or at least a small town; but it is also true that to live in that small town entails a gradual dimming in our understanding of what the global or international really means, and a growth of paradoxically parochial pre-occupations and excitements. 'A great event has recently occurred in our parish . . .' says the narrator of *Sketches by Boz*, describing the election for the post of Beadle, '. . . which the country—or at least the parish—it is all the same—will long remember.' That 'it is all the same' is what makes Dickens' book, and *Hutoom*, which pays homage to it, so telling: both Kaliprasanna and Dickens grasped the convergence of the global and the provincial peculiar to the time (as it is to ours—our Beadle's election is the awarding of the Booker prize and other such grandiose events) and made it so comic and unprecedented.

Kaliprasanna died too soon, in 1870, to witness the final, emphatic arrival of 'high' culture in Bengal. Yet 'high' culture was indubitably on its way into that part of the world just as he was on his way out. He cared deeply, with his precocious genius, for that 'high' cultural ferment, whether in Calcutta, or in Europe, in a way that his contemporaries had still not learnt openly to. But, like many elitists, he also had a true sense of the magic of the street, of the cultish and the transitory, of the low and disgusting, of the scurrilous *battala* scandal sheets, of the non-verbal, of what Pound calls the 'barbaric yawp'. He was not yet quite an author in the canonical sense—he was *Hutoom*: all imagery and language, in a way that at once looks forward to the world of modernism, especially to the great novels about cities (*Ulysses* especially comes to mind), which increasingly abandon the notions of 'character', 'description', and 'subject-matter', and become predominantly an efflorescence of language, and also back to the world of anonymous observers and actors, the Kalighat *patuas* and, in other cultures, carnival singers. Both Bankimchandra Chatterjee and, later, Buddhadeva Bose value this confluence in Kaliprasanna, of a 'high' writer giving expression to the uncontainable chaos and richness of a vernacular or colloquial or 'low' stream. Bose, especially, bewails the vanishing of that legacy from the Bengali literature that would follow: of the setting aside of Kaliprasanna's almost invented *chalit* language for Bankim's equally invented, and inventive, *sadhu bhasha*. It is the narrow window of time, with its peculiar confluences and disintegrations, in which *Hutoom* occurs that makes its language and achievement so hard to translate; makes it, also, one of the first treasures of literary modernity. This new, ambitious, and compelling translation allows us to feel the pulse of the time and that author—we can call him nothing else—so that we may respond to what he says (breathlessly, briefly, unforgettably) of his age and our own.

Calcutta, February 2012 AMIT CHAUDHURI

Contents

Kaliprasanna Sinha the Trailblazer

KALIPRASANNA SINHA (1840-70), as he wrote so self-assuredly in *Sketches by Hootum the Owl (Hootum Pyanchar Naksha* in the original Bengali*)*, was indeed 'precocious'. He could not afford not to grow up fast as he had no time to lose. It was almost as if he had a foreboding that he was going to die early and therefore went about hungrily amassing three times the work of an average human being in each year of his all too brief life. He was just thirteen when he founded Vidyotsahini Sabha, a club for propagating Indian literatures, in the wake of an English education boom sweeping across the country. All the members in that club were older than him.

Sinha was like a high-velocity shooting star that consumes itself even as it lights up its own trajectory in a flash of blinding light. Handsome, rich, a hugely popular playwright and performer, a highly revered public intellectual and social activist, Sinha was out-and-out hero material. His daring in protecting 'seditious' elements from the wrath of the British government was awesome, as his philanthropy was of jaw-dropping proportions. Everything about him was large-scale, intense and magnified, including those that had a negative impact on his life. These were overwork, stress, familial troubles and heavy drinking, and the combination turned out to be quite lethal. The man who spent an astronomical Rs.250,000 on publishing and distributing the Bengali translation of the complete *Mahabharat* (at eighteen volumes comprising 220,000 lines, it is supposedly the longest book ever written) from the original Sanskrit was deep in debt when he died.

Sinha was born into old wealth in 1840, in a Bengal that had just about begun to hear the diffused echoes of a Renaissance knocking on the door but its city-bred English-educated elite and old-school, orthodox Hindu traditionalists were too drunk on religious bigotry, social discrimination, widespread corruption and a degenerate lifestyle to wake up and take note. Sinha went to the prestigious Hindu College (now Presidency University), where his grandfather Joykrishna had been one of the founders. In the 1830s, the Hindu College had turned into a volatile cauldron of secular and liberal ideas, the resonances of which could still be heard in its arched corridors in the 1850s. The tension between traditionalist Hindus like Radhakanta Deb and enlightened, westernized students like Krishnamohan Banerjea and Michael Madhusudan Dutt who converted to Christianity was still palpable. Kailashchandra Basu, a teacher of the college, nearly got thrown out after he converted in 1848. The rarefied air that scholars from elite homes were supposed to inhale would get charged with controversies such as the unceremonious dropping of the son of Hira Bulbul, a rich and famous Muslim prostitute, from the college rolls in 1853, after huge protests from parents of Hindu boys from 'decent' homes. Two years later, the government took charge of the college administration, naming it Presidency College and, officially, promising the end of discrimination on religious or caste grounds.

Sinha, who joined the college in the 1850s, might have, if he were around thirty years earlier, been one of the rebellious students banding under the leadership of the Anglo-Indian teacher, atheist and poet Henry Louis Vivian Derozio (1809-31) to challenge the old (conservative, Hindu) order. He had missed the bus, but there was no mistaking the traits he shared with quite a few of Derozio's disciples in Hindu College. Like them he had affluence, pedigree, a progressive outlook, plus a disarming streak of mischief. Even as he mocks the upstart Young Bengal members—self-styled 'atheists' who celebrate Durga Puja by giving in to an unbridled drinking binge in the company of disreputable 'female friends'—Sinha seems to betray a subterranean longing for that very life, their heady spirit of rebellion. Defying the establishment, even in its most frivolous manifestation, seemed to have a symbolic value for him.

He clearly enjoyed a bit of mischief, slipping easily into the mould of the insolent student-narrator (see Sketch 3, 'Idle Talk' p.108) who defeats pandits in verbal duels, claiming their *tiki* (tuft of hair sprouting from the middle of an otherwise shaven head, generic to Brahmin scholars and priests) as a trophy to build his private collection. This little anecdote had a parallel in real life. Sometimes a particularly boisterous lot of students would hop across from Hindu College to the quieter precincts of Sanskrit College and harass, even beat up, the relatively timid breed of teachers and students there. This latter group supposedly comprised the bookish lot who faithfully repeated the classics handed down from antiquity, and therefore deserved the humiliation. The rowdyism by the unruly boys of Hindu College got so rampant that Ishwarchandra Vidyasagar, the Sanskrit College principal, wrote a note to J. Mouat, the secretary of the Education Council, on 28 August, 1852, urging him to intervene. The clash between members of the two colleges was the epitome of the classic East-West confrontation—a symbolic representation of traditional Indian Sanskrit-based learning being challenged by the new western liberal secular ideas, howsoever twisted its manifestation, in this case.

Sinha was far too much of an individualist to fit into a mould or be herded. He turned himself into a one-man multi-tasking army against social prejudices, irrational beliefs, injustice, religious orthodoxy, rampant corruption, hypocrisy, lack of civic facilities and the British government's anti-people policies. Building a national character through the cultivation and development of national literature remained his top priority. Probably intuitively aware of his short life span, Sinha was eager not to miss out on life's chances.

This restlessness is evident in the way he wrote and staged play after play, adding to the repertoire of plays in the Bengali language and ensuring that the classics of Sanskrit literature reached beyond those conversant in the 'language of the gods'. His first play, *Baboo* (1853)—which by the sound of it was a lampoon based on the excesses of the Young Bengal or their prototypes—is untraceable. Vidyotsahini Sabha was founded in 1855, and subsequently the Vidyotsahini Theatre, where the first play, a Bengali adaptation of Kalidas's *Shakuntala,* was staged in 1857. These were milestone events in the social calendar of the Bengali intellectual elite. 'It is to Kaliprasanna Sinha and his Vidyotsahini Theatre that we owe the resuscitation of the Hindu drama and theatre', writes his biographer Manmathanath Ghosh.[1] The next performance was a Bengali adaptation of a Sanskrit classic *Benisamhar,* by Ramnarayan Tarkaratna, staged in 1857. The play got a lukewarm response from the local press, but Sinha's performance as Princess Bhanumati was much admired by the mixed crowd of English and Indian audience.

Before the year was out, Sinha wrote and staged *Vikramorbashi,* playing the lead as King Pururoba. *Calcutta Review* admired the freshness of the adaptation, 'singularly free of snuff'. Calcutta's who's who turned up to watch the lavishly mounted production. *The Hindoo Patriot* praised Sinha for a credible performance, inviting him to found and lead a public institution of theatre, a project that subsequently materialized in the form of Belgacchia Theatre.

The dizzyingly hectic spell of writing and staging plays was replicated in buying up a series of newspapers, an act triggered by Sinha's involvement in the Indigo movement. The resistance of the indigo peasants in the Nadia district of Bengal against an oppressive and inhuman system clamped on them by European planters was a cause Sinha adopted as his own, probably inspired by the intrepid editor of *The Hindoo Patriot,* Harish Chandra Mukherjee. Mukherjee ran a well-documented and sustained campaign against the planters with a missionary zeal, and managed to inspire a few court rulings in their favour, such as Magistrate Ashley Eden's 1859 order, banning forcible growing of indigo and protecting peasant rights. When the strain of fighting the influential indigo mafia killed Mukherjee at a regrettably young thirty-seven in 1861, Sinha bought the rights of the orphaned paper. He bought the press of *Mookerjee's Magazine* when it suspended publication, entrusting Girishchandra Ghose, the editor of *The Bengalee,* in 1862, with the task of running it on his behalf. His brief to the editor was that the paper should be 'defending Truth and Justice and faithfully and fearlessly representing the ryot [i.e. indigo peasants cultivating their own patch of land] to the ruler and the ruler to the ryot'. He also bought the Urdu newspaper *Doorbin.*

Sinha took over as the editor of *Paridarshak* in 1863, increased the page numbers and size, laying out the agenda with clarity.

> Those acquainted with English seldom care to read Bengali papers. This, however, is a great mistake of theirs, for the manners and customs of the Bengalis are altogether different from those of Englishmen and things which Englishmen consider highly objectionable may be viewed in quite a different light by us on considerations of place and circumstance ... [In the enlarged *Paridarshak*] we shall do our best to remove all the defects that have made the Bengali papers distasteful to the public. We resolve not to swerve from the path of truth, to avoid exaggeration to the best of our abilities and though it is not possible for any human being to be altogether free from bias we promise to be thoroughly impartial ... We shall always endeavour to remove national prejudices and superstitions—to improve the condition of our country ... and to prevent tyranny and oppression by the wicked and the powerful over the weak and the innocent.

A bundle of indefatigable energy and singular integrity, Sinha never hesitated to stand up for what he believed in. The trial and subsequent sentencing of Reverend James Long for translating and circulating the 'inflammatory' *Nildarpan*—a dramatized version of the planters' brutal treatment of the indigo peasants that was too close for comfort for the ruling imperial government ('Nildarpan', Sketch 3, p. 128)—inspired Sinha to openly side with the rebels. He offered to pay the Rs.1000 fine imposed on Long on the spot.

A surprised Justice Mordaunt Wells, who had thought of Sinha as a friend of the English from Calcutta's pool of Anglophile aristocrats asked, 'Why do you pay the fine for Mr. Long?'

'Because I feel for him,' was Sinha's honest answer.

Sinha followed up his act of support for the indigo peasants by reprinting and distributing the second edition of *Nildarpan* (the first had sold out completely) and assured the author, Dinabandhu Mitra, that just in case he, like Long, found himself at the receiving end of the rulers' wrath, he could count on Sinha to bail him out.

To be fair to Wells, Sinha did betray a soft corner for the English—the ones who did a modicum of service to India. When Lord

Canning, the Indian Governor-General, was leaving India, following the influential English planters' clamour to have him called back, Sinha gratefully remembered Canning's soft stance vis-à-vis the rebel soldiers of the Sepoy Mutiny. He wrote a highly effusive note of felicitation; forgetting for the moment that it was the same Canning who had gagged the press when the Mutiny broke out and whose position regarding the Indigo Revolt was, at best, ambivalent (see Sketch 3).

In fact, Sinha was never a closet colonial. He was quite comfortable with his position as a man well liked by certain representatives of the empire. He served in high administrative posts. In 1863, Sinha was made Honorary Magistrate and Justice of the Peace of Calcutta and also served as Chief Presidency Magistrate when the incumbent, Mr. Branson, went on leave.

The translation of the *Mahabharat,* Sinha's magnum opus, which took eight years to complete and had seven renowned scholars of Sanskrit working on the text relentlessly, was published in 1866. The work is dedicated to Britain's Queen-Empress Victoria. In the citation, Sinha thanks 'the British nation for liberating India from the terrible jaws of the Mughal emperors who like Rahu [an evil demon head that supposedly swallows the sun and moon, a myth to explain the natural phenomenon of solar and lunar eclipse] had eclipsed her glory when by the decree of Providence their empire established on the ruins of Hindu Kingdoms came to an end,' adding, 'An unrivalled work like the *Mahabharat* is not fit to be inscribed with any other name than that of the mighty Queen and Empress of Bharat [i.e. India].'

In the sketch entitled 'Babu Padmalochan Dutta' or 'The Sudden Incarnate' (p. 176), Sinha mentions an enlightened, benevolent and forward-looking Muslim zamindar who treats his Muslim and Brahmin subjects with equal respect and leaves baser matters like enforcing social ostracization on the culpable sort to the Hindu village heads. But on a personal level, Sinha does not seem to have been able to forgive the Muslim rulers for what he saw as their invasive nature and systematic destruction of Hindu culture.

Sinha's informed appreciation of western culture and easy camaraderie with his English friends was not at odds with his mission: to restore a sense of nationalist pride with a predominantly Hindu character in his countrymen. His way of doing it was by developing and disseminating national literature and recognizing a pioneering literary effort when he saw one. For instance, he could foresee that Michael Madhusudan Dutt's iconoclastic talent might prove to be an interesting turning point in the course of Bengali literature, even as he was apprehensive that his value might be lost on the jaded sensibilities of Bengali readers. In a review of the epic poem, *Meghnadbadh Kavya* in *Bibidhartho Sangraho,* he wrote, 'The longer Michael Madhusudan Dutt stays alive and writes poetry, the more fortunate it's going to be for the Bengali language . . . We have acquired a jewel in our home [country] worth more than we could have asked for without having to make an effort. Now whether we choose to see him as the tiara on our heads or neglect him, would not affect him in the least.'

On another occasion he went slightly overboard, placing Dutt on a pedestal higher than Homer, Virgil or Milton. Reverend Lal Behari Dey, academic, educationist and prolific writer, obviously did not agree. He complained in *Indian Reformer* about the writer's 'perverse taste' and lack of reading. *The Hindoo Patriot* responded with a riposte, accusing the *Reformer* of having 'no sympathy with anything that is Hindu.'

The publication of the translated *Mahabharat* in 1866 turned out to be a momentous event in the history of Bengali literature and social life, generating an unprecedented response. Three thousand copies were distributed gratis, with postage paid, and the entire stock was exhausted fast; a large number of these being re-sold openly, sometimes right outside the gates of the Sinha house in Jorasanko.

Krishnadas Pal was all praise for Sinha's efforts in *The Hindoo Patriot.* In the edition dated 13 August 1866, he compared Sinha's achievement to that of Raja Radhakanta Deb's mammoth Sanskrit encyclopaedia. Deb was arguably the most influential man among Calcutta's Hindu right-wingers at the time and a well-known patron of educational and cultural enterprise. 'One is in the yellow sea of life, the other in the full bloom of youth. But both have established an equally undying claim to the gratitude of the country,' wrote Pal.

Indeed, Sinha was far more open to evolving and adapting to the changing times. For example, while Radhakanta Deb was adamantly opposed to the concept of widow remarriage, Sinha was all for it. Even after it was legalized in 1856, widows marrying again were exposed to vicious attacks from the reactionaries (see 'The Mutiny', Sketch 3, p. 115). Sinha attended the first such wedding between Shrishchandra Vidyaratna and Kalimati in December 1856, and announced monetary incentives for prospective grooms. (It did take reward-worthy courage to tie the knot with widowed women as that decision was, most often, taken at the risk of facing social ostracization, being disowned by friends and family, lampooned in scandal sheets and, sometimes, getting bashed up.)

Sinha was favourably disposed to all movements towards social reform. Even as in Hootum's *Sketches,* the newly anointed Brahmo babu is pilloried for not being able to give up worshipping the black stone emblem of Lord Vishnu at home or screaming wildly invoking the Lord Supreme at the Brahmo Samaj meetings, and Brahmo leader Debendranath Tagore is mockingly addressed as 'Pope Debendranath Tagore the First' while inviting indoctrinated members of the Samaj to a feast on Founder's Day on 11 Magh (the month of Magh begins in mid-January, so approximately, 26 January), in real life Sinha did have Brahmo sympathies. He attended some of the sessions at Tattvabodhini Sabha in its initial days.

Sketches by Hootum, Sinha's tumultuous, rambunctious, often facetious but mostly dead serious take on life in Calcutta's streets, alleyways, moneyed homes and houses of pleasure was, unfortunately, overshadowed by the *Mahabharat.* The latter was considered a work of more lasting service to the cause of disseminating national literature. Sinha's *Mahabharat* proved far more popular than a similar enterprise sponsored by the Maharaja of Burdwan for its lucid and pleasing poetry. Also it got the critic's approval as being more authentic, as R.C. Dutt writes in *Literature of Bengal.*[2]

In the postscript to this work in eighteen parts, Sinha conjured up the image of Bengali-speaking people evolving into a race of bibliophiles. This was pretty much his last and most fervent wish:

May the rich and powerful men of our country engage heart

> and soul in the work of ameliorating the condition of our motherland and thus putting their wealth to its proper use, win for themselves eternal glory and fame . . . . May the prosperity of India, so long enveloped in the gloom of adversity grow like the phases of the moon. May the good men who delight in literature spend all their days in peace and in the enjoyment of our national literature, and may hundreds of poets, authors and translators be born in our country to beautify our mother tongue with the brightest ornaments.

There were far too many public facets to this child of the still-nascent Bengal Renaissance for the public to focus on his literary career, one of the reasons why an iconoclastic piece of work of such singular import like *Sketches by Hootum*—which still awaits a follow-up by a twenty-first-century Kaliprasanna Sinha—was not thought of as much more than a racy entertainer: at its best a vivid and vibrant picture of Calcutta's street life, at worst, the sum total of slang, gossip and character assassination.

Sinha's life, much like an open book, would loom large and partially eclipse what he wrote. Stories about how he impulsively gave away an extremely valuable shawl he was wearing to a charity fund for the epidemic-hit people of Ula would be consumed by the public just the same way as the updates on his property disputes with his immediate kin (see 'Of Kinsmen and Critics', Sketch 3, p. 121). The events hosted in his house, the friends he made and fell out with, the rise and fall in his fortunes were of greater interest to an entertainment-hungry public than his writing. Like a trailblazing comet, he was gone before his efforts towards building and developing a national literature could sink in the public mind.

Notes

1. Manmathanath Ghosh, Memoirs of *Kali Prassunno Singh* (Calcutta: Barendra Library, 1920): 120.
2. Ibid.

The Translator in Wonderland

THE ORIGINAL BENGALI text, *Hootum Pyanchar Naksha,* translated as *Sketches by Hootum the Owl,* is heavy-duty stuff, even for the most seasoned reader of nineteenth-century Calcutta patois. So unique is Hootum's idiom and often so obfuscating his treatment of the sometimes rather regular sights and sounds culled from city life, that one might, as Michel Foucault once said of Jacques Derrida's prose style, label him an *obscurantisme terroriste.* While Dickens' *Sketches by Boz,* which in all likelihood inspired *Sketches by Hootum,* and was written a good twenty-five years before the latter, flows without any ostensible bumps on the road, even now, Hootum's *Sketches* could appear like a series of riddles, laid out strategically on an elaborate grid, designed to tease and test the resilience of the most well-equipped reader of Bengali. Interestingly, there is more than just one way out of this daunting, engaging and seductive maze. Hootum's *Sketches* is one of the most open, fragmented, if not porous, texts in Bengali literature and the mystique of the language, which is also its enduring charm, remains ultimately un-decodable.

> 'The question is,' said Alice, 'whether you can make words mean so many different things.'
>
> 'The question is,' said Humpty Dumpty, 'which is to be Master —that's all.'
>
> —Lewis Carroll, *Alice in Wonderland*

In *Sketches by Hootum the Owl* there is no saying for certainty if the word chosen by the translator to represent the Bengali original will coincide with the author's intended 'Master'. Just one word may contain a world of meanings for those who know the context, but may not work when simply translated into English. For example, *baaje lok* (literally, bad people) may mean *(a)* wicked; *(b)* culpable and hence one from whom a penalty can be extorted; *(c)* those associated with sex trade; or *(d)* just plain riff-raff, depending on the context. The expression '*Baaje adaaye dekhe nilaam*', in fact, contains a whole story in a snappy four-worder. The mercenary appointed by the zamindar is on the prowl, looking for a suitable fall guy whom he could pick randomly and charge for a petty crime. His potential prey, trying to get lost in the melee at the Charak festival site, thinks he has been able to give the zamindar's agent a slip, and is therefore congratulating himself.

While Hootum is a master craftsman of cryptic codes, sometimes he uses words with such adroitness and verve that often they seem to drop on the unsuspecting reader like pelting rain; too fast and furious for comprehension, reflecting the robust energy and chaos in the content, the word scarcely able to contain the meaning that threatens to fill up and spill over its brim. Consider the opening paragraph of the piece, 'Nildarpan', in literal translation:

> Indigo taxes meant trouble. Peasants of the indigo districts—Krishnanagar, Pabna, Rajshahi etc.—one heard, were livid. Who excited them? Olaichandi? No. Shyamchand? Magistrate Eden's Order? The Indigo Commission? Harish? Long? The Small Causes Court? The Contract Bill? Could Grant's resignation cure the malaise? No. Only if the Shyamchandis go.

If this sounds confounding, here is the translation with clues to the subtext.

> There was trouble over taxes levied on the indigo peasants. One heard that the peasants of the indigo districts—

> Krishnanagar, Pabna, Rajshahi, and others—were livid. But who [or what] fuelled the outrage? Was it Goddess Olaichandi?[1] No. [Attempts to chastise peasants putting up a resistance against forced indigo cultivation by using] Shyamchand, the baton,[2] then? Was it the order [banning forcible cultivation of indigo] issued by Magistrate Eden?[3] Or, was it the Indigo Commission[4] report [drawing attention to the rising indignation among oppressed peasants]? Could it be Harish Mukherjee[5] [who put up a sustained fight against forced growing of indigo and made a cause for peasants' rights]? Or, was it Reverend Long, the clergyman[6] [thrown in jail for his role in bringing out the English translation of the play *Nilpdarpan*]? Was it perhaps [the emergence of] Small Causes Courts[7] [that have become instruments of perpetrating atrocities on indigo peasants]? [Could it have been the introduction of the Criminal] Contract Bill[8] [allowing planters to monitor the 'criminal activities' their native employees might indulge in]? Could the resignation by [the pro-peasant Lieutenant Governor of Bengal J. P.] Grant[9] [under pressure from the Indigo Planters' Association] cure the malaise? No. That would take the removal of Shyamchand-wielding mercenaries.
>
> 'Nildarpan', Sketch 3, p. 128

Evidently, this is the story of the Indigo revolution from 1850 to 1860 contained in a kernel. Open at your own risk.

This translation follows the 1868 edition, containing the author's introduction to both the 1862 and 1868 editions. Instead of trying to fall in line with Charles Dickens' lively descriptive tone in *Sketches by Boz*, the ring and metrical rhythm of whose impersonal immediacy resonates with *Sketches by Hootum* in the original Bengali, I have opted for a more familiar, present-day, English. In the translated work I have interpolated the text, trying to adapt *Sketches by Hootum* to a contemporary English idiom. Hootum, who easily swings from one idea to the next and, delights in non sequiturs, often brings his sentences to an abrupt halt, expecting the reader to make up the rest. For instance, 'This is probably why the city does not see much of a pompous celebration when it comes to the Rathayatra festival, but trust [the people of] Calcutta to not pass up an opportunity [to make merry].'

My interpolations, in square brackets, were added for the sake of the non-Bengali-speaking reader's ease, to give one unfamiliar with the milieu and street lingo of nineteenth-century Calcutta a little more background and lend a relative wholeness to Hootum's truncated sentences, which, I felt, might not work in English. I have tried to fill in some of the 'gaps'. Readers are welcome to make this 'whole' their own way.

I have retained Hootum's use of parentheses in the original text in the translation. Common indigenous words, transliterated in English—generally italicized the first time they appear in the text—are listed in the Glossary.

Hootum made liberal use of English words in his *Sketches.* A lot of these don't quite mean the same thing a hundred and fifty years on; nor are these used in the same sense. 'Mutton chop' as we know it now in Calcutta is a ball of mincemeat covered by a layer of mashed potatoes, dipped in a beaten egg and coated in breadcrumbs before being fried. But when Hootum uses the word, he means it in the original sense, as in a piece of meat on the bone. Again, the word 'friend' which almost always appears in the context of drinking, merrymaking or visiting 'garden houses' does not quite mean 'a person one likes and knows well', but rather a toady or a satellite of the moneyed babu, following him to the pleasure joints for a night of all-expenses-paid fun and games. The 'female friends', in this context, are companions hired for the evening. There is a power equation involved, that is, in fact, antithetical to genuine friendship. Still, for the sake of historicity, I have tried to retain the English words used by Hootum in the text, sometimes in their derivative forms. These appear in **bold.**

Tense is a tricky proposition in *Sketches by Hootum.* In this he anticipates the postmodernists, switching constantly between past, present and future (like Seamus Heaney in the poem *Digging* in which he can see his father working the shovel under his window in the present as well as twenty years back, both in the same frame) sometimes in three consecutive sentences.[10] He pushes the boundaries of sequential storytelling, sometimes twisting it completely out of a definable shape and manipulates tenses with the cool ambidexterity of a gymnast on parallel bars. Talking as he is about a decentred city, what Frederic Jameson[11] might have called a 'postmodernist hyperspace' where the reader's attempts to locate himself would be thwarted constantly, Hootum jump cuts into a story, flashbacks, fast forwards, freezing a narrative medias res and starting another. Initially, I had opted to translate using the past tense, entirely, which way, I suppose, one couldn't get it wrong, but later decided to be led by Hootum, for better or for worse.

It is rather difficult to decide on a standard spelling for Indian names of places and people, primarily because in 1860s Calcutta names would be spelt in a variety of styles. For example, the author's name was spelt as Kaly/Kali, Prassunno/Prasunno/Prossonno/Prusno, Sing/Singh/Sinh/Sinha, making it, potentially, an indeterminate number of spelling combinations. On the one hand, there was the corruption of Bengali names by the English tongue, which turned Chuchura into Chinsurah, and Mukhopadhyay/Mukhujje into Mukherjee/Mookerjee, on the other the new breed of Anglophiles liked giving an anglicized edge to their names, for example, Prasanna Kumar Thakur was spelt as Prassunno Coomar Tagore or Nandalal as Nundolaul.

For people's names I have tried, as much as possible, to stick to modern, simplified, popular versions of them, chiefly to avoid confusion as most of these have gone through several mutations (Ishwarchandra Vidyasagar signed his name as Isvara Chandra Sharma) since they appeared in English for the first time. I have opted for the neater, no-frills, Kaliprasanna Sinha, as the name is spelt by most modern-day writers, but chosen the slightly arcane Hootum, as it appears in the English advertisements of the *Sketches,* instead of the more familiar 'Hutom'. The reason being that Hootum was probably Sinha's choice and encodes the word 'hoot': a monosyllabic summary of the book's contents and the writer's purpose, in fact, its very raison d'être.

I have tried spelling names as they would be transliterated today, in order not to de-familiarize by much, while retaining the nineteenth-century style in which people signed their family names/surnames, like 'Nandys' of Cossimbazaar, Prasannakumar 'Tagore' of Pathuriaghata, Michael Madhusudan 'Dutt'.

As far as geographical names are concerned, in this translation I have tried, mostly, to follow the spellings that would be used in mid-nineteenth-century Calcutta and are, in fact, still in use—Cossipore, Burdwan, Midnapore, for example—chiefly for the sake of historicity, rather than writing these as the more indigenized 'Kashipur', 'Bardhaman' and 'Medinipur'. I have made an exception by opting for river Ganga, rather than 'Ganges', as I felt the latter does not quite lend itself to the flow and tenor of *Sketches by Hootum.*

Spellings such as 'nautch' or 'Sanscrit', current at the time when *Sketches by Hootum* was written, would sound anachronistic now. However, nautch girls do not translate smoothly as 'dancing girls', the latter being more in line with the western idea of the ballerina as opposed to the nineteenth-century cultural context, marked by decadence and private patronage of performance forms, of which the nautch girls were a product. So 'nautch' girls it is.

Deciding on some of the apparently innocuous, and rather obvious, spellings would often have my editor and me driven up against the wall. *Sketches by Hootum* is peopled with Brahmins of all sorts—from the scholar-academic, to the interpreter of Sanskrit classics, to the ones who officiate at the worship of household deities to the alms-seeking beggar. It's also a world inhabited by bigoted, reactionary, clannish Brahmins who are as hypocritical and deceitful as they can get and often equally far removed from informed wisdom.

Hootum refers to all of them by the Bengali term 'pundit/pandit', which in the English language could mean different entities, depending on whether the word is spelt with an 'a' or a 'u'. 'Pandit', according to the *Oxford English Dictionary* is 'a Hindu scholar, learned in Sanskrit and Hindu philosophy and religion, typically also a practising priest', whereas a 'pundit' is an expert in a particular subject or a field and is frequently called upon to give their opinions to the public'. Hootum's 'pandit/pundit' straddles both worlds and often neither. Often they are just conmen. In the end we decided to go with 'pandit', used more as a generic term for people belonging to the caste of Brahmins, not quite denoting what these people are, professionally.

One of the most ineluctable charms of Hootum's writing lies in being able to replicate sound effects in language. For instance, there is the sound of cartwheels dragged by tired bullocks, the vigorous beating of drums working up a crescendo at Durga Puja sites, the dull and blurred gun firing far away in Fort William to mark the hour of nine heard in residential parts of the native areas, not ever referred to as the Black Town, and so on, recreated through the use of onomatopoeic words (some of these I believe are completely fresh coinages) with an amazing clarity and imagination. I have transliterated most of Hootum's onomatopoeic words in the translated text because *(a)* often I could not find a workable English equivalent that would fit into the cultural context; and *(b)* these sounds contain a world of meanings by association. Each is a story by itself. All translations from Bengali, including that of cited texts, are mine.

Notes

1. Olaichandi is a folk variation of Goddess Durga who gets easily annoyed with people who do not pay obeisance to her and curses them with afflictions.
2. Shyamchand is a bunch of rough and thick strips of leather tied to a wooden rod; a contraption specially designed for punishing 'erring' indigo peasants.
3. Joint Magistrate Ashley Eden passed an order banning forcible cultivation of indigo in 1859.
4. On the basis of the accounts of 134 witnesses the Indigo Commission published a report in November 1860, tipped heavily in favour of the peasants. It suggested measures to curb the oppression of peasants by planters. Reverend Long, who was on the panel, informed the members about the indignation brewing in the hearts of wronged

indigo peasants.

5. Harishchandra Mukherjee (1824-61) was a self-appointed watchdog of the British government, the feisty editor of *The Hindoo Patriot,* which was his mouthpiece for recording and disseminating the horrors of the Sepoy Mutiny and the indigo unrest. Magistrate Ashley Eden's 1859 order, banning forcible growing of indigo and protecting peasant rights, was inspired by his campaign.
6. Reverend James Long was an Irish missionary whose name appeared as the English translator of *Nildarpan,* as a result of which he was tried for inciting public feelings against the planters and causing unrest, found guilty and put behind bars.
7. The government employed a group of Small Causes Court judges in the districts to look into the planter-peasant dispute over land. The courts became an instrument of perpetrating atrocities on indigo peasants.
8. In March 1861 a Criminal Contract Bill was passed in the Legislative Council, enabling the planters to monitor the 'illegal activities' their native employees indulged in.
9. J. P. Grant, the Lieutenant Governor of Bengal, was sympathetic to the oppressed indigo peasants. As a consequence he became unpopular with the planters who held him responsible for the disturbances in 1859-60. The Indigo Planter's Association put pressure on the government to ask Grant to resign prematurely, which he did.
10. Seamus Heaney, 'Digging', *Death of a Naturalist* (London: Faber and Faber, 1966).
11. Frederic Jameson, *Postmodernism or the Cultural Logic of Late Capitalism* (London: Verso, 1991): 40-44.

Introduction

PERHAPS IT WAS not serendipitous after all. That the publication of two milestone works in Bengali literature, *Hootum Pyanchar Naksha* (Sketches by Hootum, the Owl), by Kaliprasanna Sinha, *Meghnadbadh Kavya* (The Slaying of Meghnad), an epic poem by Michael Madhusudan Dutt and the birth of Bengal's most influential literary figure, Rabindranath Tagore, should happen the same year, 1861. The moment was well chosen. Bengal's literary arena, an almost unhewn patch that was being honed and nurtured by the likes of Ishwarchandra Vidyasagar,[1] was awaiting the arrival of the modern literary artist. The legacy of these three men who were as distant from each other as possible, in terms of style, intent, character and sensibilities, would change the scenario for ever.

In popular psyche, Bengali literary output in the first half of the nineteenth century was associated with fables, *panchalis,* turgid almanacs bursting with salacious gossip and adverts, vindictive tell-all satires and lewd farces. Stories from religious epics retold in the form of *Mangalkavyas* were read more as a ritual, for 'purifying the mind' and earning credits for a smooth journey to the world beyond the temporal and hardly ever for the reading pleasure. Thomas Babington Macaulay, writer, parliamentarian, who had been entrusted by the East India Company, the rulers of British India, with the job of reforming the education and legal system had made the provocative comment that 'a single shelf of a good European library was worth the whole native literature of India and Arabia' in 1835.[2] After more than two decades of imbibing the Macaulay-prescribed formula in schools, the new English-educated generation of university graduates (Calcutta University held its first entrance examination in 1857) was eagerly awaiting fresh reading material in Bengali. The coming of the triple events—two books and a newborn child who would grow to become a literary colossus—brought in their wake a promise to pull out all the stops and allow a free flow of ideas, informed by some of the finest minds in India and Europe.

Dutt released Bengali poetry from the stagnation and over-dilution of content by using un-metred rhyme, conjuring up a whole new vocabulary of beatific words, made to move in sync with the controlled music of his resonant lines. Dutt's *Meghnadbadh,* based on a lesser-known episode from the Indian epic *Ramayan,* recast in the mould of Milton's *Paradise Lost,* and inspired by a whole pantheon of literary giants—Valmiki, Vedavyas, Homer, Virgil, Kalidas, Dante and Tasso—made a noble warrior of an anti-hero, investing an oft-told story with a power-packed imaginative vision.

In 1861, the Tagore family at Jorasanko, into which Rabindranath was born, was already in the forefront of Calcutta's intellectual and cultural life. His father, Debendranath, edited the *Tattvabodhini Patrika,* the journal of the Brahmo Samaj, the breakaway society of reformed Hindus. Jnanadanandini Devi, the wife of his elder brother, Satyendranath, a writer of children's tales, accompanied her husband, the first Indian to join the Indian Civil Service in 1864, to his postings in the Bombay Presidency. She led the same kind of life as her British counterparts, and in Calcutta attended parties at the Viceroy's palace. The latter was an unprecedented and unusually bold move for a Bengali wife, derided as an act of transgression by the more conservative branch, the Pathuriaghata Tagores. Swarnakumari Devi was another brilliant older sibling of Rabindranath. She would discuss books at their rooftop literary *adda* with her musically inclined brother Jyotirindranath. She edited the influential magazine *Bharati* 1877 onwards.

The Bengali language changed dramatically in its written and spoken forms with the coming of Rabindranath, whose first writings began appearing in the Tagore family's house journal *Gnanankur O Pratibimba* in 1875. Distinctly aligned to Sanskrit, but free from its rigours and rhetoric, the language that took shape in Tagore's nimble hands was refined, erudite even. At the same time it was unobtrusively pleasant and easy on the ear. He was easily the most prolific Bengali writer of his time (1861-1941), whose output covered all genres, including travelogues, ghost stories, haiku-like brief mystical poems and tracts on the future of communism, novels, short stories, essays. Tagore also wrote over 3500 songs, the undiminished popularity of which shows how his language and themes have sustained the test of time.

Hootum aka Kaliprasanna Sinha assumed the persona of the vigilant night owl to write his personal take on a city caught in the middle of dissonant ideas and impulses on its way to becoming a bustling modern metropolis. His achievement was almost as singular as that of Dutt and Rabindranath, although perhaps on a smaller scale and hence made less impact. *Sketches by Hootum* (as *Hootum Pyanchar Naksha* is called in its English advertisement) first appeared as a slim 20-pager plus two images in metal engraving in 1861 or 1862. It contained just one sketch, 'Charak' ('Going Round in Circles', this volume), and sold at two copies for a paisa. Once flagged off on its journey, the work gathered both volume and momentum on the way. A second enlarged edition was published in 1862, containing an introduction, revised 'Charak', plus 'Baroyaari' ('The Baroyaari Pujas of Calcutta', this volume), 'Snanyatra' ('Sailing to Mahesh', this volume) and 'Hothat Abataar' ('Sudden Incarnate', this volume). In 1863, Part Two, containing 'Rath' ('The Chariot Festival', this volume), 'Durgotsav' ('Durga's Day', this volume), 'Ramlila' ('In the Name of Ram', this volume) and 'The Railways' (Sketch 10, this volume) was published. A combo-edition of Parts One and Two was published in 1864. A subsequent edition was published in 1868, to which the author, still anonymous, added a fresh introduction. It was not until 1895, twenty-five years after the author's death, that his name would appear in a subsequent edition. But at the time of the publication of the first edition of *Sketches by Hootum,* twenty-one-year-old Kaliprasanna Sinha was already quite a public figure. His elite background, enviable volume of literary output, legendary acts of philanthropy, the singular and stellar role he played in nationalist politics, his zealously rationalist and reformist endeavours and liberal outlook, informed by extensive readings of the finest in Indian and Western literatures, were all too well known for his readers to have missed the connection. As the writer mentions in the Introduction to the 1868 edition, *Sketches by Hootum* found an eager clientele on its first publication, propelled as it was by a tremendous curiosity value. In gossip-hungry, indolent Calcutta where a large section of the reading public did not have to work for a living, thinly veiled portraits of the city's chatterati had an immediate appeal.

The reason why sustained critical recognition for *Sketches by Hootum* eluded Sinha was perhaps because: *(a)* his contemporary, the novelist Bankimchandra Chatterjee (1838-94), whose comments on literature would be taken as gospel truth, dismissed the work as 'poor', 'lifeless', 'ugly' and 'without cohesion'; and *(b)* Sinha died far too soon. He never had the chance to defend himself, emphatically or in a sustained manner, or create a body of substantial work in the same genre to build on the heights he had touched, or for that matter create a fan base so that his credentials might be reaffirmed and his works re-visited and re-appraised long after he was gone. *Sketches by Hootum* was so arch and so much at an angle to the regular fare—its use of encrypted words, sense of history and obstreperous tone was unique—that it was near impossible to start a spin-off trail that would live up to the original. Many tried though. For a long time the work remained (and probably still is) the lone representative of its own genre.

By the time Chatterjee's essay on 'Bengali Literature' appeared in *Calcutta Review*, in 1871,[3] Sinha had been dead for about a year. 'Kaliprasanna Sinha or Hootum was one of the most successful writers in the style first introduced by Tek Chand [Thakur].[4] In his early youth he made several translations from the Sanskrit, and, in particular, translated the *Mahabharat* . . . But it is not as a translator that he is known to almost every Bengali, but as the author of *Hootum Pyancha,* a collection of sketches of city life, something after the manner of Dickens's *Sketches by Boz,* in which the follies and peculiarities of all classes . . . are described in racy, vigorous language not seldom disfigured by obscenity.'

Chatterjee's was a subjective view. As publishing history shows, while the popular response to *Sketches by Hootum* was impressive, it was the halo around the translated *Mahabharat* (see 'Kaliprasanna Sinha the Trailblazer') that has sustained across more than a century and a half. Few books written in that period contain such lively and intimate descriptions of social life in Bengal as *Sketches by Hootum.* It is the story of a people trying to find their feet at a time of intense and rapid tectonic shifts in history—the sanctioning of widow remarriage, the Sepoy Mutiny, the peasants' resistance to cultivation of indigo by the British planters and many such. While Rajnarayan Basu's *Shekal aar Ekal* (The Past and Present, 1874) and Shibnath Sashtri's *Ramtanu Lahiri O Tatkalin Bangasamaj* (Ramtanu Lahiri and Contemporary Bengali Society, 1903) are the standard texts referred to by those interested in the social history of nineteenth-century Calcutta, *Sketches by Hootum*—despite its in-your-face attitude and spy-cam access into the households of the rich and famous or maybe because of these very tendencies—is often construed as too frivolous to be worthy of scholarly attention.

Chatterjee's other rather rash decree that Hootum's language was not 'proper', too, was delivered from a moral position, from the point of view of the district magistrate, the imperial servant. His problem with the unrestrained use of the demotic in *Sketches by Hootum* was more an expression of his own mid-Victorian sensibilities than a rational evaluation of a deliberately adopted technique. In *Sketches by Hootum* the language not only complements the tenor and theme of a colourful, effervescent, intractable city life but indeed becomes the city; manifest in the raw, unrestrained, compulsive, head-bludgeoning overflow that is Calcutta.

It was Chatterjee's contention that *Sketches by Hootum* wallowed in malice. But if this was a work trying to expose the hypocrisy, corruption and insensitivity of some well-known and influential people, appearing under flimsy veils, Sinha was absolutely ruthless in ripping that veil off when it came to self-castigation. As *The Hindoo Patriot* editor and a feisty advocate of free press, Krishnadas Pal, observed,[5] 'In those sketches he did not spare himself for no picture in that portrait gallery is more faithful than his own.'

Although in no way comparable to the overwhelming and sustained popular adulation that Sinha's Bengali translation of the *Mahabharat* drew, *Sketches by Hootum* was, in fact, rather well taken by the public (between 1861-62 and 1868, there were three editions) and contemporary critics in Calcutta of the 1860s. *The Hindoo Patriot* wrote on 26 November 1862,

> Hootum's performance will be read with equal interest by both the two classes of readers into which the reading community may be generally divided: firstly those who read for excitement and fun, and secondly those whose pleasure consists in watching the progress of the Bengali language. We can assure our friend that the ill-favoured visage and ominous hootings for which the other members of his race are regarded with suspicion will, in his case, prove an exception. . . . We do not say that the style of Hootum will suit all departments of composition whether in didactic literature or instructive science but we may venture to hold it up as a model for general imitation. . . . His pictures . . . are sometimes so faithful as representations of current weaknesses that may well be pointed at as having sat for their portraits.

Pandit Ramgati Nyayratna, first historian of Bengali language and literature, and Rajnarayan Bose, a scholar and litterateur, were moved by Hootum's intuitive grasp of urban sensibilities: the incisive wit with which he rummaged in the trash heap of the chaos that was Calcutta and was able to put his finger on the malaise dogging the city. Raja Benoy Krishna Deb wrote in *History of the Growth of Calcutta,* 'His comical and satirical social sketch, the *Hootum Pyancha,* graphically delineates in a humorous vein several points, good and bad, of the state of society which prevailed at the time. It is a masterpiece of its kind and has never been eclipsed by the latter-day productions in the line. Time may come when one may not read *Hootum Pyancha,* but the time will never come when it will fail to give pleasure and profit to its readers.'[6]

That was about all the praise that *Sketches by Hootum* would receive in a long time. Rabindranath Tagore never seemed to have been interested in this work. His total silence on the subject comes across as a little strange, given Tagore's own flair for comedy. But then again perhaps not so. Tagore's own all too generously distributed witticisms—in everyday conversation, in his letters and in his writing in general—were refined, charming and understated. In fact, Tagorean wit was very British, not necessarily meant to raise a laugh and even less so to wash one's dirty linen in public. Tagore displayed unstinted appreciation for *Palamou*, a travelogue with a light touch, written by Sinha's contemporary and Bankimchandra Chatterjee's sibling, Sanjibchandra Chatterjee. The humour in that book fell in line with Tagore's own.

Tagore's disciple, the essayist Pramathanath Chaudhury, however, was quite taken by Hootum's smart-assed charm. '*Sketches by Hootum* is a totally satirized version of society in those days and an extremely fine piece of writing. The book's written in the language spoken in Calcutta in those days. I don't suppose there's another book as clever as this in the Bengali language. I would request those who have not read this book yet to have a go at it.'[7] Not surprising, since Chaudhury's own tastes were fine-tuned by his reading of French classical literatures—the rapier-sharp witticisms in Molière and the robust joie de vivre of Rabelais, for instance. Not for him the tedious and belaboured emotional overflow of Bengali romantic comedies or the oh-so-subtle, stiff-upper-lip English humour.

Among the literary intellectuals of the post-Tagore era, Buddhadeva Bose acknowledged Hootum's contribution to Bengali literature as one who 'first brought literary grace to the spoken tongue'.[8] Unfortunately, as Bose points out, Hootum's language of the street was discarded by the world of letters in favour of Bankimchandra Chatterjee's well-honed and spit-polished *sadhu-bhasha* (the chaste tongue) which in the hands of Rabindranath Tagore got even more cultivated, if a little distant for the common reading public to access. Tagore had pretty much set the standard for the Bengali language, as she would be written, for until at least fifty years after his death in 1941.

In 1944, literary historian and linguist Sukumar Sen, while acknowledging the vividness of the 'photographic' representation of

Calcutta's social reality of the nineteenth century in *Sketches by Hootum* and its historical value, had problems with the 'obscene' language.[9] Unwilling to concede its outstanding achievement in terms of content and craft, Sen attributed the book's success to its entertainment quotient and gossipy nature. 'This book was a minor factor, contributing to the glory and downfall of the Battala [pulp literature] publishing,'[10] wrote Sen, tarring the satirist Bhabanicharan Bandyopadhyay, who wrote *Kalikata Kamalalaya* (1824) and *Nabababubilas* (1854), and *Sketches by Hootum* with one brush.

Neither Bandyopadhyay nor Hootum were intrinsically, even generically, battala products, an umbrella term covering an amorphous range of street literature, including astrological predictions, manuals for doctor's assistants (called 'compounders' in Indianized English), do-it-yourself hypnotism, handbooks for learning English, besides almanacs, crime thrillers, farces and scandal sheets. Having said that, the duo, says Sripantha (Nikhil Sarkar), in his book *Battala*,[11] by virtue of their success with the *naksha* (sketches) genre, 'became the spiritual guru of the numerous sketch writers who followed'. Hootum himself writes in his introduction to the 1868 edition about the volley of books produced on similar lines as his *Sketches*, triggered by its runaway success. 'The battala publishers have come out with a wide variety of almost two hundred slim volumes in imitation of *Sketches by Hootum*.'

Actually, not that many obscenities figure in Hootum's *Sketches*, as a close reading of the text will reveal. There is just one really unprintable expletive hurled by a passing porter at the Vaishnavite monks who raise a cacophonous din possessed by a spiritual fervour (see Sketch 10, 'The Railways', p. 248). It does contain a great deal of direct speech by marginalized people: coach drivers, fishmongers and prostitutes. And that is authentic subaltern-speak. It was probably the 'non-literary' nature of battala publishing and Hootum's inadvertent association with it that kept the sophisticated Bengali reader, raised on a staple diet of classical Sanskrit texts and Rabindranath Tagore, away from *Sketches by Hootum* for a while.

There was at least one writer though, in the early twentieth century, whose mainstay, like Hootum's, was social satire and whose style would, sometimes, seem inspired by Hootum's characteristic staccato beat; an useful tool to build momentum in a comedy. Parashuram (Rajshekhar Bose, 1880-1960) wrote about the aspirations and foibles of the middle-class Bengali in the lead-up to Independence from British rule in 1947 and a few years thereafter with an elegant charm. He shared Hootum's concerns about the state of the nation but had no use for the latter's acerbic bite. Parashuram treated his characters (even some of the flawed ones) instead with an understated tenderness.

This extract on train travel during holidays from Parashuram's short story *Kochi Sangshad* (Tender Hearts' Club) resonates with Hootum's own piece on 'The Railways', down to replicating the pace and sounds of a steam-driven locomotive.

> Bengal's rivers and lakes, groves and hedges, the sweet smoke wafting from the burnt cow dung in village huts, filtered through the algae-covered lake, the scent of jasmine rising . . . O how absolutely soothing it is. In this wondrous autumn season, the mind wants to charge ahead with a roar, marking a rift right down the earth's middle. *Shan, shan* . . . the Punjab Mail whizzes on its way. Sprawling fields . . . rows of palm trees . . . small mounds . . . the scene changes every moment. In between [hawkers are doing the rounds with their wares of] paan, bidi, cigarette, smoking-hot tea, fried round bread—plain and stuffed with a filling of lentil paste . . . *Hameen asth, waah, hameen asth.*

It was not until the 1990s, in the wake of a revival of interest in old Calcutta and a deluge of several books on the subject by the likes of nineteenth-century enthusiasts like Radhaprasad Gupta, Sripantha, Siddhartha Ghosh, P. Thankappan Nair, Sukanta Chaudhuri and Sumanta Banerjee (see Selected Bibliography), that *Sketches by Hootum* made a quiet but eminently self-evident re-entry on the Bengali reading public's radar. In Arun Nag's painstakingly annotated *Sateek Hootum Pyanchar Naksha*, 1990, the exhaustive annotations provided by the editor pretty much took the form of a parallel story, giving the reader a full-scale briefing on the book's context. In special supplements brought out by newspaper houses at the time of Durga Puja, feature writers often tried invoking, even imitating, the Hootum-inspired style—a then-and-now picture compressed in a single story, drawing the reader's attention to the way the carnival of festive celebration has changed over a hundred and fifty years (or, rather, remained a lot similar than we care to notice).

A maverick among contemporary fiction writers in Bengali, Nabarun Bhattacharya, who seems to inhabit the antipodes of novels of social realism, quietly doffed his cap to *Sketches by Hootum* when he borrowed the word *bombachak* as part of the title for his Fyataru series of short stories.[12] The term 'bombachak', literally, a 'column of smoke' and figuratively, 'bamboozling object', referring to a particular category of *shongs* in *Sketches by Hootum*, sits easy on Bhattacharya's Fyatarus: a bizarre breed of bird/bat/men belonging to a heterogeneous underworld outfit, united in their single-minded engagement in subversive activities, testing and locating themselves in the elaborate tapestry of a fast changing urban Bengali society. The Rabelaisian carnival and relentless onslaught of images —continuously morphing and mutating into each other, as in a giant digital display board—on the human brain, in Hootum's Calcutta make an atavistic reappearance in Bhattacharya's novel *Herbert*.[13]

> On his way back, Herbert wanted to say something or the other to the trees, the familiar leper, the column on the verandah, the signboard, the tea shop, the female hospital attendant back home after doing the hours, the nurse, the prostitute, the railing around the park, the lion and the Mickey Mouse painted on the wall of the reservoir and the water, rising from the nether areas of the city. Looking at the play of lights from the moving cars on the huge advertisement hoarding, Herbert felt he was looking at a cinema screen. He watched *Fall of Berlin* standing in a crowd on the road, beside his cousin Krishna. A few more documentaries on the Second World War were on show. A naked Russian young woman ran across the dark soil, covering her tits with both hands. The German soldiers raised their guns. The woman

> kept running, not heeding what was being told. Rat-a-tat-tat-tat . . .

A few years back Sarnath Banerjee used the material in *Sketches by Hootum* to write a graphic novel, *The Barn Owl's Wondrous Capers,*[14] creating a palimpsest of images from Kalighat *pats*, paintings, maps, oleographs culled from the nineteenth century combined with recent photographs and his own sketches. The first English translation of *Hootum Pyanchar Naksha, The Observant Owl*, with a foreword by Partha Chatterjee, came out in 2007 (Permanent Black). So what was the need to come up with another translated version of the same text, one might ask. Our answer is that *Sketches by Hootum* is like *Hamlet*. Often obfuscated by a range of teasingly delicious ambiguities, this is a text that happily lends itself to more than one interpretation (see 'The Translator in Wonderland', p. xxiv).

Besides, one of our major motivations in putting this translation together was to look at what makes *Sketches by Hootum* a national treasure, read it in the context of nineteenth-century colonial history, in which it is set, and also look for clues to decode our own times and notions of modernism, liberal thought, progress and urbanity. We also wanted to explore the idea of *Sketches by Hootum* as an essential text and document the critical and public responses to it down the ages. The one hundred and fiftieth year of its publication in the original version, we felt, was an apposite moment to do a stock-taking of what we have made of this literary masterpiece.

The truly post-modern adaptation of *Hootum*'s rowdy aggression on language, taken by the horns and held tightly against the ground so as to not allow one loose word to slip by, may be traced in recent Bengali literature in the writings of song writer, filmmaker, member of the music band Chandrabindoo and newspaper columnist Chandril Bhattacharya. He begins the following piece by invoking *Hootum*.

> Just as idle boys, when they find a lump of unclaimed dough or moulded clay, invariably make toys out of these and start playing, a lot of people are using the unclaimed Bengali language to say whatever they feel like.

Bhattacharya takes off from this point by adding a contemporary gloss to *Hootum*'s axiom.

> Such *Hootumi* regret is lacking these days, for physically a Bengali does not have the grit (or guts) of growing the elixir that might sprout rapidly from the wilful man's reckless liver. Like kneading dough, one would need to apply the new-coined word-idol, suddenly, without a care. Only then can one expect the word to have a bite (byte?), like Clintoff's reverse swing.[15]

In one stroke Bhattacharya has brought together disparate and dissonant elements such as the Bengali's so-called lack of verve, a common kitchen activity like kneading dough and a cricketing metaphor. Hootum would often do the same thing, talking about the old model hackney coaches disappearing from Calcutta's streets, galvanic shocks applied to pacify agitated mental patients and the declining influence of Hindu cultural practices in the same breath (see Sketch 2, 'The Baroyaari Pujas . . .', p. 42).

One of the images published in the very first anorexic edition of *Sketches by Hootum* in 1861/62 shows Hootum as a rather deceptively benign-looking tiki-sporting pandit, sitting astride a transparent globe, releasing his *Sketches*, fitted with cute angel wings, in the sky. That globe could well have been a fence and Hootum's *Sketches* a continuous source of tension vis-à-vis his linguistic identity, if Kaliprasanna Sinha had lived long enough to write more, as he had promised in the advertisements appearing in the enlarged 1862 edition. By the look of it, Sinha was too much of a snobbish, class-conscious aristocrat to see himself as one of the hoi polloi, but realized that street language was the medium best suited to the tone and tenor of the sketch format. The dignified and luxurious prose, picked up from his exhaustive reading of the European and Sanskrit classics of literature was discarded. The intoxicating mix of street lingo, Calcutta cockney, risqué expletives, peppered with Sanskrit, Urdu and English made Hootum's language an anachronistic milestone in the time of Victorian sensibilities that no one has been able to emulate to the same effect.

Where does that place Sinha as a writer? A product of the Bengal Renaissance who translates the forbiddingly humongous eighteen-volume Sanskrit *Mahabharat* in sparkling Bengali, or a battala-induced, inertia-riddled satirist, too drunk on the effervescence of his free-flowing Calcutta patois? His choice of the *naksha* (sketch) form, as Hans Herder writes,[16] had to do with its high contextuality, immediacy and interactive nature. It paid off, both in terms of sales and evangelical impact. 'A lot of people have reformed, society has improved and instances of licentiousness, depravity and mischievousness that would take place openly have been mitigated to a great extent,' writes Hootum in the 1868 introduction to his *Sketches*. A rather quaint aberration in this context appears in the figure of Bholanath Mukhopadhyay, the unnamed 'writer of *Aapnar Mukh Aapni Dekho* (See Your Own Face)' who wrote his piece as a riposte to *Sketches by Hootum* and then came crying to him, requesting for funds to publish the book. Hootum exposed Mukhopadhyay's double standards in his second preface, publishing Mukhopadhyay's contentious letter verbatim, as proof of his depravity.

Satire as a monitor of government and public behaviour had an effect on society that was immediate and self-evident. It was a bit like sports coverage in the electronic media today, one got to see the action and subsequent repartees 'deferred live'. Foremost at the receiving end of Hootum's firing line was the Calcutta *babu*. While Bankimchandra Chatterjee's inventory of babus includes the clerk, teacher, the man of Brahmo faith, businessman, doctor, lawyer, magistrate, landlord, newspaper editor and the National-Theatre frequenter; Hootum's is a more streamlined list, comprising the landed gent, the rich patron, the neophyte Brahmo and the English-educated spoilt brat; a category that overlaps with the depraved Young Bengal prototype (see 'Kaliprasanna Sinha the Trailblazer'). In Chatterjee, the middle-class bhadralok (see Glossary) category could well be counted a babu, but in *Sketches by Hootum*, mostly, the babu commands power, pelf and/or prestige, even if he may be actually bankrupt. The professionals, like the merchant house clerk, for instance, who comes back home in the evening, has his frugal snack, and gets started on music practice, could never aspire to the exclusive and exalted status of babudom.

The elaborate physical details by which the babu is described in Hootum are generic. For example,

> Birkrishna wore a diaphanous short silk dhoti, a **collar**, a shirt with motifs of **cups** and saucers (much like the sort one uses to cover a chandelier when not in use) and a wrap from Dacca with slanting patterns, a handkerchief tucked in his waist. A gold key chain dangled on the shirt and dhoti pleats, **off-setting** the chain of the [pocket] watch.
>
> Sketch 2, 'The Baroyaari Pujas in Calcutta', p. 51.

The babu's uninformed fashion faux pas, patronage of crude entertainment, nightly visits to the whorehouses with an unfailing religious passion and the lack of real devotion for the deity he so ostentatiously worships to show off obscene amounts of often ill-gotten wealth, are made to pass through the unsparing scanner of Hootum's owl eye.

The category sometimes overlaps with the drinking, sloganeering, fisticuff-loving Young Bengal men, a twisted variation of the rebellious young men who had banded under the Hindu College professor Henry Louis Vivian Derozio in the late 1820s, with the idea of challenging the rigid, orthodox and binding practices followed in Hinduism. The sobriquet stuck with a degenerate group of foppish young men, who often, as Hootum would have us believe, were closet believers in idolatry. They would use the liberating aspects of western education and reform to satisfy their perverse ends. In one of the episodes in *Sketches by Hootum,* a drunken Young Bengal votary punches his elderly father to death. He invokes the Widow Remarriage Act (1855), freshly sanctioned by the ruling British government and says to his mother that the act now permits her to remarry and find a more congenial 'liberal' spouse.

Likewise the half-hearted Brahmo, who has not been able to shed his ritual-favouring orthodox Hindu core, is exposed: 'It is the Charak festival today. In the morning the Brahmos worshipped their one and only God who's unique, by observing the rites. A lot of them will offer alcohol to Him later on.' Similarly, the Brahmin priests, especially the ones looking for a free meal or a grant to run their non-existent schools, are not spared (see Sketch 2, 'The Baroyaari Pujas in Calcutta', p. 42).

But these mostly obvious social archetypes were, in any case, already being lampooned by Hootum's fellow satirists, as in Bhabanicharan Bandyopadhyay's *Nababababilas* (The Amusements of the Modern Babu; 1825) or Michael Madhusudan Dutt's *Ekei Ki Bole Sabhyata?* (Is This Called a Civlilization?1859). In Hootum's *Sketches* it's the professionals and the marginal people who are more interesting to watch. The wily gatekeeper who would not let a visitor pass unless he has been paid his cut: the procurer who has the uncanny ability to sniff a good deal and con his client, the sycophant who has turned his occupation into a fine art and a bona fide profession parade across the pages of *Sketches.* Between themselves, the city's small-time tradesmen and shopkeepers represent a multi-hued, layered world of experiences, their refulgent vocabulary a result of the exposure to cosmopolitan Calcutta's varied and disparate range of consumers, including the Chinese, Afghan and European clients. Words spoken in different tongues are lobbed from all directions and tossed around to make a sumptuous mishmash. For example: 'Those great souls who in their young age tried to push the sale of their goods at Calcutta's China Bazaar by shouting all day, 'Come Sir! Good shop Sir! Take take, no take, no take. But do have a see at least once, Sir' (Sketch 10, 'The Railways', p. 262).

Marginalized people from low-caste backgrounds throng the public spaces in *Sketches by Hootum.* The Duli bearers, Haris and Kaoras (procurers of herbs), the cowrie-counters and sellers of bear fur, though located in the periphery of this work, are often the source of a raw, unrestrained vitality running through the book's spine, despite Hootum's self-evident condescension towards the lower orders. They appear in their own little subplots, filling up and peopling the canvas. The attention to detail and character, comparable to William Hogarth's sketches of London's street life, is surprising, given that Hootum never hides his prejudice against the rank and file who rise to high posts, earlier held only by bona fide contenders from so-called respectable backgrounds. It is the women of the lower orders, the fishmonger, the vegetable vendor and the prostitutes who add colour and as Hootum himself calls it, 'vivaciousness', to the *Sketches.*

The piece 'Durga's Day', opens with, 'Earlier, only kings and people born into old wealth would have a puja held at their residence, but these days even the puny Teli can be seen bringing the Goddess home. The festival now is quite different from what it used to be.' The author suggests not just the mustard oil-seed-crusher's lack of respectability and lowborn status but also works as a metaphor for the 'smallness' of all those who were born low and meant to be doing mundane, menial jobs all their lives but by quirk of fate or, more often, by sheer enterprise, managed to raise enough money to host a Durga Puja at home. In *Sketches by Hootum* the prejudice, if not racial hatred, against plebeians who worked their way up is all too apparent. Unless of course Hootum was deriding the prejudice held against the marginal people he was referring to. In all likelihood that was not his position. The responsibility of taking the country forward, Sinha firmly believed, lay with the educated, traditionally rich, upper-caste aristocrats like himself. The fear of getting pecked by people from the lower orders, or the Bengali language being manipulated and abused in their hands, was a real one, as was the fear of being brought down by low-class, vicious critics, particularly after it was clear that the thin veil of the pseudonym had blown off. As he writes in the 1868 edition of the Introduction to *Sketches by Hootum,* 'The crows and lowborn rogues on the job will have poked and pierced poor Hootum, now visible during the day, to death.'

Although Kaliprasanna Sinha's sympathies with women-oriented reforms—his active support to Ishwarchandra Vidyasagar in his crusade to have the widow remarriage act implemented, for example—were well-known, in *Sketches by Hootum* he betrayed an anti-woman streak. Domesticated women have a very scant presence in the *Sketches.* Women who wear their nose-rings on the left side after the latest fashion (thereby going against the more common practice of wearing jewellery on the right nose which was supposed to ensure good health and long life of the wearer's husband) are mocked at. The act of having one's left nose pierced was no less transgressional than wives sleeping with house managers or servants, as their husbands went out for a night of unbridled drinking and whoring.

Kaliprasanna Sinha turned the stuff of Page Three and scandal sheets into literature for a cause. Apocryphal tales about godmen making gold from ash, or breathing life in a corpse—the sort that was the staple of almanacs and battala literature and circulated widely across the city through word of mouth, to which more colour was added with each retelling, enveloping everything in its way like mushroom clouds after a nuclear explosion. The elaborate detailing and adding of subplots and digressions was not only to defer the anti-climax, but also to pack in a few more episodes that tacitly or directly underscore the writer's crusade against blind faith. Hootum did what Ishwarchandra Vidyasagar was doing by raising awareness about superstition, irrational practices and orthodox notions mistakenly associated with Hinduism through his essays and pamphleteering, only on a different register.

Thanks to Rammohan Roy who argued emphatically in favour of 'a more liberal and enlightened system of instruction, embracing mathematics, natural philosophy, chemistry, astronomy and other useful sciences,'[17] trying to make the half-hearted British authorities—who feared a Hindu backlash to the introduction of scientific European education—see reason, the Calcutta Medical College became functional by 1838. Hootum's descriptions of how the Medical College students caught the 'godman' and his cohorts red-handed by applying simple science (e.g. anisette mixed in water would take on the colour of milk), are as gripping as they are educative.

Significantly, despite being a Hindu himself, Kaliprasanna Sinha realized the damage these fake promoters of 'miracles' were doing to the religion. His contempt for blind faith, excessive emphasis on rituals and the twisted forms in which these might be manifest is unequivocal. Hootum was genuinely pained to see how far Hinduism had travelled away from the Vedas. If he were around today, he probably would have something to say about the proliferation of the little hole-in-the-wall temples on Calcutta's pavements, dedicated to the supposedly vindictive Lord Shani, and the huge line of devotees who dutifully go about propitiating the virulent deity with flowers and sweetmeats every Saturday so that he may be persuaded to refrain casting the evil eye on them.

Although *Sketches by Hootum* are narrated against an almost entirely urban backdrop, there are points at which the country and the city must, inevitably, meet. These meetings are not always harmonious. The first thing that would hit the landed gentleman from the countryside, newly arrived in a highly polluted Calcutta where people lived in extremely unhygienic conditions, was a bout of indigestion. If he survived that he would be swarmed by a whole bunch of touts, brokers, lawyers' agents and conmen. Quite a few of the country zamindars in Hootum's *Sketches,* were resilient enough to withstand these elements. They did not mind putting up in the southern suburb, a humdrum residential area around Bhowanipore, for practical reasons: its proximity to the Alipore Court, where they would have a case or two to follow up. More often than not the landed gent from the country is shown as more down-to-earth, wise and well meaning than his upstart nouveau-riche city-bred counterpart.

The best example of traditional rural sensibilities coming in conflict with reason, extemporaneity and boldness in a city-bred university-product may be found in the episode involving 'guruprasadi'. It is about young Harhari, who studies in a Calcutta college and therefore has a liberal western outlook. Harhari was married to the granddaughter of an influential village head when both bride and groom were minors. When he comes of age, Harhari visits his in-laws in the village, ready to start living with his wife, still quite young at fifteen. His in-laws arrange for the girl to go through the medieval ritual of guruprasadi, whereby the family's designated spiritual guide would have to sleep with her before she could be allowed to consummate her marriage. An outraged Harhari is determined to stop this insensitive and irrational act. He sneaks into the nuptial chamber, beats the daylights out of the lecherous guru and reports the incident to the local police. Better sense dawns on the people of the village, and the primitive practice is dropped for good. Although in this story the city-bred young man's resistance to superstition and blind faith is given to triumph over country morals, Hootum did not fail to recognize the essentially provincial core of Calcutta, which would sometimes hang out jarringly, like human entrails popping out from inside a crudely stitched up slash in the stomach. In a world surrounded by lewd music, raucous women dancers, and clownish impersonators, often the city-bred babu—a package of affected speech and mindless sartorial coordination—looks funnier than the shong propped up for his entertainment. He is more of a caricature than an entire cast of characters paid to perform as cartoons around him.

The sheer lack of civic sense or hygiene must have pained Kaliprasanna Sinha, who had sponsored the construction of five tanks in Calcutta and campaigned for moving the brothels to the city's periphery. Visual, sound and environmental pollution was a part of life in nineteenth-century Calcutta, much as it is now. Scenes of competitive soliciting of customers by hawkers who spill their ware outside the shops, crying themselves hoarse, as described in *Sketches by Hootum*, are painfully familiar to Calcuttans trying to negotiate the stretch in front of Metro Cinema in Esplanade or Gariahat Road in September-October, prior to the Goddess Durga Festival. The description of Chitpore Road resembling 'a discarded [banana-leaf] plate off which *folar* was eaten . . . after a heavy spell of rain' is a reality Calcuttans residing in Ultadanga, Lake Town, Ballygunge Place and Panchanantala have been living with every monsoon season.

Sinha might be forgiven for the unsparing harshness and mockery in his tone and almost a total lack of mercy when he assumed the role of a vigilante. Some of his harshest criticisms were directed at his own ilk. There's irony that Sinha, in his persona of the caricaturist, Hootum, borrowed the language of the lower orders—the sort he seemed to look down upon—added his own spin to it and re-packaged the very same to get back at people of his own class, including himself. 'I can say this much that I did not notice anybody and yet saw everybody and, in fact, did not forget to include myself in the sketch,' he wrote in his Introduction to the *Sketches*.

Hootum's imaginary self-portrait in his *Sketches* is that of a pretentious brat, a college-educated enfant terrible, on the lines of the hip, liberated students of Hindu College who challenged the tenets and practices of Hindu orthodoxy in the 1830s. In this fictional incarnation, Hootum is shown secretly to nurse a deeply prejudiced and retrograde Hindu core. In the slew of short sketches, on the theme of gossip and urban legends, from 'Idle Talk' to 'A Tale of Two Papers', Hootum adopts the first-person narrative, weaving a fictional account of his life from infancy to old age, a narrative running parallel to Calcutta's journey through the milestones of history: the sensational 'reappearance' of the 'dead' Pratapchand, a rich heir, in 1835, Nawab Wajid Ali Shah of Oudh (Lucknow), deposed by the British, arriving in Calcutta with his entourage in 1856, the first stirrings of Sepoy Mutiny in Barrackpore, in 1857, the publication of the English translation of the play *Nildarpan* in 1860 leading to the trial and conviction of its supposed translator and publisher Reverend James Long. His fictive persona appears to age much faster than chronological time—fast-forwarded as if it were a quick recap of the piquantly conspicuous events in Calcutta's history.

At the outset, Hootum imagines himself as a regular Bengali child, cosseted and spoilt by the family elders and raised on a diet of grandmother's tales about talking birds and flying horses. The fear of ghosts and ghouls transfers to an irrational dread of child-lifters on the prowl, holy men who walk on the water and finally spirits invoked by exorcists. Even as Hootum challenges pandits well-versed in the Sanskrit scriptures in verbal duels and defeats them (ostensibly) by using his knowledge of European philosophy and sciences, or brings himself up to chucking off the amulet containing the dust collected off the feet of the holy man of Bhukailash after the godman turns out to be a fraud, in his unguarded moments, he is still haunted by the idea of the spirit invoked by the exorcist coming to get him.

Sample the picture of the dilettante whose entire existence is about public posturing.

> Gradually, my wish to become a public figure intensified. To fulfil that aim I began to dress like a Vidyotsahi[18] turned author

> and wanted to be an editor. I organized meetings and got indoctrinated into Brahmoism. I go to the Tattvabodhini Sabha[19] and broker widow remarriages.[20] I worship the stars of the group—Debendranath Tagore, Ishwarchandra Vidyasagar, Akshaykumar Dutta[21] and Ishwarchandra Gupta.[22] It is my most cherished desire that people recognize me as one of the worthies, even if a slightly less significant one, in the group.
> ('The Return of the Dead' in Sketch 3 'Idle Talk', p. 118)

But there's no knowing for sure if Hootum is counting himself as one among the hypocritical elite intellectuals, out of mock humility or genuine regret. Perhaps this self-flagellation is an expression of the guilt of belonging to a class that had all the resources to work towards the country's progress and uplift but was too lazy and self-absorbed to take up the responsibility. It's a regret that is reiterated most emphatically at the end of the piece on 'Padmalochan'—a man with considerable resource and influence who never used these except to satisfy his own base instincts (Sketch 5 'Babu Padmalochan Dutta or "the Sudden Incarnate"', p. 176).

In Hootum's hands, the language of the streets—essentially the product of a pre-print culture—was charged with an irrepressible life force. Uninhibited use of slang, risqué expressions and expletives that were the stuff of lewd musical forms such as *khyamta, kheur, half-akhrai,* and *dhop-kirtan*—the sort the lower orders would often throw at the more privileged—were appropriated by Hootum to run down his own ilk. If these forms were used by the subalterns, as an expression of a 'pungent lower order hatred of the urban successful', as Sumanta Banerjee would have put it, Hootum fell in line, by directing the mockery at both 'us' and 'them'. Notably, the obscenities in *Sketches by Hutoom* are mouthed by the lower orders, who take the advantage of the public space—the road, the train compartment, the marketplace—to give it back to the people who seem to come from a 'relatively' more comfortable social zone. 'The f—s' brothers have started a *kaloati*[23] number inside the car,' swears a passing porter when the two Vaishnavite monks in 'The Railways' start singing hoarsely, out of tune. But Hootum as narrator scarcely ever uses such un-parliamentary language. His resentment of the cook who became a college teacher because the Education Council bigwig put in a word on his behalf and the rise of the petty Muslims—the 'Idrises'—who went after the Europeans living in Chuna Gully and Kosaitolla with a vengeance in the wake of the Sepoy Mutiny, are expressed in a language that is direct, sharp and comes with no qualms and total clarity.

Some of the ideas in Hootum may seem politically incorrect to the present-day reader—his all too apparent prejudice regarding Muslims, for instance. But the sentiment seems to have been shared by other writers concerned about the fate of the Bengali Hindu post-1850, when the tussle for power between the East India Company and the Mughal rulers had come to a head. For instance, the rebel monks in Bankimchandra Chatterjee's novel *Anandamath* (1882) seem to be driven by a xenophobic antagonism towards Muslims. Between the Muslims and the English, Chatterjee would probably choose the latter, as his contention was that the English would create a congenial, liberal atmosphere for Indians to source materialistic and scientific knowledge. If Hootum seems to bear a deep-seated grudge against Muslims for the haunting spectre of plunder and vandalism they conjured up in the wake of the initial success of the Sepoy Mutiny, he was probably apprehensive that the onslaught of Islamic aggression would have a lasting impact on Hindu culture.

If Sinha's mission was to build national character and identity through an all-round revival and development of a national language (in his case, Bengali), he envisaged this development within the framework of the Empire. He dedicated his magnum opus—the translated eighteen-part *Mahabharat*—to Queen Victoria, thanking her and the British nation most effusively for 'liberating India from the terrible jaws of the Mughal emperors'. One of his perennial regrets was that the positive and praiseworthy qualities of the English had not rubbed off on the Bengalis, despite their proximity to the former during the Company Raj. The Anglophile babu has copied sartorial fashions (often disastrously), picked up a few stray words of English (using them to ridiculous effects) and taken to excessive drinking and licentiousness (for that is what he thought the defining characters of an English lifestyle were), but failed to pick up the better features of the English character (see Sketch 3, 'The Mutiny', p. 115).

Three momentous historical events are sprawled out against the backdrop of *Sketches by Hootum:* the legislation passing the Widow Remarriage Act (1856), the Sepoy Mutiny (1857) and the *Nildarpan* controversy (1860-1861). In fact, the text functions as a somewhat anachronistic register of one hundred years of England's and India's shared history from 1757, when the East India Company defeated Sirajuddaullah, the last independent nawab of Bengal, in the Battle of Plassey, to the Indian soldiers' first rebellion against the British rulers in 1857. While Kaliprasanna Sinha made no bones about his political position vis-à-vis the three historical milestones and his active role in at least two of them were well publicized; in *Sketches by Hootum*, he is interested in the impact of these events on contemporary social history, more specifically, on the little man. For example, the figure of the no-nonsense Aunt Tepi, borrowed from the first Bengali novel, *Alaler Gharer Dulal* (see Sketch 3, 'Idle Talk', 'Tekchand's Aunt', p. 127), a seasoned middle-aged woman, used to disciplining errant boys, suggests an infallible remedy for Justice Mordaunt Lawson Wells' overtly racist attitude.[24]

Hootum's anonymous, small folk were also capable of extraordinary generosity. Handloom weavers are seen paying tribute to Ishwarchandra Vidyasagar by weaving the words 'May you live forever, Vidyasagar,' on sari borders, saluting his sustained campaign to get the countless Bengali child/adolescent widows—who would be made to live in abject penury and were vulnerable to sexual assaults, often within their own homes—married again. And peasant boys spin melancholy riffs about 'the blue monkey [that is, the tyrannical and rampaging indigo planter] burning up golden Bengal'. These are moving pictures of how the momentous and epoch-making events in the nation's history touch the lives of the ordinary and marginal.

As mentioned earlier, *Sketches by Hootum* is ostensibly inspired by Charles Dickens's *Sketches by Boz* (1836-37). Indeed it brings to mind

Dickens' rambling, free-flowing documentary style, taking on the imprint of the myriad sights and sounds of the city of London, as if recorded by a sensitive pair of eyes behind the slightly uneven movements of a handheld camera. Even the metrical beat and cadence in the lines describing daybreak in 'Charak' (see Sketch 1) and Dickens' 'The Streets—Morning' are similar, to say nothing of the images of boisterous children who rule the road on their way to school in the morning in both texts.

But Dickens has none of Hootum's earthy, raunchy and robust sweep. What makes Hootum's journey more like a psychedelic romp across the city's roads is his intuitive ability to manipulate the language. Some of the interesting things he does to his prose include coining *tadbhava* words, that is, colloquialization of Sanskrit. For example, the words *'baraha'* meaning a 'boar' and *'khur'* meaning 'hoof' are punched together, and an *'ey'* sound added to turn the word into an adjective; *'barahkhurey'* would mean a cow with a boar's hooves, in other words, a man who is a freak of nature. There are examples of turning Persian into a Bengalized version (for example, Bengali *'ropte'* meaning 'to follow or move' derived from Persian *'raftahr'*), distortion of Bengali *('chhyakra'* meaning horse-drawn carriage, turned into *'chhakkar')*, copying the style of the unrefined tongue *('ficche'*, meaning 'returning', instead of the standard *'fircche')* to give the language used in *Sketches by Hootum* a more intimate feel. A shower of Persian, Islamic and English words, often in a slightly derivative form (for example, *'round'* familiarized as *'rond'* as in the police going on a *'rond')*, often come pelting down on the unsuspecting reader, throwing ajar a window on a new world in what was then the first city of the Empire.

In tone and temper *Sketches by Hootum* is more akin to that of Laurence Sterne's *Tristram Shandy* (1761), as indeed it is in terms of structure. Sterne's work, which may be read as a post-modern classic, arrived well before its time, shatters the logic of a linear narrative completely, allowing the story a free romp. Tristram, conceived in page 1, is born only in volume four and disappears altogether in volume six. In the meantime Sterne launches into digressions, leaving his characters in the middle of whatever they were doing, halts the narrative to mourn the death of Parson Yorick, making an inter-textual reference to Shakespeare's *Hamlet,* wraps up Chapter Five with a one-liner; leaves a blank page for the reader to write his own take on Widow Wadman, who is desperate to get hitched to Uncle Toby and is dying to find out if he would measure up to the job (he has a war wound in the groin which makes his virility suspect) and gives the music of 'Lillabullero', the favourite of wounded warrior Uncle Toby, whose character is a take-off on Cervantes' Don Quixote and who turns out to be the real protagonist of the story.

Compare this with the line of narrative followed in 'Babu Padmalochan Dutta or "The Sudden Incarnate"' in *Sketches by Hootum* (Sketch 5, this volume). The tale begins with a benevolent Muslim zamindar from the country who has no relation whatsoever with the main story and never reappears. Padmalochan's birth at his ancestors' home in the country is an excuse for informing readers about traditional folk rituals to welcome a newborn. Circumstances force the orphaned boy to seek his future in the city. He begins as an errand boy in an office-goers' mess and soon by dint of hard work, application and his ability to toady up to powerful people, young Padmalochan becomes the office manager in a European merchant house. Padmalochan's rise in status serves as a take-off point for launching into a digression about professional sycophants who switch loyalties in keeping with the rise and fall of their master's fortunes. The toadies pump up Padmalochan's ego to such an obscene extent he starts believing that he is indeed vested with supernatural powers: another chance for the writer to digress and talk about the miracles performed by Jesus and Lord Krishna, looking at how urban legends take shape.

Padmalochan starts wearing the typical rich man's vices like a badge of honour. His regular visits to his kept woman leads to another digression, about the Bengali babu's single-minded pursuit of licentious adventures, launching into yet another spiel about the failure of the rich and famous to lead the country. A painstakingly elaborate description of the ostentatious wedding of Padmalochan's son follows, both the pomp and show that's on public view and the women-dominated rituals taking place in the inner courtyard, delineated in graphic detail. Belles letters-style interludes, involving the Moon, the Sun and the Lotus in the pond—written in a soppy romantic style that is completely antithetical to the usual robust, often high-octane, theatricality in *Sketches by Hootum*—are inserted in strategic points to prolong the reader's anxiety over the deferral of the main story. Padmalochan then is a construct, a metaphor for the irresponsible rich: his story a pantomime of the archetypal babu's tale. Towards the end of the piece Hootum includes himself as one among them.

Hootum, writes Amit Chaudhuri,[25] 'dispenses, as modernist works later would, with conventional narrative to make the metropolis both narrative and form, doing away, radically, with the idea of "setting"; it blurs the separation between the literary and the documentary.' Indeed, in a city perpetually in transit, Hootum, the narrator, is often found detaching himself from the gushing flow of life and events happening around him to contemplate on their cause and effect and locate himself and the role played by him in the scheme of things. *Sketches by Hootum* is his anxiety-ridden response to a moment in contemporary history, informed by a sense of what preceded it and also a prescient premonition of what lies ahead.

For those of us who live in Calcutta, many of the images described in *Sketches by Hootum* are still a part of our lives; images we love, hate and are made to endure. Our roads remain just as strewn with garbage, indiscriminately chucked, even as shopkeepers strain their vocal chords to hawk their wares laid out next to mounds of muck scooped out of open drains. Highly placed officers investigating crucial human rights cases are found to be seasoned recipients of graft. Our keepers of the law, like Hootum's babu, act under a compulsion to report a quota of crimes in his fief/ patrolling area, and therefore are perennially on the lookout for the next fall guy to make the numbers. Cheap glamour and gossip have become the staple of our newspapers. Page Three is now the new Page One. While one might argue that this is a universal phenomenon, there is still a difference between *The Sun* and *The Guardian* while most mainstream papers coming out of Calcutta are now doubling as tabloids.

The Singur-Nandigram incidents of 2006-2007—marked by the resistance movements of people refusing to give up their land to make way for the Left government's sweeping industrialization drive—has an uncanny resonance with the Indigo Revolt of 1858-1861, when peasants were forced to grow indigo by European planters at the cost of the staple grains in their own plots. Some time back, the head of Calcutta's civic administration, now the West Bengal chief minister, Mamata Bandyopadhyay, had said: '*Kolkatakey London baniye debo* (I'll turn Calcutta into London.)' It is another matter that the riots in Tottenham, a part of the city of London, in August 2011, has brought to the fore the inequitable distribution of the so-called good life in London extremely violently. She has said she wants to give Calcutta a coat of blue, which is reminiscent of the scene in Hootum's *Sketches* where half the population on Calcutta's roads, cutting across class, turned out in identical red shawls as a result of Babu Padmalochan Dutta's munificence to mark his son's wedding.

A stubborn resistance to following the rule of the law, and the ability to evolve unusually creative and ingenious ways of getting past it seems to be a time-honoured tradition, as much in evidence in Hootum's Calcutta, as it is now, and as in Hootum's Calcutta, often this flouting of rules is done in collusion with the very people entrusted with their safekeeping. In fact, the aberrant is often the rule, sans pretences. The traffic in Calcutta—the crazy sea of cars, bikes, auto-rickshaws jaywalking pedestrians and gigantic trucks piled on high with cargo that look dangerously close to the tipping point, racing each other on its narrow, constricted roads—is an extreme example of flouting every rule in the book. For people who use the city's roads, it's like having to negotiate one's way through one of Hootum's frenetic carnivalesque processions, every day.

As for high culture and learning, which Kaliprasanna Sinha was so keen to build and propagate, corporate sponsorship for classical music conferences is drying up. New plays put up in Calcutta's theatres—in a city that saw its first play staged in a proscenium-style stage in Ezra Street in 1795, produced by Gerasim Lebedef—do not seem to generate the kind of excitement that made eager spectators queue up all night to buy tickets to watch Shombhu Mitra play the lead in Brecht's *Galileo* in the 1980s. We have become accustomed to 12-second attention spans and the infinite number of choices on television and the Internet. Like Macaulay's model of English-speaking, assembly-line clerks, we accept what is handed down to us by the government, civic authorities, auto-rickshaw drivers and rags masquerading as newspapers delivered to us every morning, without saying a word.

The difference with mid-nineteenth-century Calcutta and now is that we seem to have lost a culture of criticism and perhaps become too jaded to even register that loss. Hootum saw it coming.

Notes

1. Born Ishwarchandra Bandyopadhyay (1820-91), Vidyasagar was the fulcrum around whom the Bengal Renaissance in the nineteenth century grew: scholar, educationist, author and social reformer. He earned for himself the title of Vidyasagar (the ocean of learning) after spending twelve years at Sanskrit College. As the head of the institution, in 1851, Vidyasagar tried to reform Sanskrit teaching by making it more accessible, borrowing elements from western models. He also wrote the first primer, *Barnaparichay* (1857), in modern Bengali, and adapted Sanskrit and English classics into Bengali for young people.

   Vidyasagar was even better known for his sustained campaign for the remarriage of upper caste widows against tremendous hostility from conservative Hindu society leaders, a battle he technically won (the Act was passed in 1856) but ran up huge debts in the process.
2. Minute on Indian Education, 1835, by Thomas Babington Macaulay, *The Norton Anthology of English Literature*, <http://www.wwnorton.com/college/english/nael/Victorian/topic_4/macaulay.htm>

3. Ghosh, Manmathanath, *Memoirs of Kali Prassunno Singh* (Calcutta; Barendra Library, 1920: 94).
4. Pseudonym of Peary Chand Mitra, see Sketch 10, p. 263, note 2.
5. Ghosh, *Memoirs of Kali Prassunno Singh:* 6.
6. Ibid: 104-05.
7. Pramathanath Chaudhury, *Banga Sahityer Sankhipta Parichay* (Calcutta: University, Calcutta, 1944): 12 (translation mine).
8. Buddhadeva Bose, *An Acre of Green Grass: A Review of Modern Bengali Literature* (Calcutta: Papyrus, 1948/1997): 31.
9. Sukumar Sen, *Bangala Sahityer Itihas,* vol. 3, 1801-1880 (Calcutta: Ananda Publishers, 1944/2008): 450-53 .
10. Sukumar Sen, *Battalar Chhapa O Chhobi* (Calcutta: Ananda Publishers, 1984-2008): 44 (translation mine).
11. Sripantha, *Battala* (Calcutta: Ananda Publishers, 1997): 25, 61.
12. Nabarun Bhattacharya, *Fyatarur Bombachak O Anyanya Galpo* (Calcutta: Saptarshi Prakashan, 2004).
13. Nabarun Bhattacharya, *Herbert* (Calcutta: Dey's Publishing, 1993/ 2004) (translation mine).
14. Sarnath Banerjee, *The Barn Owl's Wondrous Capers* (Delhi: Penguin, 2007).
15. Chandril Bhattacharya, in fortnightly column *Uttam Madhyam* (Fine Media), *Anandabazar Patrika Sunday Supplement,* 18 September 2005 (translation mine).
16. Hans Herder, 'Modern Babu and the Metropolis', in Stuart Blackburn and Vasudha Dalmia, *India's Literary History: Essays on the Nineteenth Century* (Delhi: Permanent Black, 2004): 375-76.
17. Partho Ghose, 'Scientific Studies in Calcutta: The Colonial Period', in Sukanta Chaudhuri, ed., *Calcutta: The Living City: The Past,* vol. 1 (Calcutta: Oxford University Press, 1990): 201.
18. Literally the word suggests 'scholarly', 'enthusiastic towards learning', and so on. A pun on the word Vidyotsahini, the club Kaliprasanna Sinha founded in 1855 at the age of thirteen, leading a group of much older luminaries of Calcutta such as Peary Chand Mitra, the writer of the first Bengali novel, Radhanath Shikdar, the man who mapped Mount Everest for the first time, and so on. The idea was to raise the standards of Bengali language and literature and the members would read papers at the meets. Sinha edited the house journal, *Vidyotsahini Patrika* (1855). He also founded Vidyotsahini Theatre in 1857 to encourage study and performance of the classical Indian plays. The first play to be staged was Kalidas's *Shakuntala;* see Manamathanath

Ghosh, *Mahatma Kaliprasanna Singha,* 1915 (Calcutta, Parul Prakashani, 2008): 13-17; see also Sketch 3, p. 149, note 45.

19. There seemed to be a lack of cohesion in the Brahmo Samaj following founder Raja Rammohan Roy's departure for England and subsequent death in 1833. Debendranath Tagore founded Tattvabodhini Sabha in 1839, a society to discuss philosophical texts such as the *Vedanta.* The society was formally merged with the Brahmo Samaj in 1843. The new doctrine would be propagated through the organization's mouthpiece, *Tattvabodhini Patrika*; see R. C. Majumdar, H. C. Raychaudhuri and Kalikinkar Datta, *An Advanced History of India* (Madras: Macmillan, 1981): 868-69.
20. Sinha was a widow remarriage enthusiast. He was one of the principal organizers of the first widow remarriage between Shrishchandra Vidyaratna and Kalimati. He had made an announcement in the *Sambad Prabhakar* of 22 November 1856 that he would gift Rs.1000 to any person marrying a widow; see Arun Nag, ed., *Sateek Hootum Pyanchar Naksha* (Calcutta: Ananda Publishers, 2008): 246-47.
21. Akshaykumar Dutta (1820-86) was a scholar, polyglot, writer, editor and translator, who joined the Brahmo Samaj in 1843. He taught at the Tattvabodhini Pathshala and was the founder-editor of *Tattvabodhini Patrika,* which would carry profound, sometimes illustrated, articles on theology, literature, philosophy, history, archaeology, women's education and concerns, science and so on. Dutta also supported the persecuted indigo peasants. A rationalist, Dutta, unlike the Brahmo leader Debendranath, did not take the Vedas as uncontestable and absolute. He advocated the use of lucid Bengali instead of Sanskrit while conducting the proceedings of the Samaj. After his rift with the core Brahmo Samaj, Dutta earned his livelihood primarily from writing scholarly books on linguistics, philosophy, physics and religion. It was his mission to rid his motherland from blind faith, superstition, corruption and weakness of all kinds; see Sengupta, ed., *Samsad Bangali Charitavidhan:* 1-2.
22. Ishwarchandra Gupta (1812-59) was a poet-performer and songwriter who later turned into a popular unsparing satirist. He was the founder-editor of *Sambad Prabhakar* (1831), besides three other magazines, brought out mainly to lampoon the excesses in society. He edited and published the works of poets such as Bharatchandra, Ramnidhi Gupta, Ramprasad Sen, Rammohan Basu, Nityananda Das Bairagi, Hara Thakur, and so on. He was associated with both Tattvabodhini Sabha and the Hindu Philanthrophic Society; see

Sengupta, ed., *Samsad Bangali Charitavidhan:* 64.

23. A kaloati number could be an item of Hindustani classical music, dhrupad, kheyal, and so on.
24. The stem of dried coconut leaves are bound together to make brooms, whose connotations in the Bengali psyche extend far beyond being an essential tool for cleaning up the household. Brooms, often the sole but extremely effective weapon wielded by no-nonsense women, would be used to beat up errant people. Likewise, 'savouries from Thanthania' denotes a distinct style of slippers that could double as instruments to slap people with.
25. Amit Chaudhuri, ed., *Memory's Gold: Writings on Calcutta* (Delhi: Viking, 2008): 29.

Sketches by Hootum the Owl

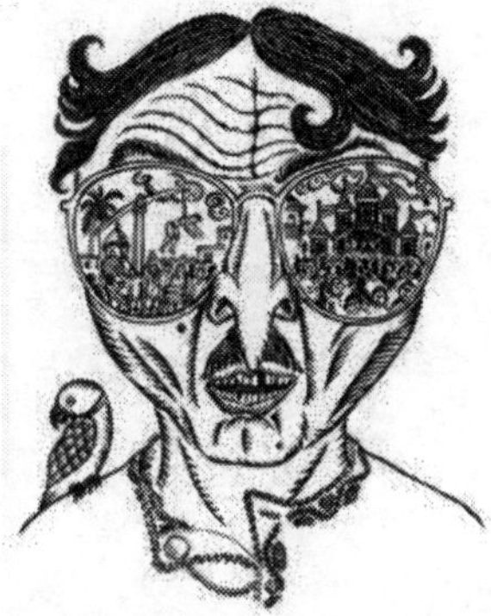

Sketches by Hootum the Owl
Part I

Published by Tala Hool Black Yaar[1]

Calcutta

Printed at the Press for the Expression of Poetry

To the most generous, crown of society, the
Right Honourable Muluk Chand Sharma,[2]
engaged in the well-being of Bengali society and literature

His most humble
Servant
Hootum
Offers, as flowers unto his feet
(This, his first bouquet of writings)

ADVERTISEMENT

FROM now on Hootum Pyancha will be writing sketches like these from time to time. As to what good that will do, you won't know right now but will realize only after a time what Hootum was trying to get at. But, alas, by that time, the crows and lowborn rogues on the job will most likely have poked and pierced poor Hootum, now visible during the day, to death. Therefore, whether it's censure or applause, Hootum won't be around to hear any.

Notes

1. The code denoting the identity of the publisher has been variously interpreted. Arun Nag cites Pareshchandra Das's explanation, which goes like this: Tala (Arabic) = God; Hool (Arabic)= to offer/dedicate; Black (English) = Kali (Bengali); Yaar (Persian) = friend, favourably disposed = Prasanna (Bengali). Therefore, Tala Hool Black-Yaar translates into 'Kaliprasanna, God's dedicated servant' (Arun Nag, ed., *Sateek Hootum Pyanchar Naksha,* Ananda, Kolkata, 2008: 180-81).

   It was a standard practice to assume separate names while writing the introduction and the main body of the text.
2. By all indications, Ishwarchandra Vidyasagar; Kaliprasanna Sinha, the author of Hootum's *Sketches,* was an ardent admirer of this great intellectual and moral hero of the nineteenth century, and provided financial support to him in times of need; see also Introduction, p. lix, note 1. The name Muluk Chand Sharma appears again in an advert in *Sambad Prabhakar* (25.3.1864), throwing light on the Vidyasagar-Kaliprasanna association:

Muluk Chand Sharma sponsors
[essay contest]

First, an article on
'The areas in which India has progressed since ancient times'.
Not less than twenty pages.
The prize money: Rs.10 only.
Judge: Babu Kaliprasanna Sinha
Second, an account of the life of the most famous king of Bengal, King Ballal Sen, not less than 100 pages of a twelve-page form.
The prize money: Rs.40.
Judges: Pandit Ishwarchandra Vidyasagar, Babu Rajendralal Mitra and Babu Kaliprasanna Sinha

A Word by Way of an Introduction

THESE days, many of us, veritable bands of poets, are making a living out of the Bengali language. Just as idle boys, when they find a lump of unclaimed dough or moulded clay, invariably make toys out of these and start to play, many use the unclaimed Bengali language to say whatever they like. Were the language inherited by its rightful heirs, it would not be so abused by **schoolboys** and idiots like us. By this time, many authors would have either been hanged or imprisoned. But since there aren't any, the Bengali language is now taken.

But there isn't anything new in it for us to engage with—every writer is trying his hand at every possible genre, leaving nothing for others, as if they have a copyright [on all forms of literary expression]. Therefore, writing sketches is my only hope. Legend has it that once a rich man employed a clown who would entertain him by performing a new set of gags every day. But after a few days, he found it difficult to come up with a fresh piece of buffoonery. He racked his brains and finally hired a porter, climbed inside the latter's wicker basket and went to see the master. Seeing the clown sitting in the basket on the porter's head, the rich master asked, 'What's this?' 'Your Honour,' said the clown, 'This is today's new item.' Similarly, I would say these sketches, my gift to the readers, are new. Now it is up to you to censure or applaud.

The aim of circulating the sketches will be clear to all kind souls as soon as one has looked at the first two pages. That's because not a single word written here is untrue or unnecessary. It's true that many people might recognize themselves in the sketches, but needless to say, in reality it is not who they think it is at all. I can say that I did not notice anyone and yet saw everyone and, in fact, did not forget to include myself in the *Sketches.*

I could have presented the *Sketches* like a mirror, knowing that no one, if he were intelligent, would break a mirror because it made him look ugly. Instead, he would work towards gradually improving his looks. But now having seen the trouble that ensued over *Nildarpan,*[1] I am afraid to hold up a mirror to the dastardly beasts. Therefore, at this old age,[2] all I could do was to put on make-up and play the fool. Venerable Readers, please excuse the impertinence.

The Skies
1784 *Shakabda.*[3]

Notes

1. Published anonymously in 1860, *Nildarpan* (The Indigo Story) by Dinabandhu Mitra was the first political drama in Bengali. A powerful play against the tyranny and exploitation of the indigo planters, it caused a sensation and touched a raw nerve with the English rulers. After an English version of the play, translated anonymously by Michael Madhusudan Dutt, was edited and published by Reverend James Long, the Landholders' and Commercial Association, comprising a large number of planters, filed a suit. To protect the printer, C. H. Manuel, whose name appeared on the pamphlet, Long went public, claimed responsibility as translator and publisher. He was given a month's prison term and fined a thousand rupees, paid off on the spot by Kaliprasanna Sinha. Interestingly, *The Englishman*, which had initially reacted quite acerbically towards the play, later came round, as did the connoisseurs among the Europeans, and wrote, after a special performance for an English audience on 19 April 1873: 'The really conspicuous talent for histrionic art possessed by the Bengali cannot be seen to better advantage than in this drama.' For further details, see Sketch 3, p. 154, note 68.
2. Kaliprasanna Sinha was twenty-one at the time of writing this.
3. This calendar, marking the era of King Shalibahan commences from 78/79 AD. But Hootum seems to have got the year (1784 + 79 = 1863) wrong here and later in the book, as this preface to the second edition was published in 1862; see 'A Note on the Bengali Calendar', p. 267.

Preface to the Second Edition

READER! Here is the second edition of my *Sketches by Hootum the Owl* (Part I), now reprinted and in circulation. At the time of its publication, the writer of this piece did not expect, not even in his dreams, to be so appreciated by Bengalis or to be read across most of the country—openly or in secret. Good-hearted people—who always wish for the country's well-being and put their body and soul into praying for the betterment of the luckless Bengali race—liven up their leisure time by reading Hootum's *Sketches* most adoringly. The unfortunate ones, too, Hootum's targets—meaning, the members of Goddess Lakshmi's groom's party,[1] the ace among scoundrels and the king of rogues—saying, let me find out if Hootum has ticked me off, or what names he has called me, have, at least, read Hootum clandestinely. And it's not just about reading. Many people have reformed, society has improved and instances of licentiousness, depravity and mischievousness that would take place openly has been mitigated to a great extent. This may sound like bragging about one's work, but this is common knowledge [even] in the domestic circles—that is, **household words.**[2]

Reader! A few ignorant people have spread the rumour that *Sketches by Hootum the Owl* is an abominable book, full of slander, gossip, obscene verse and foul language typical of panchalis, and that in it a few decent people have been travestied out of pique. But that's an error on the part of the hallowed critics. I'll say it not once but more than a hundred times—it's a mistake on their part. It was not the author's aim to do so; neither did he do it by design. Hootum is not so mean that he would use his pen to get his own back or abuse people. By the grace of the Lord of this World, the pen which has produced Hootum's *Sketches* has also translated the greatest Indian book[3]—a repository of the finest history of the nation's major religion and moral sciences, and various other elements—that exalts the mind and serves as the most unique support system to a dying householder, roving mendicant and the king himself. Therefore, know this for sure that a cobra does not eat cockroaches to satisfy hunger, nor does it raise its hood when bitten by ants. This author's relationship with the wicked lot described in Hootum's book is similar to that of a cobra's with a cockroach.

You might ask why then did the author target only a select few babus of Calcutta? What crime did Bagambar, Pyalanath and Padmalochan commit to be made part of the show? Why were Chhuncho Seal and Pyancha Mallik named? And what was the fault of Anjanaranjan Bahadur and Huzur Ali of Burdwan[4] that they, and not the other feudal lords who were around as well, should be dragged into this? The answer to that is this: *Sketches by the Hootum the Owl* is like new jewellery adorning Bengali literature, and a new puzzle Bengali society might try to figure out. Unless the point was hammered home, common folk would not be able to make sense of it, and Hootum's aim would have remained unfulfilled. Indeed, despite the work being such a thinly veiled account, many people are unable to recognize themselves or their ever-familiar friends or even realize why they have featured in the *Sketches*; while reading they completely forget their own attributes and faults, as mentioned in the text.

The maharaja of Mayurbhanj's lawyer sent the maharaja a pair of high-quality *lopeta* slippers, with designs sewn in gold thread, bought from Mechhuabazar. The maharaja, used to the Orissa-made variety of footwear, thought the gift was an accessory with which to dress up one's turban. On his birthday he fastened the slipper to his turban with great flourish and made an appearance at the party. Therefore, lest the readers fail to recognize the 'imaginary hero' described in this book, the author himself has appeared in public with his relatives and dear ones from society, dressed like a shong. [As they say], 'One might well be blessed by Goddess Chandi in foreign climes, but ignored in one's own.'[5] So this is the way things are in Bengali society, especially in the cities. And Saraswati, the Goddess of Learning, is so exhausted having to work up her imagination relentlessly that she does not have any strength left to take up themes concerning more superior beings than these [the ones I mentioned above].

The battala publishers[6] have come out with a wide variety of almost two hundred slim volumes in imitation of Hootum's sketches. Some, claiming these were ripostes to Hootum, wrote *Aapnar Mukh Aapni Dekho* (See How You Yourself Look)[7] and, in fact, ended up exposing themselves in the process. After Hanuman burnt down Lanka[8] and saw his charred face reflected in the waters of the sea, he prayed for a boon wishing that the same fate befell people everywhere. This writer, looked upon as being in the same league as Hanuman, is now in a similar situation. How far he has succeeded, of course, will depend on how you, the reader, rate it. But it needs to be said that it does not become a gentleman to go begging door-to-door carrying written petitions [asking for funds] to publish slander and calumny.

The writer of *Aapnar Mukh Aapni Dekho* has stolen the matter regurgitated by Hootum and, like a dwarf trying to reach out and touch the moon, has tried to write a rejoinder, published a book and passed it off as an answer to Hootum, thus throwing dust into the eyes of the gentlemen to whom it was sold. Unfortunately, the business did not run for long. As in the cases of the seven-legged cow, the horse that came from the sea and the genie of Hossain Khan,[9] this time too the good-hearted people found out about the motives of the author. In fact, the author wrote to Hootum himself asking for help and a small donation. I quote the letter here:

SALUTE TO THE LORD OF THE WORLD

'Dear Sir,

I never expected the first part of *Aapnar Mukh Aapni Dekho* to be accepted and adored by the community of readers. But now, by the grace of the Lord of the World, many of the readers who read the book have said, "It's an excellent book for reforming social practices." That is reward enough [for me] and makes the hard work worthwhile . . .

Since it was stated in the first part that the second part of *Aapnar Mukh Aapni Dekho* would be published, many people are looking forward to it. That includes the readers and subscribers. This grand project could never be executed without hard work, funds and the encouragement and monetary help from noble and magnanimous souls. But I'm a pauper. I don't have any money to spend. Therefore, this issue will, by no means, be sorted out unless this great work finds a place in the vortex of great men's patronage. Seeking support from ordinary people will not help. Only a rich, wise person like your magnanimous self who would encourage such work, wishing to contribute towards the improvement of the language of one's land and the good of one's country, could help in this respect. The earth smells sweeter, perfumed by the fame and fragrance of your generosity, philanthropy and gratitude. India wears your fame as her own. You are the first to write a book with a view to initiating social reform. Following your example, I feel all of us ought to write books. So here I stand, in the vortex of your graciousness and make this request to you. If only you could look upon me with gracious eyes a little and bestow your munificence, I would be able to publish the second part of *Aapnar Mukh Aapni Dekho* very soon.[10]

Yours

. . . .

1274, 20th day of *Jaistha* (AD 1867, early June)

PS: I do not think it is appropriate to attach a postage stamp while sending this letter. Please excuse the lapse. Secondly, I will be watching the way for the arrival of orders from you. Kindly go through this and I will be most grateful if you could let me know your command.'

[An anagrammatic poem by the letter writer follows, omitted here — Translator]

In keeping with Hootum's usual and ever-familiar practice,[11] it was my duty to not publish the letter. But a few **schoolboys** and ignorant people have decided that *Aapnar Mukh Aapni Dekho,* indeed, is a riposte to Hootum. Even the retailers of Battala say the same thing and sell the strange book together with *Sketches by Hootum the Owl.* That's why I had to publish the letter sent by this hapless beggar, verbatim. Now Reader! After you have read the letter, you will know what the relationship between Hootum's *Sketches* and the author of *Aapnar Mukh Aapni Dekho* is really like.

Shatrughnapur
1 April

Shri Tala Hool Black-Yaar
The Publisher

Notes

1. In other words, fair-weather friends. Lakshmi is the Goddess of Wealth and Prosperity.
2. The resonance with Charles Dickens's journal, *Household Words*, may not be coincidental. Published in nineteen volumes between 1850 and 1859—the period immediately preceding the publication of Hootum's *Sketches* in 1862—*Household Words*, better known for its serialization of the novel *Hard Times*, also contained sketches in which Dickens could give his ideas free expression, unimpeded by editorial interference. In *A Preliminary Word*, which opened the first issue, Dickens laid out the agenda, hoping the journal would 'live in the Household affections, and . . . be numbered among the Household thoughts of our readers'. More akin to Hootum's spirit is perhaps the assertion that *Household Words* would not lend itself to 'mere utilitarian spirit . . . iron binding of the mind to grim realities', but rather would look for 'romance' . . . 'in all familiar things, even in those which are repellent on the surface.' (Source: King's College, London, Information Services and Systems: url: http://www.kcl.ac.uk/depsta/iss/library/speccoll/littre/hhwrds.html)
3. The epic poem *Mahabharat*, made up of 220,000 lines divided into 18 sections, is supposedly the longest book ever written. Kaliprasanna Sinha undertook the mammoth task of translating the original Sanskrit text into Bengali prose with the help of a team of experts in 1858, and published it in several volumes between 1860 and 1866. Sinha's *Mahabharat* is still regarded as a definitive text and a popular read.
4. All were supposedly satirical references to real people. Bagambar was probably Digambar Mitra (1817-79) of Konnagar, a disciple of Henry Derozio, the young professor of Hindu College (now Presidency University) who struck at the root of Hindu orthodox practices and inspired liberal thinking. The name 'Bagambar', given to him by Hootum, suggests he was garrulous and a show-off. Mitra was a teacher, a clerk and a tax collector before being employed as the private tutor of Kumar Krishnanath Nandy of Cossimbazar, who rewarded him handsomely for his efforts. Later, he invested the money in silk and indigo plantation and bought a few estates with the profits he made and rose in stature. He chaired Bharat Sabha and opposed the move to stop polygamy. He was the first Bengali sheriff of Calcutta, and was awarded the title 'Raja'. But Hootum seems to have

painted him as a manipulative materialist.

The identities of Pyalanath and Anjanaranjan could not be ascertained.

Padmalochan Dutta, according to Arun Nag, seems closest to Gorachand Dutta of Thanthania. He was a trader, employed with Crooke and Gray Co. at No. 2, Clive Row. He made pots of money and also squandered most of it. He bought a palatial building with a garden and a large pond on Cornwallis Street (now 2 Bidhan Sarani) but was back in his old nest in his last years. Hootum wrote a longish sketch on Padmalochan (see Sketch 5).

Chhuncho Seal, i.e., Motilal Seal (1792-1854) has a story that is one of rags-to-riches. He was born poor and lost his father quite young. Beginning as a supplier, he made a fortune from a booming business in glass and corks. Later, he began auditing the accounts of a dozen English trade establishments and became the director of three trading houses. He started an export-import business, acquired about a dozen ships and several estates. Known for his generosity, Motilal supported several night shelters, free schools and the Medical College in Calcutta.

Pyancha Mallik resembles Haladhar Mallik, a close associate of Motilal Seal.

Huzur Ali of Burdwan refers to the ruler of Burdwan, i.e., Maharaja Mahtab Chand Mahtab (1820-79), who was a sworn Raj loyalist. M. L. Wells, who was appointed the Supreme Court judge in the wake of the trial of Reverend James Long, called all Bengalis 'liars and perjurers' (see p. 126). His sweepingly racist comments triggered widespread outrage among Bengalis. But some of Wells' right-wing English colleagues called a meeting to express solidarity with him. The only Indian, according to *The Englishman* (5.9.1861), to sign the vote of confidence was Mahtab Chand Mahtab. See Subodh Chandra Sengupta, ed., *Samsad Bangali Charitavidhan,* rev. 4th edition, Part I, (Calcutta: Sishu Sahitya Samsad, 2002).

5. In other words, familiarity breeds contempt.
6. Battala (north of Rabindra Sarani and Beadon Street) was the cultural hub of Calcutta in the mid-nineteenth century and a vibrant publishing industry. Bengali religious texts, both Hindu and Islamic, illustrated with striking woodcut sketches—a fusion of biting satire and unrefined naiveté—were printed here, as were sketches, satires and fiction. The Bengali almanac or *panjika,* often full of kitschy stories and illustrations, were bestsellers. Later, the term *battala*—liter-

ally, under the banyan tree—came to connote fringe publishing activity, covering the genres of thriller, crime, scandals and chapbooks: thin volumes printed on cheap paper with crude illustrations, written by authors with sleazy names, often adopted ones.

'At least 500 farces in Bengali had been published between 1854 and 1899, most of them from Battala'; Nikhil Sarkar, in 'Calcutta Woodcuts: Aspects of a Popular Art'; in *Woodcut Prints of Nineteenth Century Calcutta,* edited by Ashit Paul (Calcutta: Seagull Books, 1983).

7. Bholanath Mukhopadhyay published the book in 1863, as Hootum suspects, to get back at him on behalf of any one or more of the people whom Hootum had satirized in his sketches. Mukhopadhyay's protagonist, Nababunion, resembles Kaliprasanna Sinha to a recognizable degree. In fact, large sections from Hootum's *Sketches* have been reproduced in *Aapnar Mukh,* which is what Hootum refers to as stealing matter 'regurgitated by Hootum'.
8. In the Hindu epic *Ramayan,* Hanuman, the ape and a staunch devotee of the warrior prince Ram, sets fire to the demon king Ravan's capital, Lanka (modern Sri Lanka), out of vengeance, and has his own face charred in the process.
9. Three instances of how swindlers used to make money by circulating rumours about supposed wonders/freaks of nature. The phenomenon of hype and idle speculation and their impact on the urban Bengali psyche is addressed in detail in Sketches 4 and 5.
10. The book was never published. It is curious that the person who wrote the first part of the book to lampoon Kaliprasanna should approach him to sponsor the second volume.
11. Kaliprasanna Sinha preferred not to go public about the financial support he offered to numerous people and institutions.

1

Going Round in Circles:

The Charak Festival of Calcutta

Says Tunoya, 'The city teaches the ways of the police station.' [1]

THE SOUND of drumbeats could be heard all across the city of Calcutta.[2] The Charak performer's back began to itch. Blacksmiths honed iron rods, *doshloki*,[3] pins and *bonti*.[4] Sundry carpenters, milkmen, spice sellers and coppersmiths were all kitted up in jewellery, from head to toe. They wore anklets, caps embroidered with gold thread, a layered, jewel-encrusted belt around the middle, and a piece of woven cloth tucked in tight around the groin, worn like a loincloth. The fabric, produced in the Dacca looms, came with woven borders, designed in memory of the soldiers killed in the Mutiny.[5] The revellers also carried a *gamccha* dyed in Tarakeswar and wore bel leaves[6] tied in a string around the neck. Today their joy knew no bounds. '[Let's go watch] Gajan festival[7] at the master's house!' [they kept exclaiming].

The great grandfather of this babu of ours had become a salt diwan, that is, collector of salt taxes,[8] soon after the East India Company started ruling Bengal.[9] That was a little before the hanging of Nandakumar [Roy].[10] At that time, a salt diwan could make quite a packet from the cuts he received. Therefore the babu's great grandfather, who spent five years in service, left an inheritance of about Rs.2,000,000 when he died. Since then the babu's family has been considered 'traditionally rich'. And now the family has accumulated the paraphernalia that might validate its claim to old wealth in Bengali society. They have acquired a coterie. A few

Brahmin pandits, that is, priests, kulin's sons, drop-outs from the kulin club,[11] Srotriya, Kayastha, Baidya, Teli, spice sellers, coppersmiths and blacksmiths from Dacca were absolutely loyal to them. They did not miss any of the rituals observed at [the babu's] home and the Brahmins in the group were well rewarded for attending the annual services held in memory of the family's departed souls. Which was to say nothing of [their presence] at the daily rituals: paying obeisance to the idol in the homestead, the black stone, that is, Lord Vishnu, and Goddess Lakshmi's measuring cup,[12] containing gold coins from the time of Emperor Akbar.

Meanwhile, the Duli bearers, Haris and Kaoras,[13] wearing anklets and garlands made of thick coarse thread, brandished arrows and doshloki—like columns erected in recognition of the courage and gracious sacrifice [they were about to display]—as they danced to the beat of drums in liquor shops, brothels and people's courtyards. The drummers—having decorated their instrument, by tying fly-whisks, feathers, bells and anklets along the binding of its left surface—worked up a beat, as they went from one neighbourhood to the other, looking for the Charak performers.

The school had practically shut shop for the day. The students preferred to spend all day at the festival site, as if this were their home. They didn't eat or sleep, just kept shadowing the drummers all day, sometimes joining in the chorus: 'Glory to Lord Shiva, the greatest among the Gods'. Some of the boys had managed to tear the leather off the drum's surface, while some kept banging thunderously on the other [still intact] end. The parents were anxious. They could only hope that the children didn't catch an infection or two.

Soon the festival day dawned. The Charak performers were all set to throw themselves on a bed of nails in the afternoon. Their leader, the head *sanyasi,* an old man, a retainer of the fourth generation of the babu's family, stuck a bel leaf in the wedge of his ear, picked another handful of these and came panting into the drawing room. He was a Kaora by birth, but since at this auspicious moment he was Lord Shiva's chosen one, the babu bowed to him. The sanyasi walked across the spotlessly clean carpet, leaving his muddy footprints on it, and touched the babu's forehead with the blessed flower. The babu was tense [not knowing how to deal with him].

The McCabe & Co. clock in the living room chimed *tang, tang, tang*... It was five in the afternoon. The sun was less intense now. The babus of the town rode their phaetons, self-driven buggies and broughams, and, depending on their status, took **friends**, bhadraloks or sycophants as part of the entourage. Some were headed towards their garden houses.[14] Most of them, except a few gentle souls, had carriages tanked up with alcohol and women following their trail. Some of them instructed their drivers and coachmen not to wear the family's insignia so as not to let people in on what they were up to. Some others did not care a whit about earning a bad name. They felt going on a romp with prostitutes was an admirable feat. They travelled with their concubines in the same vehicle, throwing caution to the winds. Those employed in trading houses peeped out of their shared carriages to catch a glimpse, thus making a worthy use of the gift of eyesight.

Meanwhile a thick crowd had gathered at the festival site at the babu's house. The drumbeats rose again. The sanyasis squatted down and started rotating their heads vigorously, praying to the idol of Lord Shiva[15] for permission to start the show. Some went down on their knees and then lay prostrate in a show of great devotion. The Brahmin priest, who officiated, kept sprinkling the holy water of the river Ganga [all around]. Half an hour passed rotating heads but the flower placed on the idol's head had not dropped. What a calamity! The news travelled inside the household. The housewives pulled long faces. They told each other that this must be the result of an error committed unknowingly, and sat down, resignedly, striking their foreheads. The assembled audience began a free-wheeling discourse: 'It seems the head sanyasi consumed something [he shouldn't have] . . .' 'Usually it's the sanyasis who are to blame for such mishaps', and so forth. Finally, the head priest presiding over household rituals and the lady of the house came to a consensus; they decided that the head of the family would have to be bound and brought forth. A jolly Brahmin and about four or five sanyasis ran across to the babu, and told him, 'Your highness will have to lift his body and come to Lord Shiva's seat. The flower hasn't dropped yet.'

It was almost evening. The phaeton was ready. The babu, fully dressed—he wore Bouquet[16] perfume in his handkerchief—was on his way out. Hearing the news he was ready to faint. But since it was not the done thing to put an abrupt halt to religious ceremonies observed by the past seven generations of the family, he proceeded towards the venue, the diaphanous shirt made from pineapple fibre still on him. Seeing him approach, the gatekeepers guarding the entrance formed a cordon in front of the babu and walked before him. The toadies followed with a morose look on their faces, sensing that the babu was in great danger.

Suddenly the drums boomed very noisily indeed. Everybody in the crowd screamed, 'Glory to Lord Shiva, the greatest among the Gods'. The babu prostrated in front of Lord Shiva's idol. Huge hand-held palm-leaf fans were being swung forcefully on either side. To the uninformed, all this looked as if the babu were being readied for a human sacrifice. Ultimately, both his hands were tied together, a garland of flowers wound around them. Silk scarf still wrapped around his neck, the babu stood on one side [of the arena of worship], ready to cry. The priest kept pleading with Lord Shiva: 'Baba, drop the flower, drop the flower, please.' An extra pot of water from the river Ganga was poured over the Shiva idol, hoping to put an early end to the babu's plight. The sanyasis rotated their heads vigorously. After half an hour's struggle, a wad of bel leaves fell down from the idol's head. The crowd was rapturous with joy. People cried out, 'Say glory to Lord Shiva.' 'And why shouldn't things go smoothly,' they said, 'after all, the babu comes from an illustrious family, doesn't he?'

The drums picked up a different beat. The sanyasis danced all the way to the pond nearby to fish out the twigs that had been dropped into the water two days back. Twenty bundles of hay had been spread out at the venue. Thorny twigs laid out on a bed of straw were hammered into the ground. After these were securely planted, the priest sprinkled holy water from the river Ganga on them. Two sanyasis tied a gamccha of **double**-width at either end, spreading it out taut, for their fellows to throw themselves on, one by one. Oooh! 'Lord Shiva is great indeed!' [The divers cried, as they took the plunge]. They were not supposed to breathe a word about how badly the thorns hurt!

A few shrewd ones among the shady people in the audience took full advantage of slinking into the melee and avoiding notice. Some of them, like the invisible Gods in heaven, congratulated themselves for having given the babu, who would invariably have slapped a fine if he caught them,[17] and everybody else, a slip. Ultimately, the diving exercise was over. One of the divers, trying to show off his valour, fell on his back in a reverse dive. The drums hit a crescendo. The audience began to pull at the thorny twigs, [one of them saying,] 'My wife says that the twigs are blessed, keeping these at home would drive the bedbugs away for good.'

The bells and gongs indicating the arrival of evening had stopped ringing. All the street lamps were lit now. Peddlers' cries could be heard: 'Want to buy jasmine?' 'Kulfi, anyone?' The liquor shops were shut, in keeping with the laws of the excise department, but it was not as if the customers went back [empty-handed]. Soon it was dark enough to conduct business under cover. It was difficult to tell the bhadraloks on the street from the lowly folks. They all wore English shoes, striped wraps from Santipur and Simla-style dhotis. Smart-assed *yaars* went around in groups, knocking on people's doors, laughing raucously and spitting out English words, fast and furious. The house lights coming on in the evening were their cue to step out. They would return early next morning, only after the grinding of wheat in flour mills began. Huge crowds assembled in the pots and pans market of Mechhuabazar, the crossing of Chorbagan, Poddar's shop at Jorasanko, Notun Bazar, Battala, the lanes of Sonagacchi and the four-point crossing of Ahiritolla.[18] Some of the people [visiting these places] covered their faces and heads, thinking nobody would recognize them. Some others spoke louder than usual, coughed and sneezed pointedly to let people know that they 'enjoyed a little fun and games after sundown'.

[Back home from work], the merchant office clerk—a man of fine tastes—washed, had a small bite and was now settling down to play the sitar. Right next door, children screamed out the lines from Vidyasagar's *Barnaparichay*.[19] Wayward young men were getting their first taste of the world of forbidden pleasures. The goldsmiths were about to start soldering under the light of the *durgapradip*. A few shops selling clothes, wooden items and utensils on either side of the road closed down for the day. Gold merchants, pawn-shopowners and shopkeepers who only accepted cash down payments to buy and sell gold were updating the account books, taking stock of the day's sales. The market owned by the rajas of Sovabazar[20] was about to wind up for the day. Lamp-in-hand, fisherwomen urged people to buy inferior quality rotten fish and hilsa harvested from the sea: 'O man-with-a-gamccha-on-your-shoulder, like to buy some nice fish?' 'O bloke-with-a-bristly-moustache,' one of them says, coquettishly, 'got four annas to spare?' Occasionally, a customer trying to get fresh with a fisherwoman was having his forefathers abused [in return]. Penniless opium-eaters, drug addicts and drunkards mingled in the crowd posing as blind men, feeling their way about with a walking stick. 'Please spare something for the blind Brahmin, dear donors,' they said, trying to raise money to buy their daily fix.

Once again loud drumbeats were heard at the festival site in the babu's house. 'Say glory to the name of Bhadreswar, the Lord Shiva,' screamed the crowd. A clamour was heard: it is time to suspend the sanyasis. Planting and securing the contraption [from which they would hang] in the field in front of the house was complete. The juniors, the next generation masters of the house, hung around the site, clutching the hands of gatekeepers, servants and maids. And then, the sanyasis lit a bunch of straw and held it beneath the rotating grid. Having suspended a person, head-down, from the contraption, they began dropping the dust of resin to raise the flames, right next to his face. More people were made to go through a similar exercise, one by one, until the hanging ritual was over. In half an hour, the city was back to its more restful state. The sitar started playing again. The chaps hawking jasmine, ice and fresh cream got a moment, as they normally would, to sell their wares. That's how Friday night passed.

It was the evening before the big celebration, and moreover it was a Saturday. The city was [usually] in high spirits on Saturday nights. Bell-shaped lanterns and wall-lamps were lit up in paan shops. The sweet fragrance of jasmine gushing out with the lovely breeze sent the city into throes of excitement. In a couple of the houses along the street, dancers were training in the *khyamta* form. Quite a few people had gathered on the road; they listened to the music, in open-mouthed wonder. To them just getting to hear the mild tinkling sound of the anklets and tiny cup-shaped cymbals was like a ticket to heavenly pleasures. A skirmish ensued somewhere in the city. Elsewhere, a guard caught a thief, who was now being bound and taken away. About four or five thieves hung around them, laughing. Thoroughly entertained by the spectacle, they congratulated themselves on their alertness [at having evaded arrest], not stopping to think what would happen the day they found themselves in a similar fix.

If X was getting a player from Chitpore[21] to impersonate Lord Shiva at the Gajan festival in his house today, Y would host a Singhi Bagan-style[22] performance at his space. And the next neighbourhood would hire all-women groups singing a panchali. Large-scale celebrations were on at the festival sites in the city today. Policemen posted at the four-point crossings were in luck. Although the liquor shops were closed, liquor would be sold throughout the night [on the sly]. Opium would fly [from the shelves], non-stop. Tomorrow morning you would hear complaints such as, 'The big brass pot kept near the well in Ghosh's house is missing', 'The Pals have lost a basket full of brassware' and 'the spice traders' valuables were cleared out'. Tonight it was quite impossible to get any sleep, thanks to the intermittent sound of drums, the sanyasis' hurrahs, and shouts of 'Say glory to Bhadreswar, the Lord Shiva'.

Meanwhile, the clock on the church tower chimed. *Ding dong ding, ding dong ding,* it went. It was 4 am. The babus who preferred to stay out [at night] were now on their way home. The cooks [who came here to work] from Orissa began kneading the dough. The street lamps were now dim, having lost their glow [as daylight appeared]. A soft breeze blew. Cuckoos started cooing on the balcony of the whorehouse. Crows cawed. The subdued barking of street dogs was heard on the road, intermittently. Except these occasional sounds, this huge city seemed to be quite deserted at this hour.

Now Reader, look over there. Women were out in groups, going for a dip in the Ganga, exchanging gossip [on the way]. Comments such as 'Ram's mother can't move any faster', 'The fourth daughter-in-law of that family is unbelievably wicked' and 'That woman's so tight-fisted' got bandied about. The butchers from Chitpore carried large pieces of **mutton chops**, heaped together. Police sergeants, inspectors and head constables—whom the poor people found no less monstrous than Yama, the God of Death—now through with their **rounds,** went back to the police station, their shoes squeaking noisily. Their purses and pockets bulged with quarters, crowns, half-rupees and smaller change. These lords would not give up [small things like] a piece of firewood, a bowl of tobacco or a roll of paan if they could lay their hands on any. Quite a few of them were displeased with a posting in the city, as the haul was less than what they had expected. Bodies itching with rage, they went on their way, trying to hatch fresh schemes so that they might grab a harmless guy from a decent family the next morning and show him what they truly excelled in. The **superintendent** was a simple guy, oblivious to viciousness or deceit [in his ranks]. He spent most of his time in the company of four or five friends, playing the harmonium, the piano or playing with his pet dog. So the inspectors had a rare astral combination working in their favour.

The canon went off with a dull *vroom.*[23] The crows cawed noisily, preparing to take off from their nests. Shopkeepers opened shutters, bowed to Devi Gandheswari,[24] sprinkled holy water from the Ganga around the shop and changed the water in the hookah, preparing to have a smoke. Gradually, the sun shone brighter. Porters carrying fish ran past, quarrelling fisherwomen ran after them. Barge after barge arrived, carrying potatoes from Baidyabati[25] and aubergines from Hasnan.

Doctors, foreign and native, were like [the incarnations of] Lord Yama. They visited patients, riding on cars or palanquins, depending on their status and income. One did not see them smile unless there was an outbreak of typhoid or cholera. And since the epidemic in Ula[26] a lot of quacks, who would otherwise be unemployed except for putting a stamp on cows after treatment, had made quite a bit of money. Some of these cow-markers could be seen **practising** in Calcutta as well. They prescribed bizarre medicines. If one of them tried piercing through the patient's nostrils—as they would do with bovines—to give him relief, the other would administer only pure water [instead of medicine]. The city's own Ayurvedic physicians were one up on these quacks. Whatever the ailment, they ensured that the ultimate panacea was death itself. A lot of them started practising medicine right after they had finished reading the *slokas* of Chanakya and the book of the generous Karna.[27]

Tucking clothes in a bundle under the arm, Brahmins who doubled as priest and grammar school master were on their way to the river for a dip. Today they were in a great hurry, eager to reach the client's house early in the morning. Rheumatic, middle-aged folks went out for a **morning walk.** Palanquin-bearers from Orissa rushed towards the river to have a bath, grabbing fibrous twigs to brush their teeth with. *The Englishman, Harkara, Phoenix* and *Exchange Gazette*[28] had by now reached the doors of the subscribers. Certain Bengali papers reached their subscribers only after the news in them got somewhat stale, like deer meat. But it was different with the English papers; they must be served fresh, with **breakfast,** hot off the press. Gradually the sun came up.

After the pair of bullocks that pushed the wheel at the oil mill was replaced, just as clerks who keep accounts [in merchant offices] are made to work shifts, the turbaned [white-collar] employees started appearing in **instalments.** Ship chandlers and **booking clerks** arrived first, followed by the barbers and menders of clothes. Today since the **government offices** were closed, we did not see the **clerks, bookkeepers** and **head writers.**[29] Now that English education was widespread, people wore all sorts of [fashionable] clothes to work. The turban seemed almost on its way out. Only the old-timers among the clerks believed in giving the ever-familiar turban its due respect. Once they began drawing a **pension,** we would have seen the last of turbaned clerks serving in merchant houses. One of the drawbacks of wearing a turban was that it covered the Prince Albert-style of parting one's hair asymmetrically at one side,[30] which was now in fashion. Menders of clothes and hairdressers had almost given up wearing the turban.

The procurer had little respite. He skipped breakfast before stepping out in the morning. Not that he had much to do, except he could not possibly go through his day without showing up at the houses of cash-rich babus and moneylenders who offered instant loans at exorbitant interests. Primarily, his job was to keep track of who might be selling a house, who was on the lookout for a garden house to buy and who wanted to borrow money. Moneylenders used to fleece customers, traders with whom the high castes did not mind mixing and quite a few city-bred babus had these procurers on their payroll. They brought home the prey for the babu who swallowed it whole, in a single gulp.

Being a procurer was not a bad thing. Like the proverbial cat running away with the cream, there was money to be made in this business. In fact, quite a few young men from decent families travelled daily to work as procurers. Penniless accountants, declared **insolvent** four times over, had now turned procurers. The Padmalochans[31] of this world had built solid pillars[32] resembling banana tree trunks on the money made from cuts. These people were like mangoes that did not show their true colours from the outside. It was hard to recognize them for what they were. They would stop at nothing.

Professional moneylenders, wannabe traders and other rich men usually had a fishermen's net cast in the river of deceit. The procurer, holding onto the buoy of trust, floated, pushing the water [in the desired direction]. Therefore, when the tide was good, even the smallest fish could not slip past the net.

The clock on the church tower struck seven, to the sound of loud gongs. The din on the city streets was deafening. There was a sea of people on the roads. The sound of drums playing, smoke billowing from burning resin and the foul smell of alcohol circulated all around. Piercing themselves with arrows, doshloki, *sutoshon*, hooks, snake-shaped rods and pieces of bamboo, the sanyasis arrived from Kalighat,[33] dancing like crazy all the way, as if their lives depended on it. The verandah of the whorehouse teemed with yaars of the genteel sort, besides amateur panchali-singers and those who sang the choral numbers in **half**-akhrai concerts. Most of these people were indoctrinated **members** [votaries] of the garden house culture, gathered here early in the morning to watch the Gajan festival.

Meanwhile, there was major excitement in rich men's drawing rooms as the guests arrived, depending on the stature of the babu in question. Some of them, in keeping with the demands of living in a civilized society, **hated** the Charak festival. Someone else, in spite of being a Brahmo, participated in the fun, as 'his forefathers had been doing the same thing since the last seven generations'. Indeed he was quite annoyed being made to do so against his will. But with his elder brother and third uncle by marriage still around, and his grandmother yet to depart for Kashi,[34] he didn't have an option.

It was fun watching performers whirl around the pole and have their bodies pierced with arrows and swords. They took the grandchild, the young son and the infant daughter to watch the immersion of clay idols [after the worship was over]. Even elderly blokes were not ashamed to go out wearing diamond-studded caps, loose long shirts embroidered with gold thread, pearl necklaces, diamond chokers and ten rings on either hand, trying to pass themselves off as young lads, even when the son by their first wives may well be sixty years old and the nephew had grey hair.

Often a zamindar or a raja from the country came visiting Calcutta. When they wanted to push the cases pending at the Chief Nizamat Court[35]—whether it was to wait their turn or trying to jump the queue by availing of a special provision—they usually put up at Bhowanipore.[36] The air here was too warm for those who came from the districts. Earlier, those who came to Calcutta from the rural areas suffered indigestion. Nowadays there was a bigger affliction that left those affected gasping with shock. Conned by seasoned swindlers, one often ended up losing the last paisa before heading back home. Some of the zamindars from the country preferred living in the city all the year round. If you saw somebody who looked like one of the panchali or *Chandi*-singers, wearing a **crepe** wrapper around his head, a pearl necklace and a costume like the *baiji's* servant, riding a phaeton at noon with about a dozen sycophants for company, you would know at once that here was a puny fox who was treated like a king in his village, in intelligence very like a mule, and in learning an ignoramus incarnate. He was a connoisseur of idol immersions, community pujas, khyamta dances and *jhumur* who occasionally went into hiding to escape an arrest warrant or the moneylender's decree. But on Sundays and days when festivals, immersions or a bathing ceremony was held, he was sure to dress up and go out in his carriage.

It was not as if all the zamindars from the country had a rib less [in other words, lacked the spirit and integrity of a normal, upright man] than the regular count. One or two of them who came to Calcutta occasionally did get back all feted and having made a name. They might have put up at Sonagacchi but refused to get ruffled by the entertainment it offered. In fact, often city-bred people found the ways of country zamindars quite awesome. Again, some of them, who put up at Cossipore,[37] Barisha,[38] Bhowanipore or Kalighat, ended up spending their time at Sonagacchi, round-the-clock. They broke into people's homes and started a fight. The very next day, they might show up at the police station, accompanied by fathers and uncles, holding the hand of their lady love, like a couple. They bought elephants on credit. And then there was a major fight with staves and clubs at the time of **payment**. When the pressure mounted they slipped back into their own territory, which was no less than Lord Ram's own country.[39]

Procurers were no different from the small-time agents[40] swarming in on a **sailor** who had newly arrived in the city. When a rich man from the country visited the city, the procurers at once presented themselves in his court. By the kind permission of the attorney [who was handling the babu's assets], the agent was assigned a variety of jobs such as renting a house, organizing a car and making a booking with the khyamta dancers. He also worked as the babu's **political agent**. He took him to the garden house with seven tanks, Asiatic Society's museum, Bally Bridge, the lock-gate at Baghbazar,[41] the well-decorated drawing rooms of different babus and the houses of a few well-known prostitutes. If he could strike the iron when it was hot, the agent could exert tremendous influence on the babu. It was party time for a while. By the time the babu went back home, either because he was cash-strapped or had other business to attend to, the procurer was [recognized and] employed as a bona fide professional.

These days the westernized babus of the city belonged to two groups. The first could be called 'the stylish Englishman's cow-dung **bust'**. The second were an abominable prototype of the declassed white man. The first did everything in English style. They chatted sitting at the table, drank tea from cups. Cigars, jugs filled with water, brandy in **decanters** and glasses covered with a lid made of pith were laid out on the red cotton table cover, the *Harkara, The Englishman* and *The Phoenix* kept within easy reach. **Politics** and the **best news of the day** were the only things that excited them. They ate sitting at a table, defecated in a **commode**, and wiped their bottoms with paper. They had a lot of positive qualities, such as sympathy, generosity, philanthropy, modesty, and so on. It was just that they were ill all the time, having drunk themselves to decrepitude. They were slaves to their wives and had banished all feelings of enthusiasm, unity and the desire to improve completely from their hearts. They belonged to the **old class** [meaning old school].

Among the second group, Bagambar Mitra and the likes were more dangerous than a snake and more ruthless than a tiger.[42] You could say they were a monstrous breed of animals. Just as thieves put a little alcohol on their lips to pass themselves off as drunks when they go out to steal, these people pretended to work towards the country's welfare with only their own benefit in mind. All that they were interested in at any given time was: 'How can I make more money?' and 'How can I keep the others under my control?' It was their **policy** to push others into misery and cash in on the crisis. The very idea that these people might make donations was far-fetched. You could not expect them to donate more than a quarter of a rupee.

The drawing rooms of the rich were most lively in the mornings. The head clerk of the lawyer's firm sat like a crow in a pilgrim's haunt [waiting for the goodies to come his way]. Several cases—three-to-four **equity**-related and two others having to do with the **common law**[43]—were pending in court. Creditors, collectors who produced bills, lenders who collected their pay in instalments, have been doing the rounds for the last three months, clutching ledgers, bills and handwritten notes. The family manager kept asking them to come the next day. The babu wore the **summons**, **warrant**, lawyer's note and **subpoena** he had received like a badge of honour. Criticism and humiliation did not mean a thing to him. But his heart burnt with rage as he remembered each instance of being conned and fooled. 'This too shall pass' [he told himself]. He wore a specially designed ring [to facilitate a turnaround in his fortunes], but didn't seem to have any peace of mind, however much he tried.

A [just-deceased] rich man's son who had come into a lot of money at a young age roamed around like a kite whose alignment with its central axis had gone awry. Only the other day he was playing brides and grooms, blind man's buff and riding human horses. But now he was vested with the job of identifying the subtle manipulations made in the ledger by the manager. He would also need to keep an eye on the lawyer's seasoned moves and be on his guard to avoid getting checkmated at the outset. While crows are known to snatch at edibles in the hands of a child, human beings are hardly any better. A lot of people showed up [at his door], passing themselves off as 'a very close friend of the late master's' or 'his second aunt's husband's maternal uncle's father's brother's aunt's son's cousin from his mother's side'. 'Job-seekers' and 'people saddled with the responsibility of marrying off a daughter' (some of these saddled-with-a-nubile-daughter-to-marry-off people were probably not yet married themselves) and sundry others turned up. The real motive remained submerged, way under the water in Dwaipayan Lake and would reveal itself only at the right moment.[44]

Now that some time had passed, the roads swarmed with people. The trader's shop at the four-point crossing was packed with visitors togged up in all sorts of outfits. One of them wore a shirt with **cuffs** and **collars**, sporting silver **buckles** fastened on **shining leather**. Another one had donned a **Chinese coat** in combination with shoes made of **India rubber**, a **crepe** shawl and a **guard chain** made of horsehair around the neck [to secure the pocket watch]. He was also carrying a **walking stick** and had styled his hair after Prince Albert.

Calcutta was like a treasure trove. There wasn't a single type that you would not find here. [Just look at the] people, determined to get their share of entertainment, lined up on either side of the road. Lawyers from the Small Causes Court, **section writers**, moneyed spice sellers, oilseed grinders, blacksmiths who were natives of Dacca and Brahmins who made a living by officiating at household pujas and consuming *folars* comprised most of the crowd; someone was carrying two daughters, another had three sons [in tow].

A clergyman distributed Bibles by the basketloads, with a catechist by his side. The latter, dressed like a **suburban** watchman, wore trousers, a flimsy long shirt and a black conical cap. He wielded his hands and mouth a lot, extolling on the greatness of Christianity, exhorting as they do in court. If you saw him all of a sudden, you might think he was playing the chorus in a puppet theatre. Basket-carrying porters, schoolgoing boys and peddlers stood attentively around him, not able to make out a word of what he was saying. Earlier, wayward young men would quarrel with their parents and run away to the western part of the country or convert to Christianity. But nowadays, after the railways were laid, it was very difficult to run away to the west [and not get tailed]. Besides, given the miserable lives the native Christians led,[45] one was afraid to convert.

A cloud in the sky was enough to turn Chitpore main road into a muddy mess. The Gajan procession moved on, right through the piles of dust, strewn all around, followed by bands of drummers. In front were two porters, carrying a huge brass dial, suspended from a bamboo log, on which boys kept beating with clubs. Sundry flag-bearers followed, haphazardly. A group of Haris in the middle sang a *bhajan*—'Bhola's a forgetful soul, a colourful bloke/The naked lord of the three worlds wears matted hair and a garland of bones'[46]—in sync with the beat of the drums. Behind them came a liveried gatemen, postmen and guards, dressed in keeping with the status of the babu [who employed them]. In between were impersonators, dressed up as Shiva—smeared all over with chalk and ash, wearing tin headgear resembling a snake's hood—and his divine consort, Parvati.[47] Behind them came a group of sanyasis, stuck all over with doshloki. They [carried pots containing] burning resins, dancing all the way. Other performers lined up on either side kept driving more arrows into their tongues and hands. Long fishing rods, with lobsters made of pith suspended from the hook were carried along. *Danak, danak* . . . the drum went. The drummers played short, peppy beats, non-stop, on several **sets** all at once. The babu's nephew, younger brother and cousins followed in carriages. They were up since 3 o'clock last night. Now their eyes were bloodshot, and heads covered with the dust from the roads of Bhowanipore and Kalighat. The audience watched on, awestruck. Suddenly a horse got agitated by the sound of the music. People ran, some of them stumbling over, landing inside shops. Some fell into the gutter. The sun was strong enough to crack open the skulls [of the assembled audience], but they refused to budge.

Ultimately, the processions went back, following police orders. The police **superintendent** who surveyed the roads on horseback, checked his pocket watch and found it was past the cut-off time. **Martial law** was on: anyone playing the drum would be taken to the police station. As soon as the constable's baton hit a drum or two, the city became absolutely silent. Many people tiptoed back to their homes, carrying the drums on their backs. The audience swore at the rules of the **Queen's** kingdom as they went back home.

The city cooled down for a little while at least. Those who had pierced themselves with arrows took these out and stepped inside liquor shops. The tired sanyasis went home to enjoy the breeze from a hand-wielded fan and swigged down several pots of *amani*. The shrine of Shiva at the Gajan venue closed doors. The fun of driving arrows through one's body was over for this year. That's how Sunday passed, in a jiffy.

Today was the last day of the year. Young men and women were saddened to see a year of their youth pass by. The hapless prisoner on the other hand was ecstatic to find he was through with another year of his term. Today the old year took leave; tomorrow the young one would dawn on us, and we would chuck the pains we have suffered, the losses we have made—in the space of the old year—with the year itself, for the sake of the future, which brought us hope. The past made a face at us on his way out. The present arrives and took his seat solemnly, like a schoolmaster—inspiring fear and joy, bringing us both surprise and tension. With the departure of the old and the coming of the new, the world was made to feel the way indigo peasants' hearts fluttered when the incumbent district magistrate was transferred,[48] the way the hearts of the boys promoted to the new class beat ominously when they saw the new master, the way the lady who gave birth to a series of stillborn children was sceptical when finally, well past her prime, she produced a child that was alive.

The English celebrated New Year in great style. They rang in the new by offering paan and betel nuts [as one would to the new bride, poised to enter the household][49] and rang out the old with drunken revelry. The Bengalis, whether they had a good year or not, munched on horseradish stems as they drove the old year out to the sound of drums, consigning it to the roads, with the dust. Only the drunken babus who offered pots of alcohol[50] to have these sanctified by the Gods and those who opened fresh ledger books treated the Bengali New Year's day with due respect.

It was the day of the Charak festival. In the morning the Brahmos worshipped their one and only God who was unique, following the rites. A lot of them would offer alcohol to Him later on. This year a deputy priest of the Brahmo Samaj[51] performed Kali Puja with great pomp. He even swore by Lord Vishnu, not forgetting to taste cow dung at the [staunch Hindu] zamindar's house to make amends for attending a widow's second wedding.[52] It was difficult to make sense of the way Brahmos behaved these days. They celebrated Durga Puja at home and yet visited the Samaj every Wednesday where they would close their eyes and howl like bereaved souls. Was the Supreme Being an unrefined upcountry man or a Maharashtrian Brahmin that he would not get the message unless he was addressed in Sanskrit couplets borrowed from the Vedas?[53] Or was he so engrossed chatting with his buddies so as not to care? In due course the paraphernalia surrounding Christian and Brahmo rites would be quite the same. There is a move in that direction it seems.

The pole, now lifted from the pond, had been planted on the ground. A rotating crescent-moon shaped contraption was fixed on top, with ghee and bananas in between.[54] Once the glare of the sun mellowed a little, multitudes swarmed into the festival venue. The men about town, dressed in all sorts of clothes, were out riding phaetons, *judi gadis* and state carriages to watch the festivities. Some of them rode atop the roofs of palanquins,[55] dressed like the shongs hired by the bell-metal workers community, acting out a skit.[56] The lowly, the rich and neophyte babus made up most of the crowd.

If reptiles and amphibians could pull off a feat, why not the small fish? Having seen Brahmins and Kayasthas attain sophistication, the nine lowborn sects,[57] that is, not including the Haris and cobblers, too, were trying to crawl their way up. The second incarnations of Rammohan Roy, Debendranath Tagore, Vidyasagar and Keshab Sen were getting born in low-caste homes.[58] Fowl curry and bread rolls were **introduced** for supper, instead of the regular meal of two rotis made from wheat and a vegetable.

Liquor shop owners, cowrie-counters,[59] the weaver's assistant and those peddling bear hair[60] were embarrassed about staying on in Calcutta when they found that dining at one's in-laws' and women getting their noses pierced on the left side had become fashionable.[61] Instead of sporting a shaven head with a *tiki* like Sri Chaitanya,[62] the men preferred being a votary of the Albert-cut school. Since it did not look good to go shopping wearing a short dhoti, with a bunch of keys slung on one's shoulder [in typical Bengali middle-class fashion], judi gadis, buggies and broughams, depending on one's financial status, were pressed into service. The bhadralok sycophant—who joined the brigade either for want of a job or because he was a congenital sucker—emerged on the scene, along with badge-wearing **orderlies** and postmen.

Gradually, through manipulation, craft, trade and investment, some of the city's lowly people got rich in a very short time. It was they who sponsored the traditional festivities: Ramlila,[63] Snanyatra,[64] Charak, flying balloons,[65] fireworks display and the dance of the horses.[66] Most had their pet satellites. They hired one or two thoroughbred idiots of the bovine variety whose hooves resembled that of wild boars—and raised in good families too—to say things like 'Yes Sir', 'Whatever you say is right, Sir', etc. They would not donate a penny for a good cause. But the amount they spent on the annual **garden feasts** could well have been used to support the **founding** of four or five universities.

Fun was never over too soon in Calcutta. The idol at the community puja stayed put for another twelve days after the rituals were over. Charak too could drag, become stale, rotten and putrid. This book would get longer and even more bitter if I went into all that. So here's ending the tale of Charak while the festival is still fresh.

On the festival ground, tin windmills, bamboo flutes with metallic nuts attached to them, replicas of the Charak pole, painted in yellow, rag dolls, toys made out of pith, clay models of Prahlad[67] and painted pots were on sale. Drums played on, rhythmically in sync with the following couplet: '*Danak danak dadang dang.* The lobster has two pincers'. Rolls of paan, spiked with a light intoxicant, were being sold. The Charak performer, a hook pierced to his back, danced into the venue and embraced the pole. Then he was raised by a lever and whirled around. Everyone looked up, staring at his back. He just went round and round for dear life, now holding on to the rope that he was suspended by and now letting go, his legs dangling. 'Turn him around, turn around,' the mob chanted. [As they say] when it was party time for some people, it was disaster for someone else: one man was being pierced at the back and whirled around for the entertainment of a thousand people.

Reader, by reading this minuscule piece on Charak, you have received an **insight** into the ways of Calcutta's social milieu, as it is now, and as you get more familiar with us, the more knowledgeable you would become. That was why this piece began with the **quote:** 'The city teaches the ways of the police station.'

Notes

1. Used here in the connotative sense, meaning the ways of the world. The quote is a line from a popular *tappa* number by the rather obscure poet Tunoya. See Arun Nag, ed., *Sateek Hootum Pyanchar Naksha* (Calcutta: Ananda Publishers, 2008): 181.
2. A festival to mark the last day of the year in the Bengali calendar (a month-long celebration, culminating usually on 14 April). People dressed up as Lord Shiva or the Serpent Goddess Manasa go from door to door, begging for alms which they would offer to the Gods. Devotees of Lord Shiva, putting thin iron rods and rings through their ribs, mouth and nostrils, egged on by a cheering crowd of onlookers. The climax is when these men, pierced and bloodied all over, are suspended from a rotating cross, which forms the fulcrum, pinned horizontally on a pole. As the cross is turned around fast, like a spinning wheel, the men tied to it are made to go round in circles. This is supposedly an act of purging to get rid of the negativity accumulated during the year that is on its way out.
3. Small tridents pinned on either side of a Charak performer's stomach; see also note 7. A piece of cloth soaked in ghee would be wrapped around the metal and ignited.
4. A dicing and peeling curved knife, most commonly used in the Bengali kitchen, a bonti has been historically used as an impromptu weapon, especially when it came to crimes of passion; an exceptionally sharp single blade that is made to stand at right angles to the ground, as the user's right foot presses hard down on its wooden platform placed on the floor. Bontis would be put erect inside a sack stuffed with grass, for the Charak performers to dive on and injure themselves.
5. After the Sepoy Mutiny in 1857, the first uprising of Indian soldiers against British rule, the sepoys (Indian soldiers employed by the East India Company) were looked upon as national heroes. The weavers of the exquisite saris from Dacca began a new fashion trend by weaving a special design on the borders of saris and dhotis as a tribute to the rebel soldiers.
6. Considered auspicious, the leaves of bel (its English name, not much used, is wood apple) are an essential item in any Bengali Hindu ritual.
7. The month-long Gajan festival, marking the end of the harvest precedes the Charak Festival. For more on Charak, see also note 2.
8. In 1780, the East India Company had appointed agents to oversee the manufacturing and trading of salt in each of its designated areas.

A salt diwan, i.e., a native collector of revenue from the salt trade, would serve under an English agent, often wielding absolute control on the agent's behalf. The salt trade, like most other businesses, was sewn up by racketeers. Therefore a collector, unless he was too conscientious about taking a cut, would have amassed quite a bit of money by the time his tenure came to an end. See Nag, ed., *Sateek Hootum Pyanchar Naksha:* 182-83.

9. The rise of the English East India Company was succinctly summed up by Rabindranath Tagore, who wrote '*Baniker maandanda neme elo rajdanda hoye*' (The trader's scales turned into the ruler's sceptre). The English merchants had obtained trading rights in Bengal by paying Emperor Farrukhshiyar a hefty fee in 1717. They also acquired the right to buy thirty-eight villages around their estate, besides having exclusive trading rights by paying a token fee annually. But Murshid Quli Khan, the governor of Bengal, Bihar and Orissa, was not ready to grant the English this special privilege, and his successor, the hot-headed Nawab Sirajuddaulla even less so.

   Siraj was defeated by the English force in the Battle of Plassey in 1757. The deal with Mir Jafar, who became the new titular head, was that the Company would protect him against the French and other colonialists, in return for more land and autonomy. Mir Jafar, who had betrayed Siraj and taken his place, did not last long. When Mir Kasim, another kinsman, removed him with the help of the Company forces, the latter decided that the revenue earned from Burdwan, Midnapore and Chittagong would be spent to support the Company's soldiers.

   Soon Mir Kasim fell foul with the English. Mir Jafar made a second pact with the Company, whereby he was reinstated and allowed to keep only a small force. The Company claimed the three contentious districts. On 12 August 1765, Emperor Shah Alam II handed over the governing rights, i.e., the diwani, of Bengal, Bihar and Orissa to the Company. It was decided that they would collect the taxes and pay an annual fee to the emperor in Delhi and the nawab in Bengal. 'In this respect the Company was merely a substitute for the nawab of Bengal who had collected revenues and paid tribute [to the emperor in Delhi] in like fashion.' See Antony Wild, *The East India Company: Trade and Conquest from 1600* (London: Harper Collins, 1999).

10. Nandakumar Roy (1705-1775) held high offices in the government of Murshid Quli Khan. He was a part of the conspiracy hatched against Siraj, and was given high posts in the Company as a reward. After

Mir Jafar was reinstated, Nandakumar, his aide, was given the title of 'maharaja' by the emperor in Delhi. After Mir Jafar's death, Nandakumar's stock fell. He hastened his death when he got on the wrong side of the Company's Governor General, Lord Warren Hastings. He had complained to the Company about Hastings's corrupt ways (apparently, the latter accepted a bribe of Rs.300,000 to procure a job for Nandakaumar's son Gurudas Roy). A vengeful Hastings had him framed in a fraud case. Justice Elijah Impey found Nandakumar guilty and sentenced him to be hanged on 5 August 1775: 'more as an exemplary lesson than as a dispassionate act of justice, to teach the natives what would happen to them if they dared to oppose the British rulers'. See Sumanta Banerjee, *The Parlour and the Street: Elite and Popular Culture in Nineteenth-Century Calcutta* (Calcutta: Seagull Books, 1998). This was an incident that shook up the otherwise unruffled Bengali psyche, as Nandakumar had been extremely influential.

11. This is an inventory of caste Hindus, hierarchically arranged: *(a)* Kulin denotes an exclusive group of high-caste Brahmins and Kayasthas: the 'pure race'. For many of them, taking a series—the number could run into hundreds—of nubile and younger women as wives was a vocation. The much-married kulin would often support himself by paying an annual visit to each of his many in-laws, where he would be given a meal and money and get to spend the night with a wife whose face, or name, he could hardly remember. It was quite easy to lose one's kulinhood by marrying into a non-kulin family, for instance. *(b)* Srotriya, a Brahmin who is a level below that of a kulin, in the caste hierarchy; *(c)* Kayastha: High-caste Hindus, traditionally associated with employment in government offices; *(d)* Baidya, high-caste Hindus again, Ayurvedic practitioners; *(e)* Teli, low-borns, traditionally engaged in grinding mustard seeds to make cooking oil.
12. A small wicker container to measure rice, often worshipped as a symbolic representation of the Goddess of Prosperity.
13. They were the untouchable subalterns. Duli bearers would traditionally bear a carriage, transporting people on their backs. Haris still exist as Harijans, traditionally engaged in waste disposal. A Kaora is a procurer of herbs by profession.
14. It was imperative for a rich babu to have a private pleasure retreat, somewhere in the periphery of the city, preferably on the banks of the river Ganga, where he would entertain his friends and guests with an abundant supply of wine and women.

15. This would normally be a Shivling, a phallic symbol denoting the God of extraordinary might and virility; also the creator and destroyer of the world.
16. A popular perfume brand at the time. See Nag, ed. *Sateek Hootum Pyanchar Naksha*: 187.
17. This is a penalty the zamindar would slap on his subjects for their involvement in petty crimes such as theft, forgery, and so on. Ibid.
18. Together these formed the most vibrant and crowded stretch of Calcutta. In modern Calcutta, the area corresponds to the stretch beginning north of Tiretta Bazar, off Calcutta's vibrant China Town, through Batakrishna Pal Avenue, till it cuts into Rabindra Sarani (erstwhile Chitpore Road), which used to be the Ahiritolla four-point crossing. Mechhuabazar now corresponds to Jorasanko, the site of Rabindranath Tagore's ancestral house. The small presses, which produced chap books and chemolithographs, were distributed in and around Battala. Chorbagan today is best known as the site of the spectacular Marble Palace, Raja Rajendralal Mallik's ode to European classical art and architecture, built in 1835. The market in Notun Bazar, off the northern-most parts of Rabindra Sarani and opposite the eponymous Kochuri Galli, is where one might still find traditional Bengali sweetmeats. 'Chitpore Road is where the most spectacular stately homes in Calcutta are situated but survival strategies are at odds with gravity.' See Soumitra Das, *A Jaywalker's Guide to Calcutta* (Mumbai: Eminent Designs, 2007).

    Sonagacchi, along Rabindra Sarani—right next to the slew of clay modellers' workshops—is the hub of Calcutta's notorious red-light district. Sonagacchi looks much the same even today, although the women working out of the tiny, ill-lit quarters in these labyrinthine bylanes are now into campaigning for safe sex and rights of sex workers in a major way.
19. The first definitive Bengali primer that Ishwarchandra Vidyasagar wrote for school children, published in 1855 and still in circulation.
20. A thriving, overcrowded, bursting-at-the seams market in the heart of north Calcutta, close to Batakrishna Pal Avenue, with a slew of jewellery shops threatening to spill over on the road from either side. Sovaram Basak, the merchant who set up the market, was hardly a raja/zamindar, but belonged to the weaver caste. 'But being fabulously rich, his middle-caste lineage was ignored.' See Das, *Jaywalker's Guide to Calcutta.*
21. One of the four villages (the other three being Sutanuti, Gobindapur

and Kalikata) that grew into the modern metropolis that is Calcutta, Chitpore, since Hootum's time, has been the city's famed theatre district and the hub of battala publications. A slew of booking offices for *jatra* performances (high-octane melodrama or mythological plays, performed in open spaces to huge crowds) are still lined up on either side of Rabindra Sarani, but the audience for this sort of entertainment has evidently moved from the city to the districts and rural areas.

22. The house of the Sinhas was a sprawling mansion near what is now Belgacchia in north Calcutta. They were great patrons of art. Michael Madhusudan Dutt's first play, *Sharmistha,* was performed here.
23. Canons were fired from Fort William three times a day to mark time: at 9 am, 1 pm and 9 pm.
24. A deity worshipped by spice sellers.
25. These are Calcutta suburbs, metaphorically speaking, a sort of a kitchen garden in Calcutta's backyard, still servicing the city's vegetable markets.
26. Malaria swept through Ula (present-day Birnagar in Nadia district, West Bengal) in 1856, killing three-fourths of its population. See Nag, ed., *Sateek Hootum Pyanchar Naksha:* 189.
27. Moral tales a Bengali child would read at the primary stage of his education. Chanakya was India's own Machiavelli who lived in fourth century AD. A minister to Chandragupta Maurya, he wrote several guidebooks containing tenets of good governance, the most famous being *Arthashashtra* (Economic Theories); treated as a seminal text when it came to moral education in Hootum's time.

    The popular version of the story of Karna, which has the hero from the *Mahabharat* and his wife, Padmabati, cutting up their son to feed a guest, was also a must-read for children.
28. *The Englishman,* originally *John Bull,* was first published on 1 October 1833. J. H. Stocqueler, a well-known journalist, bought the rights of *Bull,* gave it a liberal spin and rechristened it as *The Englishman.* The paper was run with financial support from Dwarkanath Tagore. *Harkara* is a shortened version of *The Bengal Hurkaru and Chronicle,* first published as *The Bengal Hurkaru* in 1798, edited by Charles Maclean. The paper suspended publication after the editor who had apparently arrived in India 'without permission' was asked by the government to leave the country. *The Bengal Hurkaru* was revived in 1828, had a tie-up with *The Bengal Chronicle* 1836 onwards. In Hootum's time, the paper, now rechristened *The Bengal Hurkaru and the India*

Gazette, assumed a pro-planters, anti-peasant stance vis-à-vis the *Nildarpan* case. The *Phoenix,* first published in 1855 as a periodical, became a daily from June 1856. Edited by H. D. Chick, the paper was well-known for its reliability and authenticity. Later it was merged with *The Citizen.* The last editor was J. W. O'Sullivan. *The Exchange Gazette* was a daily newspaper (excepting Sundays) published first in 1818 from The Calcutta Exchange Press, 5 Council House Street. Primarily a trade and commerce-related paper, featuring advertisements. There was a Bengali edition as well. See Nag, ed., *Sateek Hootum Pyanchar Naksha:* 191.

29. In an era preceding typewriters, photocopiers and computers, writers were hired to make copies of all official documents. The person leading the team would be a head writer; ibid.
30. Queen Victoria's husband's visit to India in 1853, it seems, set a trend in hairstyling, that of parting one's hair at the side; ibid.
31. See 'Preface to the Second Edition', p. 10, note 4.
32. Greek pillars, big and circular at the base, tapering upwards.
33. Kalighat, on the southern fringes of Calcutta, beside a narrow and muck-filled canal cut from the river Ganga, comes with an obvious etymological connection with the city's name. Famous for the temple of Goddess Kali and the adjacent burning *ghat,* Kalighat is a bustling slice of life in Calcutta as much as a seat of votive offerings and impromptu weddings.
34. Sending Hindu widows—both elderly and young—to Kashi (modern Benaras) or Vrindavan was a common practice. The idea was that the ladies, condemned by fate, would spend the rest of their lives in the holy city, in an ambience of abstinence and spirituality. In reality this would often be a ploy to pack them off to a life of penury and isolation and deny them a share in the family property. In Tekchand Thakur's *Alaler Gharer Dulal,* arguably the first Bengali novel (1858), Motilal, an English-educated upstart, misbehaves with his widowed mother and sister who leave home and end up leading a life of utter penury—although somewhat redeemed by their total absorption into spiritualism and compassion—in Vrindavan.
35. This was a criminal appeals court that dealt with cases from outside of Calcutta. The court was functional till the Calcutta High Court was set up in 1862. See Nag, ed., *Sateek Hootum Pyanchar Naksha:* 192.
36. In Hootum's time Bhowanipore, now a crowded residential area in central-south Calcutta, was a suburb on the southern fringes of the city, a place where only zamindars from the districts would put up

while their more urban cousins would treat south of Park Street as the back of beyond; another reason could have been the proximity to the Sadar Diwani Adalat, the Company's highest appellate court, and the fact that some of the country's most illustrious lawyers lived there. See P. Thankappan, in 'The Growth and Development of Old Calcutta', in Sukanta Chaudhuri, ed., *Calcutta: The Living City: The Past,* vol. 1 (Calcutta: Oxford University Press, 1990): 18-19.

37. One of the oldest up-market locations in north Calcutta, preferred by the city zamindars and moneyed people, later best known as a location for a gun and shell factory and in the 1970s as the site of the police massacre of Naxalites.
38. Located in the southern suburbs of modern Calcutta, this is where the descendants of the family of Sabarna Roychoudhury still live. The Roychoudhurys had zamindari rights over the three villages—Sutanuti, Govindapur and Kalikata—which were transferred to Job Charnock's son-in-law Charles Eyre in November 1698. This was the base on which Calcutta grew. See Nair, 'The Growth and Development of Old Calcutta': 11.
39. There was no discontentment, want or unrest during Ram's rule in Ayodhya, in the epic *Ramayan,* in other words, it was a utopian situation. But the expression has been used in a pejorative sense in the present context, meaning the ruler's absolute and total control over the land he surveys.
40. These were conmen who offered to take the sailor, who obviously carried a lot of money, his salary for the months he had been on board, around the city, in other words, take him for a ride. See Nag, ed, *Sateek Hootum Pyanchar Naksha:* 193-94.
41. The garden house with seven tanks was located north-east of Chiria More on Barrackpore Trunk Road; the Cossipore English School is located on the estate; the Asiatic Society on Park Street was founded by Sir William Jones in 1784 to facilitate research in Oriental themes. It has a museum and a rich archive; the Bally Bridge, constructed over the Bally Canal, connecting Bally with Uttarpara in 1846 was regarded as an example of technological achievement at the time. The circular canal skirting the north and north-east of Calcutta was connected to the river Ganga near Baghbazar. A lock-gate was installed at this junction in 1833; ibid: 194.
42. See 'Preface to Second Edition', p. 10, note 4.
43. Provisions complimentary to each other which help give redress to the wronged party, widely practised in England before the Judicature

Act was passed in 1875. See Nag, ed., *Sateek Hootum Pyanchar Naksha:* 195.

44. In the epic *Mahabharat,* Duryodhan, the anti-hero, had hid himself in the deep waters of the Dwaipayan Lake, to escape the righteous wrath of the valiant Bhimsen. The connotations here are of viciousness, treachery and a hidden ulterior motive.
45. Converted Christians had a hard time in a largely bigoted Hindu-dominated society. Apart from social ostracization and being disowned by one's own folks, they often had their own moral dilemmas to contend with. The most celebrated example of this was the poet Michael Madhusudan Dutt (1824-73) who being westernized, thought he would find Christianity conducive; he also wanted to avoid marrying the bride, from his own caste, whom his father had chosen for him. Dutt's conversion to Christianity was abetted by Reverend Krishnamohan Banerjea (1813-85), but he never got to marry Banerjea's daughter—a major reason why he had converted in the first place. Subsequently, Dutt was disowned by his father and thus began a life of abject penury and stress, albeit marked by flashes of brilliant poetry.
46. Bholanath is the other name of Lord Shiva, the third of the holy trinity in the Hindu pantheon, immensely powerful, as the Destroyer, he seems oblivious of his own powers. He represented an alternative lifestyle presenting both austere and more flamboyant aspects like smoking pot, living in the cremation grounds, and so on. Women even now keep a fast in his name, wishing for a husband like him.
47. Shiva's divine consort is the Goddess Durga as Parvati. She married him against her father's wishes, which ultimately ended with Parvati dead and an enraged Shiva going berserk, dropping her body parts all across India. A holy shrine was built on each site where a body part landed, Calcutta's Kalighat being one, constructed over her little finger.
48. See 'Nildarpan' Sketch 3, p. 128; p.154, note 68.
49. This combination is given to the new bride waiting to enter her in-laws' house as a welcoming gesture.
50. In idol worship, offering fruits and sweets to the deity is a part of the ritual. The worship over, these are consumed by the devotees as *prasad* (food blessed by the God). According to Hootum, since alcohol is the staple of the babus, that's what they will offer the Gods as well—one more excuse to get drunk on *prasadi* liquor.
51. Founded in 1828 by Rammohan Roy, this monotheistic society came

into being as a reaction to Hindu orthodoxy and bigotry. A meeting place for the elite intellectual reformists, the Samaj had its flaws: perceived and real. See Sketch 2, p. 100, note 89.

52. See Sketch 3, p. 147, note 34; Sketch 5, p. 195, note 11; and Sketch 8, p. 233, note 12.
53. A rift developed in the Brahmo Samaj, between the camp led by Debendranath Tagore and the rationalists led by Akshaykumar Dutta (see Introduction, p. lxi, note 21; Sketch 4, p. 174, note 12), who wanted the Samaj to concentrate more on social service rather than popularizing the Brahmo religion. See Nag, ed., *Sateek Hootum Pyanchar Naksha:* 196.
54. These were applied to the pivot as lubricants to make the pole rotate smoothly.
55. The two handles would be cut off, wheels added and the vehicle pulled by a horse.
56. This was an annual roving performance on the last day of the Bengali year, funded by the bell-metal merchants. Usually the actors would do a satire on contemporary society; ibid: 196-97.
57. These include the low-caste Shudras, namely, betel-leaves growers, blacksmiths, potters, gardeners, milkmen, confectioners, barbers, weavers and mustard-seed-grinder; ibid: 197.
58. Roy was the founder of the Brahmo Samaj, a pioneer in stopping the practice of sati, a champion of English education. He was also the Mughal emperor's envoy to England. Debendranath Tagore headed the Brahmo Samaj from 1842 to 1862, appealed to the British Parliament for autonomy, but is generally better known as the father of Rabindranath Tagore. For Vidyasagar, see Introduction, p. lix, note 1. A writer and ideologue, Keshab Chandra Sen, parted ways with Debendranth to form his own group in 1866. He was severely criticized for flouting the marital norms of the Brahmo Samaj that he himself had introduced in marrying his under-age daughters off to the royal families of Cooch Behar and Tripura.
59. Cowrie was the lowest unit of currency, therefore, having to count them indicates one's poor status.
60. Bear hair worn inside an amulet was supposed to cure remittent fever. See Nag, ed., *Sateek Hootum Pyanchar Naksha:* 199.
61. These are references to practices that were considered a social taboo in nineteenth-century Bengal. No self-respecting son-in-law would live off his in-laws and neither would a good woman have her nose pierced on the left side, which would be considered an act of transgression.

'The ladies of the house would say, if the wife wore gold on the right of her nose, the breath purified by the metal did good to the husband when it touched him, probably the reason why Hootum ridiculed the trend of piercing the left side of one's nose.' See Kalyani Dutta, *Thor Bari Khara* (Calcutta: Thema, 2004): 84.

62. Sri Chaitanya was the biggest exponent of the Bhakti movement in Bengal in the sixteenth century who inspired an unimaginably huge cult following in his time and still holds sway over a considerable part of the world. His typical hairstyle would be a tonsured head with a tiki in the middle.
63. Traditional theatre based on the life of Lord Ram, the central character of the Indian epic, *Ramayan.* See Sketch 9.
64. A festival around the ritual bathing of Lord Jagannath in summer. See Sketch 6.
65. Mr. Wintle who rose in a gas balloon on 29 July 1785 from Esplanade, was probably Calcutta's first flier. Mr. Robertson sailed in Calcutta's skies in a balloon several times between 1836 and 1838. Robertson would pool in money from rich sponsors to fund his flights. See Siddhartha Ghosh, in 'Calcutta's Industrial Archaeology', in Chaudhuri, ed., *Calcutta: The Living City.*
66. Horses were made to dance in sync with live music; a major source of entertainment in Calcutta in the 1850s.
67. The child incarnate of Lord Vishnu who was born to a family of demons and propounded a cult of non-violent resistance.

2
The Baroyaari Pujas in Calcutta

'And these what name or title e'er they bear,
— I speak of all —' ~ *Beggars Bush*[1]

ALMOST as if in mourning for the just concluded Charak festival, horseradish stems begin to crack open. Dust and pebbles on the road get swept hither and thither, churning restlessly. Drummers let go of their drums and turn cobblers. Milk sells cheaper. During this time the milkmen get little time to dilute milk with water [preoccupied as they are with the Charak festivities]. Spice sellers start selling bear fur. Carpenters gather bits of wood, bundling these up in scarves with floral motifs made in the looms of Dacca. The Brahmins who make a living out of eating folar and performing puja at their clients' now greedily await the next *adya shraddha* [where they might officiate]. Seeing this, the summer heat could not hold itself together any more. It spread out in all directions, singeing houses under high heat, causing death by drowning, cholera, and so on.

Rotten litchis and mangoes pile up high in shops set up on the roadside by agents who buy from planters and sell to wholesalers. Flies buzz on the discarded pulp of a ripe jackfruit. Elsewhere mango stones lie scattered. Boys rub these hard [against a surface] to make slits, playing on them like a whistle. After a recent spell of rain, the main road at Chitpore looks like a [banana-leaf] plate off which folar was eaten. *Kothiwallahs* stand underneath the balcony of the whorehouse and in roadside shops, shoes in hand [unable to walk through the mess on the road]. Those who drive hackney carriages are having a field day.

Calcutta's *cranchees*[2] are a blessing for rheumatic patients. Its effect [on the rider] is like exposure to **galvanic shocks**.[3] The sky-blue hackney coaches of yore that made the passengers swing this way and that seem to have disappeared from the streets of Calcutta, going the same way as the Hindu religion. Only one or two of these still seem emotionally tied to [the lanes of] Khiddirpore,[4] Bhowanipore, Kalighat and Barasat,[5] the reason we still see them.

'Four annas [for a ride]', 'Four annas [for a ride]', '[Going to] Lal Dighi',[6] '[This one's headed towards] the Treasury',[7] 'Come Babu, let me take you to the Small Causes Court',[8] the coachmen call out, after the current fashion. A kothiwallah or two sit inside the car like a new bride, bereft of company. Some of the clerks who work in **government offices** begin haggling with the coachmen. Disgusted, one of them decides he would walk to work. The coachmen laugh and hoot. 'Why don't you go in a porter's basket? You don't seem the sort who can afford a car ride,' they said, throwing a [back-handed] **compliment.**

It is ten in the morning. Boys, carrying books, walk to school, laughing boisterously along the way. Old junkies rub oil on their bodies, throw a gamccha on the shoulder and collect inside shops selling opium and smoking joints. Traders, now through with their business at the *haat,* are on their way back on empty barges. Calcutta is abuzz with activity. The rattling of cars, swish of whips cracked by drivers of horse-drawn carriages, and the sound of the hooves of Normandy and Weller horses on the road make the earth vibrate. It is difficult to walk on the road without something or the other getting in one's way.

Birkrishna Dan's **manager,** Kanaidhan Dutta, hired a hackney coach of good-if-not-the-best standards, to go around collecting the annual subscriptions for a baroyaari puja.[9] Birkrishna was the adopted son of Kebalchand Dan. They had a trading office in Haatkhola, around a dozen barn-houses to hold the harvested crop, five godowns to store wood and lime in Beleghata, and cash worth ten to twelve lakh rupees invested in the moneylending business. They also traded in company shares every now and then. Dan stayed in the city round the year, going home only to attend the Durga Puja for about ten to twelve days annually. He had a buggy, a Weller horse, a prostitute, two sycophants—both Telis by caste—a garden house in Garpar and a *bhouliya*[10] boat with six rowers dedicated to his exclusive use, the tools to aid his relaxation and pleasure.

Birkrishna Dan was dark, short, stocky and potbellied. He wore a gold amulet, a thick gold waistband, a double-layer gold necklace, and a huge gold good luck charm—shaped like a flat playing card—that he would put on at the time of offering his daily prayers. He bathed in the river Ganga every day, and would decorate his forehead, neck and ears by drawing the holy mark without fail. Dan could sign his name in Bengali and English. He knew a few English words like 'come' and 'go' [picked up] from the English clients who came to see him and the **contract** papers of a few English companies. But he was not all that involved when it came to running the business. It was Kanaidhan Dutta who managed his affairs. Dan spent his time enjoying the breeze from hand-drawn *punkhas*,[11] riding the buggy and playing the esraj.

Initially, a dozen-odd people would pool in money to fund a puja[12] [to propitiate a God or Goddess]—be it Kali or any other—at the time of a raging epidemic. But since then the Mother Goddess, moved by the yaars' entreaties, dripping with devotion and respect for her, has ended up with them. The baroyaari puja was organized primarily by moneylenders, wholesalers, tradesmen and retailers who sold their ware at the haat. Every year, one, two or five cowries per maund [37.3kg] of goods sold or exported would go into the baroyaari puja fund. The money accumulated over a year or two was deposited with a prosperous man with a taste for the pleasures of life, one of the yaars, that is, who was made the chief executive. It was his job to collect subscriptions from other sources, go from door-to-door for collections, organize the shongs and other entertainment that would take place on the days of the puja.

This time Birkrishna Dan of Dacca was [nominated] the chief executive of the baroyaari puja. So Kanaidhan Dutta, Dan's chief manager, was given the responsibility of collecting the annual subscriptions and performing other tasks.

Dutta's car jingled-jangled musically all the way before pulling up at the door of a rich Kayastha at Noorighata.[13] He jumped down from the car quickly and walked up to meet the gatekeepers. The gatekeepers posted at rich men's houses in the city did not usually—even if it were the raja of Nadia [at their door]—announce the visitor inside [unless there was an incentive]. It was difficult winning them over. Even after one had offered a tip for Holi, a bonus for Durga Puja or a gift to celebrate Rakhi Purnima,[14] it would be unlikely to cut any ice. Dutta haggled for a long time and finally convinced a gateman to take the news of his arrival inside, promising to pay him four annas.

Even when a visitor came to collect the interest on money loaned to the master of the house or to buy his ancestral property and sent in a message to that effect, whether he would be granted an audience depended on the consent of his highness, the gateman. Only a few wealthy houses were open to all. But one could not really blame the rich men in question. Beggars in the forms of 'Brahmin pandits', 'job-seekers', 'people saddled with marriageable daughters', 'bachelors' and 'Brahmins arrived from distant places' drove the city's affluent people crazy. It was difficult to find out who was actually desperate to buy a fix and whose need was genuine, even if one produced an **affidavit** [to establish one's claim].

Dutta waited at the door for half an hour, introducing himself to a dozen odd people, explaining the purpose of his visit. The gatekeepers cracked a few rather impertinent jokes. Dutta was beginning to lose his cool when the gateman, whom he had promised four annas earlier in the day, ambled in lazily and took him to the master of the house.

Reader, speaking of rich men's gatekeepers, I am reminded of another story which I cannot resist telling you at this point. Ten or twelve years back, a gentleman who lived in Baghbazar had called a few **friends** over to lunch at his house on his birthday. It was not as if we have **copied** the idea of celebrating birthdays from the English. For generations, we too have been [observing birthdays by] drinking jaggery with milk, planting sesame seeds and releasing fish in the water (to each his own), wearing new clothes, lighting wick lamps, calling friends and relatives over for a meal and celebrating to the sound of conch shell blowing, as one would at the time of having one's last meal as a bachelor.[15] But these days certain city dwellers prefer to celebrate birthdays in un-conventional ways. Somebody who turned sixty[16] by the grace of Mother Shashthi[17] was seen to indulge in excesses of substandard entertainment by decorating the gate with gas lights, hosting dances and inviting Englishmen for a meal. The idea was to have the guests bless him so that he could keep himself entertained likewise for the next sixty years: so that he could dye his hair and moustache, wear a shirt embroidered with golden thread and a diamond choker when he went to watch a dance, and turn out in full splendour at immersions, bathing processions and chariot festivals.

Sometimes, the most acute impact of the babu's birthday celebrations could be felt in his garden house. The guests would have to take a week off from work to get rid of the hangover. But this babu of ours from Baghbazar did not go into all that. He just wanted to treat a few close **friends** to a nice meal. The guests arrived one by one on the day of the feast. The food was ready. Only the fish for the meal had not been caught, as it was rather cloudy in the morning. But since fish was a staple of the Bengali diet, the host got extremely worried [about its absence]. He had sent people to look for fish in different places, but couldn't get any. Finally a fisherman arrived with a carp weighing about ten or twelve seers [0.93kg]. The host was overjoyed to see the fish. He thought he would pay anything that the fisherman asked for. 'How much do you want, old chap? Just say the price and it's yours,' he said. 'The price is twenty blows [on my back], struck with [your] shoe,' said the fisherman.

The host was truly amazed. He thought that the fisherman had drunk too much liquor on a cloudy day, else he was mad. But the fisherman was adamant; he had resolved not to sell the fish except for twenty blows struck with the master's shoe. The host and servants called him a lunatic and a drunkard and made fun of him. But the fisherman stuck to his resolve. Finally, the host, who was in a quandary as there was no way he could let go of the fish, agreed to strike, albeit softly, the fisherman, who bared his back absolutely unflinchingly. After the tenth blow, the fisherman said, 'Sir, please stop. I have a partner who will have to take the rest of the blows. It's your gatekeeper, sitting at the door. Please call him. He had said he wouldn't let me in unless I paid him half of what I earned for the fish. So I agreed to pay him half my share.' That was when the host realized why the fisherman had asked for twenty blows struck with the shoe as the price of the fish. The gatekeeper did not have to wait too long at the door for his share of what the fisherman had earned. The host paid him the remaining part of the twenty blows immediately. Reader, especially the rich men among you, I hope you would care to remember this piece of fiction.

The master of the house sat on a mattress, one-and-half feet high; his bare torso reclined against a cushion. Next to him sat his bespectacled secretary, engaged in a discussion with the clerk. In front of them a few account books were left open, besides a basket full of waste paper. On the other side [of the room] four or five Brahmin pandits waited, looking for opportunities to please the babu by telling him that he had been born in a rare auspicious moment and that he was really a heavenly being, who had lapsed when his meditation was interrupted and thus he came to be born on earth. Twenty yards from the mattress sat two jobseekers and an old person saddled with a marriageable daughter, pulling sad faces to make themselves look exactly like the archetypes of unemployed people and those with daughters to marry off. The sycophants stuck around the master, one of them whispering a thing or two in his ears. The master sat stiff, like Lord Kartik without his peacock.[18] Dutta walked up to him and bowed.

The master of the house was devoted to baroyaari puja. On the days through which the Durga Puja was held, he stayed put at the venue, round-the-clock, even as his nephews, sons-in-law and sisters' husbands were kept on their toes.

Dutta informed him about several things related to the [impending] puja and collected a **subscription** worth a thousand rupees before leaving. The manager took a cut of Rs. 2 per 100 during the **payment** but Dutta, who was keen on holding onto the burnt wood from a charred house [so that at least something is salvaged from the ruined heap] and keeping the manager in good humour, did not protest. The babu busied himself with the thought of what to wear on each night of the baroyaari puja.

Until two in the afternoon, Dutta, who hadn't got a chance to eat in the meantime, visited several houses with his subscription book. He did manage to raise some money. A big amount was entered in the book and signed [by the donor] (assuming that's a guarantee for the money to materialize!). Elsewhere he was taken by the scruff of his neck and driven out, jeered at and even got his chin tweaked.

Twenty years back, those who went collecting subscriptions for a baroyaari puja were much like a bailiff who had come to enforce Regulation Eight.[19] They would trample over the clay stove in the house and force the householder to pay up, quite like an extortionist persecuting a Brahmin for occupying duty-free land.[20] Some of them managed to sweet-talk rich men into paying up.

Once, the organizers of a baroyaari puja went to collect subscriptions from a trader who was one-eyed. This man was extremely miserly. It hurt him even to provide for his father's wife (meaning his mother). He would preserve the pale tubes made from banana leaves used for smoking, for a year, trading them for free laundry[21] for the entire family. When the baroyaari puja authorities asked for a subscription, the businessman was enraged. There was no way he was going to indulge in one paisa worth of wasteful expenditure on the baroyaari puja, he said. The executives scanned the premises closely for a long time, but couldn't find any evidence of wasteful expenditure. Tobacco was rolled into small balls and kept inside the same box as company shares. The man himself sewed pillow covers and the boys' clothes, when he found the time. The servants (actually just an old guy from Orissa) had to account for the number of tobacco balls and broomsticks [used to sweep the house] twice a day. Old dhotis were exchanged for utensils.[22] He owned company shares worth Rs.3,000,000, made a handsome packet from interests drawn from investments and also by lending money on a daily or weekly basis, but couldn't be persuaded to spend a paisa. His family expenses were covered by the money earned from pushing the spindle—that's what the family occupation had been, traditionally. His only unnecessary investment seemed to be the pair of spectacles he wore. It had two lenses, while he had only one eye. The baroyaari organizers made a note and pleaded with him once again, 'Sir, we have caught you making a bad investment there. You ought to take off a lens or pay us.' The trader was pleased to hear this, and finally agreed to pay two quarters, extremely grudgingly.[23]

On another occasion, a group of baroyaari organizers called on the Sinhas' house. Sinha was going to **office** at the time. Four or five of the organizers surrounded him and began screaming, 'We've got him!', 'We've got him!' A crowd gathered on the road [outside the house]. Sinha was taken by surprise and asked what the matter was. That was when one of the organizers said, 'Sir! As Mother Bhagawati [Durga's other name] was travelling from her abode in Kailash to our baroyaari venue at such-and-such place, the lion she was riding broke a leg on the way and now she is stranded. She appeared in our dreams, saying that she could come only if we got her a spare lion to ride on. We have been looking for one in various places for a month now but couldn't find any. Today by a sheer stroke of luck we have found you.[24] We are not going to let you go, come what may. Please come with us. It is up to you to make sure that our Mother, the Goddess, can arrive safely.' Pleased with the way the organizers had put it, Sinha made a handsome contribution.

There are more bizarre tales about collecting subscriptions for a baroyaari puja, but there is no need to go into all that here. Earlier, the baroyaari puja at Chinsurah was quite extraordinary. They would feature shongs of the *achavo* (i.e., incredible) and *bombachak* (i.e., bamboozling) variety. Babus from the city and other places would hire **boats**, barges, **pinnace** and bhouliya to watch the shong. The puja drew such huge crowds that banana-leaf plates were going for a rupee a piece, and thieves were a dime a dozen. Of course poor people in dire straits could not afford to light the stoves in their kitchens.

For the last few years, baroyaari puja has been celebrated with great pomp in Guptipara, Kanchrapara, Shantipur and Ula, villages not too far away from Calcutta. There would be a major struggle for one-upmanship [among these villages]. Once, the residents of Shantipur spent Rs.500,000 on the baroyaari puja. It took them seven years to prepare for the event. The idol was sixty-feet tall. Finally, on the day of the immersion, each idol had to be torn apart from the frame[25] and immersed individually. The residents of Guptipara held a baroyaari puja satirizing [the achievement of their Shantipur counterparts]. They hung a *kaccha*[26] around Lord Ganesh's neck to commemorate the Divine Mother's death by accident. Huge amounts of money were spent on that puja as well.

Times have changed since then. Quite a few rich Bengalis have become more civilized. One does not hear any longer of people cleaning their posteriors with rose water, tearing the border off a Dacca-style dhoti before wearing it,[27] and using the dust of pearl instead of lime as a filling in one's paan. Things like spending a hundred thousand on dogs' weddings, throwing 100-rupee notes at the performers in a *jatra* and going to bathe in the river in a carriage drawn by four horses to the sound of trumpets, flaunting well-oiled bodies, have been few and far between. Incidences of a babu encouraging servile behaviour, taking a seat at a level higher than the rest, wearing one's hair in layers like Lord Kartik, employing a band of useless sycophants, keeping women and having the back pleats of one's dhoti crinkled and twisted happen only 'occasionally'. Like rising waterspouts and earthquakes, these too have become rare.

The Kayasthas and Brahmins among the rich (unless we're talking of a country-bred nincompoop) did not generally have sycophants on their payrolls. Only a few rich men from the business class had proved lucky for the parasites. One sees these toadies—with inflated chests, side hair partings, a sacred thread around the neck, eyes red like the *koonch* fruit, pieces of cotton dabbed in *ittar* [perfume] stuck in the ear (they were educated in all departments, just did not know their alphabet)—only in the company of rich gold traders.

Doubtless, when sycophancy ceased to be a profession,

baroyaari, khyamta, substandard revelry and flippant entertainment would go that way too.

Looked like winter would settle down any moment now. Milkmen carrying pots on their shoulders were on their way to stores. Fisherwomen, having washed the platforms [on which they laid out their ware], blades and baskets, put the lamps out. The men whose job it was to ignite the gas-lit lamps on the streets rushed past, carrying ladders on their backs. The guards finished **parading** in front of the police station (they were supposed to get into action [when required] but were too intimidated by the drunken men to do so). Clerks working in banks now had leave to go home.

There was a buzz of activity at Birkrishna Dan's office. The organizers had assembled to demonstrate to the potters the kind of shongs they would like to commission. The potter would deliver the shongs, made to order. Dan and Kanaidhan Dutta began [the discussion] by stating their choice.

Twenty multi-coloured **bell lanterns**—white, **green** and red—borrowed from the barrack where criminal cases were tried[28] had been put up. A layer of straw was spread on the courtyard, topped by wattle and finally a carpet of red coarse fabric from Madras that seemed to glow, smiling almost. Weighing scales, mats made from palm leaves, trays used to de-husk the grain and sieves peeped in from behind the **gunny bags** and a worn-out piece of jute cloth. Today these would be counted among the resident sons-in-law and dependent nephews [who do not command much respect in the household and are generally shoved in a corner].

Birkrishna wore a diaphanous shot silk dhoti, a **collar**, a shirt with motifs of **cups** and saucers (much like the sort one uses to cover a chandelier when not in use) and a wrap from the Dacca looms with slanting patterns, a handkerchief tucked in his waist. A gold key chain dangled on the shirt and dhoti pleats, **off-setting** the chain of the [pocket] watch.

Reader, the era of the nawabs had come to an end, like the setting sun in winter. The power of the British Empire grew like the sun after the disappearance of the cloud cover. Large bamboo groves went to seed, while puny twigs acquired deposits with a medicinal value.[29] [Riff-raffs like] language teacher Nabo,[30] small-time tradesman Shree[31] and puny Telis[32] were now being counted among the zamindars. The title 'raja', like armed guards, and the weapons in one's armoury, were consigned to the streets, woods and waste bins, discarded like shoes made of **India rubber** and the striped scarves from the looms of Shantipur. The families of Krishnachandra,[33] Rajballav,[34] Man Singh,[35] Nandakumar,[36] Jagat Seth,[37] and similar well-known and highly respected people went to the dogs. The Hindu religion, the respect commanded by poets, people's enthusiasm for learning, philanthropy and the staging of plays disappeared from the country as a result. Bands of **half**-akhrai, **full**-akhrai, panchali and jatra performers were formed. The young men of the city signed up with different drug-addicts' clubs—Shit-eaters, Trouble-makers and the Birds.[38] Money counted more than family name now. Rama the undertaker,[39] Keshta Bagdi, Pyancha Mallik and Chhuncho Seal were now the godfathers of Calcutta's Kayasthas and Brahmins. They became the city's leaders.

This was when **half**-akhrai and **full**-akhrai genres of music came into being. The city's moneyed people have been enjoying **half**-akhrai numbers ever since. The rich men of Shyambazar,[40] Rambazar, Chowk and Jorasanko who had nothing much to do began promoting a **half**-akhrai group each. Sycophants, job-seekers, and the hapless homebody-types from [different] neighbourhoods and clubs joined the amateur group of *dohar* singers. Some of them secured jobs, thanks to [their expertise at] **half**-akhrai. The grandpa-like family priest who once earned his keep by officiating at household pujas now lived like a king.[41] In a short while he managed to acquire a family coat of arms, a garden house, a judi gari and a two-storey house.

To come back to the baroyaari puja we have been telling the readers about, Birkrishna Dan took the initiative of organizing a **half**-akhrai concert at the venue, on the first night of the puja. Preparations were on.

The **half**-akhrai singers rehearsed at house no.2 on Dhopapukur Lane. Birkrishna rode his buggy to the venue every day, to keep a check on how things were going. [This is where] the dohars met up at 10 in the evening, after they had returned from the merchant's office [where they worked], washed and had a light meal. Blacksmiths from Dacca, farmers, laundrymen, puny Telis and folar-consuming Brahmins constituted most of the crowd. They were led by the youngest member of the Mukherjee clan. This man was an Ace among his friends, a Jack of Clubs in the company of a prostitute and a seasoned junkie who could match up to Lord Shiva's father.[42] He had a lean body and wore the sacred thread bunched together around his neck. Roasted tobacco leaves pressed to his teeth, he wore a dhoti with half-a-foot-wide red and black borders, made in the looms of Chakraberia. Two hundred and seventy grains of opium, a hundred and fifty bowls of *ganja* and a pitcher full of country liquor were kept ready for his daily fix. He would go for a bigger dose on festival days and Saturdays.

It was a moonless night, pitch dark. Clouds rumbled, lightning flashed intermittently. Leaves on the trees were absolutely still. The earth emitted heat as if it were on fire. Travellers occasionally stopped to look up at the skies as they hurried on their way. Dogs barked. Shopkeepers were preparing to down the shutters and go home. *Goodum!* The guns went off. It was 9 o'clock at night. There was major revelry at house no. 2 in Dhopapukur Lane. Birkrishna of Dacca, Pyalanath of Chowkbazar, the baroyaari leaders and a few expert musicians were expected to meet here. The song [to be performed during the puja] sounded like a good enough composition. The dohars on their part were adept at keeping the rhythm and singing in sync.

Time is not beholden to anybody. Like a river in flow, a prostitute's youthful looks and the age of every living being, time does not wait for anyone. The clock on the church tower struck the hour of ten. *Dhong dhong*, it went. A huge storm buoyed by strong winds began to rage. The dust on the roads rose, adding to the darkness. The cloud gnashed its teeth angrily, making small boys curl up on their mothers' laps. A heavy spell of rain came down, dropping like clubs.

A crowd had begun to accumulate at house no. 2. A lot of them turned up all soggy, unable to refuse the invitation. Four-chamber lamps fixed to the wall were lit. The stage glittered in the light. It looked like a battlefield, littered with paan, discarded straws made from rolled banana leaves [used for smoking the hookah] and flat-bottomed smoking bowls. Mukherjee junior exchanged pleasantries with the guests. All this while he had been trying to get the attention of people with a 'Hey you' and 'You there', and now had a cracked voice. The Telis, blacksmiths from Dacca and the laundrymen among the dohars, who between themselves had polished off a curry with some rotis made from wheat and had a stomach full of firni, sat tight, wearing clean dhotis and wrappers. Some of them found it difficult to keep their eyes open. The light from the lamps dimmed in their line of vision, appearing like fireflies. Sometimes they would sit up with a start, their stupor broken. It felt like flying. The room resembled a thick forest of people, sitting around in clusters, forming a loose circle. Somebody would crack a joke or break out into a *tappa* number, at times. The smarter lot carried their custom-made pair of shoes inside their pockets, or sat tight on these. When it came to shoes, dohars did not trust one another. The rehearsal was being kept on hold as people waited for Pyalanath of Chowkbazar to arrive. The singing would begin as soon as he stepped in. One or two of the dohars got tired of waiting [and said so]. A few others drummed up support [for the impatient members] by reiterating words like, 'Quite right'. But Pyalanath happened to be one of the chief **managers** of the baroyaari puja, a man of style who was always turned out in the finest of clothes. He was the life force of the yaars. Therefore not waiting for Pyalanath would look like a deliberate show of disrespect. Be it storm or lightning, or the end of the world, Pyalanath was sure to arrive, being a connoisseur of such cultural activities.

Fed up with waiting, Gobinda, the lead singer began singing a tappa number composed by Jikku, affecting a nasal tone. The pot of ganja was **passed** around from one cluster to the next. In one corner of the room the embers dropped from the hookah. People sitting nearby sprung up and shook out their clothes and dhoti pleats, creating a lot of hullabaloo. Each person had fifty odd **depositions** to make as to what made the embers drop. At that point a carriage rolled in and stopped at the door. Mukherjee junior sprang up from the meeting and ran towards the portico, shouting, 'It's Pyalanath Babu. He is here.' The dohars hurrahed, crying out in ecstasy. Drums were being beaten with great flourish. Pyalanath ascended the stairs. It took him half an hour to get through the series of **handshakes, good evenings** and greeting people [the traditional Bengali way] by putting both hands together.

Babu Pyalanath of Chowkbazar was a short guy, of small build. He had crossed fifty last year. The babu was a staunch Hindu who fasted on the eleventh day of the waxing moon, the first hour of the twelfth and the eighth day of the lunar cycle in the month of Bhadra and did not drink any water on the days when the moon waxed or waned. He had a poor man's temper, but a king's tastes. He had studied English for just three months at Sherburne's school[43] in the Bengali year 1219 [1812 AD]. So far he had managed to get by with what he had learnt there. He wore a costume and a cap at all times (tilted at such an angle that sometimes one could not help wondering if the babu had a right ear at all!). His favourite outfit comprised churidar trousers cut in Lucknow style (which made him look a bit like a baiji's servant), a long loose shirt, a dupatta tied across the middle and of course the tilted cap. He was held in high esteem in the baiji and khyamta circles, all too willing to bend over backwards to help sort out their troubles. He was ready to forget being a Hindu at the baiji's request and wouldn't mind undoing the back pleats on his dhoti and giving a fatwa or counting the prayer beads in the name of his twelve yaars. The babu was highly influential in Muslim circles. Even the Iranians with thick-set beards and Muslims resident in Lucknow [kept praising him, thereby] doing justice to the wisdom and skills of the babu at all times. The babu was not very fond of English ways. He felt an English education was required only for practical reasons. Having spent most of his time with the Muslims, he preferred their culture. He liked talking about the splendour of the *nawabi* era, its extravagant styles and grandiose temperament.

In the meantime the dohars began a new song, set to a different tune. The noise vibrated across Dhopapukur. Children sleeping in their mother's laps woke up with a start. Dogs started barking.

The song sounded something like that of Haris beating swine to death. Everybody [at the meet], pleased with the new tune, began cheering and congratulating the singers, showering praises on them. The dohars, now greatly encouraged, doubled the volume. The laundrymen's [donkeys] had been sleeping most soundly after a hard day's work. The extraordinary sound of the vocals made them start and run away, with the rope and tether. The singing continued till two at night after which Vedavyas[44] [on whose text the songs were based] got some respite, at least for the rest of the night. The dohars, the connoisseur babu and the executives took great pains to find their way back home in the dark and, finally, having reached there, could go to bed.

They were making clay idols modelled after the [typical] shongs at the baroyaari puja site for a while. Now they were ready. For a month, readings from the *Mahabharat* were held at the venue. Tomorrow that too would be over. The interpreter sat on a raised platform, garlands of blossoms wrapped around his head. He looked like the sacrificial bull or buffalo about to be beheaded, and made a complete travesty of the exercise. He hardly ever looked at the original text. In fact, whatever he said was either regurgitated from Uncle Kashiram's work,[45] or concocted stuff. Being an interpreter of religious texts was not a bad idea. [One could expect] fine food and sweet air from the hand-wielded palm leaf fan [in the bargain]. Only sometimes one had to take a few blows that came as a part of the package, along with the good meal and entertainment, and that could be a major pain. Earlier, Gadadhar Shiromoni,[46] Ramdhan Tarkabagish,[47] Haladhar Panchanan,[48] and so on, were the leading narrators. Sreedhar[49] [too] became quite famous at a very young age. Nowadays interpreters did not bother to read the scriptures. As long as they had a trained voice, and had read two words of Chanakya's slokas [i.e., had a bit of primary education] and picked up two verses of *kirtan*, they performed for money, butchering Vedavyas as they sat on the podium [interpreting the *Mahabharat*].

A big crowd had turned out to listen to the readings and to have a look at the clay models. Potters, postmen who brought in the tinsel that would be used to decorate the idol and the organizers smoked the flat-bottomed hookah, shouting themselves hoarse for no apparent reason. Some dubious types cried out, 'Move, move,' trying to show off their 'influence'. Some of them sought out a couple of coquettish women to whom they interpreted the [significance of] the shong in question. It was difficult to grasp the essence of a shong unless it was explained, as had been done in the Bengali translation of the *Mahabharat*, sponsored by the maharaja of Burdwan.[50]

There was a tableau depicting Bhishma on a bed of arrows,[51] and Arjun sending an arrow through the earth, releasing the water of river Bhagabati, to satiate the guru's thirst. Duryodhan stared vacantly, watching the mighty act performed by his cousin. All the characters wore similar costumes and had faces cast in the same mould, only Bhishma's was milk white in colour, Arjun's black like the shoe polish manufactured by Day and Martin and Duryodhan's was **green.**

Another tableau showed the nine jewels.[52] King Vikramaditya, dressed like a drug peddler, sat on the throne held up by thirty-two figurines. Kalidas, Ghatakarpar, Baraha, Mihir and the rest of the nine jewels stood in a circle. All of them were dressed similarly, wearing a dhoti, wrapper and a tiki each. If you saw them all of a sudden you might think they were *agradaani*.[53] Brahmins, paying obeisance to the gatekeeper for allowing them to enter a house of ceremony.

Elsewhere Srimanta was seen singing in praise of Goddess Bhagawati, decorating her name with thirty-four honorifics. The constables stood around him. Srimanta wore a woollen wrap around his head, a loose long shirt with **English** (well, partially) cuts, and trousers. He looked like a **High Court pleader** on the job.

One of the models was about a sacrificial rite being performed by a monarch to establish his sovereignty over several other kings. Kings from across the country and abroad sat in a circle. The Brahmin leaders, dressed in shabby clothes, sat at the centre, surrounding the sacrificial flame. They looked, and dressed, like gatekeepers, guarding a goldsmith's shop.

There was also Ram[54] at his coronation. Bivishon, Jambuban, Hanuman and Sugreeb—the monkeys—stood around him, dressed like city-bred accountants. Lakshman held the umbrella.

Shatrughna and Bharat waved the fly-whisk. Sita sat on Ram's left, her sari wrapped [stylishly] at an angle, a piece of jewellery pinned to her hair brushed against her forehead. Her hair was tied in an English-style bun. Indeed, the look was totally over the top.

'He's given to ostentatious display when he might actually be starving', now that is a tableau that has turned out truly wonderful.[55] The babu may be all togged up in a tasselled cap, pineapple fibre shirt, belt, silk handkerchief, a guard chain made of [horse] hair, but he doesn't have a house to live in. He eats at his aunt's, sleeps in the temple and hangs around at the Sens'[56] drawing room where people meet for chitchat. He does not have the money to buy food to appease his empty stomach, but sits up all night thinking of ways to bring about a **reformation** in the country. (It's another matter that he does not own a mosquito net and therefore would have lost sleep anyway.) During the day he roams around, spending his time in the police station, the High Court, Tulloh's auction house[57] and the Small Causes Court. In the evening, he attends meetings at the Brahmo Samaj, and then moves on to the **club**, to his utter relief. The money earned through spying, working as a broker, flattery and hack writing is usually exhausted paying for tasselled caps, getting pineapple-fibre shirts mended and shoes polished. Therefore, sometimes, the babu has no other way but to accept a badly-paid schoolteacher's job.

Another tableau showed how unable to endure the ludicrous behaviour of certain people, the protagonist preferred to take refuge on a shelf suspended from the ceiling. This one was about Young Bengal[58] members dining at the table. They wore trousers and silk shirts with an English **cut** (even in times of severe heat), and glasses (although they were able to see well enough without them). At night they lay in the gutter, caught muskrats and had them for dinner, while during the day they would be delivering **speeches** [advocating] **reformation**. Unable to bear with these [atrocities, the shong on display] decided to perch himself on the suspended shelf.

Besides these, a variety of other tableaux were put up at the venue of the baroyaari puja, [with titles] such as, 'Won't do good, will do harm, stop me if you can', 'The heart cracked open like a door ajar', 'The dung cake burns while the fresh dung smiles', 'The slit-eyed boy is called Mr. Beautiful Eyes', 'How to drink and not get de-classed', 'The wretched and the destitute', 'The sugar-coated pill', and so on. It was no use going into all that here. But the tableaux of 'Heron the Hypocrite' and 'The Little Nawab' on either side of the idol were really excellent. The hypocrite sported a well-nourished body, much like that of the cobbler's dog, and a paunch resembling a pumpkin. His head was shaven, except for a tiki gathered in the middle, like Sri Chaitanya's. He wore a necklace and gold amulets the size of small drums and a good luck charm on the arm. His hair and moustache were dyed. He had on a black-bordered dhoti, a loose long shirt and an asymmetric tiara embellished with gold thread. Last year he had crossed eighty. His body had almost disintegrated into three, but his spirit was still in its crawling stage [like an infant's]. He eyed the women from regular, decent homes, even as he counted the prayer beads in Lord Hari's name. A few coins inside the beads' bag were jingled to entice [the women].

The Little Nawab was quite nice to look at. He had a complexion resembling lac-dye stirred in milk, and wore his hair Prince Albert-style. He was stout, like a Chinese hog, carried a red handkerchief and a walking stick made from peach wood. He wore a diaphanous dhoti made in the looms of Simla, tucked in like a loincloth. At first glance he could have been mistaken for the scion of a royal family, but in reality he was only the weaver Hriday's grandson.

The baroyaari idol was almost 20 cubits tall. The frame was decorated with images of Scottish **highlanders** on horseback, fairies, birds of all kinds, lotus and other flowers made of pith. Mother Bhagawati, the world's nurturer, appeared at its centre. The lion's body was coated with silver foil and the elephant's with green velvet. The idol's face was that of a European woman; her figure and complexion resembled authentic Jewish and Armenian styles. The Gods—Brahma,[59] Vishnu, Shiva and Indra—put their hands together and prayed to her. Little English fairies played the horn above the idol, carrying the Union Jack. The royal **crest** with the **Queen's** lion and the **unicorn** appeared in between.

Today was the first day of the baroyaari puja, a Saturday. Birkrishna Dan, Kanai Dutta, Pyalanath and Birkrishna's friend Radhamadhab from Ahiritolla engaged themselves in various duties at the baroyaari venue till three in the afternoon. Three giant wild buffaloes, a hundred lambs and three hundred he-goats were sacrificed. The sweetmeat placed on top of the [pyramid] of the main dish offered to the Goddess alone weighed one and a half maunds. The liveried and badge-wearing Brahmin pandits, kitted out in silken dhotis and scarves, sporting tikis and holy marks on their foreheads, the sort who were patronized by the city's big-time zamindars and their cliques, led by Sinha, Ghosh, Dey, Mitra and Dutta, were paid and sent back. Those who had arrived to make a case for themselves, those who came uninvited, those who did not belong to a group and those looking for a meal of folar stuck around like vultures at the Nimtolla Burning Ghat. A lot of beggars, gatecrashers, agradaanis, professional paean singers and dervishes had accumulated. The guards sent them back. Many poor people were arrested. It was only after they loosened their purse strings did the police inspector and the head constable's fine sense of judgement prevail and set them free.

It was almost evening. The crowd at the baroyaari venue now resembled a thick forest. Quite a few of the city babus arrived in their carriages to watch the shong. A lot of spectators forgot about the shong and watched the babus instead. A couple of chandeliers had been lit. The **bell lanterns** lit above the tableaux looked quite spectacular. The babus organizing the show collected one by one. 'Do this', 'Do that', some of them cried, issuing orders to the people around while carrying a flat-bottomed hookah fitted with a pipe and munching on paan. Tonight Dhopapara would be pitted against Chowk. One and half maunds of opium, two maunds of cannabis, seven large tumblers full of milk, besides cardamoms—small, large and medium—camphor and cinnamon, were culled together from the shops of twelve [i.e., several] spice sellers. A mountain of mild, strong, rather nice ambergris-scented and Iranian tobacco was put together. Many more items were ready, kept under wraps like a subterranean river, to be revealed only when required.

The news had spread all over the city. Tonight a **half**-akhrai would be performed at the baroyaari venue at such-and-such place. Be it a yaar like a **schoolboy** or a seventy-two-year-old **invalid**, everyone was crazy about **half**-akhrai numbers. Business was good. The laundrymen made quite a packet. The hiring charges of a pleated dhoti, a clean, well-ironed shirt, and a striped Shantipur-style stole for one night shot up by a quarter of a rupee. The very same **crepe** and **net wraps** that were found useless by four–five generations together and put away in chests since the nawabi era now seemed to dominate the fashion scene. The black ribbon worn as a waist-band, and key chains suddenly, like the babu himself, changed places and were used to **offset** the chain attached to the pocket watch. Like whores, a single pair of shoes came to service all sorts of people.

A huge crowd thronged the baroyaari site. On the one hand there were the clay models, cordoned off by a railing, on the other were the human shongs, both inside the railing and out, dressed in different costumes. The rich, who turned out in tasselled caps, long shirts, cummerbands and walking **sticks**, looked more bizarre than the demon in the *chalchitra*. Birkrishna, the chief organizer, went pottering about like a spinning top, looking like a dandy. Red spittle, from eating paan, ran down the corners of his mouth, like the image of the blood-toothed demoness one finds in the almanac. Servants, postmen, accountants, clerks and **managers** had no time to breathe.

The clock on the church tower went *dong dong*. It was 2 am. The singers from Dhopapara, completely sozzled, arrived on the performance arena, reeling and tottering all the way. Some of them lay down in the green room. When someone else is paying for the meal, by nature, Bengalis do not restrain themselves (unfortunately the stomach is not always as accommodative). Drums, violins, **flutes**, mouth organs and sitars were played individually and in unison. Those with conservative tastes cheered two hundred times, praising the music. Finally, [the Dhopapara team] sang a number about the

Goddess (we tried very hard to make sense of what the song was about, but there was no way we could succeed) and left, after which the singers from Chowk took over.

The team from Chowk too sang as well as their predecessors, earning themselves a lot of cheering and congratulatory shouts before they took leave. The stage was empty for an hour. [The audience who wore] **Chinese coats** and wraps of **crepe** and **net** with striped, floral and angular patterns dispersed, like columns of ants moving in several directions. The paan shop was empty. The smoke from cheroots, tobacco and hemp created a terrible darkness, far more intense than the sort one saw at the fireworks display to celebrate Queen Victoria's **proclamation.**[60] That kind of smoke does not ensue even when guns are fired to mark large-scale **reviews** [of soldiers]. For half an hour the idol could not be seen and it was, in fact, difficult to recognize one another in the crowd.

Gradually, like a babu's wealth, the fog in springtime and the clouds in autumn, the smoke made itself scarce. The audience could stand at ease. The singers from Dhopapukur took the stage. They began a song about pining away for one's beloved. Having sung for about half an hour, they packed up and left once again. The team from Chowkbazar came on stage and responded to Dhopapukur's tragic ditty. Diehard supporters were now divided into two camps, like soldiers lined up for a **review**. The judges looked at the lyrics written on paper, trying to make up their minds. Uncle Mitra was on one of the teams while Dadathakur anchored the other.

The tragic theme would be followed by demotic, vulgar numbers, although somewhat understated. These performances would determine the winner, which way the judgement was going to swing and whether the show would end happily or in the inevitable fights.

Guns were fired [to mark time] a little while ago. The east was beginning to look brighter. A light breeze was blowing. The Dhopapukur team took to the stage and began a raunchy number. 'Well done', 'Congrats', 'Bravo' the fans cried, cracking their voices in the process. The divine Sun rose early, as if to enjoy the farce. The Moon was ashamed to show his face in civil society, embarrassed at the Bengalis giving in to vulgar entertainment in this day and age. The Water Lily hung her head. Fie! Fie, the birds chirped loudly. The Lotus smiled from her base in the mud. Since the Dhopapukur guys had scored by coming on stage and singing a vulgar number, the Chowk team had to give a fitting reply. After the Dhopapukur people had finished screaming for one and a half hours, the team from Chowk took to the stage. The band played. The riposte to the number was being readied in the green room. The Chowk team sang it with great energy. 'We have won', 'We have won' screamed their staunch supporters, flush with excitement (fist-fights were not left out). The judges too decided that the singers from Chowk had won. The sounds of booing, wild laughter, **hurrahing** and claps made the team from Dhopapukur feel less than a sod. The hangover from the drinks, the strain of having stayed up all night and the shame of losing made Mukherjee junior and a few dohars who had led the singing to wilt.

The singers from Chowk fastened the drums [on their backs], held the flag aloft and sang all the way home. Some walked barefeet; some had only their socks on, not being able to find the shoes. The diehard fans had great fun following them. It was ten in the morning. The audience, who had had their fill of fun at the **half**-akhrai concert, started looking for a drink of whey laced with hemp to help cool them down, once they reached home. Their duty done, the Chinese coats, dhotis, wraps, shirts and shoes, which had been hired or borrowed, were returned to their owners.

It was Sunday. Panchali and jatra would be performed at the baroyaari venue. The baroyaari puja organizers arrived after ten at night, a lot of them still nursing a hangover: 'belching due to acidity', 'headaches' and 'a sluggish body' [being some of the complaints]. The panchali performance began. The first group performed *Gangabhakti Tarangini*,[61] the second started on the tale of Mahiraban.[62] A panchali rendition on the lines of a small-scale **half**-akhrai followed. Most of it had to do with reciting rhymed verses, so the performance was over by one o'clock at night.

[Let's move on to] jatra. The proprietor of the jatra company was seventy-six years old. He wore his hair in waves, tattoos on his body and a ring in the ear. [This evening] the proprietor cast himself in the role of the messenger, a dozen rather grown-up boys were made to dress up as maids in waiting and brought on stage. First Lord Krishna danced to the beat of the tom-tom, next came Vyasdev and Mani Gosain,[63] singing their parts. The maidens and the messengers, who accompanied Lord Krishna, entertained the audience until early morning with dialogues such as, 'Tomorrow, I am not going to drink water', 'Tomorrow I'm not going to watch the clouds (I'll have a marquee set up)', 'Tomorrow I'm not going to change clothes' and songs about a young lady from the foreign shores. A mountain of plates, pots used for ablutions, pitchers, torn clothes, old **bonnets** and shawls had piled up. Rupees, half-rupees and quarters were being thrown at the performers. Occasionally shongs appeared to perform numbers like, 'Get me married, Father' and 'I am called Sundar the fisherman, I cast *bauti* nets to fish in the water'.[64] The jatra was over at eight in the morning. A babu who had been drinking and watching the jatra in a completely inebriated state, put the end of his dhoti [as a mark of devotion] around his neck and bowed to the idol (meaning that of Goddess Jagadhatri, created in a form sanctioned by the Hindu religious scriptures) after the jatra was over. But seeing that the Goddess's lion was biting the elephant, the large-hearted babu got highly enraged. He stood there for a while and began singing this sad ditty.

O Mother, deliverer, dear,
  why does the elephant make you so angry?
Slaying human beings instead
  would have landed you in Harinbadi.[65]
Your crown would be left lying,
  breaking pebbles make you weary,
The police would have tried you
  and submitted to the **grand jury**.
Uncle Lion would have felt the heat;
  to the lawyer's he would hurry.

He finished his song, bowed and left.

The reason we found the depraved lot among the city's drunkards (actually drunks are not much different from one another. When one is drunk, be it a raja bahadur[66] or an utterly undistinguished commoner, they look quite similar) in the gutters, roads, police stations, police lock-ups and liquor shops, going wild, because there was no one at home to hold them back. There was no dearth of drunkards among the rich men in the city, either. But they did not go carousing on the streets just because they had people at home to lock them up. Some of them got so wild [in private] that if one saw them from the skies above, one would curl up in fear and start nursing a racial hatred towards the rich Bengalis. A low-class drunkard was bundled off by the watchmen and got a few blows of the police constable's baton, besides being slapped a fine of four annas and made to spend a night in the police lock-up. But the rich alcoholics among the Bengalis excelled in whatever they did. They tried to fly like birds, fell from the terrace and died.[67] They drowned themselves in tanks dug by their fathers. They destroyed the image of the lion and tried to take its place and immersed the drummer with the Durga idol. They boozed and went wild at the **cantonment fort, railway stations** and **auctions** and landed up at the police station. Besides, they indulged in excesses of generosity, singing, giving tips and lectures [in a drunken state].

Once, the play *Vidyasundar* was being performed at a rich man's house in Shyambazar, of old wealth. The middle son of the house sat in the audience with his group of yaars. Fistfuls of money were being thrown at Malini, the female gardener. Vidya sang, 'The foreigner cast a spell on me and now I am doubly aflame with desire.[68] Two young boys aged about sixteen—**stud bred**[69]—dressed up as maids and moved around, dancing to a khyamta number. Brandy was being served in silver glasses at the soirée. Even the lizards and the black stone representing Lord Vishnu were dead drunk.

The episodes in which the lovers decide to meet, Vidya conceives, the Queen is reproachful, the thief is caught and Malini is heartbroken were played out, one by one. The chief of police tied

Malini up and began hitting her. Malini urged the babus [to save her]. Wailing loudly, she raised quite a ruckus in the house. The babu was jolted out of his drunken stupor, to find that the cop was beating up Malini and would not let go, even as she desperately swore by the babu's name. This made the babu very angry. 'Let's see who can take her away from me,' he said, and grabbing the silver glass kept in front of him hurled it at the cop's temple. 'O Father!' said the cop. The glass had hit the target. The cop turned a circle and dropped down on the ground. Anxious people rushed in from all directions. The body was lifted and carried inside. Water was sprinkled on his face and other measures taken [to revive him], but to no avail. He had been bumped off with single stroke.

On another occasion, *Vidyasundar* was being played at the Ghosh's house in Thanthania. The babu, completely inebriated, lay on his side as he attended the jatra performance, snoring noisily. He lay knocked out all night. At dawn the ruckus made by the cops in the execution scene woke him up. The absence of Lord Krishna on the stage irritated the babu. 'Get Krishna,' 'Get Krishna,' he cried, raving mad. Others tried to reason with him, 'Your honour, there is no Krishna in the play of *Vidyasundar*.' But the babu could not be convinced. He felt Lord Krishna—who was otherwise favourably disposed to the babu, was now being excruciatingly heartless—and had chosen not to show up. He began crying his heart out.

On another occasion, a *gosain* was harassed very badly by a drunken babu. I cannot refrain from telling the story here. Dwipchand Goswami of Benetolla[70] had quite a few rich disciples, the Boses of Ba'ar Simla[71] being the prominent ones among them. One day Ramhari of Amtah wrote a letter to Bose, saying, 'I would really like to be indoctrinated [into the Vaishnav cult], but I have a few questions and unless those are sorted out, I shall remain a follower of the *Shakti* cult.' Bose, who was a sworn Vaishnav, was very happy to receive Ramhari's letter and sent Nader Chand Goswami to him so that he could clarify Ramhari's doubts and counsel him vis-à-vis the teachings of the Vaishnav cult.

Ramhari lived in Sonagacchi. He would have a few yaars and musicians hanging around him. He went out in the evening and came home in the morning, and was a heavy drinker. He had got embroiled in mild riots before, and had given written undertakings to the police [that he would be liable to punishment if the offence was repeated]. After dark, Sonagacchi was all pomp and splendour. It seemed as if the Hindu religion—manifest in smoke from burnt resin, the sound of the blowing on conch shells and the sprinkling of holy water from the Ganga in each house—went about purifying the air of Sonagacchi.

Nader Chand Goswami arrived in Sonagacchi after dark, carrying Bose's letter. Goswami was huge, had a shaven pate, except for a Sri Chaitanya-style tiki worn at the back of his head—it looked like a stem attached to a watermelon. The name of Lord Sri Hari was inscribed all over his body. He had drawn a *tilak* on his nose and bore a splotch of sandalwood mark on his forehead, which could be mistaken for bird droppings. Goswami was born in Calcutta but had never been to Sonagacchi (many of the city's prostitutes came within the jurisdiction of the Ma Gosains of Simla).[72] Goswami took great pains [finding the way] and finally reached Ramhari's house.

Ramhari had been drinking since he came back from the kothi, and the drug in his drink had a stupefying effect. One of the sycophants sang, 'Now Hazrat would go to London,'[73] to the beat of the drum. Another tied a wrapper around his head and was about to start dancing like a baiji. That was when Goswami arrived with Bose's letter. Now who would not be disgusted seeing that fat oaf of a Goswami amid such merriment? Everybody was extremely irritated. Goswami was spared the spanking only because Bose was his referee.

After he had read the letter, Ramhari asked Goswami to take a seat most cordially. Rama, the servant, changed the water in the hookah meant for the 'Brahmins' (this one was actually used by the Muslim Khan Sahibs), offered it to Goswami, and winked at his sidekicks. Someone ran and paid a quick visit to the tailor. The singing and joking was **postponed** for a while. A debate on the scriptures was about to begin. Goswami finished the smoke, put the hookah down and engaged in the usual formalities. Ramhari responded extremely politely.

Ramhari told Goswami, 'My Lord, I have major doubts about certain aspects of the tenets of Vaishnavism. You would have to sort these out. First, since Radhika is Lord Krishna's maternal uncle's wife,[74] how could Lord Krishna take her [as his consort]? Second, how could a man (all right, God) satisfy the desires of sixteen hundred wives? And third, I heard Lord Krishna had roast lamb on the day of Doljatra, so why restrain us [his followers], from having **mutton chops**? Besides, drinking among the Vaishnavs is sanctioned. Lord Balaram would drink round the clock,[75] Lord Krishna too was a confirmed alcoholic.'

The questions made Goswami sit up with a start. He began looking for a way of escape. The babus smirked, gesticulated at each other and drank the 'elixir' from silver glasses. Seeing that Goswami could not come up with a fitting reply, one of the sycophants said, 'Master, I think Goddess Kali is superior. As you can see there is a generation gap between Kali and Krishna. Kartik is Kali's son. Now the plumes on the tail of the peacock, which Kartik rides on, are stuck in Krishna's hair, above his crown. That makes Kali the greater of the two.'

A huge wave of laughter rose. Goswami, who was rather headstrong by nature, could feel his blood boil. He was looking for a way out when a sycophant reeled and fell over Goswami, licking the holy marks on his nose and forehead with his tongue. 'Watch it, watch it,' said another, as he cut off Goswami's tuft. Goswami felt that these people would end up conducting his funeral [if he did not watch out]. He let go of his shoes and bag of prayer beads and ran for dear life, heaving a sigh of relief once he hit the road. Ramhari and his cronies were overjoyed. Many among the rich liked to be entertained this way and incidents like these were common in many places.

Newer instances of drunkenness would be seen in Calcutta every day. All were rather bizarre and quite queer. The father of Danukarna Mitra of Chorabagan was the accountant at Nat Drive Monkisson Company. He was also into moneylending and company stocks. Danu had cleared his exams and now went to college, listened to **lectures** and, sometimes, would write **articles** in English papers. A lot of the rich men's sons in the city had a donkey's sense of judgement and such a fine intelligence that it was almost not there. They were not at all interested in education, their minds forever raced towards flippant things. Going to school was a pain, like gulping down a bitter pill for fear of one's parents. Therefore, by the time Danukarna cleared his exams, he was a father of four sons and his eldest daughter was already married. A few schoolmates of Danu would visit him all the time, sometimes clandestinely. Cannabis, drug-laced candies and drinks prepared from hemp leaves would be consumed. Occasionally they yearned to taste sherry and champagne, but since the master of the house was a self-made man, he kept a strict vigil and made it a point to tell the boys off [when necessary]. But [on this occasion] his towering authority was challenged.

The college had closed for the **summer vacation**. The schoolmasters went shopping and fishing in other people's garden houses. The pandits went to their homes in the country and started tilling the soil with a hoe (evidently, that was the class most of the pandits teaching in English schools belonged to, anyway). In the evening Danu sat in his study with a few **schoolfriends**. Pyari, from the same college, tip-toed into the room, carrying bottles of brandy and sherry, hidden under his wrapper. The doors and windows of the room were shut at once. Initially the bottle was uncorked very carefully, and the drink sipped very cautiously as well (it was like cats lapping stolen milk). After a while the brandy had disappeared, and the drinkers began to warm up. The doors and windows were opened, the men howled and hooted. Finally, the sherry too was finished. **Speeches** in English and loud thumping on the table continued. Fear herself ran away in shame. Danu's father sat in the *Chandimandap,* counting the prayer beads. Hearing the shouts and the terrible noise, he went up to his son's room to find that the boys, now wildly drunk, were screaming, kicking up quite a rumpus. He was terribly vexed at this and started blasting Danu, saying whatever came to his mind. One of the friends got highly enraged at the invectives being spewed. He and Danu charged at the father, and punched him. The master of the house had grown old. A Young Bengal-style punch (heavier than a monkey's hit) made him swerve around and fall. The wives of the house rushed to the spot, gasping and panting. The master's wife came out of the inner chambers, weeping and duly chastizing her son. Even as reprimands were given, tears shed and a general chaos raged, the friends, who were scared of the police [arriving on the scene], had scooted. Danu took pity [on his mother]. He went to her and said, 'Ma, long live Vidyasagar.[76] What do you have to fear? Let the **old fool** die. We never wanted him. Now I will get you the kind of father with whom you and I could sit together and drink to our health. Let that **old fool** die. I want a father who is **quite reformed**.'

Ramkali Mukhopadhyay was the treasurer of the office of Supreme Court lawyers who took up the cases of **Messrs Thieves, Rogues and Pickpockets**. On his way back from work, he went across to Radhabazar, making it a point to stop by at the [liquor] shops on either side of the road. [Towards the end of his journey] his turban was tipped to one side, the dhoti unfurled and tied itself in knots and his legs were buckling. When he reached the pots and pans market in Jorasanko, he just had to let himself go. He felt as if his legs had been tethered to the ground. Finally, he stood there like a piece of stone. A servant of the Tagores' was passing by at that time, tottering under the influence of booze as he went. Seeing him, Ram said, 'The chap's drunk,' and moved aside, still swerving. The servant stopped and asked, 'Who the hell are you to say I'm drunk?' 'I'm Ram,' was the reply. The servant said, 'In that case, I'll be Ravan.' 'Come, let's fight,' said Ram. But before he could land a blow, he had collapsed in a heap, utterly drunk. The drunken servant sat astride on Ram's chest. At that moment, a police sergeant had finished his rounds and was about to return. The drunken servant had not lost his senses entirely. Seeing the police sergeant, he let Ram go and was about to run away from the scene. Ram too had seen the sergeant. Now seeing Ravan slip away, he said disparagingly, 'Shame on you, son, that you should be running away for fear of Ram's Hanuman [pet monkey].[77] Shame!'

Sunday passed by, quickly. Today was Monday—the last chance to have fun, revelry, drink alcohol and show off. Today there would be performances by baijis, khyamta dancing, a singing match between poets and kirtan.

The stage was decked up extremely ostentatiously for the baijis' dance—the soirées held at Gopal Mallik's son's wedding and these at Raja Brajendra's dogs' were nowhere near this show of grandeur.[78] Pyalanath of Chowkbazar was like a [human] **directory** of the baijis. Therefore the responsibility of organizing the baijis' dance and khyamta fell entirely on his shoulders. The big-time baijis of the city: the Nanni, Nunni, Munni, Khanni and Sannis who had been awarded degrees, medals and certificates, and khyamta dancers by the names of Golap, Shyam, Bidhu, Khudu, Mani and Chuni, began to arrive with their belongings. Pyalanath received all the performers with huge fanfare, as if these were female spiritual gurus. The dancers began acting high and mighty.

The diamond-studded watch hanging from the guard chain worn by Pyalanath—a **hunting** model of McCabe & Co. make—showed it was past nine. Light from the lamps at the soirée [dazzled], making a mockery of the autumn moon. A baiji sang, 'O my beloved, know this that I am yours', to the wailing of the sarangi and the tinkling of the kettledrum and cymbals. The baroyaari organizers' young children, dressed up in miniature tasselled caps, unstitched turbans and crowns, kept running between corners and changing seats.

A chariot with the words 'God Save the Queen' written on it rumbled in, stopping near the gate of the baroyaari venue. Pyalanath ran towards the car. Someone looking like a barrel that weighed ten maunds and covered with *zari* and velvet, including zari on the shoes, accompanied by a vile sycophant, stepped down from the car. This hulk of a man wore necklaces as thick as chains used to bind people with and eighteen rings on each hand—thirty-six in all.

One of Pyalanath's toadies cried, 'That's Pachu of Burrabazar. He's made a lot of money as an agent of the cotton wool and **piece goods** trade.[79] Nice guy.' Pachu entered the scene, praised the ongoing soirée most glowingly, thanked Pyalanath and the two embraced each other. Finally, Pachu bowed to the idol and the shongs dressed up as some of the heavyweights among the Gods (such as Krishna, Balaram, Hanuman and so on) most respectfully, saluted the baijis and sat down, spreading his girth over two American cots. Two more cots were pressed into service for the time being to rest his hands, and also to place twenty rolls of paan, a bunch of keys and a handkerchief on. The sycophant sat behind Pachu so nobody could see him. When one gets too close to rich men, people say, 'One is in the shadow of the mountain,' and that's exactly what had happened to him.

The baiji looked sideways and smiled on seeing Pachu's [huge] frame. Pyalanath tried to please him by offering ittar, paan, roses and bouquets. Suddenly there was a commotion at the gate. Pyalanath's satellite, Hiralal, had arrived at the soirée in the company of Raja Anjanaranjan Deb Bahadur. The gilded, lac-filled, sceptre of the raja was held in a way so that nobody could miss it. Anjanaranjan Deb Bahadur was fair and well built. He wore a turban, open at the top, a silk dhoti, a matching scarf and gold-embroidered lopeta slippers. He was a king of the rogues and a champion among hypocrites. Seeing the raja, the baiji moved up close to him. 'I hope you patronize us at the next puja,' said the tabla and sarengi players and saluted. The riff-raffs in the assembly forgot about the shong and the baiji and gawked at the raja as if he were an amazing animal.

The crowd got bigger with each passing hour of the night. Many of the city's wealthy people dressed up in different attire got together. The venue of the dance recital reverberated [with excitement]. Birkrishna Dan was overjoyed. He was utterly pleased with himself to see the soirée resplendent with such style and grandeur. This was any day more satisfying than feeding Brahmins at his father's memorial service.

Gradually the heavyweights among the rich men attending the soirée dropped out, like stars off the sky. The older people left. The flippant ones qualifying as yaars now sat at ease. The baijis were through and the khyamta dancers took over.

Khyamta is a wonderful dance form. The rich babus of the city get to see it in their pleasure houses every Sunday. Quite a few try to get a taste of the unique flavour of khyamta in the company of children, nephew and son-in-law. Certain babus prefer to have the women dance naked. And some people in the audience would pay up only after they got **a kiss** [from the dancers]. What happens elsewhere is not fit to be written about.

Khyamta dancing began at the baroyaari site. Two dancers dressed up in jatra costume of Jashoda, the adoptive mother of the young Lord Krishna, went around, swinging their hips as they danced. 'You stole the gem on the hood of the snake/ In an alien land your life's at stake,' sang the khyamta choir. Finally, the dancing women held out incense-burners uncomfortably close to the audience's faces and wouldn't move until they paid up, behaving like beggars. The performance was over by two at night. The female khyamta dancers now went to see the organizers in their private chambers. The baroyaari venue was thus sanctified.

[Moving on to the] singing bards, Raja Nabakrishna was a major **patron** of the poets. Just as some of the greatest poets and authors were born during the reign of Queen Elizabeth in England, similarly, Ram Basu, Haru, Nilu, Ramaprasad Thakur and Jaga—the big-time singing minstrels[80]—were contemporaries of Nabakrishna.

Nabakrishna gave the singing poets a new respectability. Many rich men, in keeping with his requests, or just by imitating his tastes in music, got hooked to the singing poets. The Birds of Baghbazar came into being around this time. Shibchandra Thakur,[81] the founder of the Birds, was a yaar of Nabakrishna. Shibchandra played a role similar to Rammohan Roy's when it came to reforming the Birds of Baghbazar; he taught them how to fly. So, for a while, this band from Baghbazar became the ace among their kind in this city. They nested in a **public** *aatchala*. This was where they would congregate. Here they would behave like birds, make speeches and try to fly. There were a few more hemp-smoking joints in Bosepara as well. Now the Birds were no more, the Shit-eaters and the Trouble-makers too have disappeared. The Birds have [mostly] grown old and died. Only a few old ones, half-dead almost, were still visible. Dejected at the group having disbanded and not having much money left, they listened to jhumur songs after sundown. The **municipal**

commissioners have dismantled the club, only its **ruins** remain.

Earlier, rich men would not be so hassled by their involvement in the British Indian Association,[82] having to give [public] addresses, hold meetings and handle the press as they seem to be these days. Almost each of them kept a woman (many do so even now), got up from bed only in the afternoon and would perform the daily puja with great fanfare (this would take at least two to three hours and an oil massage another four). The sound of the servant slapping oil on the master's body pounded like an earthquake. The babu would sit naked to take the massage, even as he looked into property-related matters, signed documents and put his official seal on them. By the time the babu had rinsed his mouth after a [midday] meal, the sun would have set. If he were a zamindar, the babu would stay up at his office until two at night, packing in a bit of song and musical performances at times. He would argue about petty rivalry between his camp and the rest and get all puffed up, listening to the sycophants' flattery. Among these, the musicians were the babu's favourites, they would be rewarded even when their performance was torn to shreds. But decent folk were not allowed in. Guards with unsheathed swords [who did their job] with great flourish would be posted [to prevent intruders].

Some of the babus would sleep all day, get up and work only after sundown. [For them] the day was like night and night day. Gradually, with the coming of Rammohan Roy,[83] Gopimohan Dev,[84] Gopimohan Thakur,[85] Dwarkanath Tagore,[86] and Joykrishna Sinha,[87] these practices disappeared. *Samachar Chandrika,*[88] the first paper of the Bengalis, came into being. The Brahmo Samaj[89] was established, and the Dharma Sabha,[90] as a reaction. Raja Rajnarayan[91] tried to set a new trend by making Kayasthas wear the sacred thread. Sati[92] was abolished. Hindu College[93] was established. [David] Hare[94] arrived on the scene. Gradually the Bengalis began to recognize honest effort.

The battle of the poets, on the theme of the behaviour of feudal lords, began at the baroyaari site. Jaga, a resident of Bhalco and Rama from Nimtah had begun playing the drum, to the beat of numbers like 'An Ode to the Greats', 'In Praise of River Ganga',

'The Three Bones of the Bhetki Fish', 'Gopinath of Agar Island', 'Go If You Would, Go, Run, Run'. The bard pitched his song rather high (four keys above the fifth note):

(TO BE SUNG ALOUD)
You keep coming to my house,
slipping through the arms of the law,
Now like Surpanakha's nose[95] in the trap,
we have managed to catch ya.

(OPENING LINE)
Now, you who snatched property dedicated to Gods,
and to Brahmins
Have to sleep on a blanket [in jail], how about that?

Now it's declared, and your notions cleared,
such oppression
Can't continue!
By the laws of the Penal Code, the Mukherjee's son's[96]
Been cut to size
His illegal dealings brought to book and vile ways penalized.

(PROLOGUE)
In the Queen's Empire, in her land,
the subjects would have no worries,
Which is bad news for the highly-respected,
most venerable Mathuranath.[97]
E.D. Latour, the monster-blaster, has arrived in this district.
Now there will be no secret murder, arrests,
starting a brawl or riot.

These tales of [country] zamindars made the urban audience quite happy. Only a few Raychaudhuris, Munshis and Roys who had come from the villages hung their heads in shame. The pleader's agents, loyal to their masters [from the country], shot angry glances. The bards danced in sync with the beat of the drums.

The scavengers came out, their carts lining up in a row. The sweepers pushed the trash carts, moving towards Jackson's Ghat.[98] The bauls began a riff in the Lalit raga, singing to the accompaniment of cymbals, big and small, chanting the thousand names of Lord Krishna and went around singing from door-to-door:

> What's the use of counting the prayer beads in God's name?
> It's just wood knocking against each other, all in vain.

The oil grinder set the mill in motion. The laundrymen went their ways, carrying clothes. Bullock-drawn carriages screeched as they moved, occupying the entire road. Gradually the sky cleared up. The performance of the poets at the baroyaari site was over. The yaar-like organizers and the audience left. The elderly and the middle-aged, who were told that there would be kirtan singing, stayed back. Spiritual gurus, orthodox Hindus, roving mendicants and the Vaishnavs gathered together. [It was time for] Shyam from Simla and Nistarini from Baghbazar to start kirtan singing.

Shyam from Simla was a fine kirtan singer. She was young, not bad to look at, and had a voice resembling the clanging on a bell-metal plate. The singing began. When the songstress sang, '*Ta tathaiya, ta tathaiya,* Gopal twists and turns, dancing, he steals the cream and eats it.[99] Oh, dear, he steals the cream and eats it. *Ta tathaiya, ta tathaiya,*' everybody was moved. All around the name of Lord Hari was being chanted. The tom-tom players knelt down and started beating the instrument with great gusto. The songstress, who went down on her knees and stood up again, sung in dulcet tones, letting the music pour on the audience like a shower of honey. A gosain was possessed by the spirit of Lord Hari. The rest lifted his body and kept dancing. Some of them licked the dust off the ground where he lay.

By the grace of the founding fathers of the Hindu religion, a gosain could be quite an ace among frauds. I have never seen a lean, weakling of a gosain since the day I was born. Since childhood, the word 'gosain' conjures up the image of a monstrous mountain of a man in my mind. Money could not buy rich men the kind of meals, drinks, travel and luxurious life that the gosains enjoyed on other people's accounts. As incarnates of Lord Krishna, the gosains had access to some of the most invaluable things, without having to make the slightest effort or having to move out of their homes to achieve these. Ignoring the dispensable acts[100] performed by Lord Krishna, such as quashing Kaliya, the snake, killing Putna, the ogress, lifting Mount Gobardahan on the tip of his finger, they preferred to engage in the choicest sports the Lord had indulged in, such as whisking away the milkmaids' clothes, trying to make peace with an angry lover and spending time playing pranks as a young boy in Vrindavan. They had their fill of sweet pancakes and kheer and gave the following sermon, picked from *Chaitanya Charitamrita*,[101] to the multifarious variety of their disciples:

> The guru's Lord Krishna himself,
> just in case you're wondering,
> When the guru's pleased, so is Krishna, it's a proven thing.
> Young maid, like Radha, you deserve love and worship,
> Trust your senses, the guru's honour is for yours to keep.

Besides this, the gosains sometimes worked as undertakers. They were ready to indoctrinate a disciple even if they were paid a measly five quarters, dispose off dead bodies and keep an eye out to catch a childless widow, so that when she died they could claim to be her heir. Once a gosain from Midnapore, with a rather oversized paunch, was chastized severely. The fable needs to be told here.

The Vaishnavites in east Midnapore followed the tradition of *guruprasadi,* that is, the newly married bride had to offer herself to the guru first before she was allowed to live with the husband. Rameswar Chakraborty, who lived in Betalpur, was regarded as a distinguished person in the [surrounding] rural area. He had a residential house and a homestead beside the river Subarnarekha, surrounded by a garden sprawling over five bighas of land. All the rooms in it were made of bricks and stone, only the roofs above the Chandimandap and the drawing room adjacent to the doorway were covered with reed on top. There were two temples of Lord Shiva in front of the house, and a tank paved with stones, with fish in it. Chakraborty did not need to worry about buying fish when there was a ceremony in the house. Besides these, five hoes, five cowherds, five pairs of bullocks would be engaged in tilling the 200-bigha tax-free land given to the Brahmin. There were two huge granaries in Chakraborty's courtyard. The bhadraloks of the village had a lot of respect for Chakraborty. They would play the game of dice sitting in his Chandimandap.

Chakraborty did not have a son, only a daughter who was married to Harhari Chatterjee, the son of Brikabhanu Chatterjee, from the city. At the time of the wedding the bride and the groom were no more than five and ten years old. So the son-in-law's visits and the daughter's going to stay with her in-laws were postponed for a few years. Only gifts and pleasantries would be exchanged [between the two families] on the occasion of festivals, such as the year-end pithe-making,[102] and son-in-law's day.[103]

Harhari finished college. He was about twenty-one years old now. So Chakraborty came to the city to see Brikabhanu and talk to him about taking the son-in-law for a visit to his in-laws'. Brikabhanu offered Chakraborty heartfelt hospitality for the few days that he stayed with him. Finally, on an auspicious day, he sent Harhari [with Chakraborty]. A gateman, manager and servant accompanied Harhari.

It took the son-in-law around three to four days to reach Betalpur. The whole village was abuzz with the news that Chakraborty's city-bred son-in-law had arrived. The village women left whatever they were doing and came running to see the son-in-law. The young boys had hardly ever seen a city-bred person; they came in droves and surrounded Harhari. There was a great hullabaloo around Chakraborty's Chandimandap. The women peeped from this side and that. A few infants who still held their shit in their stomach stood in one corner, naked. The courtyard spilt over with the huge number of riff-raffs crowding it.

Finally the son-in-law was taken inside the house so that he might have some food. Everything was set. Four betel nuts were hidden underneath the wooden seat. When the son-in-law stepped on it, the seat skidded and he fell with a thud. The sisters-in-law laughed loud. Each item served as refreshments was meant to be a joke. The purple jaam [sour plums] were made of clay, the 'milk' candy of flour and rice powder, the sugarcane was actually a piece of wood, the sugar syrup turned out to be straw soaked in water. The glass of 'water' was stuffed with cockroaches and spiders underneath the cover, and moles and mice were found inside the container meant to hold paan. The son-in-law endured the hazards of this tomfoolery and stepped out of the household. He found a few young men of his age, brothers-in-law by extension, and spent the rest of the day exchanging tales of the city for country-bred jokes and having fun.

Night was all set to arrive. Evening had settled in. The cowherds played the flute on their way home, returning with the herd. As each of the exquisitely beautiful women came to the river, pitchers balanced on the hip, the Moon—an ace debauch—seemed to peep from behind the bamboo groves and the palm trees, as if to catch a glimpse. Crickets and similar insects buzzed for dear life. Civet cats, polecats and otters had begun to roam about in the ruins of the temple of Lord Shiva and abandoned houses. Bats and vampires were out, hunting for food. Suddenly a herd of jackals howled. The first quarter of the night was over. The boys took the son-in-law inside the house. Once again, he was made to consume a lot of fake and real food, after which he went to sleep in the room allotted to him.

The son-in-law had not been to his in-laws' since his wedding, not even when the marriage was renewed. So the last time he had seen his wife, she was only five years old. Both his wife and he were children then. The situation pretty much ensured that Harhari was not going to get any sleep tonight. Tonight he would be meeting his wife for the first time. If the wife were offended with him, he would have to put his college education and knowledge of the Brahmo tenets on the backburner and try and break the ice by touching her feet. He would also have to make a special effort to persuade her to get educated so that she might please his heart at all times. Why couldn't a Bengali wife be a second Miss Stowe, Miss Thomson, Miss Barclay or a Lady Lytton, [the wife of] Bulwer-Lytton?[104] After all, they are more intelligent and virtuous than an [average] English wife. Why then did they have to spend their time making *boris,* playing with dolls, quarrelling and engaging in petty jealousy? Sita, Savitri, Sati, Satyabhama, Shakuntala and Krishna[105] too were gems extracted from the same mines [that is, same stock]. Therefore, the reason why Bengali women lie trapped inside a **furnace** and burn, themselves and others, like coal, is only because their parents and husbands did not try or push the matter enough. The fact that hardly ever were both the man and the lady in a Bengali household well educated remained a wondrous mystery. Vidyasagar's wife probably did not know her alphabet. [She was probably] too taken up with sprinkling holy Ganga water, Shah Farid's amulet and the water washed off the feet of the idol at Balsi.[106] The son-in-law fantasized about a lot of other things besides these. Gradually, these thoughts and the strain of the journey made him slip into a deep sleep. Finally, at the first hour of noon, he woke up at the sound of women's voices, calling [one another]. He found that it was late and he was still lying in bed—alone.

The women in the Chakraborty household told one another, 'Now that the son-in-law's here, and the daughter, by the grace of Mother Shashthi, has completed fifteen years, the guru should be sent for.' Chakraborty consulted the almanac, decided on a good day, and sent a message to the guru, who arrived with a shuttle, a ladle-shaped sceptre carried by Vaishnavites and a tom-tom. It was time to set the stage for a guruprasadi.

Harhari did not know anything about the preparations. The gosain arrived with his cohorts. Everyone in the household was in a state of nervous excitement. [Harhari's young] wife went around, wearing new clothes and a lot of jewellery. Since his arrival Harhari was not allowed to spend any time with his youthful wife. So he became rather suspicious and asked a lad, 'What's all this pomp and show about?' The boy said, 'Don't you know, dear brother-in-law, today we are going to have a guruprasadi performed here.'

The words, 'We are going to have a guruprasadi here', made Harhari's blood boil. He was determined to save his wife from the menace and went about it in right earnest.

When it came to doing one's duty, there was no stopping the holy men. Almost as if to abet the process, the Sun went down, not caring for the aching Lotus. Evening, like a bride, waited as the conch shell was blown, bells rung and the crickets buzzed, for the husband to arrive. Dusk, her maid-in-waiting, now playing the messenger's role, took the news to the lord of the night—the Moon. The Stars came out one by one to make merry at the post-wedding party. The Water Lily blossomed on the transparent water of the lake, not minding one bit when she found out that her beloved was about to get a taste of an illicit affair; the reason being that the Moon had thousands of water lilies to choose from whereas for the Water Lily, there was only the Moon. The Moon came out. The jackals howled as if singing a paean to him. The Flowering Trees showered their blossoms like gifts which made virginal Nature laugh.

A major celebration was on inside the Chakraborty household. The gosain, dressed like a groom, went to the room meant for the son-in-law and lay there. Harhari's wife, wearing lots of jewellery, entered the room. The women eavesdropped and began peering through the slits in the window.

Before the gosain could enter the room and lie down, Harhari, who had been briefed by the boy, had hidden himself underneath the bed, armed with a short club. Now he saw his wife enter and touch the gosain's feet. She stood self-consciously and started crying. The gosain got up, took her by the hand, made a huge effort to make her understand and finally took her to bed. What could the poor girl do! It had been drilled into her head that to defy a family tradition was a grievous sin. So she did not make any more protests but went and lay in the 'Lord's' bed, in meek submission. The gosain touched the girl and said, 'Say, 'I'm Radha and you are Shyam.' The girl, as instructed, repeated, 'I'm Radha and you are Shyam,' three times. Harhari could not take it any longer. He came out from under the bed and said, 'And here comes Balaram, cudgel in hand,'[107] and started beating up the gosain with the club.

Shaven-headed Vaishnavs were waiting outside the door with tom-toms and cymbals. They would start playing when the gosain took Lord Hari's name [to indicate] that the job was done. They mistook gosain's screams for the holy chant and started playing the tom-toms with great fervour. The women began ululating, the sound of bell-metal plates, bells and conch shells kicked up a ruckus.

All of a sudden Harhari opened the door, walked out and went straight to the police station. He met the inspector and reported everything. The inspector was a decent guy (which is a rarity). He asked Harhari to have faith in him, took him to his house and put him up there, treating him with due respect. The next day he sent Harhari home with armed guards as escorts.

Meanwhile, everybody [at the Chakraborty's] was quite awestruck. 'Goodness, how could he [Harhari] have been inside!' they said. Finally they went inside to discover that the gosain had lockjaw. He lay unconscious in a river of blood flowing on the bed.

That was the end of guruprasadi. People came to their senses. The gurus too became wary. Now in the villages where guruprasadi is still in practice, the gurus do not actually engage in such activity. Their oral consent is good enough.

On another occasion, a city-based gosain was chastized at a businessman's house while trying to enact the heroic deeds performed by Lord Krishna. Let me give you the story at this point.

Ramnath and Shyamnath Sen were brothers. They worked as accountants in four or five merchant houses in the city. For a while the babus seemed to flourish in a big way. [They rode] four-horse-drawn carriages, blew trumpets and kept sycophants and women in excess. Their drawing rooms would be crawling with jobseekers, unemployed people and those carrying letters of recommendation. The babus were obsessed with visits to the garden house, consuming alcohol and low-brow entertainment. It was left to the relatives and friends to look after the family business. One Sunday, the babus were visiting the garden house when the household guru arrived with the ladle-shaped insignia, tom-toms and a horn. The news of his arrival reached inside the house. The guru was taken inside with a great show of respect. When the household women showed up, all together, the guru chose the risqué episodes from *Chaitanya Charitamrita* and Bhagvad Gita[108] and staged a demonstration. The performance over, the gosain was about to wrap up and go when the younger Sen arrived.

Sen junior had a temperament somewhat like the English. He was extremely livid to see the guru but suppressed his real feelings with great difficulty and asked, 'How are you, my lord? Did you discuss the amorous sports from the Bhagvad Gita?' The guru, who was scared, fumbled and tried to get away by saying, 'Yes sir.' Sen junior was accompanied by a straight-talking sycophant of his. He said, 'Sir, gosain has performed all of Lord Krishna's adventures, excepting balancing the Gobardhan range on his little finger. If you would allow it, the good lord might be persuaded to hold the mountain. Why leave out that particular feat?'

Finally the gatekeepers were asked to bring around a boulder weighing 10-12 maunds that had been lying beside the door and place it on the gosain's shoulder. The weight fractured gosain's hip. Since then the good lords refrain from going personally to certain households to engage in amorous sports. Instead, they have a variety of female disciples who board a palanquin and arrive at their lords' houses at their bidding.

Kirtan singing at the baroyaari site was over. After the performance, a baul put this number to tune and sang.

Calcutta's a strange city.
Whores, houses, *judi gadis* and lies delivered
  with such felicity.
Here dung smiles as the dung cake burns,
  so much for solidarity.
Herons and cats pass off as monotheists,
  lay traps driven by depravity
The puny Teli wants to sport walking sticks,
  the distiller affects the gold trader's prosperity.
Khyamta dancers live in lovely houses,
  decent people under a canopy.
I'm tired of watching the Hindu rites,
  and their hidden insincerity.
Defecating on the streets and frowning [still],
  such is their duplicity.
Gold coins have a filling of copper,
  gilded and polished well.
Poor Hootum can see through it all,
  and would rather be away from the city.

The song pleased everyone who heard it. The baul was given four annas as reward. Quite a few people wrote down the lyrics and picked up the tune with great care.

The baroyaari puja was over, but the idol was held back for another eight days, after which the preparations for the immersion began. Kanaidhan, the law agent, got [the paraphernalia they would be employing as part of the procession] passed by the police department. Four bands playing English instruments, impersonators dressed up as Turkish riders on horseback, flag-carrying *firinghis,* bell-metal discs to beat on and mark time and fifty drums were assembled. Wheels used to move huge logs were joined together to create a platform and the idol mounted on it. The organizers marched with the idol, with shongs in two rows, on either side. The main road in Chitpore was like a sea of people. The whores stood on terraces and balconies, watching the fun as they smoked their hookahs decorated with silver. The people on the road gaped at the idols, both moving and static. From Haatkhola the idol was taken to Jorasanko and Mechhuabazar in a procession, and, finally, to the bank of the river Ganga for immersion. This was the final phase of blowing up the twenty to twenty-five thousand rupees that had been raised so painstakingly. The process was now complete. Birkrishna Dan and the other organizers came back home with extremely sad looks on their faces. Had their clothes been wet, people would have mistaken them for people returning from the burning ghat after cremating a dead body.

Within a year Birkrishna Dan had accrued enormous debts in the market. His office and storehouse had to be closed down. Ultimately he was declared insolvent and went away to live in Farashdanga.[109] After a few days his house collapsed and he was buried under the debris. Kanaidhan Dutta, the attorney, was found guilty of perjury at the Supreme Court. Sir Robert Peel[110] ruled that he be deported across the seas [to a penal settlement]. His family members went through extremely hard times for a while and later had to start a shop selling puffed rice to make a living.

The great lord who lived in Noorighata Lane had gone to

Benaras to attend to something important, even as the puja was on. One day Pyaĺanath was going on a pleasure trip to the Company's garden house[111] with a few baijis and other [dubious] women by boat. A storm took them unawares. The boatmen tried very hard but in vain. Finally, the boat got stuck in a shoal, turned upside down, crashed to bits and drowned. The babu was a rich man's son who had never learnt to swim. He got washed away in the current, and nobody ever found out where he landed.

Mukherjee junior turned into a hemp addict over the years. He developed tuberculosis from smoking hemp, non-stop. He grew a beard, having pledged it to Lord Shiva of Tarakeswar,[112] drank the bathwater of the deity at Balsi, tied amulets prescribed by Shah Farid, hoping to get some relief, but nothing came of these. Finally, he renounced the world, left home and has not been traced ever since.

Gabaram, the leader of the dohars, stopped singing and took to the family business of coating metal with gold to meet the family's expenses. He died of paralysis during the last puja.

Pachu, Anjanaranjan Deb Bahadur, puja organizers and a few other dohars are still alive. What happened to them will be told in the following sections.

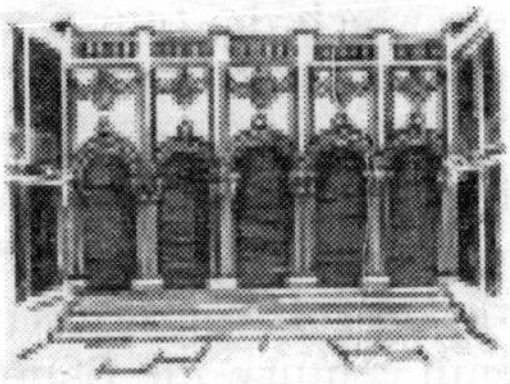

Notes

1. A Jacobean 'political tragicomedy' by John Fletcher and perhaps Philip Massinger, 1622; see Ira Clark, *The Moral Art of Philip Massinger* (Lewisburg, Pa: Bucknell University Press, 1993). The plot line involves palace intrigues and the rightful ruler, Gerrard, the duke of Brabant, being thrown out of his kingdom. Gerrard joins a gang of petty thieves and beggars, living like Robin Hood. 'The play is interesting by reason of its examples of early thieves' cant and its realistic picture of vagabond life', which Hootum probably found resonating with his descriptions of low life; see Paul Harvey, ed., *The Oxford Companion to English Literature* (London: Clarendon Press, 1960).
2. 'A kind of rickety and sordid carriage resembling . . . the skeleton of an old English hackney coach of 1800-35 . . . drawn by wretched ponies, harnessed with rope and standing for native hire in various parts of the city.' See Henry Yule and A. C. Burnell, *Hobson-Jobson,* (London, 1886; Delhi: Rupa, 2007): 272.
3. 'Entrepreneurs in the 1800s began manufacturing items out of the same materials as Volta's battery and claimed that a galvanic current [named after Luigi Galvani's who made this discovery in 1791] was produced when worn next to the skin . . . human sweat would act as the salt solution and produce electricity, which was presumed to be good for all sorts of illnesses, including paralysis, rheumatism, nerve disorders, heart and blood diseases.' Applying Galvanic shocks to rheumatic patients, evidently, was part of the current trend in medical care in Calcutta of the 1850s. (BBC webpage on Victorian Medical Care.)
4. This is the point from which the river Ganga turns south-east, and the Khiddirpore Nullah officially marked the southern boundary of Calcutta in 1779, by a Supreme Court Order. Around 1857, after the Sepoy Mutiny, fugitives from Bihar and UP entered Calcutta through the Khiddirpore docks. Some of the landed gentry, dislodged at the time of the construction of Fort William, were given land around here. In the early nineteenth century, the Church Missionary Society set up eight schools in the area. The first Indian-owned press was set up in Khiddirpore by a certain Baburam in 1807. The government built a modern market in the area in 1859; see Sukanta Chaudhuri, ed., *Calcutta: The Living City: The Past,* vol. 1 (Calcutta: Oxford University Press, 1990).
5. Northern suburb of Calcutta, beyond the airport at Dum Dum.
6. Lal Dighi, or the 'Great Tank' as it was known, is in the hub of

Calcutta's office district and the major administrative blocks.

7. The Government Treasury building, Council House Street, is among the several grand colonial structures, including the Town Hall and the Imperial Secretariat building, all at the west of the Governor's residence.
8. The Small Causes Court dealt with complaints regarding lending and borrowing of money and would declare people insolvent. It kept changing its address at the time Hootum wrote. From 9/2 Old Court House Street it moved next to the present High Court, according to Heysham's map, published 1856. Sanders & Cones's *Annual Directory* (first published 1858) shows the Calcutta Small Causes Court at 19 Chowringhee Road. See Arun Nag, ed., *Sateek Hootum Pyanchar Naksha* (Calcutta: Ananda Publishers, 2008): 200.
9. This refers to the very affluent Shibkrishna Dan (1837-73) of Jorasanko; and Kebalchandra, his adoptive father, is a slight variation on the name Gokulchandra. Kanaidhan Dutta, the manager, was modelled after Shibkrishna's brother-in-law, Krishnadhan Dutta, who looked after the business. Shibkrishna was one of the pioneers of baroyaari puja in Calcutta. He dabbled in coal mines, iron ore and was also a supplier to the railways; he put up the money in celebrating Durga Puja festivals with great pomp and show. Arun Nag quotes Amritalal Basu who wrote in *Smriti O Atmasmriti* (Memories and Reminiscences about Myself): 'There was a popular saying in Calcutta in those days: Mother Goddess dresses herself up in jewellery at Shibkrishna Dan's house in Jorasanko, has her meals at Abhaycharan Mitra's in Kumartuli and goes for entertainment to the Sovabazar raja's house. Few could match up to the flawless decking up of the Goddess at Shibchandra's.' See Nag, ed., *Sateek Hootum Pyanchar Naksha:* 202, 215.
10. A lighter version of the barge, given out on hire.
11. A manually-operated, large piece of cloth, arranged in neat and equal folds, hung from the ceiling, used extensively in pre-electricity colonial India. The punkha-puller would sit outside the room of the master, drawing a string attached to the fan to push the wind in and out.
12. Literally, this means *baro* (twelve) *yaars* (friends) pooling resources to pay for the expenses of a public worship of a deity, most often Goddess Durga; a community puja, and not the usual ones sponsored by rich patrons, in which everybody could participate.
13. Noorighata is the other name for Pathuriaghata (*pathar* and *noori* mean 'stone'). The man referred to is the cash-rich and foppish

Khelat Chandra Ghosh. Ibid: 203; also see Sketch 3, p. 157, note 83; Sketch 8, p. 233, note 8.

14. A full-moon day in the monsoon month when people tie *rakhi*, a band that protects the wearer from misfortune, on each other's wrists. Traditionally sisters tie these on their brothers' wrists.
15. Both girls and boys are treated to an elaborate meal on the last day of being single as a part of Hindu wedding rituals, a prelude to fasting on the wedding day.
16. A dig at Khelat Chandra Ghosh once again, his birthday was the stuff of Page Three and got into the Bengali newspapers like *Sambad Prabhakar.* See Nag, ed. *Sateek Hootum Pyanchar Naksha:* 204.
17. A highly-domesticated goddess on the lines of a loving, if sometimes a little temperamental, aunt. She presides over pregnancy, childbirth and the well-being of children.
18. One of Goddess Durga's two sons, a warrior, supposedly the most good looking of Durga's brood and also a dandy. Kartik's flamboyance shows in the choice of a carrier, the peacock.
19. By the Permanent Settlement enforced by Lord Cornwallis, the zamindar was legally bound to pay up the annual revenue or have his estate auctioned. By the provisions of the Regulation Eight (made effective in 1819), which defined the rights of the various classes of tenants, greater power was given to the zamindar to collect rents from his tenants. The zamindar was made liable to arrest if he failed to pay up the annual rent; R. C. Majumdar, H. C. Raychaudhuri and Kalikinkar Datta, *An Advanced History of India* (Madras: Macmillan, 1981): 792-93. To facilitate the process, the zamindar leased his property to the lease-holders and gave them the responsibility of collecting revenue and would auction the leased-out land when the target was not achieved. The lease-holder sublet his land and more middlemen were created. The result, expectedly, was unmitigated suffering for the poor peasants. The bailiff as revenue collector was absolutely ruthless. See Nag, ed., *Sateek Hootum Pyanchar Naksha:* 204.
20. Often generous patrons would give a Brahmin a plot of tax-free land for him to earn his living; but the bailiff empowered by the Regulation Eight would not spare him when it came to extortion.
21. When guests smoked the lone hookah in the miser's house, each person used a pipe made by rolling a banana leaf (a rigidly followed caste system prevented sharing of the pipe between people belonging to different castes). The miser saved the used pipes and sold them to the laundry man who would extract the alkaline substance from

these and, in exchange, wash the family's clothes.

22. The practice of exchanging old clothes for utensils made of steel and plastic is still quite common in Calcutta.
23. The stories of the blind miser and the missing lion that follows are sourced from *Nadia Kahini* (Tales from Nadia) by Kumudnath Mullick. The blind miser also has a resonance in an incident involving Joykrishna Mukherjee, the zamindar of Uttarpara, who wore dark glasses after he went blind. A Brahmin who had gone to ask for support for his daughter's wedding apparently told him that it was a waste of money for a blind person to wear glasses (see also note 96 below). See Nag, ed., *Sateek Hootum Pyanchar Naksha:* 205.
24. The story involving the missing lion had to do with Gangagobinda Sinha who was a minister at Hastings. He was mobbed by the Brahmins of Birnagar in Santipur, and persuaded to sponsor the puja that year. There is a pun on the word 'Sinha' which is the Bengali word for lion and also a surname. Ibid.
25. These were the days when the Durga idol and her four children would be part of a single frame, the *ekchala.* The practice of making each member of the family of five standing separately came much later.
26. A Hindu post-funeral ritual whereby the deceased's son/nephew wears a piece of coarse cotton with a key attached to it hung from his neck during the thirteen-day period of mourning.
27. Some of the babus were so delicate that the woven borders felt too rough to tuck in. The man best known for setting the trend was Ramtanu Dutta of Haatkhola who 'wore no dhoti more than once and though these were of the finest Dacca muslin, he would have the borders torn off lest they chafe his skin'. See Chitra Deb, 'The Great Houses of Old Calcutta', in Chaudhuri, ed., *Calcutta: The Living City: The Past,* vol 1: 59.
28. Now located at the junction of Colootolla Street and Rabindra Sarani, this house served multiple purposes: a criminal cases court, a barrack for the guards and was also let out for festivals. Furniture and props would be available on hire too. See Nag, ed., *Sateek Hootum Pyanchar Naksha:* 208.
29. Puny twigs developed deposits with a medicinal value: Translucent white deposits sometimes develop around the knobs of a mature bamboo shoot, also known as *tabasheer,* of supposed medicinal value. When a relatively green bamboo shows a similar phenomenon, in Hootum's world-view, it is a metaphor for the plebeian, low-caste families growing in influence. Ibid.

30. Nabakrishna Deb, né Kundu (1733-97) was a polyglot who knew Arabic, Persian and English. He taught Persian to Warren Hastings. He also taught Governor Francis Drake and became the external affairs secretary who played a key role in helping the English to overthrow Nawab Sirajuddaulla. After Siraj's death he, with co-conspirators Mir Jafar, Amir Chand and Ramchand Ray, pilfered Rs.8 million from a secret royal treasury. Lord Clive recommended him for the title of Maharaja Bahadur and made him a magistrate on a salary of Rs.6,000 in 1766. The same year Warren Hastings declared him the lord of Sutanuti. Deb was a patron of Brahmin pandits and poets' duels. See Subodh Chandra Sengupta, ed., *Samsad Bangali Charita-vidhan,* 4th rev. ed., Part I (Calcutta: Sishu Sahitya Samsad, 2002): 242.
31. Refers to Lakshmikanta, alias Noku Dhar of Posta, an anglophile who helped the English with money and advice to consolidate the empire. Dhar was a close friend of Robert Clive and Warren Hastings who supported the Company's wars against the Marathas in return for the zamindari at Posta and the title of a raja. Ibid: 495.
32. This turn of phrase, meaning the riff-raff, or the low-born person of no consequence seems to be a favourite with Hootum. But in the present context, as Arun Nag suggests, the writer might be referring to Krishnakanta Nandy, the founding father of the royal family of Cossimbazar. He began life as a grocery shop accountant and went on to become a clerk in a British merchant house. In 1756 he saved the life of Warren Hastings who was threatened by Nawab Siraj-uddaulla. Krishnakanta joined the East India Company and became Hastings's trusted lieutenant, becoming a minister when Hastings was appointed Governor-General in 1773, receiving land and farms as a gift from the Company. Besides these, he acquired profit-making estates and was a successful trader of salt and silk. He played a key role in the hanging of Nandakumar (see Sketch 1, p. 33, note 10). Ibid: 81.
33. Krishnachandra Roy (1710-82), the maharaja of Krishnanagar, was given the title by Emperor Shah Alam. A conservative Hindu, he had sided with the British against Nawab Sirajuddaulla. Well versed in Sanskrit and Persian, he was a patron of the arts. The well-known poet Bharatchandra and Ramaprasad, the kirtan singer, were two of the most luminous jewels in his court, to say nothing of Gopal the jester. Krishnachandra revived certain traditional Hindu practices and patronized pujas and festivals. He celebrated Jagadhatri/Durga Puja,

opening it up for the public. (See also Sketch 8, p. 232) Ibid: 103.

34. Rajballav Sen (1698-1763) came from a zamindar family in Dacca. He was employed by Nawajis Khan, Alivardi Khan's son-in-law, after whose death he served as a minister to Ghoseti Begum, his widow, and hence became a pawn in the war between Sirajuddaulla, the last independent nawab of Bengal, and the East India Company. Siraj accused him of looting the revenue and put him in jail. He took revenge by turning into a trusted aide of Lord Clive. When things turned out in the Company's favour he was awarded the title of a maharaja and made the minister of the pan-Bengali region: Bengal, Bihar and Orissa. Mir Kasim had him assassinated because of his growing influence. Rajballav was the leader of the Baidyas in Bengal; he tried to introduce social reform in the community by marrying off young widows but was unsuccessful. Ibid: 468.
35. The Mughal emperor Akbar had made Raja Man Singh of Ambar his general. He defeated Rana Pratap of Mewar and helped consolidate Muslim rule in Bengal and Bihar. See Nag, ed., *Sateek Hootum Pyanchar Naksha:* 210.
36. See Sketch 1, p. 33, note 10.
37. A family name given to a line of Jain traders from Rajasthan who settled down in Bihar towards the end of the seventeenth century. As they gained control of the Bengal treasury, they were the kingmakers. Fatehchand was a trusted aide of Murshid Quli Khan and instrumental in making Alivardi Khan the nawab by removing the legal heir, Sarfaraz. His grandson, Mahtab Chand, helped the East India Company to defeat Siraj and later joined them to work towards the undoing of Mir Jafar. Mir Kasim arranged to have Jagat Seth assassinated. The kind of wealth this family had amassed was the stuff of legend. See Sengupta, ed., *Samsad Bengali Charitavidhan:* 163-64.
38. Clubs formed with the aim of drinking and smoking pot, the dancing and singing was just a peripheral activity. The Birds (Pakshir Dal) could be a reference to Rupchand Pakshi, the 'front man' of a well-known hemp-smoking club at Baghbazar. Rupchand went around town in a carriage designed as a bird's cage and wrote light songs in a mish-mash of English and Bengali, reflecting contemporary social reality. See Sumanta Banerjee, *The Parlour and the Street: Elite and Popular Culture in Nineteenth Century Calcutta* (Calcutta: Seagull Books, 1998): 151-52.
39. The first two names may be references to real people or imagined. The real-life Ram, the undertaker, used to supervise the cremations

at Nimtolla Ghat. He left a fortune worth Rs. 400,000 or 500,000 at the time of his death in 1837. But Arun Nag is doubtful about whether he was the same as Hootum's man. Keshta Bagdi could be a grandson of Raja Nabakrishna Deb, who was so dark that people called him the Bagdi (Bagdis were weavers, fishermen, palanquin bearers, considered to be low caste) raja. Members belonging to one line of the Sovabazar rajas too had the middle name Krishna/Keshta, but it is not certain if Hootum meant one of them. For Pyancha Mallik and Chhuncho Seal, see 'Preface to the Second Edition', p. 10, note 4; Nag, ed., *Sateek Hootum Pyanchar Naksha:* 211.

40. Areas where the elite Bengalis lived. The Shyambazar market was founded by Sovaram Basak in the 1740s and named after Shyam Ray. It is one of the busiest traffic intersections in present-day Calcutta; see P. Thankappan Nair, 'The Growth and Development of Old Calcutta', in Chaudhuri, ed., *Calcutta: The Living City:* 16; A. Upjohn's map of Calcutta drawn in 1794 shows Rambazar located at the crossing of Rabindra Sarani and Vivekananda Road, towards the north-west, near Harinath Dewan Street; see Nag, ed. *Sateek Hootum Pyanchar Naksha:* 211. Chowk (meaning a marketplace) could be either Sovabazar or Baghbazar. Jorasanko, of course, was the seat of the famed Tagore family.
41. Arun Nag believes the grandpa-like priest (dadathakur in the Bengali original) could be a reference to Haru Thakur, aka Harekrishna Dirghangi (1738-1813). Haru, who came from a family of priests, became a poet-singer who found favour in the courts of the maharajas of Burdwan, Krishnanagar and Sovabazar in Calcutta. Later he became the resident poet at the court of Raja Nabakrishna Deb which marked a turnaround in his fortunes. See Sengupta, *Samsad Bangali Charitavidhan:* 622.
42. The expression suggests somebody who can beat Lord Shiva, known to be under the spell of a drug-induced trance at most times, at his own game. See Sketch 1, p. 39, note 46.
43. Founded at Jorasanko in 1800-1801; Sherburne, it was believed, was born of an English father and a Hindu Brahmin mother. His illustrious students included Dwarkanath Tagore, Harakumar Tagore and Prasannakumar Tagore, who paid him a pension for as long as he lived. See Nag, ed., *Sateek Hootum Pyanchar Naksha:* 212.
44. The author of the Hindu epic *Mahabharat*—the longest book ever written—and also a character in it.
45. Kashiram Das's early seventeenth-century Bengali adaptation of the

original Sanskrit *Mahabharat* used to be quite ubiquitous in Bengali households, loved for its poetry and easily accessible language. The first four sections *(parvas)* were published from Serampore Mission Press in 1801-03. The complete set, edited by Joygopal Tarkalankar, was published in 1836. Hootum seems to suggest that Kashiram's version is still an adaptation of the Sanskrit original and hence not the real thing. See Sengupta, ed., *Samsad Bangali Charitavidhan:* 95.

46. Among the interpreters of Hindu mythological texts and the epics, Gadadhar Shiromoni was a pioneer. A resident of Sonamukhi in Bankura, sometime after 1760, Gadadhar because famous for his interpretation of the Bhagvad Gita. He was employed by the royal house at Burdwan and spawned a whole school of interpreters who followed his style. See Nag, ed., *Sateek Hootum Pyanchar Naksha:* 213.
47. A much-venerated pandit and a professor of Sanskrit, Ramdhan received widespread acclaim for his interpretations of scholastic texts and skill in music. He excelled in adapting stories from the Bhagvad Gita and stringing these together with suitable songs. Ibid.
48. Details about the life of this interpreter are unavailable. Ibid.
49. He lived in the early to middle 1800s (1816-?). Born into an interpreter's family at Bansberia, Hooghly, Sreedhar began as a singer of panchali and performed as a singing bard but moved on to interpreting classical texts which brought him fame. He was also a musician and a lyricist, specializing in the tappa genre. He was a contemporary of the more famous tappa exponent Ramnidhi Gupta. Hence some of his compositions are supposedly ascribed to Gupta. He wrote in Bengali, Hindi, Arabic and Persian, on the themes of love and spiritualism. See Sengupta, ed., *Samsad Bangali Charitavidhan:* 538.
50. Mahtab Chand Mahtab (see Preface to the Second Edition, p. 10, note 4 and p. 91, note 37.) employed a huge panel of pandits well-versed in Sanskrit to translate the *Mahabharat* in 1858. The translated work began to be published in volumes (parvas), and after Mahtab's death in 1879 the project was completed by his adopted son, Aftab, in 1884; Nag, ed., *Sateek Hootum Pyanchar Naksha:* 214. This was a precursor of the mammoth project Hootum himself would undertake in a few years' time, which turned out to be a definitive version loved by generations of Bengalis including the present.
51. In the great war in the *Mahabharat,* Bhisma, the commander-in-chief of the Kauravs, had his body so badly pierced by arrows from all possible sides that when he fell, he was lying a few feet above the ground, on a bed of arrows. But Bhisma could not die unless he willed

it. His favourite archer, Arjun, who was in the enemy camp, released an arrow which struck the earth to hit a subterranean river from where water gushed out in a fountain and fell on Bhisma's parched lips. His thirst satisfied, Bhisma could die in peace.

52. King Vikramaditya or Chandragupta II, who lived in the 4th and early 5th centuries AD, was a patron of scholarship and the arts. Legendary talents in various fields, the 'nine jewels', are supposed to have adorned his court although it is uncertain if all of them flourished at the same time; see Majumdar et al., *Advanced History of India:* 142. Among these nine jewels, Hootum has mentioned Kalidas, one of India's poetic geniuses and the writer of such classic plays as *Abhigyan Shakuntalam, Bikram Urvashi* and *Malavikagnimitra,* in the text. His epic poems *Raghuvansham* and *Kumarsambhav,* and the fragments *Meghdoot* and *Ritusanhar* have inspired Indian poets for generations. Ghatakarpar was famous for writing the eponymous *Ghatakarpar,* an epic poem. It is believed that Ghatakarpar is the other name of the great poet Bhasa. Baraha and Mihir could have been the same person or a father and son. They were mathematicians and astrologers who could predict the future with amazing felicity. See Nag, ed., *Sateek Hootum Pyanchar Naksha:* 214.
53. De-classed Brahmins, or those of low status not allowed to officiate at a puja or a ceremony or teach the scriptures; could be called to eat the food offered to the deceased's soul at the time of a memorial service.
54. This episode appears towards the end of the Hindu epic *Ramayan* where Ram, eventually defeats the demon king Ravan, and is crowned the ruler of Ayodhya with due ceremony. Among the people standing in attendance are Bivishon, Ram's trusted ally, who deserted his elder brother, the demon king Ravan, to join the righteous one. Jambuban, Hanuman and Sugreeb are the apes and Ram's trusted lieutenants, who helped him win the war. Lakshman, Shatrughna and Bharat are Ram's younger brothers, extremely loyal and devoted to him, and Sita, his wife, who had been abducted by Ravan, the reason why the war had to be fought.
55. The Bengali aphorism, *Baire konchar pattan bhetore chhunchor kettan,* literally would translate as 'outwardly he flaunts the finery while the musk rats sing inside', in which 'inside' could mean an empty stomach or impoverished house. This was a popular theme that inspired nineteenth-century woodcut prints made mostly in Battala about the decadent babu culture in the city. See Nikhil Sarkar, 'Calcutta

Woodcuts: Aspects of a Popular Art' in Ashit Paul, ed., *Woodcut Prints of Nineteenth Century Calcutta* (Calcutta: Seagull Books, 1983): 30-31.

56. Could be a reference to Gauri Sen (seventeenth/eighteenth century), who from utterly modest means rose to become a flourishing merchant engaged in export-import. His philanthropy was the stuff of legend, hence the Bengali proverb, '*Laage taka, debey Gauri Sen*' (If you need money, ask Gauri Sen). See Sengupta, ed., *Samsad Bangali Charitavidhan:* 148.
57. Tulloh & Co's auction house was located at 1 and 2 Tank Square, i.e., present-day Dalhousie Square. See Nag, ed., *Sateek Hootum Pyanchar Naksha:* 215.
58. Henry Louis Vivian Derozio, a teacher with radically atheist views, inspired a band of young men who went to Hindu College (now Presidency University) to follow a line of enlightened, rational thinking; see also note 93. The group of firebrand leaders of the movement who challenged the orthodox ways of the Hindus and embraced western enlightenment came to be known as 'Young Bengal'. Illustrious members included Tarachand Chakraborty, Rasikkrishna Mallik, Radhanath Sikdar, Krishnamohan Banerjea, Dakshinaranjan Mukherjee, among others who imbibed the doctrine and tried to propagate a new world-view. Later, Young Bengal came to represent the decadent face of the western-educated babu. In favour of radical reforms, they went about eating beef and drinking in public and greeting the deity as they went past Kalighat with a 'Good Morning, Madam,' to shock the daylights out of a conservative Hindu society. See Banerjee, *The Parlour and the Street:* 52.
59. The Gods who keep the cycle of life in motion according to Hindu mythology. Brahma, the four-headed father figure, creates life forms. Vishnu appears on earth in his different incarnations from time to time to deliver it from evil. Shiva destroys the cycle when it has completed its time, making way for a new one. Indra is the king of the Gods who is apprehensive of being dethroned. He often assumes the forms of other heavenly and human beings, trying to seduce their wives.
60. On 1 November 1858, the British government on behalf of the Crown, took charge of the administration of India. Victoria became Queen-Empress. Grand celebrations were held in India of which an integral part was the fireworks display. The programme was a flop. There was literally more smoke than fire. *The Hindoo Patriot* on the following day wrote a rather unsparing critique: 'The Fireworks—Lieutenant

Pearson's farce in three acts has in acting turned out a miserable failure . . . The sight of a pile of bamboos burning is one too common in Bengal to have much delighted the expectant spectators. The siege of Delhi as represented pyro-technically on the Maidan suggested remembrances of the terrible reality only by presenting a contrast in its wretched mildness . . . The monument promised well at the beginning but immediately after began shrouding itself in a thick volume of smoke; Nag, ed., *Sateek Hootum Pyanchar Naksha:* 221.

61. A paean to river Ganga, narrating the story of her journey from the heavens to earth, written in the late eighteenth century by Durgaprasad Mukhopadhyay, adapted to be sung like a panchali. Arun Nag cites literary historian Sukumar Sen, in whose opinion *Gangabhakti Tarangini* was written in the last twenty years of the eighteenth century. The book was first published by Gangakishore Bhattacharya in 1816. Ibid: 221-22.
62. Mahiravan is the arrogant, powerful but slightly daft son of demon king Ravan. During the siege of Lanka in *Ramayan,* as the only surviving son, he had managed to take princes Ram and Lakshman captive and was about to sacrifice them at the altar. But when Mahiravan asked Ram to bow down so that his head could be struck off, he pleaded that being of royal lineage he did not know how to bow down. Mahiravan tried helping him by demonstrating the art of putting one's head for the sacrifice and had his own sacrificed instead.
63. Mani or *muni* (saint) gosain was one of the archetypal characters in a typical jatra performance who appeared to provide comic relief in the interludes. Ibid: 222.
64. A net laid out in the river into which fish swarm in during high tide and get trapped.
65. A generic name for a prison; there was an Old Harinbadi Lane near the Tiretta Bazar and Petty Court Jail, inside the National Medical College Campus, the Harinbadi referred to here was the Grand Jail located at the east of the present-day Victoria Memorial; ibid.
66. This was a much sought after title given to the native zamindars who found favour with the British rulers. Most often such titles would go to the zamindars indulging in extortion and severe repression.
67. Such anecdotes about the babu going berserk under the influence of liquor were the stuff of gossip in nineteenth-century Calcutta. Instances of the babu taking the lion's place as Goddess Durga's carrier may be found in Tekchand Thakur's *Mod Khaoa Baro Dai, Jaat Thakar Ki Upai* (How to be a drinker and keep one's caste). In it a

rich man takes his surname Sinha (the Bengali word for lion) a bit too seriously under the influence of liquor to think that indeed he might be the chosen one for the role of the lion carrying the deity. So he breaks the idol, crawling in to take the divine carrier's place. In the same book, Thakur narrates a story about a babu who insisted on drowning the drummers with the idol at the time of the Goddess's immersion. The real-life protagonist of this story could have been Joynarayan Mitra, who was notorious for making a fool of himself. See Nag, ed., *Sateek Hootum Pyanchar Naksha:* 223.

68. This is lifted from the extremely popular version of the play *Vidyasundar,* played in a tradition popularized by Gopal Ude, or Gopal from Orissa. 'For the contemporary audience, Malini's overtures echoed the immediacy of the familiar soliciting heard in the red light areas of Calcutta in those days.' See Banerjee, *Parlour and the Street:* 142; also see Sketch 6, p. 212, note 6.
69. A metaphor borrowed from breeding of horses. Stud bred horses are products of genetic engineering, or unnaturally bred. The suggestion is that the offspring are illegitimate; See Nag, ed., *Sateek Hootum Pyanchar Naksha:* 223.
70. Nabadwip Chandra Goswami, who was Hootum's contemporary, founded a Gouranga temple with a golden idol at 57, Beniatolla Street. He had quite a few gold traders among his disciples, and tried promoting their cause. Ibid: 224.
71. 'Shimulia' or Simla, so called because of the abundance of shimul (silk cotton) trees in the area, was a 1000-bigha area owned by the raja of Nadia. John Holwell, the collector of Calcutta, rented the area on behalf of the East India Company in 1754 for Rs. 2281 per annum. The area extended to Dihi Bahir (or Ba'ar, meaning extended or greater) Simla, which is shown in A. Upjohn's 1794 map as lying outside the Maratha Ditch. When the area around Gobindapur was cleared to build Fort William in 1757, many prominent families of Calcutta were given alternative land in areas just outside what was then central Calcutta; Bahir Simla being one of these. See Nair, 'Growth and Development of Old Calcutta', in Chaudhuri, ed., *Calcutta: The Living City:* 11, 14.
72. Ma or Mother Gosains were the female counterparts of the gosains (spiritual gurus of the Vaishnav cult). Often the gosains kept prostitutes, passing them off as disciples. Hootum's implies that Nader Chand Gosain did not need to visit prostitutes at Sonagacchi as the prostitutes coming 'under the **jurisdiction**' of the Mother Gosains of

Simla would attend on him if he so wanted. The Ma Gosain of Simla referred to here was Madhumukhi Devi, the second wife of a certain Loknath Goswami. See Nag, ed., *Sateek Hootum Pyanchar Naksha:* 224-25.

73. A popular song in Hootum's time, lamenting the state of India after Wajid Ali Shah (1822-87), handed over Awadh (Lucknow), the last bit of Mughal-ruled India, to the East India Company in 1856. Wajid Ali Shah, who was living in Garden Reach/Metia Buruj area of Calcutta at the time in virtual imprisonment, had thought of going to London to request Queen Victoria to restore his kingdom to him, but could not do so because of his failing health. Wajid Ali, who was a patron of the arts and himself a poet, could have written this song. For more on Wajid Ali, see Sketch 3, p. 146, note 29. Ibid: 225.
74. The greatest love story in Hindu mythology is based on an incestuous relationship. Krishna, the eternal lover of women, was in love with Radhika, or Radha, the wife of his maternal uncle, Ayan Ghosh. The affair is symbolic of the divine's reaching out to the human and the human being's attaining divinity, and is on a different plane altogether from those happening within the parameters of restrictive society.
75. Balaram, Krishna's elder brother, was the maverick sort with some human foibles.
76. Ishwarchandra Vidyasagar is being invoked, as against huge odds he was instrumental in passing the Widow Remarriage Act, 1856. Since widows are now free to remarry, Danu will get a more suitable husband for his widowed mother. For more on Vidyasagar, see Introduction, p. lix, note 1; p 2, note 2.
77. See note 54 above; The word 'hanuman' in Bengali denotes a biggish monkey, figuratively speaking a mischief-maker.
78. These are examples of what the babus did when they had money to burn and were desperate to be noticed by the public. The hype over Ramgopal Mallik's son's mega-buck (Rs700,000-800,000) wedding in 1819 touched public life. *Samachar Darpan* of 16 January 1819 described it as unprecedented. The family's fortunes took a nosedive as a consequence. Brajendranarayan was the adopted son of Raja Rajnarayan of Posta (see note 31, above) who supposedly spent more than a hundred thousand rupees on the 'wedding' (marrying off cats and dogs was a popular sport among the babus) of a pet cat kept by his mistress. See Nag, ed., *Sateek Hootum Pyanchar Naksha:* 225-26.
79. A technical term for the business of importing Manchester cotton in India. Ibid.

80. The leading singing poets of the time. *Kobigaan* (the duel of the poets) was the predecessor of modern poetry in performance. Usually, a poet, backed by a team of supporting singers, would start on a theme, and have a rival poet respond to it. Ram Basu pioneered the tradition of extempore banter and repartee between the competing poets/teams. Harekrishna Dirghangi began as an amateur but was later made the leader of the poet's company patronized by Raja Nabakrishna. Nilmoni Chakraborty began as a disciple of Haru Thakur but later formed his own team with elder brother Ramaprasad. Jaga could have been Joggeswar the washerman or Jaga the trader, who was known for his rivalry with the very famous Bhola Moira. Ibid, 227-28.
81. Shibchandra was born rich and worked as the minister of the customs house. He had amassed great wealth through fair and dubious means but blew it all up by giving into a life of unbridled hedonism. He was the chief patron of the Birds. See note 38, above.
82. Landholders' Society and Bengal British-India Society came together to form the British Indian Association on 31 October 1851, aiming to make the British rulers in India more capable administrators by looking after the interests of both Britain and India. Raja Radhakanta Deb was the chair, Debendranath Tagore the secretary and Digambar Mitra the joint secretary. See Nag, ed., *Sateek Hootum Pyanchar Naksha*: 228.
83. These were the faces of the new emerging Bengal, a mix of western enlightenment and conservatism, and the founding fathers of the Hindu College (now Presidency University). For Rammohan Roy, see Sketch 1, p. 39, note 51; notes 86, 89, 92 below.
84. Gopimohan Deb (? – 1837) was the adopted son of Nabakrishna Dev of Sovabazar and the father of Raja Radhakanta Deb. He was one of the founders of the Hindu Dharma Sabha and one of the five principal donors who set up the Hindu College. See Nag, ed., *Sateek Hootum Pyanchar Naksha:* 228.
85. Gopimohan Thakur (1760-1819) belonged to the house of Darpanarayan Thakur of Pathuriaghata, a polyglot who held high posts in the British administration. He was one of the chief patrons who funded the setting up of Hindu College by donating Rs.10,000 at one go and became its first governor. See Sengupta, ed. *Samsad Bangali Charitavidhan:* 141.
86. Now better known as the grandfather of Rabindranath Tagore, Dwarkanath (1794-1846) was one of the most illustrious entrepreneurs of nineteenth-century Bengal. Well versed in English and French, he

began his career in law and later became a collector of salt taxes in 24-Parganas. Six years later, he was sitting on the taxation, salt and opium boards. He founded the Union Bank with a capital of Rs. 1,600,000, ventured into shipping and supposedly went to England on his own ship. With his friend Raja Rammohan Roy, Dwarkanath tried to propagate social reform, emphasizing English education and liberal thought. A founding father of Hindu College, Dwarkanath was on its governing body from 1833 till his death. He also started a Bengali school as part of the prestigious Hindu School in 1840. He supported the Calcutta Medical College and helped found the Calcutta Public Library. He owned the papers, *Bengal Harkaru, Bengal Herald* and *Bangadoot* and supported *The Englishman*. He advocated the suppression of sati, freedom of the press, setting up juries in civil courts and reforming the police force. Ibid: 223.

87. He (1770-1820) was Kaliprasanna Sinha's grandfather. Beginning as a secretary to Postmaster General Hall and Calcutta's magistrate William Rumbolt, he made a lot of money from service and trade, a major donor to Hindu College and a prominent figure on its board of directors. A man of liberal views, he argued in favour of Derozio when the orthodox Hindu governors of Hindu College tried to throw him out of the institution; see Manmathanath Ghosh, *Mahatma Kaliprasanna Singha* (Calcutta: [1915]; Parul Prakashani, 2008): 6, 11.
88. The weekly *Samachar Chandrika* was the party mouthpiece of Dharma Sabha, a club of orthodox, traditional, conservative Hindus. First published on 5 March 1822, the paper was edited by Bhabanicharan Bandopadhyay who had initially collaborated with Rammohan Roy to launch the *Sambad Kaumudi* in 1821 but parted ways owing to irreconcilable differences on religious and social issues; see Banerjee, *Parlour and the Street:* 181. Contrary to Hootum's claim, it's not the first Bengali periodical. *Samachar Darpan* was published on 23 May 1818 from Serampore, the hub of pioneering activity in Bengali publishing. *Bangal Gejeti* (Weekly Bengal Gazette) edited by Gangakishore Bhattacharjee is supposed to have preceded these, but no copies of the journal exist. See Nag, ed. *Sateek Hootum Pyanchar Naksha:* 229.
89. As a reaction to the orthodoxy, casteism and other regressive aspects of traditional Hindu practices, Rammohan Roy began a reform movement to rationalize and modernize, and remove idol worship. The central idea of monotheism was taken from ancient Hindu scriptures which had instances of the formless Brahma, the Supreme Being, being worshipped. Roy published notes on the Vedanta and the

Upanishads in support of his contention. In 1815 he founded the Atmiya Sabha, the predecessor of Brahmo Sabha/Samaj, which had its first meeting on 20 August 1828. 'It was meant to be an assembly of all who believed in the unity of God and discarded the worship of images.' The Vedas and Upanishads would be read and interpreted at the Samaj's weekly service and songs dedicated to the Supreme Being sung. Notably, Rammohan Roy remained a confirmed Hindu all his life and even wore the Hindu Brahmin's sacred thread, categorically denying that he had founded a different religious sect. For further details see Introduction, p. lxi, note 19 and p. lxi, note 21. See Majumdar et al., *Advanced History of India:* 868-69.

90. In support of sati, the conservative traditionalist Hindus formed Dharma Sabha on 17 January 1830, to 'protect the interests of the Hindu religion'. *Samachar Darpan* wrote on 13 February 1830 that Dharma Sabha members would boycott those trying to stop sati. Distinguished members included Ramgopal Mallik, Gopimohan Deb, and Radhakanta Deb (see note 84). *Samachar Chandrika* served as their mouthpiece. See Nag, ed., *Sateek Hootum Pyanchar Naksha:* 230.
91. Rajnarayan Ray (Kar) belonged to the zamindar family of Andul. He became a champion of the Kayasthas after he was prevented by the priests at the Govindaji temple in Vrindavan to touch the idol, as he was a non-Brahmin who did not wear the sacred thread. As a result, he took up the Kayasthas' cause with missionary zeal. He went through a sacred thread ceremony, the rite of passage into Brahminhood, and wrote a book called *Kayastha Kaustav,* to prove that Kayasthas came from a superior stock to that of the Brahmins. Ibid.
92. Among the upper castes, burning 'chaste' Hindu widows on the funeral pyres of their husbands was prevalent in Bengal in the eighteenth and nineteenth centuries. 'Not only would such a woman enjoy eternal bliss in heaven along with her husband, but her action would expiate the sins of three generations of her husband's family.' But often the burning, which took the form of a public spectacle, was executed by avaricious male relations, out to grab the widow's inheritance. Sometimes, the helpless victim would be drugged and tied forcibly to the pyre, lest she should change her mind about sacrificing her life. The British government in India dragged its feet over the issue for fear of hurting popular sentiment. The government passed a resolution in 1812, supplemented by two more in 1815 and 1817, forbidding the burning of widows who had been drugged, were pregnant or pre-pubescent. In 1817, there was a ruling that widows

with children younger than seven years would not be allowed to commit sati. In 1817, orthodox Brahmins appealed to the government to nullify the earlier measures. Rammohan Roy submitted a counter petition, in which he wrote, 'all these instances are murders, according to every *Shastra* as well as to the common sense of all nations'. Roy wrote a pamphlet on the subject and organized a vigilance committee to ensure that the government regulations were being followed. He was vehemently opposed by orthodox Hindus, like Radhakantha Deb, and his life was under threat.

As the new Governor-General, Lord William Bentinck advocated immediate abolition of sati, declaring conducting sati a criminal offence. On 4 December 1829, Regulation XVII was passed, banning sati. Any person associated in any way with sati would be considered a criminal. The battle between the pro-sati lobby and its opponents reached the British Parliament. Rammohan went to England and submitted an appeal with the House of Commons. The Privy Council dismissed the appeal made by the pro-sati lobbyists. See Majumdar et al., *Advanced History of India:* 816-19.

93. The hub of learning, culture and revolutionary ideas, Hindu College was founded on 20 January 1817, initially located in Garanhata. In 1819 the college was moved to Jorasanko and to College Street (adjacent to Sanskrit College) in 1826; see also note 84 above. Hindu College in Hootum's time, contrary to its name and the expectations of orthodox Hindus like Radhakanta Deb, one of its chief patrons, turned out to be a seat of secular and liberal ideas. Prominent students such as Maheshchandra Ghosh, Krishnamohan Banerjea, Gnanendramohan Thakur and Michael Madhusudan Dutt converted to Christianity. In their resistance against what they felt was a concerted effort by Christian missionaries to strike at the root of Hindu integrity, Radhakanta Deb and other like-minded patrons tried removing a teacher of the college, Kailashchandra Basu, when he turned Christian and Henry Louis Vivian Derozio, the leader of the 'Young Bengal' pack was thrown out of the college 'without even the mockery of a trial' for propagating atheist ideas. About twenty-three years later, in 1853, once again the 'liberal' and 'secularist' credentials of the college were put to test when the son of Hira Bulbul, a high-society Muslim prostitute's son was admitted and then dropped, following huge outrage among conservative Hindu guardians, many of whom withdrew their wards. Two years later, the government took over the institution, renamed it Presidency College and abolished all considerations of religion and

social status while admitting students. See Subir Roychoudhuri, 'The Lost World of the Babus', in Chaudhuri, ed., *Calcutta: The Living City: The Past:* 72-4.

94. David Hare (1775-1842), who came to India to sell watches, made higher education his mission. He was actively involved with the Calcutta School Society and personally financed its model schools, particularly the Arpuly School, when they fell in hard times, and was keen that students should acquire proficiency in their mother tongue, even as they received an English education. To meet the growing demand for English education, parallel English classes were begun at the model schools where only students proficient in Bengali would be admitted. See ibid: Poromesh Acharya, 'Education in Old Calcutta': 90-92. Hare was against conversion and all for the freedom of the Press. He joined the movement against the sending of Indian coolies abroad. A true lover of India and its people, Hare was not allowed any space in the cemetery after his death by the Christian missionaries who saw him as a heretic. See Nag, ed., *Sateek Hootum Pyanchar Naksha:* 231.
95. Surpanakha was the demon king Ravan's sister in the epic *Ramayan.* When she proposed to Ram, who had been banished to the forests with brother Lakshman and Sita, Lakshman cut off her nose.
96. Joykrishna Mukherjee (1808-88) began his career as a clerk in the British Army at Meerut. Later he became the zamindar of Uttarpara. While he was a nationalist and a liberal who would donate generously for the cause of education (the Uttarpara Public Library founded by him is still considered one of West Bengal's most valuable collections), he was infamous for his heavy-handed ways, forgery of property deeds and seizing land gifted to Brahmins or dedicated to a God. He had the rules at his fingertips and an elephantine memory that would store the details of land transfer and taxation in flawless detail. In 1858 Joykrishna was accused of kidnapping Madan De of Baluti and ransacking his household. The district magistrate of Howrah found him guilty and gave him a prison term. Joykrishna appealed to the Sessions Court. The civil and sessions judge of 24-Parganas, E.D. Latour ruled that the punishment would remain effective. A subsequent appeal to a higher court saw Justice A. Sconce ruling in Joykrishna's favour. Joykrishna was released after spending forty-three days in prison. The imprisonment of the mighty and tyrannical Joykrishna pleased a section of the general public, so much so that his fall from grace was lampooned in poems and songs (see also note 23 above); Nag, ed., *Sateek Hootum Pyanchar Naksha:* 231-32.

97. Ibid. The sessions judge E.D. Latour was a righteous man who disliked tyrannical zamindars and was extremely sympathetic to the movement against the indigo planters. Mathuranath Munshi, the zamindar of Taki, thought it was beneath his dignity to show up at the lower court and appealed to Latour to that effect. Latour dismissed the appeal but a higher court granted it, which *The Hindoo Patriot* (5.5.1859) treated as a cause for celebration. The zamindars ganged up against Latour under the leadership of Digambar Mitra and tried to have him impeached in 1861, but did not succeed.
98. Ibid; a very old wharf (appears in maps published in 1784) slightly north of Clive's Ghat. Between Jackson's Ghat and Canning Street lay Jackson Ghat Street (now Jackson Lane). Also known as Moylah Ghat (dumping ground).
99. This is perhaps the most endearing image from the folk version of Hindu mythology. Lord Krishna, as an adorable mischievous child is shown stealing cream from the pot suspended from the ceiling; an iconic image of mischievousness, humanizing a child God.
100. Considered 'dispensable' from the point of view of the slovenly and rascally gosains, actually these are the tasks young Lord Krishna performed to rid the world of evil and protect its inhabitants. Kaliya, the multi-hooded venomous serpent, was quashed to death by Krishna as he played the flute. Putna was a demoness sent to suckle the infant Krishna who pulled so hard on her poison-smeared paps that it sucked the life out of her. Gobardhan was a mountain range. When there was a deluge, Krishna lifted the range on his little finger for the people to take shelter underneath. The gosains were more interested in the amorous sports that Krishna engaged in: hiding the milkmaids' clothes left on the bank while they went to take a dip in the river; trying to conciliate with the offended beloved and cavorting in Vrindavan with his beloved.
101. A seventeenth-century text containing 2500 slokas written by Krishnadas Kaviraj on the life and achievements of Sri Chaitanya, an extraordinary scholar of Sanskrit who left home to propagate ideas of universal love as the leader of the Vaishnav cult. Certain slokas in the text have been borrowed from the works of Roop Goswami, Kabikarnapur, Vrindavan Das and Raghunath Das Goswami. The life of Sri Chaitanya is read against this backdrop. See Sengupta, ed., *Samsad Bangali Charitavidhan:* 104.
102. A variety of sweetmeats made with batter and fresh jaggery or

molasses, sometimes stuffed with sweet potatoes or made into a pancake and stuffed with kheer and coconut. This is done to celebrate the harvest on the last day in the winter month of Poush beginning in mid-December.

103. Celebrated at the height of summer when mangoes, jackfruits and other summer fruits are ripe and luscious; the son-in-law is invited to his in-laws', treated royally with a feast and plied with gifts.

104. Miss Stowe is the first in the line of Hootum's well-educated, accomplished English women with progressive views who are worth emulating. She could be Harriet Beecher Stowe (1811-96), the author of *Uncle Tom's Cabin* (1852), a scathing critique of slavery based on her personal experiences in Cincinnatti, Ohio; see Paul Harvey, ed., *The Oxford Companion to English Literature* (London: Clarendon Press, 1960): 753. Thompson was possibly Katharine Thomson, the author of several historical biographies and novels. She knew Lady Lytton (the last name on Hootum's list) closely and wrote about her in *Recollections of Literary Characters*, 1854; see Charles Dickens, *The Letters of Charles Dickens,* vol. 2, edited by Madeline House, Graham Storey, and Geoffrey Tillotson (London: Oxford University Press, 1969): 39. Miss Barclay could have been Lydia Ann Barclay (1800-55) who selected and edited the letters and a short spiritual autobiography of her more illustrious ancestor, Lydia Rawlinson Lancaster; see Gil Skidmore, *Strength in Weakness: Writings of Eighteenth-Century Quaker Women* (Altamira, Ca: Rowman, 2003): 32-34. Lady Rosina Doyle Bulwer Lytton (1802-82), who was the author of twelve novels, was married to the Earl of Lytton, Bulwer-Lytton, and separated from him in 1836. Three years later she portrayed her husband as a villain in the novel *Cheveley, or the Man of Honour.* The bitterness was sustained throughout their lives. In June 1858, when her husband was contesting parliamentary elections, she ran a vituperative campaign against him. That Hootum sees Lady Lytton as a feisty, liberated woman who would go to any lengths to get her own back, rather than as an embittered virago, rejected by her public figure of a husband, shows that Hootum probably had great respect and empathy for women; Marie Mulvey-Roberts, 'Rosina Bulwer-Lytton'. *The Literary Encyclopaedia.* 2004, http://www.litencyc.com/php/speople.php?rec=true&UID=637)

105. They were the six 'satis' (women of virtue) in Hindu mythology, to which Hootum has added Shakuntala. These women were loyal to their husbands through thick and thin. Sita was the loving wife of

Ram in *Ramayan,* who followed him to the forests and was abducted by Ravan, the demon king. She was won back by Ram in a fierce battle, but he abandoned her soon after, bowing to popular demand, as she could have been touched by a man other than her husband during the kidnap. Sita underwent a trial by fire and survived it. Savitri was an extremely clever and scholarly woman who married for love, knowing that her husband would live for only a year. When the God of Death came to take Satyavan away, Savitri defeated him in a war of words and thus won her husband's life back.

Sati chose Lord Shiva, the wayward one, who had not much to recommend him except his predilection for drugs, much against her father's wishes. When King Daksha, her mighty father, humiliated her husband, Sati died. Satyabhama is Lord Krishna's wife, loyal to him despite his many dalliances.

The myth of Shakuntala, a story from the *Mahabharat,* has the virginal girl growing up in a hermitage in the forest. She falls in love with King Dushyanta. But later he refuses to acknowledge her or the child she is pregnant with. The crisis is resolved much later when the king recognizes the ring he had given her and remembers everything. Krishna, or the dark lady, is Draupadi, the wife of the valiant five Pandava brothers in the *Mahabharat.* Draupadi's whole life is a series of challenges which she faced courageously.

106. Vidyasagar's scholasticism was legendary as were his efforts to better the lot of women in Bengal, primarily through education. But his wife is not known to have received a formal education. It is indeed quite curious that one does not get to hear much about the activities of the wife of the man whose mission was to educate and empower women. While one is told that Ishwarchandra's mother was keen on setting up girls' schools in the ancestral village, Birsingha, there is no knowing if the daughter-in-law of the house was encouraged to study.

Hootum imagines her as a country-bred housewife, without urban refinement and progressive ideas, taken up with rituals that underscore her backwardness. Sprinkling holy Ganga water has to do with a near-obsessive ritual practised by women terrified of defilement by touching the 'impure' elements. The logic is that a few drops of Ganga water have a purifying effect on the dirtiest object.

Shah Farid used to be a Muslim saint or dervish vested with healing powers. Roving mendicants would wear an amulet whose touch supposedly was a panacea for a lot of ailments. The stone named after Lakshmi and Narayan kept at the Teli residence was supposed to be a rare specimen, the reason why the water washing it was considered to be so precious and therapeutic. See Nag, ed., *Sateek Hootum Pyanchar Naksha:* 233.

107. Lord Krishna's sibling, usually appears with a hoe on his shoulder. Here he is imagined carrying a cowherd's cudgel.
108. The part of the *Mahabharat* where Lord Krishna tells a reluctant Arjun that the results of the great war are pre-determined, and that he must perform his task (i.e., fight and kill his kin, if necessary) without thinking of its outcome, and opens up a world-view informed by studied stoicism that has endured. The risqué episodes Hootum talks about must have been interpolations rather than a part of the original text.
109. Farashdanga, as the name suggests, is where the French had settled down, in other words, Chandernagore, which, in any case, was miles away from the glamour and high life of Calcutta. See ibid: 234.
110. Ibid; it was Sir Lawrence Peel who was the Chief Justice in Calcutta from 1842 to 1855.
111. The present-day Shibpur Botanical Gardens.
112. The beard would be grown till one's wish was fulfilled, after which it would be sacrificed at Lord Shiva's temple in Tarakeswar.

3
Idle Talk

AS THEY say, you can tell a Chinese from the way he applies his skills and a Bengali by the way he employs his mouth. To this Hootum would like to add the following: you can tell a Calcuttan by the way he engages in idle speculations. In this city a fresh piece of rumour [circulates] every day, all of which are quite outrageous and fantastic. When one does not have much to do, one could always pack the elder kinsman off on his final journey to the river Ganga.[1] Therefore, it is hardly surprising that idle people who spend time chatting round the clock, hookah in hand, fiddle with playing cards and pawns on the chess board, and break wind, would be engaged in whipping up cock-and-bull stories. Dear Reader, until the day the Bengalis acquire a **better occupation**, and until the social norms and the domestic regulations followed by them are **reformed**, there is no way this huge aberration [in society] could be eradicated. Those who were never taught the principles of morality do not realize [the damage] lies could cause. So they conveniently spread these falsehoods, using them like everyday wear and are not ashamed of them or embarrassed to do so.

The Child-Lifter

Soon after I was born, I was told that child-lifting was rampant in the city. [Apparently] the peddlers from Kabul who sold dry fruits were on the lookout for children whom they stole and took back home. Delicious fruits grew in the many orchards of that country.

The [stolen] boy was let loose in one of them. And when he, having eaten his fill of fruits, non-stop, became swollen and the colour of his skin resembled lac-dye mixed in milk—it were as if his skin would crack and bleed if one clicked one's fingers against it—they put a cauldron full of ghee on the stove and hung him upside down above it. When the ghee started boiling in full steam, blood oozed out of the boy's face, falling in large drops on the cauldron. When all the blood in the boy's body had drained out, a garnishing of fruits and sugar candy was scattered over the victual, before removing the cauldron from the heat. It was food for nawabs and aristocratic Muslims. After I heard this story, I wouldn't step out of the house on my own, not even if my life were under serious threat. And since then I developed a racist hatred for low-caste Muslims.

Pratapchand

I grew up, went through the chalk ceremony.[2] One day, I hid in the servants' quarters to give my tutor, of whom I was terribly scared, the slip. I heard the servants saying to one another, 'Pratapchand,[3] the maharaja of Burdwan who died, is back again. He has lodged a legal complaint to reclaim his estate, and eminent people of the city are planning to go and see him. It is going to be disaster for Paranbabu. The adopted son doesn't stand a chance [now that the real heir is back].'

Anything that's new tends to intrigue young people. Ever since I heard about this incident, I would prod people to find out more about Raja Pratapchand. Somebody said, 'He can stay underwater for a whole day and night.' Somebody else said, 'He survived a bullet wound. The maharani has confirmed that he is indeed Maharaja Pratapchand. He had cut his ear trying to fly a kite. His sister recognized him by the cut mark.' Another one said, 'He must have committed a major crime, and that's why he went into hiding like King Yudhisthir.[4] He hadn't really died. During his funeral at Ambika Kalna, only his coffin was burnt, he was not inside it.' This started a major rumour across the city. The story of Pratapchand was the talk of the town.

After some time had passed like this, one day, suddenly, one heard that the Supreme Court, through a rather copiously conducted trial, had found Pratapchand to be a fraud. Different people of the city, with good intentions and otherwise, began saying, 'He's not the real Pratapchand.' Another one said, 'Thank God for Dwarkanath Tagore, it's because of him that the fraud could be **proved.** Else, Paranbabu would be in big trouble.'

Meanwhile, Pratapchand, now a proven fake, started living in Baranagar. In spite of being an impostor, he managed to attract a huge following of whores, closet whores, housewives and daughters. Nothing, it seems, was too tough a job for Pratapchand. Gradually, just as a trendy piece of music [loses its appeal], Pratapchand too became passé. And I started going to school.

The Holy Men

Reader! A school is more terrifying than the abode of Yama, the God of Death. To me the pandit and the schoolmaster appear no less fearsome than a tiger! One day, at about 1 pm, we were riding on each other's backs like horses, when the old gardener who usually watered the plants, said, 'A holy man has arrived at the house of the raja of Bhukailash.[5] He was born way back, in the Age of Truth.[6] Ant hills cover his body, from which large peepul trees have sprouted. He is sitting in meditation, with eyes closed. If his concentration is broken and his eyes open, he will turn all that he sees into ashes.'

I was terrified. School over, I went back home, still thinking about the holy man. Tops, kites, **cricket** equipment and pigeons[7] lay neglected. The wish to visit the holy man grew strong [inside me]. Ultimately I ran to my grandmother.

My aged grandmother would tell me tales in bed at night. These were about the talking birds *Bengama-Bengami*, the pigeon king, the friendly foursome—king's, courtier's, trader's and soldier's sons—the ever-vigilant palm-leaf scimitar and flying horse, golden and silver magic wands and so on.[8] She recited verses from the works of Kabikankan Mukundaram[9] and Kashiram Das's *Mahabharat.*[10] I fell asleep listening to them. Alas, [those were the days] I would surely remember those lovely days of my childhood, even at the moment of my death. My soft lotus heart, which had not yet known the ways of the world, was more delicate than tender flower buds. Everything seemed believable. My hair would stand on end when one took the name of ghosts, she-ghosts or the Lord Supreme. [That was a time when] the heart knew nothing about regret and sorrow. I would not want to lose that state of innocence even if I were made immortal.

When I went to bed, I told Grandma about the holy man the gardener had been talking about. Grandma looked sombre for a while. Then she asked a servant to bring her the dust of the holy man's feet the next morning. She told me a few more stories about holy men.

Grandmother said, 'About eighty years ago (Grandma was newly married at that time), our friend Varanasi Ghosh[11] saw a similar holy man inside a forest, on his way to Kashi. This holy man too was deep in meditation, unconscious of his surroundings. He was lifted by the boatmen and brought inside the boat. Varanasi hosted him in the boat and took very good care of him. In those days the place where the river split into two at Chhapghati[12] was barely navigable, so the passengers travelling by the river took a detour through a swampy patch of forest. Varanasi had to do the same thing. One day, as the boat was being towed through the marsh, the boatmen and the rest were slightly distracted. Suddenly another holy man who was a spitting image of the earlier one appeared beside the water. The first one was meditating, sitting on the prow of the vessel. The holy man on the river bank walked across to the boat, smiled, took the one on the boat by the hand and the two walked away over the water. The boatmen and the rest were left gaping, their jaws dropped. Varanasi scanned the marshes thoroughly but found neither of the two [holy men]. These were saints from ancient times. They have been meditating for ten, maybe twenty thousand, years. They could perform any feat if they wished it.

'Once the Duttas of Jhilipur, while digging a plot of land in the Sunderbans, unearthed a holy man thirty yards under the topsoil. Huge roots of peepul clung to his body, shrivelled up like a piece of desiccated wood. The Duttas took a lot of trouble to bring him to Jhilipur and the holy man stayed there for about a month. Finally, one night he went away and nobody could locate his whereabouts.' I fell asleep, listening to the story.

The morning after, Rama, the servant, brought home the dust of the holy man's feet. Grandmother packed the dust inside a huge amulet, almost as big as a giant drum, and fastened it around my neck. And since that day I have managed to escape the evil eye of ghosts, she-ghosts, ogresses and monsters to some extent.

After a few years, I left school, joined college, met classmates who were rich men's sons and hence of my own ilk. One day, at 1 pm, as we chased grasshoppers in the field next to Gol Dighi, the pandit who taught us in class came wandering in our direction. Earlier, the pandit used to be a cook at a rich man's house. Thanks to the much-thought-out deliberations by the **Education Council**,[13] the recommendations of Mr. Sen,[14] and the generosity of the principal, he was now a teacher.

The pandit loved to chew paan, which is what anyone trying to please him would offer. As soon as the pandit arrived on the scene, the boys began offering paan to him. I gave him a roll of sweet paan [as well]. The pandit liked it sweet. He was pleased with the gift and showed it by taking my name. 'Hello Hootum! Heard about the holy man brought to the raja's house at Bhukailash? An English doctor has managed to interrupt his meditation. First, the raja's people poured burning hot balls made from coal dust on his body, and dunked him in water. But that was not enough to break his trance. Ultimately the doctor held a bottle of tincture under his nose, and he was conscious again. Now the holy man is consuming whatever he can lay his hands on. He is giving people massages and fanning zamindars by drawing the punkha[15] to earn a living. The hallowed aura about the holy man has shattered.'

The pandit's words left us awestruck. The reverence one had towards the holy man disappeared like camphor without the black pepper that lends it substance, or, to give another example, like the contents in an uncorked bottle of ether. Grandmother's amulet was chucked away the very next day. The fear of ghosts, ogresses and she-ghosts returned to haunt me.

The Ruckus at the Lala's

I was promoted to a higher class at school, which meant I could now avoid the pandit who used to be a cook. One day, I failed to answer in class and hence was made to wear the donkey's cap, stand on the bench and be **confined** to it during the recess hour. The master had gone to the smoking room to have his afternoon snack. (While he could not cope with hunger, the boys, obviously, were expected to pass this endurance test!) [In the meantime] the youngest son of a Brahmin mimicked the sound made by the shyama birds, the cooing of pigeons and was simulating the strides of a **pony.**

That's when a young lad who lived in Cossipore said, 'Yesterday afternoon, in the house of the Lalas,[16] I mean the Lala rajas (Holy Lord Vishnu, even people like these have attained the status of a raja!), a group of drunken Englishmen appeared, and struck the gatekeepers with spears. The rajas were so scared that they hid inside an abandoned well like Hassan and Hossein[17] and managed to save their lives.' (There weren't too many chameleon-like traitors to turn them in at that moment.[18])

Another lad quipped, 'No, it wasn't like that at all. I heard the story from my elder brother. The sahibs had killed a crow which sat on a tree in front of the raja's house. So the chief of the guards stepped out to hit back at the sahibs.' Another chap stood up and flailing his arms close to my face said, 'Not at all. That's rubbish. My house too is in Tala. You know the huge ditch behind the raja's house? The rotting pond next to it is at the back of my house. A brother of one of the clerks working in the raja's office has a face just like a monkey's. So a sahib had made a face at him, and the clerk grimaced back. That's what made the sahibs come back with guns, pistols and their henchmen and fire at the raja's men.'

Even as people exchanged different versions of the story, the **master** returned from the smoking room. The Brahmin's youngest son stopped horsing around and making bird sounds. The rajas were spared [for the time being]. *Dong, dong,* the clock struck. It was 2 pm. The class resumed. So much for my tiffin break!

Back home I heard a lot more terrifying stuff about the Lalas from many others. Owners of Bengali newspapers started filling up their pages with absurd gossip, such as: 'A group of white men were passing by, marching to the tune of loud music. One of them was thirsty. When he went to ask for water at the raja's house, the captain of the guards held him by the scruff of his neck and threw him out. That's when the colonel, who was travelling with the group, ordered his people to open fire.'

Earlier, the Bengali newspapers of the city were quite strange. The pages were full of trivial news items on the lines of 'Is there a donor as great as Babu X?', 'Babu Y spends a crore on his mother's memorial service (the babu, by the way, is just an accountant)', 'A drunkard drowns himself to death', 'A prostitute has lost her nose-ring. The finder will be rewarded by being made the editor's assistant', etc. Some of these papers engaged in slander campaigns to make a profit, some lavished praises with an eye on monetary rewards. Such sleazy activities continue to happen in many papers, even now.

Finally, we got the facts right. A firinghi hunter had got into a row with a gatekeeper and ultimately shot him down.

The Excitement over Conversions

The crisis involving the Paikpara rajas had subsided, but there was a fresh rumour that Duleep, the son of Ranjit Singh,[19] had been indoctrinated into the cult of Jesus, and with him all the Sikhs had converted to Christianity. We were told that a few Brahmins from Bhatpara too would become Christians. The Bhatpara brood of Brahmins belonged to pure Hindu stock. Therefore the news that they would convert to Christianity shocked a lot of people. Ultimately, it was revealed that rather than the Bhatpara [clan], it was Babu Gnanendramohan of Pathuriaghata, the son of Babu Prasannakumar Tagore[20] [who had converted]. Krishnamohan Banerjea,[21] who was also a Christian, married his daughter to Gnanendramohan. Thus there was no dearth of married women.

When a new trend catches on in the city, it does not die down too soon. Therefore, in keeping with the current fashion, a schoolmaster, a certain Mr. Haldar from Kalighat, a businessman and a Kayastha added to the tribe of Christians. A few ladies from elite households came out of the shadows to step into the realm of light. Finally, the hallowed light beamed out through the roofs of certain people. Some of them lost their property; some regretted the damage done and began remedying it. Like portable lamps carried along the way, the excitement over conversions lit up the space around itself and moved on, leaving it in darkness. I had grown up and didn't like going to school any more.

The Mutiny

Dear Readers! One day I was wandering around aimlessly, when I heard that the soldiers serving in the west [of India] were wild with fury.[22] Anointing Nana Saheb[23] as their leader, they wanted to wrest the kingdom from the hands of the English. The Muslim **chief** in Delhi would once again be made the sovereign of Delhi, and by extension of the world. All this meant trouble.

The Idrises **volunteered,** hoping to finish off the Gomezes and De'Souzas living in Chuna Gully and Kasaitolla.[24] English guards were posted in the houses of the heavyweight [officers of the Company]. All kinds of strange rumours had begun to circulate: 'Delhi was taken today', 'Yesterday Kanpur was conquered'. Gradually, as the way it often is when one starts losing in a game of dice, the English lost almost all the territories in the north and west. Their wives and small children were killed. Like the Hindu God Panchananda,[25] the 'do-gooder' British,[26] unable to harm the elder son, tried breaking the neck of the younger one. Angry with the [rebel] soldiers, they took it out on the Bengalis.

Lord Canning[27] was asked to seize the weapons in possession of the Bengalis (they did not have much besides blades and scythes). Efforts were on to make sure that Bengalis did not get high posts in government offices. Muslim constables who worked in post offices lost their jobs. Indigo planters became honorary magistrates, and using the Mutiny as an excuse (the thief would always look for a crack in the fence) forced loans, torture and the punishing rod Shyamchand[28] on [the poor peasants]. Shyamchand isn't a small, trivial thing, mind you. It can stop the law [from taking its course], to say nothing of its influence on the soldiers. The Badshah of Lucknow[29] was taken prisoner and locked up in the fort. This was the English soldier's chance to burgle a few rich households. A **martial law**[30] was made effective. The printing press, by the grace of which Hootum is able to say so many things without fear or difficulty, the press which apportions the same status to the king and his subjects, to the man who lives in a well-guarded house and the one living in a hut with a tiled roof, had its freedom—traditionally inherited from its British origins—in shackles[31] for a while because of the Mutiny.

Now pushed to a corner, the Bengalis called a meeting at Gopal Mallik's house[32] and impressed on the British that despite the [wonderful British rule] for a little more than the last hundred years, the Bengalis have remained the luckless blockheads that they used to be. Despite having lived with the British, having received British education and training in British etiquette for years, Bengalis were not able to match up to the Americans [in adapting British ways] (it was doubtful if they ever would). Some of the rich Bengalis never sailed on a boat on the Ganga for fear of getting caught in a storm. If they needed a piss at night they would grab their wives' or servants' hands to lead them out. The only weapon they knew the uses of was knives used at the [dining] **table** and to sharpen **pens** [made from reeds]. It was quite improbable for these people to go to war, given that their own shadows made them jump. I might as well say that all that they borrowed from the British at a superficial level were food habits and a few hand-picked rituals, which, like borrowed garments, would have to be returned if the government ordered them to do so. Mr. Roy would sack his Burmese cook, the anglicized babus would go back to eating folar, Ghosh's son would take to opium and Bagambar Mitra would dissociate himself from wearing tweed trousers and practising English hooliganism.

The loss of wives, children and fellow men had made the English so desperate that these protestations failed to placate them. They sent a memorandum to Parliament, demanding that Lord Canning be **recalled**. The city was in the grip of a new craze. Soldiers from Britain began arriving by the shiploads. A new song was being circulated in the market.

> Here come the British soldiers
> With headgears on their skulls.
> Each stride shakes up the land,
> They are from the Highlands.
> Now the glory of Tantia Tope[33]
> Will be on the wane,
> Delhi will easily be won,
> And Nana Saheb in chains.

The Bengalis are adept at striking the iron when it is hot. The sworn Hindus (and everybody seemed to be a sworn Hindu during the day) went around telling people that the soldiers were angry because the Widow Remarriage Act[34] had been passed and widows were being married off. [They said] the government had annulled the Widow Remarriage Act and all Vidyasagar's efforts have come to naught and that Shrish,[35] the first person to have married a widow, would be hanged.

Somewhere else there was a buzz that the Mutiny was triggered off by the conversion of Duleep Singh, the seizure of the assets that the ranis of Nagpur[36] had brought at the time of their marriages and also by the fall of the Badshah of Lucknow.

Opinions differed widely. Someone said the English had tried fiddling with the Hindu religion, and that's what led to the Mutiny. The whore kept by the abbot of Tarakeswar, the wife of the priest officiating at Kashi Bisweswar, and the ladies of the house of Haldar the senior [it was said] had dreamt that the British Empire would not last. A couple of Brahmin pandits opened the book of the future and showed evidence [to prove the same].

Gradually the hype over the Sepoy Mutiny was on a downward slide. Delhi was conquered, Nana Saheb fled, Lucknow was won with the help of Jung Bahadur.[37] Almost all the soldiers involved in the Mutiny were either hanged or blown up in front of a canon or stabbed with a sword. The rest, following Lord Canning's **policy**, appealed for a reprieve and were spared.

The East India Company was on its way out, like the old year [coming to an end]. The **Queen proclaimed** her sovereignty. Hope, the elusive one, went around from door to door, singing 'In the Queen's reign, the subjects would not have any woes,' to the accompaniment of fireworks, firing of canon balls and illumination. The tension over the **Queen's Proclamation,** until it finally came through, was akin to people speculating about the sex of an unborn child until the pregnant woman in question actually gave birth,

The turmoil over the Mutiny was over. The Bengalis had a close shave: similar to the noose put around a condemned criminal's neck snapping [providentially]. They were spared physically and their honour survived, for the time being. Innocent people were condemned to death, while certain criminals were rewarded with a rent-free land. A lot of Brahmins made a fortune. The proverb—every dog has its day—was vindicated. Just as men realize the worth of devoted wives in times of illness, sorrow and danger, the government too had an occasion to find out a little bit about the word 'Bengali' because of the Mutiny. The 'do-gooders', their hopes and honour now dashed, were left singeing in their heart of hearts, and began casting vengeful eyes at the Bengalis.

I left school. What a relief it was; like having a cool breeze soothe one's body.

The Return of the Dead

Right from early childhood I was highly precocious. When I left school, the precocity spilt over, like starch from a pot of boiling rice. I assume the readers would get an idea of the extent of my precocity in my work *Sketches by Hootum.* My precocity assumed monstrous proportions. Certain people started calling me a 'Clever Bugger', out of affection.

As a child I had a high regard for the Bengali language, and was not averse to learning it. My aged grandmother would tell me folk tales before I went to sleep. She could recite verses by Kabikankan Mukundaram, Krittibas and Kashidas[38] from memory. I too learnt them by heart and would recite these verses at school, at home and to my mother who would be very pleased and sometimes gave me a sweet for each couplet. As a child I believed that eating too many sweets could give one a stammer. So I had some and scattered the rest on the terrace for crows and pigeons to feed on. We had a nice white cat called Munjuri who would have the rest (poor thing, it died yesterday morning and hadn't even left a litter).

A pandit was hired to teach me Sanskrit. He worked very hard on the job. It took me four years to wade through *Mugdhabodh,*[39] read two pages of Maagh[40] and three of *Raghuvangsham*[41] and that was when my precocious self took over. Now whenever I saw a Brahmin pandit teacher dressed in red, sporting a tiki and wearing a sandalwood mark on the forehead, I would start a debate with him. If it were a young man in similar attire, I defeated him in the debate and cut off his tiki.[42]

I wrote treatises in the papers, tried to write poems and lifted from articles written by others, passing them off as my own with great pride. I had steered clear of Sanskrit College[43] and yet became very like the young men who went to that institution. My desire for fame surpassed Himalayan heights. Sometimes it felt that before long I would become something of a poet: Kalidas the Second (Holy Lord Vishnu, wasn't Kalidas a champion lech!). All right, not Kalidas then. What about Samuel Johnson,[44] the renowned scholar in **Britain**? But he was a poor man's son, that's not fair. Rammohan Roy? All right, one day I might as well be Rammohan Roy. But to have to die in Britain? Spare me.

Gradually, my wish to become a public figure intensified. To fulfil that aim I began to dress like a Vidyotsahi,[45] turned author and wanted to be an editor. I organized meetings and got indoctrinated into Brahmoism. I went to the Tattvabodhini Sabha[46] and brokered widow remarriages.[47] I worshiped the stars of the group: Debendranath Tagore, Ishwarchandra Vidyasagar, Akshaykumar Dutta[48] and Ishwarchandra Gupta.[49] It was my most cherished desire that people recognized me as one of the worthies, even if a slightly less significant one, in the group.

Alas, I had been quite mad at times, driven by the wrongheadedness of youth. I feel like both laughing and crying when I think of those days now. And my present madness would have to be atoned for in old age. When the terrifying images of these past misdeeds appeared beside my deathbed and my body became aflame with fear and shame, it would be only the Supreme Lord—one's last resort, the nonpareil one—to whom I would turn to for succour. Just as young boys wail, taking the names of their parents even as the latter are beating them up, screaming 'O Father, O Mother'; I too, when I got into trouble by disobeying the rules laid down by God, would take His name, dear Reader, and would get away as I made faces and cocked a snook at you.

One day I was walking around, wearing a heavy wrap in the time of maddening heat to pass myself off as a philosopher, when a lawyer's clerk from Nadia district told me: 'There's a strong rumour doing the rounds in my neighbourhood that on Sunday, the 15th day of Kartik [i.e., early December], all those who have died in the last ten years are going to return from the abode of Yama, the God of Death.' Just as traders, sometimes, pay for the release of a prisoner or two as a part of the rituals performed during the worship of the Goddess who rides the lion, their household deity, a certain God in heaven, was going to release a few of the prisoners held by Yama to mark the wedding of his son. That was what Ramsharma Acharya of Nadia district had prophesied, based on astral calculations. I was amazed to hear about this extraordinary speculation.

And then the news was all over the city. The dead shall return on the 15th day of Kartik [31 October/1 November]. Proprietors of Bengali newspapers got something with which to fill up their pages. Just as when you tie one knot over another, the earlier knot gets slightly loosened, the stirrings of devotion for Vidyasagar—

who was campaigning for widow remarriage—in the hearts of tender young widows of the city slid down by several notches, the way the mercury in the thermometer nosedived during seasonal change.

Wherever I went, there was no escaping the false exuberance over the return of the dead. Hope was the best friend of ignorant men and women. Conmen and rogues started visiting affluent and vulnerable homes, posing as returnees. Many families were dishonoured, money and jewellery were swindled and yellow arsenic[50] sold at a premium in the market.

Gradually, like evening arriving at the end of a gloomy Asharh [mid-June to mid-July] day, like the way time moves for a newly bereaved person, the 15th day of Kartik arrived, in kingly fashion. Just as those who believe in idol worship wait for the auspicious moment in the evening during Durga Puja, just as the relatives of a dying patient wait for the doctor and school boys and office-goers wait for a holiday, widows and families who had lost their sons and brothers waited for the 15th day of Kartik. The day had acquired the connotations of a Delhi laddoo.[51] Seeing the grandeur associated with and the extreme faith that people seemed to have in the 15th day of Kartik, even non-believers joined the band-wagon. In my young days I had a pet Chinese rabbit that had died about eight years back. Expecting it to return I plucked some very tender green grass. The old broken hutch was dusted and a bed of cotton laid inside. I waited for it to return.

Today's the day. A lot of people waited at Nimtolla and Kashi Mitra's Ghat[52] for the dead to return. Evening descended. And then it was 10 at night. But the dead had not returned. Having waited all day long for the dead, many were half-dead by the time they came back home at night. The excitement over, the return of the dead was over.

Of Kinsmen and Critics

And then I turned into a fully grown adult. Certain people were jealous of my situation. To some of my relatives [my coming of age] felt like the husking pedal pounding their chests. They would simper and celebrate when I landed in trouble and were ready to give an eye if that would make me blind in both. [They were like women] who did not mind drinking shit out of the co-wife's bowl as long as that spoilt her utensil. The babus and the ladies related to us began to behave similarly. It was better to be childless and live in the forest than to be with one's kinsmen and a whole bunch of children, as I was doing then. My relatives were like Duryodhan's father, and their daughters were one up on Kaikeyi and Surpanakha.[53]

Over the years, I saw an entire race of enemies being born and also acquired a group of **friends.** Those who mingled with the enemies would only find faults and criticize me. The **friends defended** me as far as they could. The enemies had sworn that they would be criticizing me, just as they ate and slept every day, so there was no stopping them. I looked very hard for instances of my having wronged them at any time; reasons for which they might be offended with me. But there were not any. Rather, it was clear that I had not even met some of my critics. Just as some people went about helping others in a sustained manner with a missionary zeal; certain people of this city have taken up the job of criticizing others for no apparent reason. They treat this occupation of theirs as something they must do and as a mission.

I fervently wish that these critics live for some more time, so that people recognize them for what they are. Like the speakers who go on and on, and ultimately get tired and stop, these people too would stop on their own. But then many are critics by profession. Be that as it may, I am not talking of professionals here.

Nana Saheb

After the excessive expectations over the return of the dead collapsed, in a span of a few days Nana Saheb died about ten to twelve times; he was arrested and revived all over again like the demon Raktabeej.[54] Like the seven-legged cow, the horse that came from the seas, the Badshah of Lucknow, Shibkrishna Banerjee, Justice Wells, the arson by the monkey-faced indigo planters and the jail term given to Reverend Long, the major ruckus—the sort one associates with crocodiles, sharks and wolves—created by the two blue papers, *The Englishman* and *Harkara,* factionalism and conspiracy marking the memorial service of the late wife of Rammohan Roy, the proponent of the Brahmo Samaj, and finally the rumours about the incarnate-arrived-lately grew and spread.

The Seven-Legged Cow

A room was rented in the market to display the seven-legged cow.[55] The tickets cost two paisa per show. A lot of cows got together to look after this one. And the rest of the cows would be summoned by ringing a bell. In a few days' time, the seven-legged cow collected a booty and went home.

The Horse That Came from the Seas

Likewise, the horse that came from the seas too was making money. To attract better sales, it visited a few houses that had giant pillars, vigilant guards and light-skinned coachmen: the sort of households where horses congregated at all times, even in the female quarters. But who would buy this one? The asking rate was a hundred thousand rupees. Certain rich people in our city were worth three to four million, and were absolutely the right kind to be put in a cage and showcased at the zoo. Unfortunately, there were no takers for them.

Weren't there any people of great style left these days? Among the zoos in Bengal, the one in Burdwan[56] was unlike any other. It had a lot of wonderfully bizarre creatures like the maharaja himself, Tattva, Ratna, gibbons from Sri Lanka and bears, and some of these were absolutely unmatched.

The Badshah of Lucknow

The horse who lived in the seas spent some time in the city and ran right back to the sea when it did not find enough to eat here. Its place was now taken by the Badshah of Lucknow. The new rumour in the city went like this: 'The Badshah of Lucknow is staying at Muchikhola, before he leaves for England. He dresses like a nautch girl, and applies lac-dye around his feet.' Someone said, 'He is slim, quite nice to look at, just like a dancing maiden descended from the heavens.' Someone else said, 'Oh, no, he is a stocky no-neck fellow with crooked arms. But he sings rather well, if at all there's anything to recommend him by.' Another one said, 'Tut, that's all rubbish. I was on the same steamboat as he, the day he came here. He's dark, thin, wears glasses; looks a lot like our very own maulavi.'

The Badshah of Lucknow's arrival at Muchikhola after he had been released from prison added spice to the life of the city for a few days. Thieves and rogues, among others, made quite a killing. Shopkeepers managed to sell damaged and old stock at exorbitant prices. A few khyamta dancers were promoted to the ranks of a begum.[57] The Badshah occupied half of Muchikhola area. At the outset, snake charmers keep their big catch—that is, cobras—inside earthen pots, and only after the snakes' energy saps do they tease them out of the pot. Similarly, the government had held the Badshah inside the fortress for a while, and let him go out and play only after his poison fangs were extracted. The Badshah started dancing in sync with the tabor's beat. The Rudras, Bhadras, Sheikhs, Khans and Dans and other artful watchdogs in the city dressed up for the occasion and joined the lamentations. Monkeys and goats joined in as well.

Once the Badshah of Lucknow had settled down in the city, a few rich men had cast their nets wide.[58] They had high hopes [of landing a prize catch], but ended up losing [everything, including] the net. Some of them said, 'The fish was fat [and hence escaped the net].' Someone else said, 'He was [actually] royalty from Rajasthan.' Others said, 'He was a fake.'

Shibkrishna

Shibkrishna Banerjee was the new talking point in town.[59] For a while, the babu had discarded restraint altogether. One day he would whip somebody, use his shoes to beat up someone else the next. If today he conned a north Indian simpleton, tomorrow it could be the hat-wearing Englishman. Finally, he deceived himself. He got himself entangled in a net, sullied the reputation of the Bengali race and was put behind bars for fourteen years.

Some Englishmen would do anything for money. And this was made evident, thanks to Shibkrishna. There was a doctor in his team [of frauds] with a thirty-two-letter honorific—**MD, FRCS** etc.—preceding his name.

Shibkrishna Again

Many rich people in our city did not have any good qualities, only vicious ones. [Their attitude was like this:] 'I would do you only harm and no good, do you mind?' They had given the adage, 'Fool to others, himself a sage,' some currency. The babus paid to acquire other people's disputes [and filed suits]. Sometimes, they did it just to get their own back on others. Had it not been for such professionals, who could have touched Shibkrishna? After all, he was only trying to dupe his sister-in-law and nephew and claim their property!

Why, many rich people in our city, Calcutta, have poisoned their brother's wife with the help of a doctor and were still moving around in carriages and horses, without a care in the world! Why didn't the law prevail in those cases? The sort of fraudulent activities that Shibkrishna was involved in were happening every day in the houses of rich men and a lot of them got away with it. A rather naive rich man, originally from Kashmir, had once regretted, 'There are plenty more blokes like me in the city. It's just that I got caught.' Shibkrishna was in a similar situation.

Justice Wells

When the trial of Shibkrishna was about to begin, Justice Wells was inducted as the new judge. He came with a preconceived notion that Bengalis as a community were almost entirely made up of liars and fraudsters. Therefore, when he brandished all four limbs and made a speech during court proceedings, Wells would very often, say, 'Bengalis are liars and perjurers.' Bengalis, of course, might well say, 'If ten in a hundred are liars and perjurers, it does not follow that the remaining ninety would be liars as well.'

There was a buzz of discontentment all around. The leaders of influential groups were given a memorandum. Major discussions were held in high places. Ultimately, after much effort had been spent, it was decided that a meeting would be held and a petition submitted before [Secretary of State] Sir Charles Wood. But where might one hold the meeting? The Bengalis did not have one foot worth of 'public' space [to call their own]. The Town Hall was meant for the English. The terrace at Nimtolla was government property. There was no **hall** at Kashi Mitra's Burning Ghat. The open portico of Babu Prasannakumar Tagore Ghat was a possibility. But Tagore was friendly with the English, so it would be difficult to get him to agree. Ultimately, it was decided that the Nabaratna *naatmandir* at Raja Radhakanta Deb's residence would make a spacious venue. It was advertised in the papers that on such and such date a meeting would be held at Raja Radhakanta Deb Bahadur's Nabaratna naatmandir to try and find a remedy for the affliction troubling the mouth of Justice Wells. The remedy, of course, was in the deep waters.

Quite a few rich men in the city were ashamed to acknowledge their Bengali lineage. They were far happier if taken for the grandson of Andrew Pidroos who lived in Chuna Gully. Therefore, they stayed far away from the activities that might add to the well-being of the Bengalis and enhance their reputation. In fact, it was actually the other way round. They were constantly engaged in trying to bring disaster on the people of their own race. These people were really sorry to find that the Bengalis would hold a meeting opposing Wells in Raja Radhakanta's naatmandir. At the time of thanking [their English friends] for the meal, they were reminded of it, and put their heart and soul into ensuring that such a meeting did not take place. They made a case [for Wells] and submitted it to the raja. But the raja believed in keeping promises. He had pledged his support, so despite the recommendations by influential people, he refused to listen to them. The supporters [of Wells] were swept away like junk in the tide by the powerful waves of the ocean.

A meeting was held on the appointed date.[60] The people of the city turned out in droves, with great enthusiasm. The idol kept inside the Nabaratna hall and the Garuda carved out of stone that stood with folded hands in front of it too were ecstatic beyond all limits. It was evident at the gathering that Bengalis had acquired a little bit of courage. Only the babus who had been trying to make a case for Wells and the rich gold traders stayed away from the meeting. The Wells supporters lost face. As for the tradesmen, they never get involved in any activity, so that was that.

The Wells-related fad was almost passé. A petition signed by one million people was submitted to Mr. Wood. Wells has been cut to size ever since.

Tekchand's Aunt

When she heard that a meeting was held to cure the malaise dogging Wells, Tepi, Tekchand Thakur's aunt,[61] said, 'Dear me, these days you only follow English styles. We would have cured this affliction by feeding him coconut mixed with puffed rice and savouries from Thanthania.'[62] Indeed, puffed rice with coconut was a great panacea, far better than Holloway's [medicine].[63] Quite a few rich men in this city and a few maharajas from the districts suffered from different ailments round the year. They travelled to Darjeeling, Simla, Sapatu, Bhagalpur and Raniganj but still did not get any better. I would request them to try coconut with puffed rice and savouries from Thanthania. **Immediate relief** [is guaranteed].

Nildarpan

There was trouble over taxes levied on indigo peasants. One heard that the peasants of the indigo districts—Krishnanagore, Pabna, Rajshahi, and so on—were livid. But who [or what] fuelled the outrage? Was it Goddess Olaichandi?[64] No. [Attempts to chastize peasants putting up a resistance against forced indigo cultivation] by Shyamchand, the baton, then? Was it the order [banning forcible cultivation of indigo] issued by Magistrate Eden?[65] Was it the Indigo Commission[66] report [drawing attention to the rising indignation among oppressed peasants]? Could it be Harish Mukherjee[67] [who put up a sustained fight against forced growing of indigo and made a cause for peasants' rights]? Or was it Reverend Long, the clergyman [who was thrown in jail for his role in bringing out the English translation of the play *Nilpdarpan*]?[68] [The emergence of] Small Causes Courts[69] [that had become instruments of perpetrating atrocities on indigo peasants], perhaps? [Could it have been the introduction of the Criminal] Contract Bill[70] [allowing planters to monitor the 'criminal activities' their native employees might indulge in]? Could the resignation of [the pro-peasant Lieutenant Governor of Bengal J. P.] Grant[71] [under pressure from the Indigo Planters' Association] cure the malaise? No. That would take the removal of Shyamchand-wielding mercenaries.

The indigo planters assumed that there would be a second **revolution**[72] [As the Bengali proverb goes,] 'Is there anybody there in the prayer room?' "But I did not eat the banana offering!"[73] They asked for more ammunition and soldiers from the government.

Regiment after regiment comprising English soldiers, guns, boats and a special commissioner were despatched. Small town jails were overflowing with innocent people. It made sensational news in the papers. Walter Brett became a cult figure.[74]

The Indigo Commission would hold sessions to listen to the peasant's woes. Queen Victoria, Aunt Royal of the Indians,[75] woke up with a start (she was hooked to opium, you see). One of the many uncles married to her represented the Bengalis as commissioner. The Commission was digging for worms, but found a snake instead. And the venom that it released was the source of the play, *Nildarpan.* The tax officials were desperate. Instead of beating about the bush and mounds of ash, they trained their guns on temples, churches, palaces and the press. Finally, a big **Hungarian hound**[76] bit Father Long.

Ordinary constables turned deputy magistrates and moved to the districts. There was tremendous activity. The tiger living in the marshy jungle, that is, the Planters' Association, now under duress, changed its name to the Landholders' Association and moved to a garden of tulsi shrubs.[77] Harish was dead, Long got a prison term. Wells was ticked off. Grant resigned. But the problem remained unresolved. This was real monkey business. A variety of songs on the theme were circulating in the market. As they steered the hoe and munched on puffed rice and radish, the peasant boys sang:

The happy days are over at last, it makes us sad.
By the grace of the Great Queen, happily did we live here.
Gone are the farm, the home, the harvest,
  the worthy has lost all honour.
The blue monkeys[78] have burnt up golden Bengal.

To retaliate, the indigo planters passed the Cattle Trespass Bill. Some of them offered champagne and women to the judges and lawyers of the lower courts. Some increased the taxes and having won the verbal duel felt that they had got their own back.

That was the end of the Lanka episode, as performed by the blue monkeys. The captains got some rest. The Aunt Royal took another dose of drugs and got real high. Some of the well-known uncles, brandishing weapons, started a rigorous regimen of penitence dedicated to the light-skinned Gods, praying for the posts of honorary inspector, or deputy magistrate or **accessories** for their children. So be it.

Even ghosts are unable to suffer a Shyamchand's blow. Little wonder then that it would lead to peasant unrest. Our 'do-gooders' were already quite cut up about the Mutiny and the protest meeting concerning the Black Act.[79] Now with the ruckus over the blue monkeys, their discontent grew deeper roots. Just as when a second wife arrives in an affluent household, the master and mistress have a stressful time trying to please both daughters-in-law, the governments of India and Bengal too got into a similar situation by trying to please both the 'do-gooder' **sweeping class** and **native community**.

Ramaprasad Roy

Dear *Hootum* readers! We have already told you that time is not someone's slave, that time is like the water in a river, the prostitute's youth, and the life-span of living beings. It does not wait for any man. I was growing up fast, the years passed by in a jiffy. Hardly ever was I reminded that one just might die some day. Instead, with the advancing years, the desire to live longer became more powerful in me. I began pampering my body. I dyed my straggly, jute strand-like moustache in front of a mirror. It broke my heart to deny myself [the pleasure of wearing] black-bordered dhotis made in the Simla looms. My body now was ready to disintegrate into three. I couldn't see without wearing my glasses. But my hopes and desires remained the same. Rather, these kept growing, rather than diminishing. In fact, I was doubtful if I would be satiated even if I had been granted a boon of immortality and lived as long as nature existed.

Just as a traveller, excruciatingly tired from walking in the sun and hurrying towards his destination with single-minded zeal, would be startled if he suddenly saw a cobra lying on the road; I too, when confronted with this world's grave dangers, sometimes found myself in a similar situation. And that is when this singed heart was jolted into consciousness. If the aforementioned traveller had a thick club in hand, he could kill the snake and go on his way. Similarly, I too could survive a great danger by taking advice and help from friends. But the unfortunate person who does not have anyone to call a friend finds himself in a sorry state of affairs indeed, when danger arrives. In those moments God is his only refuge. The aura of religion is so pure, and its spirit so sombre, that it drives hypocrisy, disbelief and wickedness away. A heavenly and pure stream of love floats all around. And the sea of troubles seems softer than the mother's lap, steeped in affection. Alas! Blessed is he who, in times of danger, has had a chance to experience this sense of pure joy. Because once you were able to hit hard and shatter the stony coldness and get to the heart of the matter, it would be yours forever.

I was an adult now. I would hear the terrifying sound of the sea of this worldly existence, swathed in the fog of deception, which left little scope for optimism. One day, a few of us, all of the same age, had got together and were debating some trivial matter, when somebody in the group said, 'Heard this one? There would be a big do at the food offering ceremony for Ramaprasad's deceased mother.[80] A hundred thousand rupees has been earmarked. All the [eminent] people in the city, even those living in Kashi [now Benaras] and Karnataka are going to be invited.' Gradually we began hearing a lot more about the memorial service. And wouldn't it make one's curiosity grow, given that Ramaprasad's father was a preacher of Brahmoism, and a trustee of the Brahmo Samaj, that the son should be such a slavish follower of idolatry when it came to performing the memorial rites for his mother? So I tried getting a blue print of the rituals that would be performed at the service, from start to finish.

The day when the offering would be made gradually drew near. Goldsmiths parked themselves at the venue. The gluttonous Brahmins began hiring **apprentices**. The professor from Sanskrit College specializing in the subject of folar began lecturing on the variety of fruits and sweets that might be offered. Those studying the Vedas wrote **voluminous** notes on the subject. The Bhattacharyas [i.e., Brahmin pandits] running Sanskrit grammar schools received invitations stating whether they would be given a regular or half payment [as an honorarium for attending the memorial service]. The pandits who did not have a school to run and hence came uninvited turned Ramaprasad's house into something much worse than Nimtolla and Kashi Mitra's Ghats (how many vultures inhabit these burning ghats, after all?), trying to plead their case and claim their bonus in cash. It was another matter that bulls shat all the year round in some of these schools. On Saraswati Puja day the Brahmin pandit's wife and their infant daughter tried to pass themselves off as students. Tiny clay idols of Goddess Saraswati, embellished with tinsel and lotuses made out of pith were installed. A few [gullible] bhadraloks, let loose on the scene would earn the pandit some money.

It was only when they were young did the Brahmin schoolmasters have any contact with Goddess Saraswati. Once past childhood they did not see her again in their lifetime. All that they saw was her clay idol, once a year, and that too just because for them it was an opportunity to make measly little amounts of money.

Dear Readers! Don't underestimate the liveried and badge-wearing Vidyalankars, Nyayalankars, Vidyabhushan and Vidyavachaspatis.[81] There is nothing they would not do for money. Left to these, the Sanskrit language, driven by worries for its future, is shrinking to the point of disappearing altogether. The man who performs street shows with animals would make the monkey dance, wear costumes and stand atop a goat to make money. Brahmin pandits do not mind dressing up as monkeys and dancing if they get paid for it. Even if you scanned the prisons where criminals were sent to serve a life term with a toothcomb, you would not find samples of the sort of terrible crimes that these pandits were capable of.

The ceremony of offering food to the dead was due tomorrow. These days many people belonging to the influential groups in the city look like hooded snakes [but have little venom]. Their reputation was like a bloated drum that was empty inside. Ramaprasad was one of the leading lawyers practising at the district high court. And given the way the English have been favouring him, he would be likely to hold other even higher offices.[82] Therefore it did not look good for Brahmin pandits to refuse Ramaprasad's invitations. But there were differences of opinion over Ramaprasad and—[*missing in the original*]. A few fresh, newly inducted society leaders, strong in their conviction and having no fear of humiliation or of displeasing Ramaprasad, expressed their views in a **proclamation** meant for the members of his group. The written **proclamation** was circulated among the Brahmin pandits in the group, which meant trouble for a lot of people who had a foot each on either boat. [Ramaprasad's] yaars who ate from the same plate had always believed in heads I win, tails you lose. They would quickly rinse their mouth afterwards but found themselves in big trouble at this moment. So Uncle Mitra took **leave** and went out for some fresh air. Chatterjee became bedridden. The **proclamation** circulated by the group leader became more terrifying than the summons issued by the jury. It read like this:

Reposing faith in the Lord Sri Hari
My most worship-worthy,
the infinitely well-versed and a
repository of the gems among the scriptures, like the sea,
Brahmin pandits, dear sirs,
At your feet let me offer [the following letter]
Your servant, Chunder Das Ghosh.[83]

I prostrate a hundred thousand times and touch your feet before stating that due to the blessings of your respectable selves, this servant has been keeping well. Given that Babu Ramaprasad Roy, son of the late Rammohan Roy, is going to have a grand show at the annual memorial service for his mother, and as the renowned kulin member of this association and my brother-in-law Babu Dhinikrishna Mitra[84] *has learnt from a written document that the aforementioned Roy would send an invitation to all the associations in the city, therefore there is an immense possibility that he would be sending one to this association as well. But since the associations that have affiliations to our Sri Sri Sabha have no truck with Roy, in terms of dining together or any other dealings, therefore, even if he sends an invitation, please do not attend.*

Chunder Das Ghosh
Noorighata

Seconded by
Hobiswar Sharma, A jewel among philosophers
Pandit of the Nobleman's Court

The Brahmin pandits, and the folar-eating types, disappeared after they received the proclamation. Some of them stuck around, flowing unobtrusively, like a subterranean river. After all, when someone is drinking water while still submerged in it, even Lord Shiva's father [i.e., the canniest person around] would fail to catch him. Police outposts manned by guards came up in various places. But to no avail. The smell of money grew stronger than that of onions and garlic, purifying the air in the memorial service hall. Even the idols of Madanmohan[85] in Baghbazar and Shyamsundar[86] in Sreepat Khardah began rolling in the spirit of Brajadham.[87] On the appointed day, since the morning the house of Ramaprasad turned into a thick forest of people. Brahmin pandits were packed together, [the queue stretching] from the portico to the kitchen. One did not find such huge crowds assembling at Sreekshetra to see the lovely face of Lord Jagannath, even on Rathayatra day.

On the morning of the service, Ramaprasad, dressed in silk from Benaras, looked as if he were a living embodiment of devotion and respect. The crowd grew as the day wore on. At one end of the hall, the panegyrists chanted the glory of King Ballal Sen[88] and Adisura.[89] At the other, the Brahmin priests got into a dispute. A few kulin leaders of the association who would not usually venture out of their homes now arrived on the scene and took their seats, driven by fear and shame. Several groups began to sing, all at once. The glass and plates in the dining room shook in terror at the din made by thumping at the tom-toms and the chanting of Lord Hari's name. Seeing his stepbrother[90] perform his mother's memorial service with great pomp and show, Brahmoism started crying out of sheer sibling rivalry, which made **ambition** laugh.

Finally, after the chief guests had been garlanded and decorated with sandalwood[91] and the gifts given away, the service was over. It was quite interesting to watch Brahmins being fed in Calcutta. The revered sirs did not hesitate to bring along the newborn infant whose mother was still in post-natal confinement to a meal of folar. It was on days like these that a Brahmin would round up all his children. Folar-hungry Brahmins entering the venue [with their entourage] sometimes resembled a schoolmaster walking in with the entire school. On their way out they looked like some of the heavyweights among laundrymen. Even a donkey would find it difficult to carry the huge bundle of luchi and sweetmeats [the Brahmins took back home]. The Brahmins left after getting an honorarium of a half rupee, a quarter or two annas [depending on the pecking order]. Mounds of curd-smattered banana leaves discarded after one has eaten off these, broken earthen cups, and mango stones piled up like the Nilgiri Hills. Flies hovered, buzzing. Crows and dogs waited expectantly. The air stopped circulating underneath the marquee. As a result, the swishing of water, mixed with the suffocating smell of luchi, sweetmeats, curd and mangoes, swept across the household. It was a smell those who had not been to a house of ceremony would find difficult to imagine offhand.

Meanwhile, in the afternoon, alms-seekers had begun to line up on the road. As the evening progressed, their number grew with the darkness. Water-carriers, shopkeepers, palanquin-bearers from Orissa and opium-eaters mingled with the alms-seekers. The neighbourhood reverberated with cries of the assembled public. At 7 pm, the neighbours and visitors from houses with big courtyards were taken inside the house [to clear up the space], for distributing alms to the beggars. Those who had been conducting the service now stood at the door, bags full of half rupee, quarter rupee, two annas and paisas in hand. [Servants carrying] torches, lanterns and ushers went from street to street, calling out for alms-seekers. Alms were distributed till 3 am.

Around thirty thousand alms-seekers had accumulated. There were quite a few pregnant female alms-seekers among them, and since they gave birth at the time of the alms distribution, the numbers grew significantly.

Food was distributed among the nine sects, Kayasthas and Baidyas at the same time. When it comes to helping themselves to a meal of folar, it was difficult to say who was the most adept among all of these. If there were highly skilled eaters among the Brahmins, there were still more of them among Kayasthas, nine sects, and Baidyas. Rather, in certain matters, the latter are one up on the folar-eating Brahmins who come with a **certificate** of merit.

When there was a ceremony in a house in the city, pint-sized little boys of the family wearing jacket, trousers, cap and a belt, tied a red handkerchief on one hand, like the town-crier in a theatre, went out to invite associates and relatives. The rich or solvent people took a Brahmin professional along to do the invitations. Sometimes, the household accountant or a Brahmin priest on the lines of a family elder was good enough to perform the task. The Brahmin or the accountant carried a huge list in his hand, had a **wooden pencil** stuck to his ear, munching on paan as he went about doing his job. The boy accompanied him like a **true copy** of a signature.

Now that English etiquette prevailed, many did not **like** going to messy feasts serving folar. Some people managed by sending their children. Some dropped by on their way to the garden house, pretending to be terribly ill when they were requested to eat something. At home they would eat gigantic quantities of food that even a pair of Kumbhakarnas[92] would find difficult to consume. Even if they ate up the elephants and horses in the stable they would still be hungry.

Dear Reader, I am a true devotee of the folar. What a piece of iron is to a magnet, I am to luchi. So if you have a folar ceremony coming up at your house, please do not forget me—I am the cousin of Raghu,[93] who could consume a maund of edibles at one go. If someone mentioned the word 'folar', I would be ready to land up in hell or jail [to sample it]. The other day I had folar at the circumcision ceremony of the son of Maulvi Halum Hosain Khan Bahadur. I even had a sit-down dinner at the second wedding of a widow, which is quite outside the sanction of the Hindu religion. I have also tasted the food—mountains of rice heaped together for the public to feast on—at the house of the Pope, that is, Debendranath Tagore **the First**, on 11th Magh, the anniversary of the Brahmo Samaj of Calcutta.[94] Incidentally, on the day of the feast, the wide sprawling field of a courtyard in the house of the Tagores, where Goddess Durga is installed during the puja, was overflowing with Brahmos. But on Wednesdays, when it was time to pray, there were just about ten to twelve people of the Samaj, eyes closed, heads shaking, replicating the elegiac numbers in the Masjia[95] in a Sanskrit adaptation, as it were, in a sing-song chant. What about the rest? Perhaps they were Brahmos only on formal occasions. Or were they cats looking for the cream in times of a sacrificial ceremony, like me?

I have earned quite a number of **diplomas** and **certificates** for my proficiency in consuming folar. If the universities begin granting a degree on the lines of BA or BL, for excellence in consuming folar, then I would be the first **candidate** [to claim it].

There was great pomp and show indeed at Ramaprasad's mother's memorial feast. The finest of food items were collected and brought together for the service. It was quite a treat watching people feasting in the city. For one, lunch or refreshments could go on till 2 am. Secondly, [one finds] all sorts of animals coming together at such dos. At the first glance it might seem that those who sit down to a meal have shoes nailed to their feet, like horses. But watch more attentively and you would know that the guest, such is his trust in the hosts of the ceremony and fellow folar-eaters, is not sure if he should remove his shoes before sitting down to eat.

Finally, the Kayasthas were fed most elaborately. Heads of carp and sweetmeats were distributed among the kulins, in keeping with their hierarchical status.[96] The spectacle of middle-aged opium-eating kulins munching fish-heads scared small boys. Some people had their plates looking much worse than a dumping ground for cattle carcasses. This is how, after a show that lasted almost fifteen days had run its course, the celebration of the memorial service for Ramaprasad's mother came to an end. Those who thrive on fads rested for a while.

The leaders of different groups—the great ones who did not go to the service—now began playing the group members against one another. Many of the Brahmins who had had their fill of folar and picked up the remuneration [for attending the event] now came to the leader of the clique formed by the great grandsons of Sri Sri Dharma Sabha hopefuls, touched the holy water from the Ganga and swore in front of the holy black stone that in all these years of their stay in the city, they had never heard of Ramaprasad Roy. They claimed they associated only with the pure breed. One of them added that his forefather (the late Uncle Tarkabachaspati) had said at the time of his death [to the group leader], 'Your Honour, there's no one like you in this whole world.' But certain venerable people, who did not have titles, were caught. [To atone for the sin] they ate cow dung, offered prayers to Lord Vishnu and shaved off their eyebrows.

The first widow remarriage in Calcutta was attended by quite a few Brahmins from Bally, Uttarpara, Ambika and Rajpur. They had their folar, took the money and then began to slip away, surreptitiously. A lot of them atoned for their sins by consuming dung. A good number of them who were present at the wedding venue said, 'I was confined to bed on that particular day.'

Until such time as these great men prevailed, there was no way Bengalis could lead a decent, civil life. Just as the spiritual gurus must co-exist with lowborn people like the Haris, cobblers and the undertaker, these great men had managed to survive because of the hopelessly blockheaded Kayastha and Brahmin leaders. Each of these was an embodiment of wretchedness and roguish behaviour. But there was no knowing what they had in mind, given the disposition they affected. They seemed to be absolutely decent, harmless people, on the surface. In reality, all that was affectation and hypocrisy.

A Tale of Two Papers

Atending the memorial service for Ramaprasad Roy's mother was an issue that led to huge disputes. Sons parted ways with fathers. Aunt disowned her nephew.[97] And the nephew, whom the aunt had provided for, all along, trampled on [what ought to have been] an everlasting sense of gratitude and joined the opposite camp. When I was in school, a boy called Shambhu, who came from an affluent house of gold traders, was my classmate. One day, as we talked pronouncing the words with guttural 'r's, he said, 'Brother, last night I teased my wife to no end. She had said, "You are a monkey." I retorted at once, saying, "Your father-in-law's a monkey."' The nephew's jokes [on his erstwhile patron] were on the same lines.

Rasaraj,[98] the newspaper, started appearing again. There was a stream of scurrilous poems and trash [in it]. As if on cue, a well-educated young man from Sanskrit College, forgot all about Brahmoism and **college education**, and published a paper full of trashy stuff on the lines of *Rasaraj*, by the name of *Jyamon Karma Temni Fal*[99] (As you sow, so you reap). A fight ensued between the two papers. The two collected their share of ammunition and soldiers and plunged right into the ocean of warfare. Schoolboys got together hordes of mindless fellows and joined either camp, as if this were a battle between the warring clans, Kauravs and Pandavs [in the *Mahabharat*].[100] Vile ones, clerks, vicious and wicked people closed in on the battlefield, like crows, headless demons, jackals and vultures, waiting to drink the ugly juices oozing out of the skirmish. The awesome war between the two papers continued apace. *Rasaraj*, which ran features with titles such as, 'The Fair of the Muslim Saint Gorachand', 'An Account of the Birth of the Fairies', 'The Ghostly Horse', and 'Conversations with a Brahmin's Ghost' sold five hundred, thousand, even two thousand, copies a day, when *Brahmo Dharma*[101] would sell hardly a copy a month, even on credit. *Tilottama*[102] and *Sitar Banabas*[103] did not seem to have any takers.

After the struggle between the two papers had continued for a while, the government, assuming the plaintiff's role, complained to the police, against the editor of *Rasaraj,* for writing obscene articles. The editor of *Jyamon Karmo,* lest he too was made to reap the fruit [that matched the kind of seeds he had sown], went into hiding. The choir members and percussionists [who had been drumming up support for] *Rasaraj,* keeping in mind the adage, 'every man for himself', scooted from the scene of the concert, leaving behind the drums, cymbals and the lead singer. The nephew (alias Uncle Mitra) locked himself up in the indoor lavatory for fear of being subpoenaed by the court. The greatest among the giants [of journalism], Kshetramohan Vidyaratna, entered the portals of the prison house at Harinbadi[104] for three months, carrying anklets and a fly-brush. The remaining part of the song of Muslim Saint Gorachand was sung there. The sound of hammers breaking stones, whips lashing and chains jangling substituted that of cymbals and drums. The prisoners, passing themselves off as the audience, and [seemingly] moved by the song of the saint, cheered and paid the singer a tip. [As they say], 'Ramakanta ate the curd, but Gobardhan fell ill.' The same was true of the nephew (alias Uncle Mitra) and the *Rasaraj* editor.[105] I had grown old over the years and now could not do without a pair of glasses.

Notes

1. An idle brain would think of ways to bump off the elder kinsman and take him to a burning ghat on the banks of the river Ganga, and leave him like that till he died.
2. A symbolic ritual performed to initiate a child to the world of learning. The child is made to write his first letters, literally hand-held by a Brahmin priest, on the morning of Saraswati Puja, Saraswati being the Goddess of Learning and the Arts.
3. Pratapchand (born 24 Oct 1791), was the only son of Tejchand Ray, the maharaja of Burdwan. When Tejchand declared Pratap his legal heir and the inheritor of his estate, his stepmother Kamalkumari and her brother Paranchand, who had immense control over the estate, conspired to get rid of him. An ailing Pratap was left beside the river Ganga in Kalna where he 'died' in 1821. Tejchand adopted Mahtab Chand, Paranchand's youngest son, as his heir. In 1835 a roving mendicant arrived in Burdwan, trying to pass himself off as Pratapchand and acquired an instant following. 'Pratap' was persecuted, arrested and held without trial for eight months, and had a lot of his followers killed by the magistrate. There was a concerted bid to prove that 'Pratap' was, in fact, a person named Krishnalal Brahmachari. The magistrate of Burdwan, E. A. Samuells, who was obviously convinced that Pratapchand was a fake, went out of his way to write to Dwarkanath Tagore (see Sketch 2, p. 99, note 86) to mobilize witnesses who would testify that Pratap was actually Krishnalal.

   The trial at Hooghly Court was one of the most-publicized reality shows of the time, attracting thousands of spectators, most of them sympathetic to Pratapchand's claim. Dwarkanath testified, saying that the person concerned was not the Pratapchand he had known closely; but educationist David Hare, known for his honesty and steadfastness, (for Hare, see Sketch 2, p.103, note 94) identified Pratap as real, as did Pratap's personal physician, Dr. Scott. Finally, Pratap was declared a fake, made to pay a heavy fine and renounce any claim to the name. He spent his last days at Moyradanga, Baranagar, as a spiritual guru and had a huge following; see Arun Nag, ed., *Sateek Hootum Pyanchar Naksha* (Calcutta: Ananda Publishers, 2008): 235-36. Goutam Bhadra says the Pratapchand saga captured public imagination and endured as it was a reflection of popular culture. There were spin-offs in different popular cultural forms: verses, panchali, rumour and scandal.

In the form of rumour, the story created social expectation and apprehension. As verse or panchali, the Pratapchand episode was meant to serve as a moral tale; see Goutam Bhadra, *Jaal Rajar Katha: Bardhaman-er Pratapchand* (Calcutta, Ananda Publishers, 2002).

4. In the epic *Mahabharat,* King Yudhisthir, his brothers and their wife, Draupadi, went to live in the forests, after the king lost everything to his evil cousin Duryodhan in a game of dice. The thirteenth and last year was spent incognito, assuming a different persona, in the employment of King Virat, preparing for the great war. The thirteen years spent in hiding has a resonance in Pratapchand's fourteen-year absence. During the trial Pratapchand claimed that a guru had asked him to go into hiding and practice penance for fourteen years to absolve himself of the sins he had accumulated. So he pretended to have died and had escaped during the cremation at Kalna. See Nag, ed., *Sateek Hootum Pyanchar Naksha:* 235-36.
5. *Samachar Chandrika,* dated 30 June 1832, reported about an ascetic staying with the Ghoshals at Bhukailash in Calcutta. In a state of trance, he could go without food for days. Huge crowds arrived to see him. The same story could also be found in Akshaykumar Dutta, *Bharatbarshiya Upasak Sampraday,* vol. 2, 1883; Nag, ed., *Sateek Hootum Pyanchar Naksha:* 237-38.
6. Ancient Hindu texts divide time into four eras: the first of these is Satyayug or the Age of Truth, when all is pure, honest and truthful.
7. Breeding and flying pigeons in unoccupied afternoons was generic to Babu culture, and bird perches could still be found on many terraces in north Calcutta.
8. An inventory of the archetypal themes in fairy tales of Bengal. Bengama and Bengami are the talking birds whose job is to enlighten the ignorant traveller who stops to rest under the tree in which they live.
9. Mukundaram Chakrabarty (1547—?) is the author of *Chandimangal Kavya,* written between 1594 and 1606; a milestone work in medieval Bengali literature for the simple appeal of its poetry, attention to detail, creation of dramatic moments and an exposition of the deep truths of life, which earned him the title of 'Kabikankan'.
10. See Sketch 2, p. 92, note 45.
11. Varanasi was a minister to Gladwin, the district collector of 24-Parganas, who amassed a lot of money and built a huge house at Jorasanko, on a road that was later named after him. He was related to Kaliprasanna Sinha's family by marriage. See Nag, ed., *Sateek Hootum Pyanchar Naksha:* 238.

12. A place near Jangipur, Murshidabad district. This was much before the Farakka Barrage would channelize the water down Bhagirathi. The river would be dry at most times, so those travelling by boat would take a detour and come through the river Mathabhanga. The area around Chhapghati had turned into a swampy bog. Ibid.
13. The Council was set up at the time of Lord William Bentinck and Thomas Babington Macaulay to promote English education among Indians; a parent body which supervised the setting up of different schools and colleges and, evidently, was not above prejudices and playing favourites. Ibid.
14. Ramkamal Sen (1783-1844) an apprentice in government departments, moved on to the role of compositor and later supervisor in Dr William Hunter's Indian Press. Soon he became the treasury manager of the Bank of Bengal and later an eminent educationist. He helped set up the Indian Museum and the Calcutta Medical College. He was principal of Hindu College and secretary of Sanskrit College. He compiled the first English-to-Bengali dictionary and was a regular contributor to the *Journal of the Asiatic Society*. Therefore, it is not unlikely that he had some influence in the academic and other circles. See Chitra Deb, 'The Great Houses of Old Calcutta' in Sukanta Chaudhuri, ed., *Calcutta: The Living City: The Past,* vol. 1 (Calcutta: Oxford University Press, 1990): 63.
15. See Sketch 2, p. 87, note 11.
16. Pratapchandra Sinha and Ishwarchandra Sinha were descendants of Krishnachandra Sinha (1775-1821) who came from an extremely wealthy family in Uttar Pradesh, where Kayasthas were referred to as Lala. Krishnachandra renounced a life of affluence and went to live in Mathura-Vrindavan as a mendicant. Pratapchandra had acquired the title of Raja Bahadur.
17. Prophet Muhammad's grandsons who were killed at Karbala.
18. When Prophet Muhammad was meditating inside an abandoned well, his enemies came looking for him. While the spider wove its web to hide him, the chameleon turned him in. See Nag, ed., *Sateek Hootum Pyanchar Naksha:* 239.
19. Duleep Singh (1832-93) ascended the throne of Punjab at age five, after Maharaja Ranjit Singh's sudden death. After the annexation of the Punjab to British territories, young Duleep was converted to Christianity and brought to England in 1854, where Queen Victoria grew exceedingly fond of him and he grew up in the royal household. An extravagant playboy and an avid hunting squire, he led an

extravagant life. Later, shunned by the British establishment, Duleep looked for allies among other European superpowers, with little success. He died alone and poor in a hotel room in Paris. (http://www.duleepsingh.com/Biography.aspx?evid=21)

20. Prasannakumar Tagore (1801-68) of Pathuriaghata went to Hindu College, which his father Gopimohan helped found. A member of the English-educated elite and moneyed class, Prasannakumar was on the governing board of Hindu College, and involved in the running and funding of School Society, Benevolent Society and the Hindu Free School. He was also the founder-president of the British Indian Association (1867) and edited *Reformer,* a weekly magazine. He was enthusiastic about women's education and theatre—the founder of Hindu Theatre (1831), the first theatre house for staging Bengali plays. A conservative Hindu who supported Rammohan Roy's anti-sati campaign, he was not against polygamy. When Gnanendramohan, a student at Hindu College and later at the Medical College, was inspired by his teacher Reverend Krishnamohan Banerjea to embrace Christianity in 1851 and married his daughter the same year, Prasannakumar disowned his son. Gnanendramohan went on to teach Hindu law and the Bengali language at London's University College; see Subodh Sengupta, ed., *Samsad Bangali Charitavidhan,* 4th rev ed., Part 1 (Calcutta: Sishu Sahitya Samsad, 2002): 184, 313.
21. Krishnamohan (1813-85) was a polyglot who translated Sanskrit texts into English. A staunch believer in the freedom of the Press, he edited *The Inquirer* among a handful of other journals in Bengali and English. He put together the first Bengali encyclopaedia and the mammoth 13-volume bi-lingual *Bidyakalpadroom.* One of the leading lights of the Young Bengal, his conversion to Christianity and subsequent moves to get more people in the fold cost him his job and earned him a degree of notoriety. He inspired Gnanendramohan Tagore to convert so that he could marry his daughter and also had a role in the conversion of the poet Michael Madhusudan Dutt. Ibid: 106-07; see also Sketch 1, p. 39, note 45.
22. The Indian Mutiny, arguably the country's first war of independence against British rule, following which the ruling East India Company was absorbed by the Crown, by the Queen's Proclamation on 1 Nov 1858. There was a growing unrest among Indian soldiers employed by the East India Company. The immediate provocation for the first attack on English soldiers at Barrackpore by Mangal Pandey on 29 March 1857 seemed to be the introduction of a special set of cartridges

for the new Enfield rifles, supposedly greased with animal fat (touching beef was offensive to Hindus and pig fat offended Muslims). The incident grew to a full-blown Mutiny by the rebel soldiers in Meerut (whom Hootum is probably referring to as 'soldiers serving in the west') who seized Delhi on 10 May 1857 and declared Bahadur Shah the emperor of India. See *Papers Relating to the Indian Mutiny*, vol. 1 of 6, London, 1858; Antony Wild, *The East India Company: Trade and Conquest from 1600* (London: Harper Collins, 1999): 175-85.

23. The adopted son of Peshwa Baji Rao II, Nana Saheb's claim to succeed Baji Rao was dismissed by the English after Baji Rao's death in 1851. When the Mutiny began in Kanpur (Cawnpore), the Company commanders, who thought Nana was a British loyalist had put him in charge of the Government Treasury in Nawabganj, but Nana joined forces with the rebel soldiers. On 5 June 1857, the Second Cavalry rode off to Nawabganj, where helped by Nana Sahib's men, they broke into the Treasury. The First Native Infantry followed. A deputation of mutineers called on Nana Saheb, asking him to lead them and he agreed to do so. See Christopher Hibbert, *The Great Mutiny: India 1857* (London: Allen Lane/Penguin, 1978): 172-76.
24. Chuna or Chuna Gully is a lane north of Bipinbihari Ganguly Street. Kasaitolla, the eponymous hub of abattoirs, in Chitpore area, corresponds to the modern Bentinck Street. These were two among the places where the white population preferred to live. See Nag, ed., *Sateek Hootum Pyanchar Naksha:* 242.
25. Ibid: a spirit who supposedly casts an evil eye on small children and makes them fall ill. The lore of Panchananda has to do with two brothers, one devoted to the demi-god, the other a non-believer. Panchananda visited their mother in her dreams, telling her that he would wring the neck of the devoted brother. But why him, asked the mother, isn't it the non-believer who deserved the punishment? True, said Panchananda, but it's impossible for me to harm someone who doesn't acknowledge my existence.
26. Arun Nag comments these were primarily the indigo planters and traders, who were supposedly working towards the growth and prosperity of the British Empire. Ibid: 245.
27. The Earl of Canning was the Governor-General of India during the Mutiny. In the wake of the Mutiny, and the growing insecurity among the European community living in Calcutta, when he was requested to initiate military rule in Bengal he passed the Act XVI of 1857, whereby native regiments were liable to be disarmed when there were

good grounds for belief in their disloyalty; civil and military officers could summarily try and punish all distributors of peace, making native citizens even more vulnerable. Canning was against the rampant plunder, rape, arson and genocide perpetrated by the English troops in the name of controlling the Mutiny. On 30 July 1857 he banned such activity. When he passed a resolution advocating that the captured sepoys should not be punished without regard to the gravity of their offences, the Europeans in Calcutta, who began calling him 'Clemency Canning', petitioned the Queen for his recall to England; see Hibbert, *The Great Mutiny:* 162-67.

28. See The Translator in Wonderland, p. xxx, note 2.
29. Wajid Ali had put up at Metia Buruj, around which a small township emerged (see also Sketch 2, p. 98, note 73). Wajid Ali was given a privy purse of Rs.12,00,000 a year, the lion's share of which would go towards patronizing music and maintaining a private zoo. In 1857, when the Mutiny began, the British government held him in suspicion and therefore took him and his thirty-three followers, to Fort William as prisoners; see ibid: 242-43; William Dalrymple, *The Last Mughal: The Fall of a Dynasty: Delhi, 1857* (Delhi: Viking, 2006): 126.
30. Martial law was made effective in areas where the Mutiny was most pronounced. There would be instant trials and 'rebels' were hanged by the thousands. One of the most iconic images of the quashed revolution is that of soldiers hanging by the neck from trees lining either side of the highway.
31. Following the Mutiny, the government issued warrants against *Samachar Sudhabarshan* and *Doorbin* (Persian). The printers and publishers of these papers were arrested and tried at the Supreme Court. The Suppression of the Press Act (no. 15 of 1857) directed all press owners to acquire a licence, and submit a copy of every paper printed for scrutiny by the government departments. Publishing seditious material that could encourage the masses to go against the government rules was strictly prohibited. Doubting the government's intents or insinuating that the government was interfering with the religious practices followed by the natives was forbidden. Also, publishing any material that could potentially damage the government's relationships with the rajas and feudal lords was not allowed; Nag, ed., *Sateek Hootum Pyanchar Naksha:* 243. Interestingly, 'all press owners' included the European printers in India. The English journalists who were clamouring for a more rigorous suppression of the Mutiny were outraged when subjected to similar

restraint as their Indian counterparts; see Hibbert, *The Great Mutiny: India 1857:* 166.

32. At least two meetings were held at the house of Ramgopal Mallik (Hindu Metropolitan College), condemning the Mutiny and expressing solidarity with the British government, in fact, pledging support to it. One of these was attended by Kaliprasanna Sinha, presided over by Raja Radhakanta Deb. The news of the other figured in *Bengal Harkaru,* 26.5.1857: 'Several gentlemen, large landed proprietors, demanded that the government should be solicited to arm their retainers, on behalf of the authorities and declared that the peasants and the inhabitants of the country were so loyal and faithful as themselves and were waiting anxiously to hear that the government had with a strong hand put down its enemies.' See Nag, ed., *Sateek Hootum Pyanchar Naksha:* 243-44.
33. A trusted lieutenant of Nana Saheb's who continued to resist the British army after the fall of Kanpur. In March 1858, Tantia Tope joined forces with Lakshmi Bai to resist the capture of Jhansi by General Hugh Rose but could not hold out for long. Lakshmi Bai was killed fighting at Gwalior, Tantia Tope fled across the Chambal ravines into Rajasthan. In 1859, Tantia Tope was betrayed by Man Singh, raja of Narwar, who wanted to redeem himself in the eyes of the British. Tope was publicly hanged in April 1859; see Hibbert, *The Great Mutiny:* 252-86.
34. Since the banning of sati in 1829 by Lord William Bentinck, upper-caste Hindu widows were spared martyrdom but relegated to a life of neglect, utter penury and systematic domestic oppression and violence. The idea of letting young widows re-marry, first mooted in 1837, was favoured by the Chief Justices of the High Courts in Calcutta, Allahabad and Madras, but there was reluctance on the part of the government towards giving it legal sanction. The movement gathered momentum after Ishwarchandra Vidyasagar started publishing pamphlets, quoting from *Parashar Samhita* in support of widows marrying a second time. His opponents, the self-styled custodians of the Hindu religion, unleashed a series of vituperative attacks on the man and his mission. As the anti-widow remarriage papers mounted, in 1855 Vidyasagar wrote his second pamphlet, 'Whether or Not Widows Ought to Be Married', refuting the arguments cited by illustrious pandits, and subsequently the English translation of his two papers, titled, 'Marriage of Hindu Widows'. The same year he sent a petition to the government, signed by 987 Hindus,

requesting that widow remarriage be made legal. Finally, in the face of tremendous opposition and mayhem, Widow Remarriage Act (Act XV of 1856) was passed. The move did not go down well with a huge section of middle- and upper-caste Hindus. Raja Radhakanta Deb wrote a counter-petition objecting to the proposed law and endorsed by 33,763 signatories.; see Subal Chandra Mitra, *Isvar Chandra Vidyasagar: Story of His Life and Work* (Calcutta: Parul Prakashani, 2008): 177-210 also see Sketch 5, p. 195, note 11; Sketch 8, p. 233, note 12.

35. Ibid: 206-7; Shrishchandra Vidyaratna (1831-93) was the first half-hearted groom to have married a widow, ten-year-old Kalimati, who was widowed at six, on 7 December 1856. There was huge tension on the day of Shrish's wedding; and there were threats of physical harm to both him and Vidyasagar, who came as a member of the groom's party, and bore the costs of the wedding. The wedding was held at 12 Sukeas Street, in the house of Rajkrishna Banerjee. To prevent any untoward incident a large contingent of policemen was posted.
36. After the raja of Nagpur who was childless died in 1853, Lord Dalhousie annexed Nagpur. Valuable items, including jewellery and palace furniture were auctioned off to provide for the queens, who felt extremely humiliated at the way their assets were sold to the public; see Nag, ed., *Sateek Hootum Pyanchar Naksha:* 245.
37. Jung Bahadur was a rebel leader who removed the king of Nepal in 1847, put the minor prince on the throne and began ruling the country. He had been to England and awed by the might and sway of the Empire, thought it made sense to stick with the British in India. In June 1857, in the wake of the Mutiny Jung Bahadur led an army of 10,000 Gurkhas who joined forces with the Commander-in-Chief, Colin Campbell, to fight the rebel soldiers who had taken Lucknow. After the fall of Lucknow, Jung Bahadur joined the British troops to drive away the rebel soldiers who were trying escape into Nepal; see Hibbert, *The Great Mutiny: India 1857:* 358-74.
38. These were some of the earliest verse writers who would be widely read in nineteenth-century Bengal. Kabikankan Mukundaram Chakrabarty, a sixteenth-century poet, was best known for the epic *Chandimangal Kavya;* for more on Kabikankan see also note 9, above; Krittibas Ojha was the fifteenth-century translator of the *Ramayan* into Bengali, a version that is immensely popular even today and considered of seminal importance. The Christian missionaries of Serampore printed this book for the first time in 1802-03. Krittibas

interpolated elements in the original Sanskrit *Ramayan*, trying to give it a contemporary feel; see Sengupta, ed. *Samsad Bangali Charitavidhan:* 101; Kashiram Das was the writer of the Bengali *Mahabharat* (early seventeenth century) who left his work unfinished; for more on Kashiram Das, see Sketch 2, p. 92, note 45.

39. Sanskrit grammar written by Byopdeb—a primary text which all students of Sanskrit studied until Vidyasagar came up with a more reader-friendly text: *Upakramanika:* 245.
40. Ibid. Maagh was a contemporary of the poet Kalidas, famous for his epic poem *Sishupalbadh.*
41. The story of *Raghuvansham,* was written in the form of an epic poem by Kalidas, one of the greatest Indian poets ever, who lived sometime in fourth century AD. There is no historical evidence to suggest that Kalidas was promiscuous as well as stupid.
42. Hootum was notorious for punishing fraudulent and unscrupulous Brahmins by chopping off their tikis—he supposedly displayed the fifty-one tikis in his collection, in a showcase, with labels indicating the name, title and the nature of crime; see Nag, ed., *Sateek Hootum Pyanchar Naksha:* 246.
43. Sanskrit College was founded by the East India Company in 1824, for spreading Oriental education; Ishwarchandra Vidyasagar was a student and later its principal. Here Hootum has adopted the persona of the anglicized-liberal babu whose sensibilities are at odds with the classical Indian literature/teaching, practised at the conservative Sanskrit College, unwilling to admit non-Brahmins. In essence he is talking about the anglicist-Orientalist conflict, as represented in the clashes between members of the Hindu and Sanskrit colleges; see Raychoudhuri, 'The Lost World of the Babus' in Chaudhuri ed., *Calcutta: The Living City:* 72.
44. Johnson (1709-1804) is best-known for compiling the *Dictionary of the English Language* (1755); see Paul Harvey, ed., *The Oxford Companion to English Literature* (London: Clarendon Press, 1960): 16-17.
45. See Introduction, p. lx, note 18.
46. See Introduction, p. lxi, note 19.
47. See Introduction, p. lxi, note 20.
48. See Introduction, p. lxi, note 21.
49. See Introduction, p. lxi, note 22.
50. Extracted from orpiment, this would be applied as make-up by the imposters to fake deathly pallor; see Nag, ed. *Sateek Hootum Pyanchar Naksha:* 248.

51. The adage goes like this: 'Suffer if you eat the Delhi laddoo, suffer if you don't.'
52. The Nimtolla Burning Ghat dates back to the 1820s, if not earlier, and was twice enlarged with the help of private donation. The present building was constructed in 1876. The Kashi Mitra Burning Ghat was built in 1774, and used to be an exclusive cremation ground for wealthy Hindus; see P. Thankappan Nair, 'Civil and Public Services in Old Calcutta', in Chaudhuri, ed., *Calcutta: The Living City:* 228.
53. In the *Mahabharat,* Duryodhan's father, Dhritarashtra, the blind king, was too indulgent towards his wicked son who denied his cousins, the Pandav brothers, a share of the kingdom of Hastinapur.

    Kaikeyi was the second queen of King Dasharath in the *Ramayan,* who forced him to send his eldest son and heir to the throne, Ram, to an exile in the forests for fourteen years, so that her son, Bharat, could be the king instead. But Bharat, loyal half-brother that he was, placed the shoes worn by Ram on the throne of Ayodhya and ruled in Ram's name until his return. For Surpanakha, see Sketch 2, p. 103, note 95.

    As in the *Mahabharat* and the *Ramayan,* cousins were pitted against one another in a protracted legal battle that dogged Kaliprasanna's family. Santiram Sinha (1722-78) of Jorasanko, the diwan of Murshidabad and Patna, had left behind enormous riches and two minor sons—Prankrishna and Joykrishna—at the time of his death. The brothers grew up and business flourished, the assets increased by several folds. Prankrishna had four sons—Rajkrishna, Nabakrishna, Gopalkrishna and Srikrishna. Before his death in 1812, Prankrishna made a will, by which his brother Joykrishna and the grown-up sons Rajkrishna and Nabakrishna were made the manager and the executors of the property. Joykrishna, who did not have a son until late in his life, had made a will by which his late brother's sons would be entitled to his share in the property after his death, unless his wife Shivsundari gave birth to a male heir, in which case the minor son would inherit Joykrishna's share, while Rajkrishna and Nabakrishna would be the trustees.

    In 1819, Nandalal, better known as Chhatoo or Satoo Singh, was born to Shivsundari. Joykrishna died in 1820. When Chhatoo came of age he claimed his share (seven of sixteen parts) while his uncles got the rest. Later, in the 1840s, Chhatoo filed a suit against his co-sharers for blowing up and mismanaging the assets. He died in 1846, when the case was still pending. His minor son Kaliprasanna

(Hootum) was made the executor of his will. The judge directed Nabakrishna to account for the expenditures during his tenure as trustee. The legal wrangle between the two wings of the family continued well after Kaliprasanna's death. Kaliprasanna too had died without leaving behind a male heir. It was only after Bijaychandra, Rajkrishna's great grandson, was adopted as Kaliprasanna's successor, that the stand-off between the two families was somewhat resolved; see. Nag, ed., *Sateek Hootum Pyanchar Naksha:* 248-49.

54. The Indian counterpart of the many-headed snake Hydra of Greek mythology. Raktabeej could not be slain as every drop of blood from his body that fell on the ground would spawn a series of clones. Finally, it was left to Goddess Durga to annihilate him.

    After his defeat by the English forces, Nana Saheb disappeared into oblivion, having pretended to commit suicide by jumping into the Ganga after his defeat at Kanpur and leaving his seal with Tatia Tope who issued a number of proclamations in his name. After failing to enlist the help of the Emperor Napoleon III, Nana Saheb entered Nepal and is said to have died of fever in September 1859. Thereafter he was frequently reported to have been seen alive and sometimes to have been recaptured. But he was never identified with certainty. And so tired did the government become of reports that men resembling Nana had been apprehended, that when a young officer excitedly telegraphed to Calcutta from a small town near Rajkot in 1895, 'Have arrested Nana Sahib. Wire instruction,' the reply was prompt, short and deflating, 'Release at once.' See Hibbert, *The Great Mutiny:* 386-87.

55. Hootum's seven-legged cow was based on a real-life incident, the evidence of which may be found in an advert published in *Sambad Prabhakar,* 29 June 1854, urging people to visit this wonderful creature with two bodies and a common head; see Nag, ed. *Sateek Hootum Pyanchar Naksha:* 250.

56. Ibid; a metaphor for Mahtab Chand's court and the pandits he had got together to work on a Bengali translation of the *Mahabharat.* They included Taraknath Tattvaratna, Padmalochan Nyayratna and Shyamcharan Tattvabagish.

57. Ibid: 251; As a Shia, Wajid Ali Shah was permitted to enter into marriages with an expiry date; he had 'married' some of the dancing girls who performed for him and gave them the title of begums; for Wajid Ali Shah, see also Sketch 2, p. 98, note 73; note 29 above.

58. Ibid; according to *The Hindoo Patriot,* 2 July 1859, 'certain Bengali

babus have leagued themselves with one of the King of Oude's musicians and a servant of his to persuade him to pay two lakhs of rupees [200,000] for the Governor-General and a lakh and fifty thousand rupees [150,000] for the secretaries with a view to obtaining his liberation.'

59. Shibkrishna was the spoilt son of an extremely wealthy father, Radhamadhav Banerjee, a diwan who had helped build certain important landmarks in the city such as the bathing ghat at Nimtolla and the temple of Anandamoyee. Shibkrishna, who was well educated, worked as one of the managers at Smith, Ewing and Co, and lived in style in his garden house at Titagarh, from where he would travel to Calcutta for his work. He was so arrogant that he is said to have whipped anybody who came in the way when he drove the buggy. When his elder brother Shambhukrishna died, Shibkrishna tried to grab his share of the property by producing a fake will. In August, 1859, the Grand Jury issued arrest warrants against Shibkrishna and his partners in crime: Dr. J.R. Crawford, FRCS, a government-employed surgeon in charge of the dispensary at Garanhata, Nabogopal Chatterjee and Kanailal Paul. Shibkrishna and his cohorts tried to escape to Chandernagore, which was a French colony, but were turned in by the French government on 6 Feb 1860. Shibkrishna was deported to Burma for fourteen years where he died towards the end of his term.

Expectedly, *Bengal Hurkaru* and *The Englishman* were pleased with the sentencing, while *Hindoo Patriot* felt Shibkrishna was the victim of anti-Indian prejudices of the judge and the jury, writing on 26 December 1860 that Shibkrishna 'was guilty of an offence which he had committed for the first time in his life and with the object of preventing his paternal property from falling into hands which civilization alone allows to touch hereditary property.' See ibid: 251-52.

60. The meeting was held on 26 August 1861, following Wells' highhanded sentencing of Rev. James Long on 19 July. Attended by the illustrious people of Calcutta such as Raja Radhakanta Deb, Debendranath Tagore, Ramgopal Ghosh, Nawab Asaf Ali Khan, Ramanath Tagore, Satyananda Ghoshal, and so on, there was a huge turnout. Kaliprasanna Sinha gave a speech. The proposal mooted read, 'This meeting desires to record not without a feeling of regret that if confidence in the Hon'ble Sir M.L. Wells Kt. as a judge of the High Court of Judicature of Bengal has been impaired in consequence of his frequent and indiscriminate attack on the

character of the natives of this country with an intemperance inconsistent with the calm dignity of the Bench as well as from his repeated and indiscreet exhibition of strong political bias and race prejudices which are not compatible with the impartial administration of justice. That with a view to represent Her Majesty's Government the circumstances affirmed in the foregoing resolution, this meeting adopt the following memorial for transmission for Her Majesty's Secretary of State for India.' Secretary of State Sir Charles Wood responded that he hoped 'that those who hold the judicial office may be sensible of how great importance it is that their denunciations of crime may not be interpreted into hasty imputations against a whole people or community.' See Nag, ed., *Sateek Hootum Pyanchar Naksha:* 252-53.

61. Ibid: 253; old Aunt Tepi is a character in *Mod Khawa Boro Dai, Jaat Thakar Ki Upai* (1859) written by Tekchand Thakur aka Peary Chand Mitra.
62. Ibid; see Introduction, p. lxii, note 24.
63. Holloway's Pills, manufactured by Thomas Holloway, were perhaps the most famous of the patent medicines in Britain in the 1860s, and its colonies in India, Australia and North America. Marketed in Calcutta by Messers Dwarakanath Gooptu of Colootolla, Holloway's pills and ointments, frequently advertised in newspapers, had earned a following among Calcutta's delicate public; ibid; (http://web.uvic.ca/vv/student/medicine/holloway.htm)
64. A folk variation of the Goddess Durga, in a slightly more vindictive avatar, who curses with afflictions people who do not pay obeisance to her.
65. Joint Magistrate Ashley Eden who in 1859, heard the appeal of Prestwich and Warner, two planters from Habra, who wanted to make it mandatory for peasants to accept an advance for growing indigo. Instead Eden passed an order banning forcible cultivation of indigo and promised to protect the peasants against the aggression of planters; see Nag, ed. *Sateek Hootum Pyanchar Naksha:* 253-54.
66. Formed on 10 May 1860 where W.F. Fergusson represented the Indigo Planters' Association, zamindar Chandramohan Chatterjee, the British Indian Association, Reverend J. Sale, a missionary, represented the peasants while Seton Karr and Richard Temple represented the government. On the basis of the information collected from 134 witnesses and after extensive investigations, a report was published in November 1860, tipped heavily in favour of the peasants. It suggested

that planters might buy from the open market or re-evaluate the costs of the produce even as it was growing in the fields and even recommended legislation to increase the number of administrative subdivisions, reform the police and ensure civil courts 'of prompt and effective procedure'. Reverend Long, who was one of the missionaries on the panel, 'excited considerable interest in official circles . . . and stressed his belief that unless some "equitable adjustment" of the question was made, he feared for the future peace of the country.' See Geoffrey Oddie, *Missionaries, Rebellion and Proto-Nationalism: James Long of Bengal, 1814-87* (London: Routledge-Curzon, 1999): 114-15.

67. See The Translator in Wonderland, p. xxxi, note 5.

68. *Nildarpan* (The Indigo Story, 1860), a satirical play by Dinabandhu Mitra, portrayed what purportedly was a no-holds-barred exposé of the indigo planters' oppression of the peasants. 'In the author's introduction and the play, almost every section of the community, European and Bengali, was held up to scorn and ridicule. Newspaper editors, magistrates, planters and factory servants were attacked for exercising or supporting tyranny and corruption. A great deal of attention was focused on the violence and oppression by two fictitious indigo planters, Rose and Wood. Rose's attempt to violate the Bengali peasant woman Khetromani recalled a similar alleged real-life incident involving Horamani, widely discussed in the indigo districts, and carefully considered by the Indigo Commission. While those who supported the indigo system were condemned, others like the Governor-General [Lord Canning], [Lieutenant Governor John Peter] Grant and the missionaries were praised for their wisdom, sympathy or sense of justice.' [Oddie, *Missionaries, Rebellion and Proto-Nationalism:* 118-23].

The English translation of the play was done by the poet Michael Madhusudan Dutt but appeared under Reverend James Long's name; see, A Word by Way of an Introduction, p. 4, note 1. Long cut out some of the coarser passages and added a preface. W.S. Seton-Karr secretary to the Government of Bengal and former president of the Indigo Commission who had asked Grant to translate the play, had 500 copies printed with money from government funds, and secretly circulated them among the staff of the British government, MPs, newspaper editors in both Britain and India. On 25 May 1861, Walter Brett, the editor of *The Englishman* and a staunch supporter of the planters, sent a copy to W.F. Fergusson, the secretary of the Landholders and Commercial Association. Fergusson asked for an explanation from the government. Grant wrote back saying the publication was not libelous, but expressed regret that the official franking had caused offence.

Grant and Seton-Karr were ticked off by Lord Canning. A lawsuit was filed against the printer C.H. Manuel. But Long claimed full responsibility and was found guilty in the court of law; see, A Word by Way of an Introduction, p. 4, note 1. *Nildarpan* was a sell-out. Kaliprasanna printed a second edition and distributed it free with *The Hindoo Patriot.*

69. The indigo peasants of Jessore pioneered the protest movement, refusing to pay the increased taxes levied on them in 1860. Gradually the movement spread to Pabna, Nadia and Faridpore. The indigo planters filed several suits to dislodge the peasants from their lands. After considerable dillydallying, the government employed a group of Small Causes Court judges in the districts to look into the matter. Grant was against setting up too many of these, he preferred the idea of Munsif courts headed by Indian judges which were more affordable by the Indian peasants. His apprehensions came true. The courts became an instrument of perpetrating atrocities on indigo peasants; see Nag, ed., *Sateek Hootum Pyanchar Naksha:* 256.
70. Ibid; in March 1861 a Criminal Contract Bill was passed in the Legislative Council, curiously endorsed by Lord Canning which enabled the planters to monitor the 'illegal activities' their native employees indulged in. When Secretary of State for India Charles Wood protested, a second Criminal Contract Bill with certain ramifications was brought.
71. See, The Translator in Wonderland, p. xxxi, note 9.
72. If the Sepoy Mutiny was the first revolt, as the protests by wronged indigo peasants gathered momentum, the empire feared a second revolution. In May 1861, planters of the Bengal Indigo Company attacked a village, aided by armed policemen. Six peasants were killed and many injured in the encounter. The manager Robert T. Larmour said the incident could trigger a Sepoy Mutiny-like uprising, and appealed to the government to impose military rule in the indigo districts; see Nag, ed., *Sateek Hootum Pyanchar Naksha:* 256-57.
73. A Bengali proverb suggesting culpability tends to give itself away. One who stole the banana offered to the Gods in the prayer room would feel so guilty that his response to even a question only tangentially related to the crime could be a giveaway. The Indigo planters who were aware of the damage they had done had become too insecure.

74. Brett, the proprietor and editor of *The Englishman*, took a pro-planters stand and opposed Reverend Long in the *Nildarpan* case; also see note 68. Long was charged with libel against Brett and the 'planters of Lower Bengal'; see Oddie, *Missionaries, Rebellion and Proto-Nationalism:* 115-16.
75. As the reigning queen, Victoria was a mother figure to the British and by extension an aunt of the Indians; see Nag, ed., *Sateek Hootum Pyanchar Naksha:* 257.
76. Refers to the Supreme Court Judge, Justice Wells, who had a major role in Reverend Long's trial and punishment; see also note 60.
77. Refers to factionalism within the Indigo Planters' Association; W.F. Fergusson and J.P. Wise were in favour of including non-white landholders, which was opposed by the conservative planters, led by A. Forbes. In August 1860, Fergusson was made secretary of the organization whose name was now changed to Landholders' and Commercial Association; basil (tulsi), a medicinal herb, has spiritual/ sanctifying connotations (see also Sketch 5, p. 195, note 10). Hootum suggests that the change of name was an attempt to whitewash the notorious image of the planters, rather than effecting a real change; see ibid: 259.
78. Ibid; the indigo planters were referred to as blue monkeys wreaking havoc on 'golden' Bengal in the folk songs that were written in protest. A parallel was drawn with Hanuman burning up the kingdom of Ravan (now Sri Lanka). An extremely popular riff of the time goes like this: 'Now the blue monkeys have destroyed 'golden' Bengal/ Harish is dead before his time and Long is behind bars'.
79. In 1849, a Bill was proposed abolishing the exemption enjoyed by Europeans from the jurisdiction of the Company's criminal courts. Prior to this there was a 'Black Act' of 1836, by which Europeans were liable to be treated by Indian judges. Both incidents, expectedly, enraged the Europeans who called these Black Acts. There was a protest meeting at the Town Hall on 29 December 1849; see Roychoudhuri, 'The Lost World of the Babus', in Chaudhuri, ed., *Calcutta: The Living City:* 74.
80. Ramaprasad (1817-62) was Rammohan Roy's second son who left his job as a deputy collector to become an eminent lawyer. He was one of the British government's most famous public prosecutors and went on to become a legal remembrancer. He was the chair of the governing body of the Brahmo Samaj, founded by Debendranath Tagore. Roy was an active member of the Tattvabodhini Sabha, a

supporter of pro-women movements such as widow remarriage and had petitioned the government in 1857, advocating abolition of polygamy. Thus his following of Hindu rituals at the elaborate memorial service of his mother was highly controversial; see Sengupta, ed., *Samsad Bangali Charitavidhan:* 458.

81. These are various titles given to Brahmin pandits, denoting the extent of their scholarship. Literally, a vidyalankar is one who wears his scholarship like a gem, a nyayalankar is a gem among scholars in the science of reasoning, a vidyabhusan is similar to a vidyalankar, only a notch higher in the scale, a vidyavachaspati is a scholar and a grammarian.
82. Ibid. Indeed Ramaprasad would have been the first Indian High Court judge, had it not been for his untimely death.
83. Ibid: 124; Khelat Chandra Ghosh (?-1930) of Pathuriaghata, a traditionalist and prominent member of the landed gentry in Calcutta, an honorary magistrate and Justice of the Peace. The memorial service for his mother alienated Ramaprasad both from the Brahmos and the conservative Hindus, led by people like Ghosh who refused to attend the ceremony; also see Sketch 2, pp. 87-88, notes 13, 16; Sketch 3, p. 157, note 83; Sketch 8, p. 233, note 8.
84. Kumudkrishna Mitra (1844-1907), related to Khelat Ghosh, often led orthodox Hindus against liberalism and reforms; see Nag, ed., *Sateek Hootum Pyanchar Naksha*: 261.
85. Ibid; an idol of Lord Krishna, originally belonging to Chaitanya Sinha, the raja of Bishnupur. Sinha pawned the idol for 100,000 rupees, leaving it with Gokulchandra Mitra of Baghbazar. Since then the idol stayed in Mitra's homestead, which became a centre of pilgrimage for devout visitors.
86. Ibid: 262; another famous idol of Lord Krishna, one of the three crafted ostensibly from a piece of black stone found in Gaur, in the eighteenth century, during Mughal rule.
87. Brajadham or Vrindavan, the abode of Lord Krishna: the seat of devotion, dalliance and as Hootum suggests, cornucopia. In the present context, the spirit of Brajadham might be a double entendre, meaning both the devotional spirit and alcohol.
88. One of the most famous monarchs who ruled Bengal (which included part of north Bihar) between 1158 and 1179. Erudite, a patron of arts and culture. Ballal Sen supposedly initiated the kulin system; for more on Kulin system, see, Sketch 1, p. 34, note 11. See Sengupta, ed. *Samsad Bangali Charitavidhan:* 332.

89. A mythical figure, supposedly a king of Gaur, who hired five Brahmin priests from Kanauj to perform the rituals at a sacrificial offering. They stayed on and were the forefathers of the Brahmins of Bengal; see Nag, ed., *Sateek Hootum Pyanchar Naksha*: 262.
90. Both Ramaprasad and the Brahmo religion were fathered by Rammohan Roy, hence the two were siblings.
91. A practice that still exists somewhat; in the nineteenth century, it was the custom to garland important guests and put a sandalwood mark on their foreheads. The welcoming was done in a strictly hierarchical order, as decided by the host, which was often a major reason for disputes.
92. The younger brother of the demon king Ravan in the *Ramayan*; known for his gargantuan appetite and prolonged bouts of sleep. He was a near-invincible warrior in his waking moments.
93. Raghunath Bhattacharya of Ula, Birnagar, was famous for his ability to consume a maund of food at one go. He was patronized by Krishnachandra, the raja of Nadia, for his exceptional appetite. In the nineteenth century, the ability to eat like a monster was considered a feat. Often, at the time of a ceremony at home, rich hosts would invite voracious eaters, encourage them to compete with one another and eat as much as they could and, in fact, offer money as incentive. Sometimes, big eaters would make a living out of the money they made at feasts; see Nag, ed., *Sateek Hootum Pyanchar Naksh:* 263-64.
94. Indeed the anniversary (Maghotsav) would be celebrated with huge pomp at the Jorasanko Tagore House by Debendranath Tagore. Food would be served round the clock to anybody who walked in. Arun Nag quotes Abanindranath Tagore's autobiographical *Apan Katha,* where he says instances of staunch Hindus denying that they had had a meal at a Brahmo house were not unheard of; ibid: 264.
95. *Masjia* is a text containing the songs mourning Imam Hassan and Imam Hussein and the other martyrs who died in the desert of Karbala. It is read out at religious gatherings to mourn the deaths on the first ten days of the month of Muharram and chanted at the procession taken out by Shiites. In Hootum's view, Brahmos affected a similar mournful style while saying their prayers.
96. There was a rather complicated way of determining who the greater kulin was. There were about thirty-one categories of kulins, and a strict regimentation was maintained at social functions and guests were served in keeping with their social status.
97. Ibid: 264-65; the aunt in question is Nabinmani, the widow of Chhatubabu, that is, Ashutosh De, the maternal uncle of Dayalchand

Mitra. Chhatubabu was a formidable leader of the Dharma Sabha which acted like a watchdog, monitoring if anyone slipped from the staunch Hindu way of life. Dayalchand grew up in the De household, but his attending the memorial service for Ramaprasad Roy's mother did not go down well with his maternal aunt who disowned him. Articles expressing solidarity with the 'wronged' Mitra (referred to as Uncle Mitra, later in the article by Hootum) were published in *The Hindoo Patriot* and *The Indian Field.*

98. Ibid; the weekly *Sambad Rasaraj* was first published in November 1839, a precursor to today's tabloids, extremely popular, thriving on obscenities, scandals and character assassination. The most famous editor was Gourishankar Tarkabagish who had to pay heavy fines and was even sent to jail more than once for libel. Publication was stopped temporarily in 1857. Gourishakar's adopted son Kshetramohan Bhattacharya revived the paper in 1861.
99. Ibid; *Jayamon Karma Temni Fol* first appeared in 1861, as a riposte to *Rasaraj.*
100. Kauravs and Pandavs in the epic *Mahabharat* were cousins, descended from the same stock, forever locked in a battle for supremacy. The eighteen-day-long great war fought between them is the climax of the story and also a metaphor of protracted hostility and ultimately loss that cancels out victory.
101. This book analyses the tenets of the Brahmo religion in detail, based on the Upanishads, published by Debendranath Tagore in 1850. Akshaykumar Dutta was the ghostwriter; see Nag, ed. *Sateek Hootum Pyanchar Naksha:* 265.
102. Ibid; *Tilottamasambhav,* a tale in blank verse by Michael Madhusudan Dutt, published in 1860.
103. Ibid; an episode adapted from the *Ramayan* by Ishwarchandra Vidyasagar, published in 1860.
104. Ibid: 266. Both the *Rasaraj* editor, Kshetramohan and the editor of *Jyamon Karma* landed up in jail for libel and had to pay heavy fines. *Somprakash,* 9 June 1862 reports, 'The readers of *Somprakash* have already read about a horrid paper, *Jyamon Karma Temni Fol,* in this paper. It was launched to compete with *Rasaraj...* We hear this paper's editor too has been put in jail with that of *Rasaraj.'*
105. The same was true of the *Rasaraj* editor: The idea is that Kshetramohan engaged in a slander campaign to serve the interests of Dayalchand Mitra, as a result of which he landed up in prison while Mitra remained unscathed.

4
The Tricksters

READER! Uncle Haribhadra was a Kayastha and a kulin of the first order. He had a hundred and fifty bowls of opium for tiffin every day and did not have a fixed address. His meals and lodging, however, were taken care of since he knew quite a few of the town whores. Indeed, many of them would affectionately call him 'my daughter's father-in-law' or 'son-in-law'. Uncle would never fail to grace a folar ceremony by dropping the dust off his feet at the venue and never forget to bring home a bundle of luchi and sandesh. In fact, he would not leave a single pair of the invitees' shoes behind if he could target them, provided they were fit to use. I might as well say that Uncle Haribhadra was a gentleman who believed in looting indiscriminately.

Uncle talked about this and that for a while after his arrival and ultimately came to the point, 'Heard the latest? A sanyasi has arrived in our very own Simla. He's known to have acquired spiritual powers. He can turn metal into gold and read one's mind by making astrological calculations. The other day he brought a rotting corpse back to life by feeding him mercury ash. [But I think] he's a big-time swindler. We have caught fraudulent sanyasis like these a few times before, got rid of some of the most dogged ghosts and managed to expose a conman.'

At a time when the Hindu religion held tremendous sway, and as people did not know about the healing property of a substance, or the existence of chemistry and geology, they would be easily taken in. But now it was not easy to pull off a hoax, thanks to widespread English education. But then there was no such thing that one would not find in the city of Calcutta, and there was not

Figure 1. The Owl observes.

Overleaf. Figure 2. Map of Calcutta in Hootum's time.

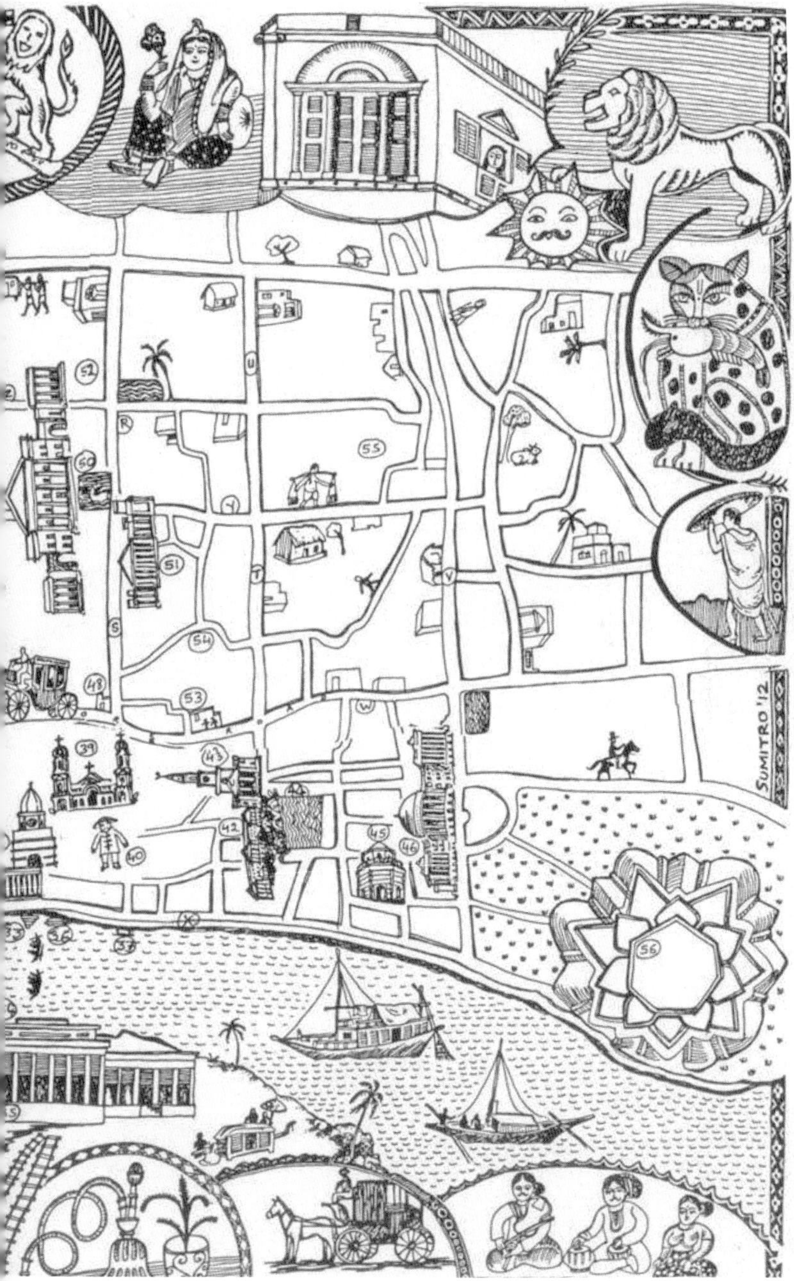

52
55
60
51
54
53
48
39
43
42
40
45
46
56
SUMITRO '12

Legend

STREET NAMES

A. Baghbazar Rd.
B. Shyambazar St.
C. Raja Nabakrishna St.
D. Hari Ghosh St.
E. Sovabazar St.
F. Ahiritolla St.
G. Durgacharan Mitra St.
H. Maniktala St.
I. Ba'ar Simla Rd.
J. Sukea St.
K. Chitpore Rd.
L. Nimtolla Ghat St.
M. Upper Circular Rd.
N. Pathuriaghata St.
O. Muktaram Babu St.
P. Mechhuabazar St.
Q. Thanthaniabazar St.
R. Mirzapore St.
S. Colootolla St.
T. Boubazar St.
U. Baithakhana St.
V. Dharamtolla St.
W. Kasaitolla St.
X. Strand Rd.
Y. College St.
Z. Amherst St.

PLACES DEPICTED

1. Baghbazar lock-gate
2. Kashi Mitra Ghat
3. Kumartuli
4. Baghbazar
5. Sovabazar Rajbari
6. Shyambazar
7. Shyampukur
8. Hatibagan
9. Ahiritolla Ghat
10. Nimtolla Burning Ghat
11. Dorjipara
12. Sonagacchi
13. Shibkrishna Banerjee's house
14. Maniktala
15. Ba'ar Simla
16. Gar Par
17. Notun Bazar
18. Dhopapukur
19. Battala
20. Pathuriaghata
21. Lalababu's Market
22. Rambagan
23. Kaliprasanna's house
24. Jorasanko
25. Adi Brahmo Samaj
26. Singhi Bagan
27. Simla
28. Kansharipara
29. Ramaprasad Roy's house
30. Mint
31. Jhamapukur
32. Badurbagan
33. Railway Booking Office
34. Railway Ferry Service
35. Armenian Ghat
36. Jackson's Ghat
37. Armenian Church
38. Portuguese Church
39. China Bazar
40. Burrabazar
41. Writers' Building
42. St. Andrews' Church
43. Lal Dighi
44. St. John's Church
45. Job Charnock's Tomb
46. Governor's House
47. Mechhuabazar
48. Foujdari Balakhana
49. Thanthania
50. Hindu College
51. Medical College
52. Mirzapore
53. Tiretta Bazar
54. Chuna Gully
55. Shankharitolla
56. Fort William

a [fraudulent] god [-man] who did not visit the city. Therefore, sometimes, the fellows who 'make gold', 'make boys', 'live without food', 'invoke the spirits', 'were experts at mixing intoxicants' landed up here, to earn their keep, try their games of trickery in different parts of the city, ultimately got caught somewhere or the other and were duly chastized.

Hossain Khan

About four or five years back, a Muslim named Hossain Khan[1] arrived in this city with similar pomp and grandeur. He had acquired powers over the genie of Hazrat. (Readers will remember Alladin and the wonderful lamp in the *Arabian Nights.* He could have anything he wanted by asking the genie to get it for him. He could make watches, rings and money disappear from inside chests, drop a bunch of keys in the river and make the genie fish it out, and perform all kinds of strange feats.)

Everybody in the city started talking about Hossain Khan. He became a hot topic of discussion [even] in the anglicized circles. If today Hossain Khan made money disappear from inside the chest in Raja Bahadur's garden house, whisked in food—bottles of **champagne,** paan rolled and spiked with drugs, stuffed in envelopes made out of banana leaves, pomegranates and currants —from Wilson's Hotel,[2] tomorrow he would generate oranges, garlands made of jasmine, ice and condiments [from nowhere] at the Rai Bahadur's house. Those who did not have faith in the God Supreme began reposing faith in Hossain Khan. [As the saying goes,] 'Five devotees can make a prophet out of a block of stone.' Gradually Hossain Khan began conning big-time idiots from Kashmir. He became entitled to a free meal at many places in the city. People from different parts of the country and outside came to watch hoaxes being performed. Hossain Khan's **premium** was on a new high.

One cannot get away with trickery forever. [As they say], 'The thief might get away several times over, but one day the honest guy will prevail.' Hossain Khan was caught in the act on one or two occasions. On some instances, he would be let off after his cheek was tweaked, or ears boxed. Eventually there was no escaping getting bashed up. [Even] those who had been treating him as a God, and fawning over him, now gave him a blow or two. In a few days' time, Hossain Khan, who supposedly had power over the genie, became something like a branded bull sacrificed at a memorial ceremony by believers in idol worship.[3] All those who had taken him home with a great show of adulation would now throw him out, after having put their mark on him. Ultimately he landed up in the government-run guesthouse: in other words, Hossain Khan went to jail. And the genie took refuge in the nether world.

The Ghostbusters

I once saw a spirit being exorcised; it was quite out of this world. Someone was taken very horribly ill in the goldsmith's house in our neighbouhood. Since the goldsmiths in question were quite well off, they spared no effort in getting the disease treated. They assembled quite a crowd of English physicians, practitioners of Ayurveda and Yunani medicine. The treatment went on for almost three years, but nobody could do anything about curing the ailment. The women of the house, seeing that the disease took an even more critical turn, began offering puja at the altar of the household tulsi bush, had rites towards a recovery performed at Kalighat, and chanted verses in praise of Kalbhairav.[4] They [also] tried mumbo-jumbo, and [praying to] Shah Farid and Lord Narayan. The patient was made to drink the water washed off the feet of the deities at Balodh, Balsi, Shahpur, Nurpur and Halumpur and wear amulets. Somebody was sent to the temple in Tarakeswar to lie on his stomach [until the disease was cured]. The eldest among the ladies in the house offered blood by ripping her chest at Kalighat and burnt resin on her hands and head. Finally an exorcist was summoned.

This exorcist was experienced in treating ghost-related ailments. These days, certain Bengali physicians called on their **patients,** dressed like a spirit. Instead of wrapping themselves in a sheet, they did so with mosquito nets and carried a rope and nails. Sometimes they arrived stark naked. It was just that instead of being borne by a magic chant, they needed about four or five exorcists to carry them. These were the **educated** ghosts from the Calcutta Medical College.[5]

The exorcist was put up at the Chandimandap. The **programme** for invoking the spirit had been finalized. A few households in the locality were informed that the spirit would show up today after dark, and that it would be reading people's minds and recommending medicines for the ailing patient. Evening descended by and by. The kothiwallahs returned home from work. Those who preferred spending the night in a prostitute's quarters stepped out. The idols [in the homestead], like the Kayasthas from northern Rarh[6] land [who do not hesitate to help themselves to a meal as soon as it is offered], consumed the cool evening snack, comprising fruits and sweets, offered to the Gods.

Boom! The gun went off as soon as the clock on the church steeple struck nine. 'Hail Kali, the deity of Calcutta,' the boys cried, clapping. The exorcist took the stage.

Our neighbour, who had been informed by the household women that a spirit was going to be invoked and had proof [that the method worked], spared no efforts putting together a meal for the ghost. The finest sweetmeats from Burrabazar, a variety of drinks and lickables prepared from sweet, thickened milk arrived on the scene. It seemed that even ten of us, seasoned folar-eaters, put together could not have polished off the huge amount of food [that was served]. The poor exorcist and his two cohorts were simply not up to the challenge!

The exorcist entered the room, sat on a low wooden stool and asked around about the details of each person inside the room. He ran his eyes all over some of the assembled people. It was clear from his looks that he simply hated some of the **boys** from the medical college and the invitees carrying thick clubs.

While the exorcist had just two disciples, there were about forty hopefuls gathered inside the room, who wanted to see a ghost. So the spirit was reluctant to appear at the outset. The exorcist, on his part, took the opportunity to make a speech on 'Our times and the Christian influence'. Finally, seeing that the audience was of the deeply devout sort and on condition that the lights would be put out, the exorcist agreed to invoke the spirit. His disciples took their seats close to the plates containing the edibles. The door was bolted. The light extinguished. The exorcist took his seat, [arranged] the brass decanters, and began invoking the spirit, performing the rituals most flawlessly. I sat stiffly in the darkness for fear of ghosts, like a shong [i.e., an inert clay model in a tableau], churned out of the baroyaari-puja factory.

Reader, you would probably remember—I have said this before—my grandmother had hung an amulet the size of a small drum containing the dust off the feet of the holy man of Bhukailash from my neck. I wore around twelve different medallions and amulets, two tiger claws and crocodile's teeth on my neck. Fish scales and rhino hide were securely tucked inside my waistband. In addition to these, I wore another amulet, shaped like an arm-plate, and a gold chain wrapped around the upper arm, in the name of the deity at Tarakeswar.

As a little child once I was taken very ill. So I was made to wear a chain around my feet: the sort thieves using a metallic rod to burrow into mud houses are bound with [as punishment]. I wore my hair matted in the name of Lord Panchananda. It had become so smeared with oil and dust that it now resembled a bell on a string, dangling from a he-goat's neck. I was still in school when driven by **ambition** at a young age I went to the Brahmo Samaj and put my name down in their book, under the printed letterhead. And that gesture of mine, I was told, sealed my induction into the Brahmo Samaj. Sometime before that, after I had heard about the kind of miseries that befell the holy man from the pandit who taught me in school, I took off all the good luck charms I wore. Today I was reminded of those. And I thought if only I had still worn them then when the spirit appeared, it would not be able to do me any harm. [At home] I had asked around where the charms might be lying, but they could not be found. A servant had [supposedly] stolen them on the day of my grandson's rice-eating ceremony. No effort was spared in trying to nab the culprit. The mistress of the house put a betel nut, coins and rice up to three-fourths of the measuring cup in a small bundle. Nepi's mother, an aged maid who had been working in this house for a long time, took the bundle to the astrologer's house. The astrologer made some calculations and said, 'The thief is an insider. He's not too ugly, nor very good-looking. The fellow is darkish, slender, sports a medium-size moustache, may be bald and again may not be so.' The astrologer's reading pointed towards the family servant. It was decided that the servant was indeed the thief and sacked. But the amulets could not be found. After this I became even more frightened of ghosts.

There's no guarantee that ghosts would not come for you if you were a Brahmo [i.e., a non-believer]. The other day the wife of one of the **directors** of the Brahmo Samaj got bewitched. She was cured only after they called exorcists from different parts of the country and abroad who went about beating [the victim], even as mustard seeds, water and pepper were sprinkled on her, accompanied by chants [to undo the evil spell]. It was common to see lamps being lit on Bhoot Chaturdashi[7] day in a lot of Brahmo households.

Meanwhile, now that the exorcist had been calling out for a while, the signs of the ghost's imminent arrival were made evident. Bones of cattle, pebbles, bricks and discarded earthen pots were pelting all around the house. It seemed someone was dancing inside the room, *goop goop*, the feet tapped. The preamble continued for a while and then there was a sharp, cracking sound. It seemed that the flat wooden stool meant for the spirit broke into two halves. 'The great one has arrived,' said the exorcist, apprehensively.

When I was young, my aged grandmother had told me that ghosts spoke with a nasal accent, and that was what I firmly believed. Today the theory was put to test. Immediately after splitting the stool, the ghost began speaking in a nasal tone. The first thing he did was to call some of the boys from the medical college by their names, declaring that they were Christians and atheists. Ultimately the ghost made every effort to scare them by saying that he would break their necks, as was his wont. The master of the house became greatly terrified when he heard the nasal speech and the fact that the ghost had taken the names of people supposedly unknown to him. He clasped his hands together (it is impossible to see clasped hands in the dark, but a ghost can see well enough even in darkness, therefore, I had a feeling that the master of the house spoke with clasped hands, even in the dark) and asked for forgiveness. But the ghost, like Sir Mordaunt Wells, believed in solving the crisis that he addressed, removing all traces of it, once and for all. Therefore, there was no going back on the promise to break our necks. Finally, after the exorcist, some elderly people in the audience and the master of the house made several pleas, the magnanimous ghost, like a brand new son-in-law who arrives [with due fanfare] on son-in-law's day, deigned to have a little snack. I was beginning to think of ways to make myself scarce.

It took almost half an hour before the sound of squishing and noisy chewing of luchis and the slurping of folar could stop. Finally, when the ghost finished eating the snack and was helping himself to opium and tobacco, the sound of severe hiccupping—the sort that's like the preamble of a cholera patient wanting to throw up—could be heard from where he sat. The bouts of hiccupping were so rapid that the spirit was unable to speak. [And then there was] the vomit, like a gushing flow. The master of the house thought it was the spirit throwing up. So he quickly had a lamp lit and brought to the room. We saw that it was the exorcist and his twin followers who had been vomiting, the spirit had left. I did not know that a young lad from the Medical College had mixed tartar emetic in the food served to the ghost. The exorcist and his cohorts had consumed this food after the spirit tasted it, hence the misery. The little faith I had in the idea of exorcising spirits disappeared after this incident. And I decided that the home-bred spirits were not worth writing home about, especially when compared to their English counterparts.

I have seen instances of spirits being invoked in a few other places besides this one, and so have the readers, so there was no point talking about them here. The Ghostbusters and Hossain Khan have been mentioned here only because they are concomitant with fraud and idle talk.

Banka, the Scar-Nosed

Although I knew that the instances [mentioned above] were extreme cases of deception, I went to Bankabehari's Simla house one evening, as asked by Uncle Haribhadra. Bankabehari was a head clerk in a lawyer's firm. He had built a house and accumulated properties and wealth by applying intelligence and strategy. He went around looking for lapses committed by people all through the year, with the sole intention of extorting money in every possible way.

Bankabehari was raised by his maternal grandfather, so the matters of his education and physical well-being were indeed neglected. One day, while playing, he fell inside a well in his maternal uncle's house and cut his nose. Since then fellow boys began affectionately calling him 'Banka, the scar-nosed'. Later, he became rather well known by that name in the lawyer's firm as well. Bankabehari was the middle one among three brothers. His elder brother was a sailor's agent and the youngest owned a retail shop. All three were into earning easy money. Since they engaged in an extraordinary variety of professions, it was little wonder that they should be dealing with all sorts of rogues. In a very short span of time, Bankabehari and company became quite famous in Simla. Just as sudden affluence tends to make people ill-tempered—you know what I mean, reader (after all, there ought to be one or two among you whose situation is similar to Bankabehari's)—over time, Bankabehari turned out to be [as painful as] a purgative to bhadraloks.

Even the bailiff and gardener posted at a High Court attorney's house were experts in law; therefore, one had expected Bankabehari to be an even shrewder one. When it came to legal counselling, training people in fraudulent practices, handling the loopholes of **equity** and the twists in the **common law,** Bankabehari performed [with the expertise of] Shubhankar the Second.[8] Any decent person would live in fear of him. He could cast a net in the skies and entrap the moon, turn reality into fiction and vice versa, and might even have had Thug Chacha[9] in Tekchand Thakur's book come to him for advice.

I reached Bankabehari's house after dark. I could not take the carriage out as the old big horse of ours, as happened from time to time, was down with rheumatic fever. I called a porter on the road and travelled sitting in a wicker basket, atop his head, instead. The journey, therefore, might have taken slightly longer than usual. It would have been even more comfortable to be carried in a constable's sling bag.[10] Unfortunately, one does not have that privilege at all times. Readers, if you most graciously check out how it feels to ride in a sling bag, you would not want to travel in a carriage or a palanquin ever again in this life. Only those who have had the experience know how cosy it is; it is just like [being in] a **coach** fitted with **springs**.

I saw a whole host of bhadraloks assembled at Bankabehari's. They too had arrived at the gathering to watch the trick of 'turning metal into gold'. And then, after the mutual introductions and the talking had stopped, we were allowed to go to the room where the sanyasi was staying. The chamber was adjacent to Bankabehari's drawing room, so we walked in barefoot. It was a square room at the centre of which sat the sanyasi, on a tiger skin, with a trident tethered in front of him. An idol of Lord Shiva riding a brass tiger and an elliptical Shivling made of agate were on display. A pipe for smoking ganja, a sling bag to carry hemp leaves in and an earthen plate used to heat up the stuff were kept by his side. His twin cohorts sat behind him, smoking pot. A little behind them lay a pair of bellows, a millstone, a hammer and a mortar and pestle, the whole paraphernalia one associates with making gold.

Seeing the sanyasi, quite a few of us behaved like living embodiment of devotion and respect, prostrating to touch his feet. Some tipped their heads a little, while a few others like me just joined the chorus that sang his glory in unison, rather noisily, like boys half-heartedly joining in when fellow students recite lessons in school. Finally, the sanyasi nodded, asking everybody to take a seat.

Glory to the great men whose manoeuvrings led to the creation of the Hindu religion! [For it's so full of] ghouls with missing heads, ghosts of dead Brahmins, Goddess Kali with blood dripping down her teeth, and the [vindictive] Goddess Shitala! The sanyasi's ostentatious get-up, whether or not they admit it, made all born-

Hindus wince. Alas! Time, indeed, is a glorious thing. If the grandfather had once bowed to a piece of stone, taking it to be a manifestation of God—[devotion to whom he thought was his] only way to salvation, today the grandson was not scared to stamp on it. Fie, faith. There is nothing you cannot make people do. What is more strange than the fact that one is ready to give one's life away for the sake of another, like a loyal slave, when asked to, and again [at another point in time] might treat the very same person like an arch enemy because of something he might have said.

Which is the most valid religion? How could one achieve proximity to God? Who knows? Therefore, there is no certainty that the people who had earlier worshipped thunder, water, earth and stone as God most resoundingly would go to hell, while we who listen to lamentations and singing of paeans with closed eyes and heads swaying in sync for an hour every Wednesday[11] would end up in Heaven. How could we, puny dunderheads, be so boastful and proud, claiming that we have been blessed [by the Supreme Being], when hundreds of theologists and men learned in the ways of nature have, for thousands of years, failed to grasp the way of achieving that blessed state? Just how stupid is that? Just as the Brahmos, that is, those who have [supposedly] achieved the true knowledge of God think that believers in idol worship, as well as Christians and Muslims are all worthless and devoid of substance, the latter, in turn, are quite sure that the Brahmos are mad and hypocritical. These days the greatest religion is the one to which the Crown pays obeisance at a given space and time. The world is changing every day, by the inevitable rule of time, and so are religious societies, their norms and regulations. Even before a hundred years had passed since Rammohan Roy gave the Brahmo religion a shape, on the basis of the Vedic principles for which he had high regard, his disciples have started dismissing the Vedas.[12] They have adopted certain Christian affectations, by way of dressing up the Brahmo religious practices. And there's no knowing what else is in the offing.

Perhaps it is things like these that make some decent folks turn non-believers. If the Supreme Being was at all materialistic, He would not have willingly let Himself be counted among 'horses' eggs' and 'flowers growing in the sky'.[13] Therefore, [given the way things are], one could, occasionally, call Him a rustic feudal lord, with little common sense.

Having asked us to sit, the sanyasi was about to move on to a different topic when Bankabehari stepped up and prostrated before him. Bankabehari wore a gold-embroidered headgear from Kabul, a shirt tailored out of red gauze, a dhoti made in the Shantipur looms, with the words 'May you live for ever, Vidyasagar' woven in the border and a striped wrapper. He held a red handkerchief from which a few keys were suspended in a ring.

Once Bankabehari was through with the prelude, sweet talk, salutation and **shaking of hands**, his elder brother explained to the sanyasi in Hindi that the assembled gentlemen were here to watch him perform the acts of trickery and [check out] his skills. He requested the sanyasi to demonstrate one or two of these when it was convenient. After he had spent some energy pleading his case, the sanyasi agreed. The prologue to the trickster's show was about to begin. Bankabehari chalked out the **programme**. After a while, a hibiscus placed on the ceremonial pot jumped with a start, like a toad popping up at the time of monsoon with a sharp whacking sound, just about two feet away from where the sanyasi sat. A sight such as this was truly quite amazing. For a while everybody in that room stared in wonder. Even as they did, the sanyasi's face, sombre and pompous, began swelling with pride. That was when one of his disciples brought in a bottle of alcohol, which would be turned to milk. Lest the audience thought that there was a second bottle or that there was anything else in the container, the sanyasi emptied the alcohol from the bottle on a fresh clay plate. The room was reeking with the smell of alcohol. Now everybody was convinced that this was alcohol indeed.

Once he had finished pouring alcohol on the new clay plate, the sanyasi roared. Small boys were startled at the noise. The aged felt their hearts rumble in apprehension. Then a disciple came up to the sanyasi and asked, 'Guru! What do you have in this container?' 'It's milk, my son,' said the sanyasi, pouring a beaker full of water in it. The liquor in the plate turned milk-white at once. We watched [the performance] completely stupefied. The exhibition of such acts of skilful trickery and stylish expertise continued till eleven at night. And then Bankabehari suggested that the sanyasi, as hallowed as the *Mahabharat* writer Vedavyas, should retire for the night with the consent of all concerned. I gave him a huge salute and came back home, feeling like a dunderhead. [By this time] I was very hungry, besides the porter had not informed that he didn't see well enough at night. So I had to take him by the hand, and walk slow for roughly a mile in a different direction altogether to reach him to the carpenter's shop before I could go home. Unfortunately, the cat had eaten my dinner that night. And the shops too were closed. The night, therefore, was spent in a bamboozled state, triggered by hunger and the strain of having walked miles.

I did say before that if the thief got away on most occasions, the honest chap too would have his day. After some time people started talking about [the dubious nature of] the sanyasi who was staying at Bankabehari's house. Finally, one day, determined to unmask the hypocrisy of the sanyasi, some of us went to Bankabehari's house. When the hibiscus jumped like it did the previous day, a Bangal student from the east country who attended the lectures given in Bengali[14] at the Calcutta Medical College, leapt from his seat and grabbed the sanyasi's hand. Finally, even as a ruckus was on, it was revealed that a fine hair from a horse's tail was used to tie the hibiscus to the sanyasi's finger nail.

Such is the way of the world that a person's shortcomings, once found out, seem to multiply [in popular imagination]. As soon as the hibiscus was revealed to have been tied to a horse's hair, everybody started rummaging through the sanyasi's belongings for other arrangements of deceit. Someone dragged out a dead goat from the corner of the room. On a previous occasion, the sanyasi had, 'restored life' by killing a goat and using its blood. Finding no way of disposing it off, he had buried it under the earth in the corner (it was not a paved **floor**, you see). He had not had the time to cover it well, and a horn was sticking out. So when somebody's foot touched it, a thorough search revealed the secret. The hoax of turning alcohol into milk, a miracle performed in front of our eyes, was exposed too. A sub-assistant surgeon said that American rum (anisette) turned white when mixed with water. Having exposed the hoaxes and embarrassed Bankabehari and the sanyasi, we, the homebodies, went back home, triumphantly. Uncle Haribhadra confiscated the brass Shivling from the sanyasi and sold it to buy hemp from an agent in Nepal. Since that day, he too had become disgusted with such charlatans.

Nowadays there were not half as many incidents involving supernatural elements as would happen before. How many saints sitting with their hands up in the air or followers of Lord Shiva did one find in the city these days? A respite from the incidents of fraud was likely as the influence of Hinduism lost currency. A business could not be sustained without buyers and profit. Therefore these deceitful exercises that were part of the religious paraphernalia would gradually become extinct. Only that Calcutta was so unusually fertile that it continued breeding such specimens of greatness who made sure that the viciousness sustained for ever, the hypocrisy and pretences of Hinduism were rampant and a thousand good deeds were trampled over.

There were three brothers, all quite mad. One day the eldest told the mother, 'Your womb was a lunatic asylum of sorts.' We too might choose to call Calcutta a breeder of gems some day. Be it the city's rich men or the middle class, each citizen is a gem of a kind. On that note we now present Babu Padmalochan Dutta.

Notes

1. Arun Nag quotes Peary Chand Mitra in *Stray Thoughts on Spiritualism:* 'We had here a Mahommedan medium named Hossain Khan who could abstract diamond rings, however carefully concealed, could bring meat and confectionary in lonely places, place before us bottles of brandy all of a sudden and give copies of letters hidden under the pillow.' Calcutta luminaries such as Jatindramohan Thakur, Dr. Suryakumar Sarbadhikari, Ramgopal Seal, Hiralal Seal and Krishnabehari Sen supposedly witnessed some of the miracles performed by him. Hossain Khan was arrested for his hoaxes and probably died in prison. See Arun Nag, ed., *Sateek Hootum Pyanchar Naksha* (Calcutta: Ananda Publishers, 2008): 267.
2. Rabindranath Tagore famously, mentions this eatery in his play *Chirakumar Sabha,* inspired by Shakespeare's *Love's Labours Lost.* This is where the English-educated Hindu young men would go to get a taste of forbidden food, i.e., chicken or mutton, and become social outcastes if they were found out.

   As is evident from an anonymous rhyme circulated in mid-nineteenth-century Calcutta:

   Jaat marley tin Seney
   Keshab Seney, Wil-seney, Isti-seney

   (The three 'Sens have defiled caste Hindus: Keshab Sen the Brahmo leader, 'Wil-sen' or Wilson's Hotel, where Hindus would feast on forbidden food and the 'Isti-sen' or railway station as the niceties of caste could not always be observed during a train journey.) See Subir Raychoudhuri, 'The Lost World of the Babus', in Sukanta Chaudhuri, ed., *Calcutta: The Living City: The Past,* vol. 1 (Calcutta: Oxford University Press, 1990): 73.
3. An ancient practice of sacrificing a bull as a part of observing the last rites of the dead; the bull was marked before being let loose to indicate that it was dedicated to the dead. See Nag, ed., *Sateek Hootum Pyanchar Naksha:* 267.
4. An inferior, slightly irascible version of Lord Shiva.
5. Calcutta Medical College was set up in 1835; the first examination performed in 1838. The first hospital with twenty beds was opened the same year. The college set a world precedent by teaching basic sciences such as physics, chemistry and botany besides regular medical courses, which is why probably its students became informed rationalists rather than just physicians. See Poromesh Acharya,

'Education in Old Calcutta' in Chaudhuri, ed., *Calcutta: The Living City: The Past:* 93.

6. Kayasthas settled in Murshidabad, Birbhum and Burdwan districts of Bengal, known as the Rarh area, are reputed to be the gluttonous sort according to Hootum. See Nag, ed., *Sateek Hootum Pyanchar Naksha:* 267.
7. The night before Diwali/Kali Puja when fourteen lamps are lit around the house to drive the spirits away.
8. Shubhankar was a title given to expert mathematicians. Primary students would be made to recite and memorize mathematical formulae in rhymed couplets ascribed to Shubhankar, an oral text, which may have been composed by more than one person. Hootum suggests Bankabehari knew his craft well, which made him a Subhankar in the field of law. See Nag, ed., *Sateek Hootum Pyanchar Naksha:* 267-68.
9. Thug Chacha, as the name suggests, was a conman par excellence, a character in Peary Chand Mitra's *Alaler Gharer Dulal* (1857), Tekchand Thakur's pseudonym. As Thug Chacha says at one point in the book, 'It's not possible to put in words the kind of devices, schemes and machinations that I employ.' See Brojendranath Bandyopadhyay and Sajanikanto Das, eds., *Alaler Gharer Dulal* by Tekchand Thakur (Calcutta: Bangiya Sahitya Parishad [1916] 1974): 78.
10. When the cops rounded up drunks from the road who were too inebriated to walk, they would put them in a sling bag and haul them to the police station. See Nag, ed., *Sateek Hootum Pyanchar Naksha:* 268.
11. The weekly day for holding a prayer service at the Brahmo Samaj, a practice that is still followed, e.g., a morning service is held on Wednesdays at the prayer hall in Visva-Bharati, Santiniketan.
12. Initially, Brahmoism was in line with the philosophy in the Vedanta. There would be readings from the Vedas at the weekly meetings (see Sketch 1, p. 40, note 53 and Introduction, p. lxi, note 21). Debendranath Tagore, who sympathized with them, 'made a compilation of select passages from the Upanishads inculcating the idea of one God and framed a new covenant embodying the principles of natural and universal theism in the place of the old Vedantic covenant in 1850.' See R.C. Majumdar et al., *An Advanced History of India* (Madras: Macmillan, 1981): 868-69.
13. Common Bengali expressions suggesting fantastical ideas/things/ situations; the idea of a formless Supreme Being was found slightly at odds with the Bengali Hindu temperament, used to worshipping

330 million deities, quite a few of these in the form of idols, each vested with distinct character.

14. Lectures at the Calcutta Medical College would be delivered in English since it became functional in 1835. Hindi and Bengali sections were begun in 1839 and 1852. Hindi was meant for doctors who would be posted in north India to treat Indian soldiers, Bengali for the benefit of doctors who would practise in small-town hospitals and disease-ridden rural Bengal. See Nag, ed., *Sateek Hootum Pyanchar Naksha:* 270.

5

Babu Padmalochan Dutta or the 'Sudden Incarnate'

BABU PADMALOCHAN alias the 'Sudden Incarnate' was born in his maternal grandfather's house—the Mitras of Natapara-mushuli. The village was rather nice, inhabited by a number of Kayasthas and Brahmins. Zamindar Muzaffar Khan, although a Muslim, did not favour atrocious practices like butchering of cows. Both Muslims and Brahmins were equal in his eyes. He knew how to treat deserving people with respect, be cordial and never missed greeting people courteously. He was proficient in Persian and knew Bengali and Urdu well.

Although Muzaffar Khan was the zamindar who presided over the village, the Mitras were given the responsibility of enforcing social ostracization [on errant villagers]. This was done by stopping the dhobi and the barber from offering their services to the errant family and discarding the hookah that they had used to smoke [in the house they visited]. The tasks of conducting and mediating a mock war between the groom's side and the bride's at a wedding and deciding on the amount the groom's party would have to pay different claimants at the bride's house were also vested in them.

Earlier, the Mitras lived in splendour. But a series of deaths in the family and its breaking up into several units pushed them into a state of penury, to some extent. Although they were broke, in the eyes of the people of the village they were still worthy of the respect they commanded earlier.

The day Padmalochan was born was not like the birthday of any other inconsequential person. Suddenly heavy clouds gathered and it rained incessantly all day. A snake parked itself in front of the *atur ghar*,[1] and hissed all night. The pet parrot, which had suddenly died, remained hanging from its perch. Padmalochan's grandmother, who thought these were good omens, was so glad that she gave a red-bordered sari of hers to the midwife. The drummer and other musicians called to play on the occasion were each given a 25 paisa coin and a pot full of coconut narus, little balls of jaggery and coconut. The eighth day of the child's birth[2] was celebrated with great joy. The young boys of the village chanted, 'Eight pulses, eight beans, how is the newborn? Let's get crapping in the father's beard,' as they beat the husking tray like a drum, collected their shares of parched peas, sugar candies and a glittering paisa each before leaving gleefully. The severed head of a cow,[3] picked up from the dumping ground, was placed in front of the door of the atur ghar and worshipped by putting turmeric and *durba* grass on it. After fifteen, twenty and eventually thirty days were over, a ritual offering was made at Lord Panchananda's shrine in the village and the mother and child were allowed to move out of confinement.

Like the waxing moon that gets enhanced each night, so did Padmalochan. Be it at a game of marbles, kabaddi, catch-the-thief or slip-out-of-the-grip, Padmalochan's sporting skills made him famous. At age five he went through the chalk ceremony. Padmalochan would crouch beside the pond, hide in reed forests and behind clusters of bamboo [to avoid school]. There was no dearth of complaints such as stomach-ache, sickness and other ailments from him.

A few years passed like this. And then Padmalochan's father died, and his mother committed sati. Then his grandfather, maternal uncles and cousins too died; some early and some at the right time. The Mitras' house was now completely bereft of male presence. The landed property was swallowed up by zamindars like Joykrishna,[4] while the rest was taken [by the government] as the taxes had not been paid for a while. Thus, from a very young age, poor Padmalochan had to depend on luck and his skills to earn a living.

Padmalochan travelled to Calcutta. He was hired by tenants of a house to do odd jobs such as folding dhotis in pleats and frying luchis in exchange of free meals. He thought he would pick up a skill or two when he had some time off. The tenants had promised to teach him to read and write.

Padmalochan entertained the tenants this way for a while. And then, to earn the munificence of some of the babus in town, began soliciting the favour of some of the really influential ones. Visit any rich man's house in town, and you would land up in a thick crowd of people. Dig a little and you would know that there are several creditors, moneylenders, loan-offerers, shopkeepers, solicitors, unmarried chaps and unemployed young men from kulin families among them. Padmalochan added a number to the crowd. He would be soliciting round the clock, with the [single-minded focus of the] Garuda bird, and after a year's continuous visits [to the houses of influential men] he did manage to get a few references. Finally, a kind-hearted manager gave him a substantial assistant's job in the merchant's **house** where he was employed.

Earlier, Padmalochan had been through a life of immense hardship. A bhadralok's son, he had to do ignominious work such as pleating dhotis, frying luchis, shopping for daily provisions, fetching water from the well. He became such an expert luchi-maker through years of practice that he was better than the Brahmin confectioners who ran sweet shops. His employers, the tenants, were so pleased with his work that they gave him the title of '**Maker**'. From that day on he began to be known as Padmalochan Dutta, the Maker.

As they say, 'When fortune favours, and a run of good luck begins, even dust is turned to gold at the lucky man's touch.' The good things that fortune had in store for Padmalochan Dutta now began to be revealed. The office manager generously gave him a superintendent's job. The English bosses were pleased with the smartness and alert nature of this scion of the Dutta family. The more they were impressed, the more Padmalochan started looking for opportunities to please them. Even venomous snakes turn merciful when worshipped steadfastly. In ancient mythology, one finds instances of people having managed to please the particularly ogre-like, vindictive sort of Gods through prolonged prayers.

Gradually, Padmalochan won the sahibs over. They now wanted to do him a good turn. One day, when the first **mate** of the merchant **house** resigned, the sahibs asked the manager to appoint Padmalochan to the vacant post.

Padmalochan was staying with the tenants in the old house, even after he was made superintendent, but it did not look good to continue residing there once he became the first **mate**. He acquired a plot of land on lease elsewhere, built a modest house and started living in it. But he did not have to stay there for long. Soon his fortune swelled, like blisters appearing on a fully-fried luchi. Padmalochan became all swollen-headed, like the way brides inflate once they go through the ritual of marriage. And then, after a while, the manager, who had not been getting along very well with the white bosses, quit his job. Padmalochan, who was the sahibs' favoured one, took his place, becoming a manager without money.[5]

Money rules the world. As soon as Padmalochan was made the manager, he felt the difference in his status. It was as if his modest house with a tiled roof was suddenly mocking the two-storey buildings. The very next morning, Padmalochan's house was filled with seekers, agents, guards, traders and retailers. If one put his hands together and went down on his knees, others sung his praise, saying things like, 'May you have a golden quill and ink-pot,'[6] 'May you be worth hundreds of thousands', 'May you have a son in a year's time', 'Only you can help this loyal friend of yours'. They tried pumping Padmalochan's ego with greater impetus than a loaf of bread baking inside a clay oven. Finally, Padmalochan began covering his face with a piece of cloth, like lecherous men [who go looking for sex] during the day to hide [from the suckers]. Good luck, like a whore, decking itself up in self-importance and vainglory, embraced him. Rumour-mongers broadcast the news to the accompaniment of drumbeats: 'Padmalochan is flying high.' Almost as if on cue, lesser Brahmins, including agradaanis, assumed the roles of roving performers, spreading the word all over the place. Now the whole city was talking about Padmalochan being a highly influential man.

There were a few unemployed opportunists in the city of

Calcutta who liked to make friends with whoever was flourishing at a particular time. They proclaimed that this was the greatest man in the entire race and worshipped him, taking him to be unique. As soon as somebody with greater influence came along, they dumped the person they used to fete and sided with the new star that was rising. When I was young, my aged grandmother had told me a story about the rope for tying the hind legs of a cow while milking and the stick to beat it with. The great men we have been talking about were a lot like that. The story went like this. The Prince asked, 'Rope and Stick, whom do you two belong to?' The answer was: 'I belong to whomever claims me.' Hootum would say the opportunists among the city's people, similarly, 'belong to whomever claims me'.

The opportunists usually came from bhadralok families. Some of them were learned, while a few were ignoramus incarnates. Most of them believed in idol worship. There were several high-caste Brahmins and Kayasthas, unemployed people, **pension**-drawers and those who were **brokes** among them as well. After a long drought, Padmalochan made a name for himself as a famous babu of the city. It was almost twenty years since the city had seen the last of a 'babu-come-lately'. Therefore the opportunists, sycophants, *ustadjis* [i.e. musicians], and the sons of Bhars, Ghoses, Boses, etc.—those with no more than bovine intelligence who were, until recently, like excreta, being swept away in the tide—now found a resting place in Padmalochan's prayer decanter.

The opportunists managed to puff up Padmalochan. They made a neat packet too. Padmalochan became **ambition's** slave. He lost his ability to tell right from wrong and, behaving like a debtor, went into hiding. When he returned to the theatre of domestic life, he had donned the mask of a sworn Hindu. He would consume the dust off a Brahmin's feet by licking them. He encouraged groupism and stirred controversies in Hindu societies. He behaved like seasoned **blotting paper** when it came to holding performances [of a slightly lewd nature] involving women.

Padmalochan was now a tremendously mighty man. His drawing room was filled with Brahmins and professors. Like the way the government had gathered **volunteers** indiscriminately at the time of the Mutiny, having attained babudom, Padmalochan too left no Brahmin pandit untouched while amassing them. He managed to put together a diverse array of strange creatures—on the lines of The Asiatic Society Museum[7]—including some live ones!

The wicked and the evil-minded among the Bengalis could not do the world any harm unless they also had money in hand. When wickedness and money came together, it would be possible to kill an elephant. Padmalochan, too, egged on by the suggestions given by a few vicious people, turned unpleasant. Criticizing all and sundry, running people down and mocking them became his major preoccupation. Ultimately, all this went to his head so badly that he began to think of himself as the incarnation of a divine being. The people who kept him company proclaimed he was a God incarnate and praised him continuously. His detractors gave him the sobriquet, 'Sudden Incarnate'. Ordinary bhadraloks, who had been watching the show, were struck with wonder and started **clapping.**

Padmalochan had actually started believing that he was either Lord Hari or a Muslim prophet or a future **messiah** of the Jews. To be a success [at playing God], he even tried staging a few miracles.

Jesus Christ of England[8] had fed a hundred people with a single piece of bread. He would cure the blind and the lame by blowing on their wounds. Lord Krishna, too, who was a Hindu God, had performed miracles such as slaying Putna, the demoness and breaking the bones of Shakat.[9] To establish his claim of being a God incarnate, Padmalochan spread a few myths about himself across the city. These included: 'he had managed to feed a hundred people on food that was meant only for twelve', 'the blind and the lame stood by his door all the time, awaiting the magic touch of his lotus hand, embellished by a clasp with motifs of a flag and a thunder-shaped hook engraved on it' and 'old women come with little children so that they could be blessed by the gentle stroking of his fingers'. The great men who ran schools for little children began dancing like vultures at the time of an epidemic when they heard these rumours. So great is the power of money that even the sea that is a treasure trove of jewels is shaken all over when pulled by the mighty moon, let alone lesser entities! How many of the variety of flies, beetles who come out in spring and droning bumble bees—the sort one sees in a confectioner's shop—would you expect to find in a bookshop? All that you get there are flimsy termites, inert cockroaches and a couple of immature and insolent mice.

Even a puff of ganja cannot match the kind of high that a sudden windfall might provide. So there was little chance that Padmalochan would remain satisfied with the title of 'Sudden Incarnate'. Soon Padmalochan became one of the major Hindu icons of the city. When he yawned, a thousand fingers were clicked in response, when he sneezed, the collective sound of people wishing him a long life volleyed through the room. There would always be a huge chaos of people saying, 'Hail Master', 'O Master', and 'As you wish, Master'. Ultimately, the major clubs in the city were told that Padmalochan was an addition to Calcutta's **natural history**.

Gradually, Padmalochan began making a goodly sum of money by various means. He bought a new house in keeping with his status. The relatives and sycophants present at his court went about collecting the objects and elements required by a rich man about town, and, in the process, filled both the babu's coffers and their own pockets. The babu personally (his eyes knew gold when they saw it) chose a mistress for himself. A kept woman was a part of a rich man's accoutrements. Some of these rich men might have died long ago, but the houses they built for their mistresses still stand like memorial **monuments**. The two-or three-storey houses built for these women were just about the only significant event in the lives of these men. There was nothing much else that the public might remember them by. Many sworn Hindu leaders and descendents of different royal families who lived in Calcutta never saw the faces of their wives at night. Just as the chief managers, accountants and advisors looked after property matters on their master's behalf, the task of looking after the masters' wives too, they felt, was vested in them, and there was no reason why they should give up the chance! Knowing this trend, a few clever zamindars locked their wives in the inner chamber while they were having fun out in the drawing room with their mistresses. It was only when the guns were fired and daylight was about to break that the mistress left in a palanquin, the babu went inside the house to sleep and the wife was released from being locked in.

Some of the younger babus, still afraid of what the parents might say, asked a servant or a peon to sleep in their bedroom when they went out to have fun. The servant bolted the room and lay on the floor. The wife made use of tulsi leaves[10] and lay in bed. The babu returned home, satiated, after midnight and knocked very softly on the door. The servant opened the door and walked out. The babu went to bed. Nobody else in the house knew that the babu did not sleep in his room at night.

Readers, it should be hardly a surprise that those who had not heard of anything called 'morality' since they were children, whose connections with the ability to tell right from wrong were extremely tangential and those who were guided by a bunch of sycophants should behave like animals engaged in vile practices. It was because of these great souls that Calcutta became a city of prostitutes. Every neighbourhood seemed to have a cluster of at least ten whorehouses. The number of whores here seemed to be increasing by the year. Indeed, it was difficult for an ordinary householder to live next door to a rich man if the former had a beautiful wife or daughter. For the lovely lady, tempted by the promise of money and comfort, was likely to pour cold water on the family honour in a short while. Until the day the beauty in question actually satisfied the babu's heart's desire, the babu was seen either on the terrace or in the balcony, round the clock. He would be smiling, or making lewd gestures, brandishing a bunch of currency notes.

The sycophants too had a tough time. They were saddled with the burden of an immense task until the day they actually presented the chosen lady to the babu. Like the nawabs of yore, the babu might order the sycophant to be buried alive, with his wife and children in the same grave, in case he failed.

Ultimately, after the virtuous wife or maiden had been violated and turned out of the house, the only way left for her was to sell her body in the market to earn a living. And that was not all. Some of the rich men in the city were so debauched that the inhuman monsters' hunger for sex was not satisfied by merely sleeping with their wives and mistresses. They turned to sisters, nieces, daughters-in-law, indeed any young woman in the household. A lot of virtuous women drank poison to avoid falling into the grasp of these criminals.

We do know that there would be an abortion a month[11] in the houses of some of the rich men. And that the credit offered for buying the periodic supply of salt and oil extended to buying roots of the red lotus, leadwort twigs and oleander bark as well.[12] Factionalism, backbiting, stirring up of controversies and spreading canards against a decent person were most pronounced in those very circles where they tried showing off an excessive adherence to the rituals of the Hindu religion. Under the surface this society was stark naked, but it wasn't easy entering it from the outside. You would be hassled at every step.

Alas! Was there any greater regret than seeing that those men who possessed immense wealth would not put their hearts and souls to improving the welfare of their own people and society? Instead they revealed horrible vices. It had been a hundred years since the English arrived, but had our situation changed at all because of that? We still followed the affluent ways of the nawabs. The same old back-pleats, wrung tight [to give it a crinkly look], pleated shawls, shoes tapering at the toe and hair arranged in layers were still in fashion. The middle class had changed to an extent, but our masters, the rich men, were just the same. We had thought that sudden affluence would create rich men of the **refined** sort, setting a precedent. But Padmalochan's example dashed our hopes completely. Padmalochan became something of a 'shroud-stealer's son, the wedge-driver'. [According to a proverb,] while the shroud-stealer only nicked the dead person's garments from the grave, his progeny would add a finishing touch to stealing [by driving a wedge through the dead body's anus].

Since the time Padmalochan kept a mistress, he stopped seeing his wife. The wife found her own pastures to graze in. Four sons were born to Padmalochan, either because of his having co-habited with the wife on earlier occasions, or because of her own expertise.

The elder son was now grown up. Talks were on to celebrate his wedding with due pomp.

Everybody started preparing for the elder son's wedding. The matchmakers,[13] both male and female, went knocking on doors, looking for a suitable girl. It was not easy to find a combination of 'kulin's daughter, exquisitely beautiful, who would bring home a dowry worth Rs.10'. After a lot of girls were considered, short-listed and checked out, the granddaughter of Atmaram Mitra, who lived in Agdom Bhom Sinha's **lane** in the city, was the lucky one; her marriage flower had blossomed.

Atmaram, who was a leader of the Hindus, had made good money. His family was as large and extensive as the clan of Ravan.[14] He had seven sons, who were employed, five lovely daughters, fairy-like, and approximately forty grandchildren. Besides, there was a crowd of nephews, sons-in-law and relatives, swarming in his house. Therefore, Atmaram, who was a vastly qualified man, was chosen to be Padmalochan's in-law. A written agreement was made between the two parties at the auspicious hour, with much fanfare. The wedding date was fixed. The assembled Brahmins were given their dues in keeping with their stature. The messengers and matchmakers happily thanked their employers. It was going to be a grand wedding. A major rumour was circulating in the city: Rs.500,000 would be spent on Padmalochan's son's wedding. Gopal Mallik had spent a huge amount of money on his son's wedding, but this was going to be bigger.

The countdown had begun. The great day approached fast, catching one unawares. And then it was imminent. The musicians arrived at the house where the wedding would take place. Bhattacharjee, the head priest, started complicated discussions with his followers. Thirty thousand pairs of shawls, iron bangles coated with gold and saris made in the looms of Dacca were distributed among more than two hundred thousand Brahmin pandits. A pair of shawls, gold-coated iron bangles,[15] saris from Dacca, sweet-scented dry kaddak blossoms used to add flavour to cooking, and roses were sent as gifts to rich men's houses with the invitation. Some of the recipients happily accepted the gifts, while some of them said, 'Are we drummers or musicians that we should accept shawls?' But Padmalochan, since he became the Sudden Incarnate, had, like Lord Ram,[16] become oblivious of who he really was and therefore did not pay heed to all that. Only the followers, sycophants and wedding organizers said [of the intended recipient], 'Unlucky fellow, he's missed the gift.'

The nautch girls began their show. Liveried servants put on silver bangles and red badges made from fabric and went around. The wedding organizers discussed hiring a military band from Fort William. The tailors, concentrating fully, were busy stitching up the groom's clothes. There was a lot of hurrahing and chaos all around. Half the population on the road seemed to be draped in red shawls gifted by the babu. While it was a practice to give old shawls to drummers and musicians at a wedding, even the bhadraloks of Calcutta found themselves wrapped in red because of Padmalochan's son's wedding.

The 12th of Poush [a day at the end of December], a Saturday arrived. We have already said that the rumour: 'Rs.500,000 was being spent on Padmalochan's son's wedding' had been circulated all over the city. Therefore huge crowds of people began to gather on the streets from the afternoon on the wedding day. The guards had great trouble making way for the carriages to pass. The groom's procession came out in the evening. First, chandeliers made of paper and base metal, shaped like the five digits of one's hand, were carried along on either side of the road. Next in line were the palm-shaped variety, and the ones that tapered upwards, step by step, like a pyramid. Two mobile bands of musicians preceded this army. A tableau followed. A **gate** opened out to a raised platform and a hill made of paper. The figures of Shiva and Parvati, Nandi, the bull, Bhringi, snakes, trees of all kinds were placed on the hill. Behind these were barges, with hulls shaped like horses, elephants, ostriches and peacocks. On each of these were twelve rowers, men and women dressed as merchants and two drums. Shongs, dressed up as European and Arakanese dancers, performed on raised platforms around these. Behind these came a hundred drummers, forty kettledrum players and about sixty large drums and ultimately a whole orchestra, playing on shehnais, drums and horns. A band from Chuna Gully, playing indifferent English music, followed a little later. In between walked the babu's sycophants, Brahmin pandits, followers, relatives by blood and marriage. They wore identical shawls, wrapped a handkerchief around the head and carried a **stick** (one might have mistaken them for **disarmed** soldiers from the East India Company's forces). On either side of the procession lamps in glittering containers of mica, wrapped in red silk, were being carried. Badge-wearing porters and small boys held silken flags tied to silver poles. The groom's father passed by in between, with the family's spiritual advisor, priest and the finest among the pot-bellied Bhattacharjee Brahmins and relatives who were particularly intimate. A little behind them rosy-cheeked men played as part of an English band, followed by impersonators dressed as English soldiers on horseback. Next went the groom's yaars, the chief of the gatemen, the **head** butler and, ultimately, the groom, who sat on a silver *sukhashan.*[17] Bell-shaped lamps were lit around the seat. Chandeliers were planted in ten silver pots in front. Two boys stood on either side, wielding the fly-whisk. In the rear the groom's trunks and cases were carried, followed by the family barber, some elderly housemaids sporting gold jewellery, and a few dubious people as well. A row of horse-drawn carriages carrying the groom's party followed. Almost each of them had a servant who sat on the roof, holding lamps with twin bulbs.

The sound of band music, drums, big and small, and kettle-drums coupled with the din raised by the crowd and the cries of the wedding organizers in the procession reverberated through Calcutta, making the city shudder. People in another part of the town hurried to their terraces, thinking there must be a huge fire somewhere in the city. The windows and balconies of the houses on either side of the road had filled up. Prostitutes gushed about the groom's looks, 'My, my, the boy is as lovely as the moon.' Hootum, the night owl, observed the events from above and collected material for his *Sketches.*

Finally, the groom reached the bride's house. The bride's father greeted the groom's party with due honour. The elderly opium addicts and wayward young men who lived in the neighbourhood surrounded the bride's father, demanding money to hold a village party where drink would flow.[18] The groom reached the marriage hall and settled down. The messengers recited poems. Women peeped from the balcony.[19] The matchmakers recited the genealogy of the Mitras and the Duttas. The Mitras were kulins. Therefore their family genealogical tree had been drawn up, in keeping with what's jokingly called Ballal Sen's registration system,[20] only the Dutta's family tree needed touching up.

Both the groom's and the bride's parties had their fill of the wedding feast and left. The groom was taken inside the house for the wedding rituals to be conducted by the household women. A low stool with *alpana* designs drawn on it in white was placed under the canopy, specially erected for the ceremony. Four banana trees were planted around it. The groom stood on the stool, cowering, as if he had come to steal. The women greeted him, with paan, a specially decorated tray, a husking tray with small earthen cups on it, signifying bliss, and earthen wick lamps. The blowing of conch shells and ululation livened up the house. The married women, including the mother-in-law, circled the groom seven times. The mother-in-law handed the groom a spindle, saying, 'Hold the spindle, boy, let's hear you bray.' The groom, who was in college, had been eyeing the married women and mentally apportioning Sri Lanka,[21] so he said, 'I did, silently, in my mind.' At once the wives of the brothers-in-law boxed his ears and the sisters-in-law tweaked his cheek. Finally, when the rituals involving jaggery and rice, other mumbo-jumbo and administering of remedies, and so on, were over, the bride was brought to the venue to be given away. The holy verses were recited, according to the scriptures. The bride was taken. The priests and Brahmin pandits collected their plates of sandesh and left. The groom was led to the *basar*.[22] A basar is the ultimate place to have fun. I may be an elderly man now, but when I remember the fun I had on my wedding night, I start craving for more; indeed, I wouldn't mind getting married all over again.

The Moon went down as the tempo of fun and games at the basar ebbed slightly. [The Sun] He, the Lotus's sweetheart, dropped his vigorous persona to adopt a more soft image and appeared again [in the lake] to court the piqued beloved. The

Lotus was amused to see the miserable state of her lover, aflame with desire. The birds cried, 'Fie, one seems to lose all sense of one's surroundings when on heat.' The Wind giggled. At this the Sun got angry and came out, shining with all his might. It scared the birds, who flew far away. People at the marriage house began preparing for *basibiye:* the post-nuptials' ceremony. The bride and groom were smeared with oil and turmeric and bathed under the banana trees. The special welcome tray was put to use, and after some more rituals, the ends of the groom's and bride's clothes which were tied up in a knot during wedding rites, were loosened.

The groom's party and his relatives had begun to arrive, one by one. Late in the afternoon the bride and groom were taken back to the groom's house with great pomp, just the way the groom was brought in the previous day. The groom's mother welcomed the new bride into the house. A cauldron full of milk was placed on a stove near the door. The bride was asked, 'What do you see my dear?' and told to respond by saying, 'My home is overflowing [with prosperity].' The bride repeated the words, silently. After this, a few housewives performed some more rituals and finally the bride and groom had some respite.

The chaos around the wedding subsided, somewhat. The drummers guzzled country liquor and entertained themselves. The organizers were such staunch Hindus that they only had a large sweetmeat each, the sort that was put on top of the pyramid of goodies offered to Goddess Durga, washed it down by drinking a pitcher full of the holy water from the river Ganga and lay down in bed. The bride and the groom slept away from each other. Since this was *kaalratri*—the ominous night—the mistress of the house decreed that it was forbidden for the bride and groom to sleep together.

A winter's night didn't get over easily. One slept in fits and starts, went out for a pee and then came back for another bout of sleep. Then the guns fired [and it was morning]. The women went to bathe in the river, chattering all the way, raising quite a din. The elderly Brahmins, the pandits, took a dip and went their ways, chanting the praise of Lord Shiva. Padmalochan came back home from the prostitutes' quarter. He had much to do today.

Generally, Padmalochan would leave the kept woman's house at seven or eight in the morning. But today he had had to leave earlier. We have already explained that many sworn Hindus, even elderly leaders, had a kept woman each. Some of them visited the 'temple' after ten at night, to return only in the morning, chanting the name of Lord Hari, after they had bathed, applied sandalwood marks on the forehead, read their *Gita Govinda* and draped themselves in ceremonial silk. If one saw any of them suddenly, without knowing the background, one might have thought that the gentleman was back from a dip in the holy Ganga. Some of them summoned their beloveds to their residences. Having spent the night in their company, the men then packed them off towards dawn, went for a bath and engaged in the morning rituals of daily worship, behaving as if they had no links whatsoever with their night-time persona. This was Padmalochan's style as well.

The relatives and in-laws arrived. The sycophants began their job of pumping up the babu's ego by saying, 'Master, Calcutta has not seen a wedding as grand as this, and won't again ever.' A little before evening, the gifts to mark the *phoolsajya*—the newly-weds' first night together—arrived. Padmalochan welcomed the servants and maids who had brought the gifts from the bride's house, giving them a rupee and a sari each, before they left. Some of the gifts were distributed among the relatives and followers of the babu. The drummers and impersonators [who had formed part of the procession on the wedding day] were given a bonus payment. The housewives in the neighbourhood, who got a share of the edibles, packed them in pots, which were hung from the ceiling. Most of these would get stale and rot, nibbled on by rodents and cats. But the women could neither eat the food themselves nor have the heart to share it with others. That was how most rich men's wives usually were. They could not bring themselves to share the food with others, even if these were rotting in the kitchen. No matter if, finally, when it was completely rotten, the whole thing was flushed down her highness's drain.

Some of the babus had a similar bent of mind. Around sixty goats were sacrificed on the ninth day of the Durga Puja at a rich man's house in the city. Traditionally, the meat would have been distributed the same day, sent to the babu's followers' and relatives' houses. But, nowadays, as soon as the sacrifice was over, the meat was packed off to a storehouse. It was only past the next full-moon day, after the puja-related chaos was over, that the meat would be sent to different houses. Reader, you could well assess how tasty the meat that would have been rotting for six or seven days might be. In fact, the recipients of such gifts would have to pay to have the meat removed from the house. I have talked about a certain 'leader of the idiots'[23] before. He was the man who indulged in such practices.

Now that the chaos around the wedding was over, Padmalochan was back in business. He never failed to observe the usual Doljatra, Durga Puja and the thirteen other festivals[24] held during the twelve months of the Bengali calendar. Even when it came to observing [something as mundane as] Ghentu Puja,[25] Padmalochan would organize an offering of sweets and hire an amateur theatre group to perform. Besides having a puja at his own home, he would also sponsor pujas that were observed with similar pomp at the homes of his mistress and about a dozen other distinguished Brahmin loyalists. Before his son's wedding he had married off forty other unmarried kulins who had lost their status.[26] With the predominance of English education, the coming of Rammohan Roy and the fact that religion was now being seen in the light of truth, the Hindu religion had fallen on hard times. Padmalochan put his heart and soul together and pledged to remove this [malaise].

Neither he nor his sons ever tried working towards the country's welfare. He never donated any money for such purpose. Indeed, he did not contribute a paisa to help the affected people the year there was a terrible famine in the north-west.[27] When people approached him with a proposal to contribute towards the country's welfare, he would label them as either Christians or atheists and drive them out. A hundred wayward Brahmins and two hundred sycophants lived off him. And that's how Padmalochan's family came to be known across the city as great and sacred.

Being educated or encouraging people to be educated was not part of the family tradition. For generations together, they had held on to the steadfast belief that knowing how to sign one's name was good enough to manage one's property and wealth. The family had no links whatsoever with Saraswati, the Goddess of Learning, or the practitioners of literature. No other moneyed man in the nineteenth century had worked as hard for the cause of the Hindu religion as Padmalochan did. And, in fact, given the times that we live in now, it did not look like anybody else would show such sincere effort in that direction. He was an orthodox practitioner of Hindu rituals, and a fierce opponent of good work. Talk of widow remarriage made him plug his ears. He did not allow his sons to learn English, as he feared they would be tempted to taste forbidden food and convert to Christianity. He did not let them learn any Sanskrit either, out of an intense hatred for Ishwarchandra Vidyasagar, and also because he was well aware of the fact that the low-caste Shudras[28] were not allowed to learn Sanskrit. Therefore, Padmalochan's sons remained, like him, 'chips of the old block'.

Padmalochan, who was engaged in many such unprecedented activities for a while, died at eighty. Ten days before he died the Sudden Incarnate felt a pain all over his body. The pain grew more intense and ultimately confined him to bed. Being a sworn Hindu, he was dead against medical treatment. Since childhood he had believed that medicines had alcohol content. So the widely famous practitioners of Ayurveda were called to conduct all sorts of treatment, but to no avail. Finally, his relatives, after consulting physicians, carried him to the bank of the river Bhagirathi. He stayed there for three nights, atoned for his sins with a lot of grandeur and passed onto death in a conscious state, chanting the names of the Lords Ram and Hari.

Reader, you have, by your good grace, travelled a long distance with us. You have not only found out about the character of Padmalochan: the chap who was born and died right in front of your eyes. [You also got to know about] many of the rich men in this city who are like Padmalochan's doubles, some even better than him. It would be pointless praying for the country's progress when the rich men in the country were dangerous and vindictive. The very people who were supposed to lead the country towards progress behaved worse than beasts at all times. They had taken the poisoned path by choice. Even burning in hell-fire was not good enough a punishment for their bad deeds.

Those working towards the country's welfare must engage in correcting the characteristic traits in these great ones, before they looked closely at the state of the nation. Else, however much you care for and wish to improve the state of Bengal, your prayers would not make sense.

Babu Tekchand Thakur, the author of *Alaler Gharer Dulal*, says, 'Drunks come in many forms in the city.' But I would say, 'It's the city's rich men that come in varied forms.' Each babu was a unique specimen of sorts. We have discussed the archetypes in the sketch on 'Charak' [Sketch 1]. Now we might discuss these at length. On the top of the heap is the sworn Hindu. The nature of sworn Hindus who live in style has been revealed in the sketch on the 'Sudden Incarnate'. It is these great ones who fiercely resist **reformation.** They are like a thorn that brings disaster in the way of Bengal's good fortune and are a pest in society.

[Reader], in the course of writing this sketch I have revealed a bit about myself.[29] As you and I grow closer, I shall keep appearing intermittently, between the colourful sketches, dressed like a shong. You are free to clap and laugh to your heart's content.

Notes

1. An atur ghar, or labour room, would be secluded from the rest of the house since birth was seen as something polluting. The newborn and the new mother would remain there for three weeks after the birth when they would be allowed to take a bath and enter the household.
2. In rural Bengal, infant mortality rates were quite high in the nineteenth century (and remain so even now in Calcutta's public hospitals, although the reasons might be slightly different). In a nineteenth-century atur ghar, often the mother was under-age and malnourished, and made to give birth in extremely unhygienic conditions, assisted by quacks. The eighth day of the child's birth would be celebrated by calling young boys from the neighbourhood. The children would beat at and destroy the husking trays and chant rhymes wishing the infant a healthy life and cursing the ancestors so that they may not take the newborn back too soon. Eight varieties of roasted beans would be distributed. See Arun Nag, ed., *Sateek Hootum Pyanchar Naksha* (Calcutta: Ananda Publishers, 2008): 270-71.
3. A dead cow's head is one of the items necessary for the rituals to be performed in honour of Goddess Shashthi, the deity presiding over childbirth and health. In certain parts of rural Bengal the cow's head would be placed in front of the door of the atur ghar, where the delivery was taking place. Ibid.
4. Joykrishna Mukherjee, the unscrupulous and tyrannical zamindar referred to earlier in the book; see Sketch 2, p. 89, note 23; and p. 103, note 96; Sketch 9, p. 246, note 9.
5. Managers would usually have to be cash rich to start with, since they had to deposit a reasonably big amount with the merchant house as security money and often provided capital to their European bosses. So Padmalochan's acquisition of the high post without capital to invest was almost unprecedented. Ibid.
6. Common Bengali adage, wishing a writer, in this case one who keeps accounts, all success in his profession.
7. The Asiatic Society was founded by Sir William Jones in 1784; the 'diverse array of strange creatures' whom Hootum compares with the assorted collection of people in Padmalochan's court, probably refers to the archaeological relics, geological and ethnological specimens in the Society's museum which were later moved to the Indian Museum. In other words, the people who graced Padmalochan's court

were veritable museum pieces, fit to be put up as rare exhibits. For the Asiatic Society, see Sketch 1, p. 38, note 41.

8. Jesus of Nazareth has been wrongly assumed to have emerged out of England. Christianity certainly received a major impetus from the British empire in the late nineteenth century. The earliest Christians in India were Syrian Christians of Kerala who are believed to have been converted by the apostle St. Thomas.
9. Shakat was the right-hand man of Kangsha, Lord Krishna's maternal uncle and chief adversary, whom Krishna killed by breaking his bones.
10. Tulsi, a species of basil, is traditionally associated with purity and virtue (see also Sketch 3, p. 156, note 77). In *Hootum* the term is probably being used to mean the opposite, insinuating that the wife may not remain as pure and unsullied when made to sleep in the same room as the servant.
11. Not all that far-fetched a comment. One of the major reasons cited by Vidyasagar at that time for advocating widow remarriage was that widows were targeted by lecherous men—often relatives and friends living in/with access to the same house. If widows were married, he argued, they would be spared undergoing abortions at home, which often turned out to be life-threatening. In support of his petition to the Legislative Council in 1855, Vidyasagar quoted a certain Major Wilkinson of Nagpur, saying the prohibition of second marriage of widows 'is highly impolitic and unwise' as, among other reasons, 'it inevitably causes a frightful amount of infanticides and abortions.' See Subal Chandra Mitra, *Isvar Chandra Vidyasagar: Story of His Life and Work* (Calcutta: Parul Prakashani, 2008): 185; for more on widow remarriage see Sketch 3, p. 147, note 34; Sketch 8, p. 233, note 12.
12. Three plant products used in performing crude abortions at home.
13. A practice that's still not completely outdated. Matchmakers visit the homes of young men and women, exchange information among the parents/guardians of likely parties.
14. A Bengali turn of phrase which suggests demon King Ravan's clan is unimaginably peopled.
15. The iron bangle, often coated in gold, is a symbol of the wearer's married status. Traditionally worn as a protective charm, it's also seen as a token of the wife's submissive bondage to her husband and marital family, according to feminist readings.
16. It's an allusion to reaching a state of extreme vanity and self-importance and generally losing a sense of balance and informed judgement. In the *Ramayan,* Ram banished his wife, Sita, from

Ayodhya to gain popularity with his subjects. This was because there were whispers that Sita could not have remained chaste in Ravan's captivity.

17. A sedan, fixed on a pair of parallely running poles, concave in the middle, to be carried on people's shoulders, also known as a *tanjaam*. See Nag, ed. *Sateek Hootum Pyanchar Naksha:* 275.
18. The groom's party/father has to pay token money to various claimants on the wedding night to be able to take the bride home. These include members of the bride's immediate and extended family, even the people of her village who would often use the money to have a party. Ibid.
19. Women in affluent homes were not allowed to participate directly in the wedding rites, conducted by the priest, as they did not usually mingle with men. They watched from behind a screen from the balcony. It was only after the priest was through that the women got a chance to take the bride and groom to the inner chamber for some of the folk rituals, which too have been described by Hootum.
20. Ballal Sen is assumed to have regularized the kulin system (see Sketch 1, p. 34, note 11). The family priest of kulin households supposedly kept a record of the families the sons and daughters of the house had been married to, as a proof that one's kulinhood was well protected. But these documents could well be fudged, as in Padmalochan's case. Ibid: 275.
21. A character in the *Ramayan* would mentally divide up the territory of Lanka between the heirs, gloating over his imagined share, in other words, count his chickens before they were hatched. In this case, the young bridegroom meeting his female in-laws for the first time was trying to assess the kind of chances he might have with them.
22. After the wedding is over, the bride and groom retreat into a room in the company of friends and cousins for a night-long celebration of the event through song, dance and general merriment.
23. There is no prior mention of 'the leader of the idiots' in this text. The figure in question, the extremely affluent but supposedly rather naïve Joynarayan Mukhopadhyay, appears in an earlier edition of *Hootum's Sketches*. Ibid: 275-76.
24. A common saying about the fun-loving Bengalis who celebrate thirteen festivals in twelve months.
25. Ghentu or Ghontakorna, Lord Shiva's follower, is a folk god, worshipped to keep small children out of harm's way. Ibid.
26. It was very easy to lose one's kulin status, and equally expensive to

have a lapsed kulin married, as one had to pay huge penalties. That Padmalochan sponsored such weddings shows he encouraged the petty orthodox practices followed in a bigoted Hindu society.

27. A horrible famine raged across present-day Gujarat, Rajasthan, Punjab, Delhi and Agra in 1861. Kaliprasanna contributed generously to help the victims. Jyotirindranath Tagore writes in *Pitrideb Sambandhe Amaar Smriti* (My Reminiscences about My Father) in *Prabasi,* Magh 1318 (mid-Jan to Feb 1912): 389-90, 'Once there was a major famine in the northwest. A meeting was held at the Adi Brahmo Samaj on that occasion . . . I remember Kaliprasanna Sinha immediately took off his very expensive wrapper (probably a shawl) and donated it.'; see Brajendranath Bandyopadhyay, 'Kaliprasanna Sinha' (Calcutta: Bangiya Sahitya Parishad [1940], 2007): 52.
28. In other words, Padmalochan did not mind being counted among the Shudras by not learning Sanskrit, because he preferred being backward and uneducated.
29. There is, in fact, not that much of an autobiographical element in this Sketch. These are more pronounced in Sketch 4 which was part of this Sketch in the earlier edition.

6

Sailing to Mahesh

GURUDAS GUIN was a **mate**, a skilled craftsman employed by the Shearwood Company.[1] He drew a monthly salary of thirty rupees, besides making around another ten rupees from the cuts. Gurudas owned a house with a tiled roof in Champatala. His family comprised an elderly mother, a young wife and a widowed aunt.

Gurudas was a big spender. He earned decent money but could not hold onto it for long. Sometimes [the monthly salary would be spent] even before the month was out. Jewellery and other valuable articles had to be pawned as a result. In the month of Shraban, just before the hilsa fish arrived in the market, Gurudas would spend two months' salary to celebrate the ritual of stone-throwing. The no-cooking festival was celebrated with great pomp in the month of Bhadra,[2] and quite a packet was spent celebrating the pithe festival as well.[3] Now it was time for the Snanyatra festivities.

Snanyatra was the ace among the festivals, the ultimate in enjoyment. Therefore Gurudas busied himself in hectic activity. He did not have any time left to bathe or eat. He acquired a few yaars to accompany him on the journey. There was constant talk of the kind of fun they would have at the festival. Unfortunately, Haladhar Bag of Champatala who, with Motilal Biswas and Haradhan Das, a **bosom friend** of Gurudas, was arrested in a theft case and sent to jail for two years. Moti Biswas had fallen inside a well in a drunken state, and broken both legs. And Haradhan, who was [wanted for not paying up] his debts, went away to Forash-danga [Chandernagore, French territory]. Without them the festivities did seem incomplete, but there was no way one could give this annual entertainment a miss. So Gurudas, even as he was really sorry [for his missing friends], began preparing for the festival.

The yaars deliberated on what they would need for the occasion. Gopal quickly rented a barge. Nabin, the perfume trader, offered to organize perfumes, anise, rum and ganja. Braja placed an advance order of aubergine and other vegetable fritters. Gurudas himself collected other items like drug-laced paan, candles, light-strong tobacco, and so on.

Earlier, the Snanyatra festival was celebrated with great pomp. Influential babus would hire **pinnace**, motor-driven and other **boats**, and barges to sail to Mahesh. A regatta would take place on the river Ganga. Post-Snanyatra, khyamta and baiji dances would be performed all night. But nowadays there was no such entertainment. Whither Ram and wherefore Ayodhya?[4] Only the [nouveau-riche] carpenters, bell-metal workers, blacksmiths and spice traders continue to organize some of the festivities. A few zamindars from Dacca would intermittently observe the festival with the grandeur that was its due. And sometimes, young lads newly inducted into babudom would have fun on the occasion.

The appointed day arrived fast. Gurudas's yaars reached his house early in the morning, all dressed up and ready to go. Gopal wore a pair of red **stockings**, a green shirt with big brass buttons and a Dacca-style woven wrapper, with floral motifs embroidered on it. He also wore a brass ring imported from England that would be used like a **seal**. Only he had not managed to pick up a pair of shoes from the shop because of the hurry and therefore was barefoot. The embroidered Dacca-style wrapper that Nabin wore had not visited a laundry in a while, and looked slightly soiled. But the dhoti he wore had a four-finger-wide black border, and was worn for the very first time that day. The short coat too was absolutely clean. Braja, a young man, had only recently found a job in the [ship] **yard** and did not have the time to organize decent clothes. He wore the dhoti and wrapper his grandmother had bought him for nine quarters last Durga Puja. Since these still had the raw, unwashed finish, he did not look all that bad. In fact, the **set** of clothes he wore was as good as new. After all, he had not worn them too many times: once on Saptami day when he visited Gokul Dan's house to see the idol,[5] and again when he went to watch the immersion, on the way to the grand baroyaari puja held at Haatkhola, and later, to a jatra performance by Gopal, from Orissa.[6] At other times, the clothes were stored inside a pot hung from the ceiling.

Seeing his friends, Gurudas got up from the bed and came out to sit on the porch. Nabin, Gopal and Braja squatted down, leaning against the poles. Gurudas's mother brought out the flint-stone, pith, a cake of charcoal dust and a dirty looking box of tobacco. Nabin struck the flint-stone, lit a fire, ignited the charcoal cake and readied the smoke. Braja brought the hookah kept inside a well. Everybody had a puff. Gurudas went for a wash after the smoke. Suddenly, a heavy spell of rain came jangling down. The frogs in the courtyard jumped upwards, landing on the porch. *Thop, thop,* they went, skipping along the way. Nabin, Gopal and Braja watched the fun. Nabin began singing a popular number: 'Who are you, calling me, a self-styled gypsy woman?'

Rain in the monsoon is as fickle as a man's fortune. It comes and goes, all the time, without rhyme or reason. And then it stopped. Gurudas finished his ablutions and asked his mother to serve breakfast right away. There wasn't any food ready to serve at home, excepting *panta bhaat,* tamarind and fish from the previous night. Mother served the food in four earthen cups. Gurudas and his chums ate this frugal meal, treating it with high respect.

Earlier, they had decided to set sail with the evening tide. But given that Snanyatra was one huge fun-filled festival [of which nothing could be missed] and the fact that sailing with the evening tide would get one to Mahesh only after noon on the festival day, now they decided to start at the time of the morning tide.

The clock on the church steeple went *toong tung, toong tung.* It was ten in the morning. Nabin, Braja, Gopal and Gurudas finished their meal, had paan and tobacco, collected their belongings, chanted the name of Goddess Durga and set out on their way. Gurudas' mother asked him to buy a fan and two large rattan baskets. His wife had asked for a painted pot, a piece of waistband

and a doll the previous night. And the widowed aunt wanted a jackfruit with big, juicy sections in it, bananas that looked like the flute of Lord Krishna and aubergines, which Gurudas promised to get.

He was not too badly attired. He wore a fine, embroidered wrap, worth not less than Rs.40. Only there were slight damages in places where bits of wood were stuck [to hold the embroidery in place]. He wore an English-style long red shirt and a **blue half-Chinese coat** on it, and a dhoti with the words 'Long live Vidyasagar, may you live for ever' woven in the border, custom-made at Shantipur. His shoes had silver buckles.

Gurudas and friends reached Prasannakumar Tagore Ghat. Others—Kedar, Jaga, Hari and Narayan—were waiting there for them. Together they boarded the barge. The boatmen were eating a meal of rice, dry fish, chillies and dal from a cauldron, and the tide too was at a low, so it would take them a while before the boat could sail.

The yaars wanted to have fun from the moment they stepped on the boat. Gopal surreptitiously uncorked the square-shaped bottle containing the hibiscus-red liquor. Braja sat down to prepare a round of ganja. The red liquor began to disappear in the usual way, the fried balls of gram flour and aubergines followed like loyal and virtuous wives. The group was in high spirits. Narayan and Kedar broke into a song, to the beat of the tabla.

'Smile while you can, as much as you like it.
You never know when you'll kick the bucket,
Who'll live in your house, ride your car.
Your watch will adorn a different pocket,
That moon face of yours will be incinerated.'

Braja, having taken a puff of ganja, sat stiff, watching the fireflies. Gopal and Gurudas were delirious with joy.

There was tremendous excitement in the city, and a huge rush among the pilgrims readying to make the trip. Old women, pint-sized wives, the sari drawn over their heads [and covering the face] *kalabou*-style,[7] and wide-eyed young women whose saris had slipped from their bosoms, filled up the roads, to watch the Snanyatra festivities. It was difficult making way for carriages and palanquins. Not thinking about the kind of load horses of hackney coaches could possibly drag, there was a struggle to squeeze as many people as possible inside the coach and at the rear. There were ten inside a coach, two on the roof, two in the driver's cubicle, which makes fifteen [including the driver] and three infants, just out of [confinement in] the atur ghar as a bonus. Stay-at-home women mingled with elder brothers, fathers-in-law, husbands, brothers' wives and mothers-in-law. By the good Lord Jagannath's grace, Mahesh today had turned into a local version of Vrindavan, the pleasure garden. Quite a few of the travellers were expected to don the mantle of Lord Krishna.

The river Ganga too was heavily decked up. The [stretch near the wharf] was thick with boats, barges, pinnaces and motor-driven large boats. Spells of laughter, drunken speech and the noise of loud jokes rose from each of these. A khyamta performance was on in one. Around thirty sycophants, totally intoxicated by alcohol and drugs, made merry. In the middle was [a boat in which] the zamindar of Mymensingh and Dacca courted influential government servants and acquaintances whom he called uncle. He spoke in a nasal tone, like a little boy. In appearance he was like the huge pitchers, produced in Dacca: an enormous mannequin, with a body like a large leather-bound vessel to store oil. He had applied black dental cleansing powder on his teeth, wore a good-luck charm on his arm and a necklace of *rudraksha* beads, with around ten amulets, shaped like small drums, hanging from it. He wore a girdle around the waist, a diaphanous dhoti and the sacred thread bunched up around his neck. He was well over sixty but pronounced 'Ram' as 'Aaum', 'Brother' as 'Braundther' and 'Uncle' as 'Aumcle'. It was people like him who called themselves the propagators of education from Rangpur,[8] practised tantric rites, guzzled alcohol and performed puja till four in the afternoon. I doubt if many among them had seen the sun rise since they were severed from their mother's body at the time of birth.

A group of city-bred neophyte babus passed by in a pinnace.

Their English speech could have made Lindley Murray[9] turn in his grave. There was a lot of adulteration in what they sang as well.

In another boat was a babu who could not afford more than the most frugal way of performing the last rites of his forefathers and hence did not have a mistress or sycophant accompanying him. He travelled with a cousin, a nephew and a younger brother. There were no drums nor paan spiked with drugs. Indeed, there was not even a flat-bottomed hookah in the boat. But such was his enthusiasm and spiritedness that he hummed a tune, [marking the rhythm] by beating on the wooden planks of his boat. At any rate he wanted to take the holy dip and cleanse himself of impurities. It did not matter if the exercise cost him tremendous hardship.

Coming back to our protagonist, Gurudas, the boatmen of his barge had finished their meal. They would set sail once they had offered *namaz* at noon. Suddenly Gopal said, 'My dear Gurudas! We are having the ultimate fun, doubtless, only it seems a little incomplete. We've got everything. It's just that celebrating Snanyatra is not quite done without a woman on board. Now it's up to you to decide.' 'Right you are,' said Kedar, at once, taking the cue. Narayan said, 'All the boats I can see are stuffed with women, it's only us who are looking like vegetables, it looks as if we're off to Gaya to offer sustenance to our dead forefathers.'

Gurudas was in such an intoxicated state that he exclaimed, 'You are right, my friends. I have been thinking the same thing. Go get a whore, commit as much money as they ask for. I don't care how much it costs. Gurudas means what he says.' As soon as they had heard this, Narayan, Gopal, Hari and Braja were ecstatic. They asked the boatmen not to release the boat from the jetty yet and stepped out to look for a woman. Gurudas and the rest of the gang sang raucously,

'You will go across the Yamuna, O my wanton one,
Have a good time at Rishdha's wharf, check out the shops,
Will buy you shampoo and a fine girdle at Baruipur,
You will satisfy us all, O my priceless one.'[10]

The carpenters who worked in the yard of Mackintosh and Burn Company had hired a boat and were having fun and games with the prostitutes as they passed by. They recognized Gurudas and cried:

'Sush, don't say a word, O nephew, Kanai,[11]
You graze cows, till the field, but there's more on your mind.'

They sang, hurrahed and mockingly threw the name of Lord Hari across as they sped past Gurudas's barge. Gurudas and his mates yelled, 'Boo!' and clapped, mockingly. But the lack of female presence in his boat, indeed, created a sense of emptiness. The crowd in the other boat continued to cry 'Boo!' and clap, embarrassing Gurudas and company immensely.

By this time Gurudas was even more befuddled with drink, and, therefore, in no mood to accept the fact that the people on the other boat had mocked them and gone ahead. Finally, he could wait no longer and went out to look for women himself, still reeling [from the effect of alcohol]. Kedar and the others sang:

'Come here, come O Makar, O fish in the Ganga water,
Rose will be married tomorrow, and we'll go fetch the water,
We'll take her by the hand and give her a fond caress,
She'd dance the khyamta with the veil on,
jangling bells on her toes.'[12]

They waited for Gurudas to return. He was gone for an hour now. After a while, Braja and Gopal too were back. They had scanned the city across its length and breadth but failed to pick up a tart. None of their sources remained untapped and none of the unattached whores were left to be checked out. Hearing the news, Kedar struck his forehead and dropped down. (When Joykrishna Mukherjee went to jail, his subjects were not this sad. When Ravan showed Sita Lord Ram's severed head in the Ashoka Garden, was she as miserable?[13]) He began a song of lament, waiting for Gurudas to return.

'Whose bird is this that lived in her heart's cage?
Go, my dear, grab it quickly, in love's cage,
Which woman kept the bird, whom did it deceive?
Whose perch did it leave, its movements are hard to gauge.'

Gurudas returned. He had thought that while he might not have found a woman his friends surely would have picked up one or the other. The yaars, on the other hand, thought while they might not have been able to find a whore, Gurudas would not return empty-handed. Returning to the boat, when he found there was no woman, Gurudas was extremely sorry but since intoxication has its victims completely in its power, he did not lose one bit of enthusiasm. Gurudas assured his friends and went out a second time to look for women, but did not know where his wish might be fulfilled. Probably the thing that had him in its power—the one whose dictates he followed—would have been able to say where Gurudas went. Seeing him go out again some of his friends followed. Only Kedar, Narayan and Braja, who remained in the boat, sang.

'The night is on its way out, alas, what to do?
The absence of Shyam will kill me too.
Look the moon has gone down, my friend,
The lotus is smiling, the moon is pale,
Will my beloved return to court me once again?'

The boatmen kept nagging them, 'The tide will ebb soon [now's the time to set sail].' The tide did indeed make more room and receded, like money from a spendthrift's pocket. The friends found themselves in the middle of unmitigated trouble.

Gurudas went around the city once more. He visited Sindurepati, Sovabazar and Siddheswaritala[14] in Baghbazar as well, but did not find what he was looking for. Finally, he went home.

We have already mentioned that Gurudas had a widowed aunt at home. Gurudas reached home and told her, 'Aunt, you must promise to do something for me.' 'What is it, dear Gurudas? Can

I ever deny you anything? But first let's hear what you've got to say,' said the aunt. Gurudas said, 'It would be very nice if you could come with us to the Snanyatra festival. Everybody else is taking a woman or two, how can we go without one? I don't mind not taking a woman but my friends are not too keen to do this trip like hermits. We will have fun on the way. You've just got to be there. No one would say anything untoward to you.' Aunt was reluctant at first, but wanted to join the trip in her heart of hearts. Ultimately, unable to stave off the very sincere requests by Gurudas and his cohorts, she went with them.

Gurudas reached the wharf with his aunt. The friends on the boat hurrahed and chanted the name of Lord Hari to see him come with a woman. They played on the *bnaya* as if it were a large drum. Finally, as soon as everyone was up on the boat, the anchor was lifted. The boatmen put all their might into it and rowed fast. The one at the hull held tight, often moving it forcefully, with a jerk.

Gurudas and his friends sang in a chorus:

'Lord Hari's sailing on the Yamuna in his love boat,
How could the cowherd women not leave their
 homes and hearths?
He sits beneath the Kadamba tree, the crooked flute vibes,
He simpers and makes eyes, seducing other people's wives.
Hurrah, ho, ho, ho.'

The boat flew like an arrow released from the bow.

Many among the wealthy had set sail at the time of the noontide. But now the high tide had lost its force and the ebb tide took over. The boats that were anchored or tied to poles on the bank were suddenly turned around. Fishermen, riding boats, started hauling up the nets they had laid in the river. The boats [going to Mahesh] had to stop where they were. The dinghy belonging to the babu of modest income and other boats and barges were anchored in the **port** area. The boat hired by gold traders tried getting ahead by staying close to the bank, testing the waters as they went. They would stop for a snack at Panihati,

Kamarhati or Khardah and sail on to Mahesh.

The sun went down. Evening, like a woman seeking her beloved, went looking for Darkness. Nature, her dear friend, gave her a bouquet of flowers to aid her in her lovely pursuit, getting herself invited to the nuptials in return. The Wind blew gently, fanning to give her relief from the stress of travel. Cranes and teals flew in droves. Dusk, the hour when the partridge meets its mate, arrived, to fill the world with more happiness. Alas. Such are the strange ways of the world that certain things, even when they bring great sorrow to an individual, might mean sheer bliss to many others.

Darkness behaved like wayward young men in the country who hide themselves inside broken old Shiva temples and abandoned houses on the roadside, beside ponds and inside bushes before women go to bathe in the pond early in the morning. He had so far been hiding inside locked rooms, wells and earthen pitchers containing water. He came out when the conch shells announced the presence of Evening. Seeing his fearful image, the Lotus, scared, bent her head down in keeping with her characteristic ladylike sense of decency. But flirtatious young women were difficult to control. The Water Lily, for example, was all smiles. The boats anchored along the riverbanks enhanced the beauty of the Ganga in a way that was difficult to describe. It seemed as if Ganga were dancing, wearing a necklace of lights around her neck. The waves, driven by the motions of the wind, kept the beat, like a tabla playing. A pinnace was anchored a little further down the canal at Bally. The babus had a good time under the moonlight on the terrace. A variety show went on without pause. The charming view of the Ganga, the soft wind and the light swinging movement caused by the waves inspired the feeling of instant renunciation—the sort one would feel when taken to the cremation ground—in some of the members. One of them was so moved by the ambience that he sang:

'Whoever wants to may go to the river, I am not going.
When I went bathing, the dark one beneath
  the Kadamba tree
Winked and said, "Put a garland around my neck, Radha".'

A boat anchored somewhere just now. The babu went to the terrace. His followers brought up the rear. One of the babu's satellites asked the boatman, 'What's this place called, Chacha?' The boatman saluted the babu and said, 'This is Cossipore, Master. And that one's Ratanbabu's Ghat.'[15] Sharing this information was a prelude to asking for a tip later on. Once they heard the word 'ghat', the babus began staring at it, wide-eyed. A lot of women—daughters and wives—had come to bathe at the ghat. When the babus started ogling, laughing and cracking jokes, most of these women stiffened out of fear and shame. One or two, however, made a sincere effort to show that they were willing to be taken. This was the big lucky moment for the sycophants. Toady Number One ran through the gamut of notes in a raga [a few times] and sang:

> 'Loyal to you, I live by your good grace,
> Please do keep this request of mine.
> If there's something else I owed you,
> I would have scooted,
> But now to pay you back I must die.
> Now it all depends on you.
> Please make sure it's justice you do.'

The elderly who had come to offer their evening prayers, little boys and women without anything much to do, stood at the wharf, in groups. Now that there was greater encouragement, the dogs in the manger yelped. The hogs that were grazing were so frightened that they stopped rummaging in the litter, grunted and ran right back into their sty.

A barge was anchored in front of the jute mills at Baranagar. The wayward young men of the village were so tickled to see the kind of fun the babus were having and the women who accompanied them that they too entertained themselves by chucking small pebbles, mud and chunks of earth at the barge. The blinds on the windows facing the riverbank had to be pulled down. Perhaps there was more trouble in store.

A houseboat moored in front of the new jewel of Rani Rashmoni[16] [the Dakshineswar Temple]. The women inside peeped to have a look.

Gurudas, our protagonist, however, was still stuck near the pole at Baghbazar. One could still hear the playing on the bnaya. Most of the people still hanging around here were the liquor and anise drinkers. The anise and rum drinkers who went inside were coming out, folded in half from waist downwards. Consumers of snacks and drug-laced paan had disappeared like Gods do after giving people a boon. Some of their prayers had already been answered. The widowed aunt, overcome with affection, was using the loose end of her sari, to fan [members of Gurudas's company]. The boat was plunged in darkness.

Suddenly there was a spell of heavy rain, and a confusing wind blew, rocking the boats. The boatmen covered their heads with the sail and pieces of sackcloth. It was almost past midnight.

Even before it could sink in, the night of pleasure was over. The Rising Sun arrived, wearing the Morning Star like a jewel in its hair parting. The Moon was having fun in the company of the stars, but seeing the Sun come out he suddenly turned wan with embarrassment and started trembling. The Water Lily pulled a veil over her face. The East had cleared up. 'The tide's up, again,' exclaimed the boatmen and set sail. All the boats sailed towards Mahesh and Ballavpur in a row. The revelry continued on the boats. In one of them someone sang in a cracked voice:

'The night is still not over, why do you want to go?
Stay a while longer, till the night's passing is due,
If it were really past, the cuckoo bird would coo,
The water lilies would go to sleep and
 the moon would go back too.'

A few of the boats were as silent as **coffins.** The sound of weeping rose from one and that of inebriated groaning from another.

The boats sailed, the tide gathered more force and the

fishermen began to immerse their nets close to the river bank, on either side. The laundryman's carrier ass—who was a **true copy** of the rich men's sons in the city, appeared on the scene. The Brahmins took their early morning bath. Men and women abandoned all sense of shame, raised their garments to squat and defecate [along the river bank]. The vegetable sellers took their barge to Baidyabati and Serampore. Boatmen ferried passengers across the river for a quarter or half a paisa. The Muslim mendicants, followers of Badar and Dafar Gazi, went around begging in a dinghy. The Lotus bloomed happily as she saw the Sun rise. Only the Hilsa fish gasped, turned and tossed with trepidation and died. That's the fate of people who are jealous of another man's success.

The babus who had a garden house in Khardah, Panihati, Agarpara, Kamarhati and similar places on the bank of the Ganga were celebrating with a lot of pomp as well. While many had observed yesterday as Saturday, some of them would consider today a Saturday[17] as well. Yet others had organized a continuous celebration; there was no end to creature comforts and the supply of liquor. A few of the garden house owners had their boats ready for a regatta match. The game would cost them a thousand rupees. For a month, animal fat was being rubbed under the boat to make it paddle faster. Red jerseys for the rowers, with badges carrying a replica of the zamindar's coat of arms stuck in the front and back, were in place. The yaars who lived in the village, the local babus of Khardah and other bhadraloks, were present. The man at the centre of this was probably Mahinder Nafar [who rose from the ranks to become], a **cabinet-maker** in the Chinese market. He was a man of very fine tastes, one with an unlimited range of favourite passions.

Some of the travellers reached Mahesh, some stayed put inside the boat and some just climbed onto the upper deck [for a good view]. A sea of people had accumulated at the venue. The space between the raised podium and the riverbank thronged with people. Shops of all kinds had come up in the middle of this thick crowd. The beggars laid out a piece of cloth to sit on and beg. The vocalists sang. Vaishnavite musicians, who played on *ananda-lahari, ektara,* cymbals and small drums, made good money. The sound of people hurrahing combined with the dust in the field and the heat to make a fine piece of sweetmeat. A lot of the spectators willingly [put themselves through the ordeal], eager to get a taste of what was much like the Delhi laddoo.

It was noontime. The sun threatened to burn one's head. Dunking one's towel, handkerchief, wrapper and ultimately torso in the water was not enough to escape the heat. The image of Lord Jagannath sat on the podium with a face like the Moon's. But the Water Lily was in no mood to respond to that lunar face. She was really miserable [because of the heat and the storm], like a fisherman's boat, tossed between the waves in a cyclone.

It was nearly one in the afternoon now. But Lord Jagannath was yet to get a bath. Unless the 'revered' zamindars from the village of Dosh Anna arrived, Lord Jagannath would have to await his turn. For some reason or the other, the zamindars had not yet arrived. The crowd, totally exhausted, filled up the shady area underneath the trees nearby, the mango orchard and the porches of neighbouring houses. Quite a few suffered sunstroke. A few of them kicked the bucket and quite a few began to hallucinate. Discarded shells of tender coconut and watermelon strewn across the ground gave it the look of a battlefield. People got noisier and almost everybody was restless. Finally, there was a buzz that the babus had arrived. Immediately, pitchers full of water were emptied on the idol's head, and the pilgrims' trip was made worthwhile. The stock of parched rice, curd, puffed rice, of the salty and sweet variety and succulent bananas disappeared fast. Even the stylishly dressed babus ate here. A lot of them had had their fill of fun and therefore did not need to eat at all.

After the people had rested a while and the clock struck three and then four, the regatta began. All the boats were let loose to see who could beat the rest and pick the flag. Obviously there was only one team that finished first. People got together to congratulate the winner and tease the losers by clapping [irreverently]. Snanyatra celebrations were over. Now everybody was homeward bound. It became consistently warmer as they sailed closer to their homes. The boats went past the sugar factory at Cossipore and the Bally Bridge. Some of the pilgrims got down at

Prasannakumar Tagore Ghat, some at Baghbazar or Ahiritolla. Everybody looked grief-stricken, their faces wan. Quite a few needed help to disembark. The excitement over the last four-five days of non-stop entertainment had died down. We failed to locate Gurudas's boat in the chaos during the return journey.

Notes

1. Well-known manufacturers of wooden furniture, catering to the high-end market.
2. Variations of the same ritual associated with the worship of Manasa, the Serpent Goddess; the stove would not be lit on the auspicious day and instead people would consume fruits, milk/curd, puffed/parched rice/grains.
3. A celebration to mark the event of bringing the harvest home after a year's toil on the fields; the new rice would be ground and mixed with milk and molasses extracted from the date palm trees to make dumplings of all shapes and sizes.
4. A Bengali adage lamenting the loss of an earlier 'golden' age. King Ram's reign in the mythological kingdom of Ayodhya in the *Ramayan* was supposedly one of unmatched bliss and prosperity.
5. For Gokulchandra Dan, see Sketch 2, p. 87, note 9. Birkrishna aka Shibkrishna was adopted by Gokulchandra, a self-made man who built his fortunes from importing iron-ore and hardware from Europe. He was a prominent patron of the Durga Puja and other festivals.
6. Gopal from Orissa came to Calcutta in search of a living as a young

man. He began as a fruit vendor but was soon inducted into a theatre company, Vidyasundar. He made his mark by playing the role of the female lead Malini in the play *Vidyasundar,* and later founded his own group, once again called Vidyasundar, borrowing the name that brought him immense fame. See Subodh Chandra Sengupta, ed., *Samsad Bangali Charitavidhan,* rev. 4th ed., Part 1 (Calcutta: Sishu Sahitya Samsad, 2002):136; see also Sketch 2. p. 97, note 68.

7. Kalabou is a manifestation of the Goddess Durga in the form of a banana tree, covered with a sari to give it the semblance of a human form. The sari end is drawn well over her 'face' and 'neck' to give her a submissive look. See Sketch 8, p. 233, note 15.
8. The zamindars from Rangpur were known to be enthusiastic about education. Arun Nag feels a zamindar from the Kakiniya family of Rangpur is being hinted here. See Arun Nag, ed., *Sateek Hootum Pyanchar Naksha* (Calcutta: Ananda Publishers, 2008): 278.
9. Lindley Murray (1745-1826) was a grammarian, born in Pennsylvania but lived in York, England. He published an *English Grammar* (1795), *Reader* (1799), and *Spelling Book* (1804), used in schools, widely and exclusively. Murray is often referred to as the 'father of English grammar'. See Paul Harvey, ed., *The Oxford Companion to English Literature* (London: Clarendon Press: 1960): 544.
10. The song describes a downward journey along the river Ganga (now Hooghly), rather than the Yamuna, which is invoked purely because of its association with the tales of Lord Krishna's dalliances with women in that river flowing past Mathura/Vrindavan. The sisters Shyama and Bama of Rishra were well-known *panchali* singers who sometimes also doubled as shopkeepers, cashing in on their popularity to sell their ware at an enhanced price. See Nag, ed., *Sateek Hootum Pyanchar Naksha:* 278-79.
11. Referring to Lord Krishna/Kanai's secret affair with Radha, the wife of his maternal uncle.
12. This khyamta number has resonances of a popular khyamta song used in the play *Lilabati,* written by Dinabandhu Mitra. The expression, 'dancing a khyamta with the veil on' is a much-used Bengali adage suggesting 'committing gross transgressions under cover'; ibid.
13. In the *Ramayan,* the demon king Ravan knew the art of creating illusions. After he had abducted Sita, and held her in the Garden of Ashok Trees, he would try different tricks to break her resistance. One of these was to show her a faux head resembling Ram's to prove that her husband had been slain. Sita, of course, had strong faith in Ram's

superior skills as a warrior and would not be taken in. For Joykrishna Mukherjee; see Sketch 2, p. 103, note 96.

14. These are three hubs of the flesh trade in mid-nineteenth century Calcutta. Sindurepati is at north of Rabindra Sarani-Mahatma Gandhi Road crossing, The Siddheswari temple is near Kumartuli, slightly north of Rabindra Sarani and CIT Road crossing.
15. This bathing ghat is to the south of Cossipore Burning Ghat. Ramratan Dutta Roy (1785-1860) of Nadhail had it constructed. Ibid: 280.
16. The Kali temple was founded by Rani Rashmoni in Dakshineswar in 1855. Rashmoni was born into a poor peasant's family and because of her great beauty, was married to the immensely wealthy Rajchandra Marh. After her husband died she inherited great wealth, which was used for the social uplift of the poor as well as for charity. The Dakshineswar Temple was controversial. The Brahmins opposed laying the foundation stone for the structure as Rashmoni was a low caste by birth. But the project went through, eventually becoming an institution where devotees across castes and religion would be welcome. See Sukanta Chaudhuri, ed., *Calcutta: The Living City: The Past,* vol. 1 (Calcutta: Oxford University Press, 1990: 61).
17. Saturday was the day to have fun/go wild before the more sombre Sabbath day arrived. Therefore 'fun' days would be labelled Saturdays.

7

The Chariot Festival

Gentle people! On the bare canvas of my nature,
I paint the characters
With a flavour of mystery—by the grace of Goddess Saraswati
Look at it with kind eyes, and make a judgement,
Giving me what you have in excess—reward or censure.
I would take either respectfully, as I bow down to you.

NOW THAT THE Snanyatra-related fun was over, Gurudas Guin dropped his embroidered wrapper and went back to his tools: the smoothing plane and jackplane. In a few days, Rathayatra, the chariot festival, would take place. This chariot festival was tremendously old-fashioned and boring. There was nothing frivolous about it. This was probably why the city did not see much of a pompous celebration when it came to the Rathayatra festival, but trust the people of Calcutta not to pass up an opportunity [to make merry].

Chitpore Road swarmed with people on Rathayatra day. Young boys put on **burnished** shoes, and dhotis woven in the looms of Dacca with borders designed as a tribute to the rebel soldiers of Sepoy Mutiny, tied handkerchiefs around the waist, and flicked back their hair. Holding on to the servants' hands, they stood on the covered sewer, in trader's shops and porches in the marketplace to see the chariots pass by. Middle-age women loitered around on the road in groups, wearing clothes that were brand new and starched.

Clay idols of Lord Jagannath, jackfruits, whistles made out of palm leaves, fans and toy birds, made of pith, sold fast. Taking a cue from children, grown-ups too played on the palm-leaf whistles. A loud blowing of trumpets was heard, rising like a storm. The chariot was ushered in by people playing on bells, drums, cymbals, chanting the name of Lord Hari and making a huge din. At the forefront were the timekeepers, flag-wielders, drummers and the band of Vaishnavite singers. They were followed by groups of mendicants, singing indifferent kirtans. Amateur hymn singers came behind them, performing. The chorus walked under umbrellas made out of circular palm leaves, as big as the thatched roof of an outhouse, fanning themselves as they went. The organizers sweated profusely, quite exhausted. Some of them were hassled, trying to coordinate the flag-bearers and the group riding on horseback. Some were at a loss, trying to fix the fans. The hymn singers stopped under balconies, at four-point crossings and in front of the square; locations where they were likely to find an audience, to perform. The prompters, who carried the verses, written on slips of paper, yelled out the words, flailing their arms from behind. Only the chorus seemed to make any sense of what they sang.

There was a drunk in the crowd of spectators. He was overwhelmed with devotion at the sight of the chariot and sang, in an inebriated voice:

'Is it you, the chariot, my mother?
Rotating wheels and nails all over.
Two wooden horses in front,
A burnt-face right on top.[1]
Ringing bells and fly-whisks
Lord Krishna sits in the midst.
Godly images on sides all,
People pull and wheels roll.
The shades in front and at the back
Serve well the flirting pack.'

Having finished the song, he bowed down, 'Chariot, my mother.

Let me touch your feet,' he said, doing the same. The chariot ambled on, going its way. By the time a few more of these chariots have passed, it was evening. The porters who ignited the street lamps running on gas show up, carrying ladders. The time allotted by the police [to parade the chariots on the road] was almost over. The spectators began to go home.

True, Rathayatra was not celebrated as grandly as Snanyatra at Mahesh was, but the celebrations that did happen were not altogether negligible.

Now that the chariot's annual trip and the return journey[2] were over, the stone-throwing ceremony in the month of Shraban, no-cooking in Bhadra and the day of Lord Krishna's birth [had all been celebrated as well], a number of potters began making the basic framework for the Durga idol. They moved to the client's house, applying one, two and finally three layers of clay on the frame, one by one. Frogs that inhabit the fields began to sing a welcome song for the Goddess: croak, croak, croak, they went on. Monsoon left the scene, having had a taste of mango stones, jackfruit fibres and the discarded parts of the palmyra fruit. Durga Puja arrived in no time.

Notes

1. It could be a burnt-face monkey perched on the chariot's steeple.
2. The biggest festival observed by Vaishnavites is Lord Jagannath/Krishna's annual visit to his aunt's place. Idols of the Lord, in his truncated limbs avatar, and siblings, Balaram and Subhadra, are taken to their aunt's place on a seven-day trip at the end of which there is a return journey.

8

Durga's Day

THE DURGA Puja, Bengal's very own festival, was not heard of or seen in the north or west of the country. I suppose the rampant celebrations in Bengal began at the time of Raja Krishnachandra.[1] Earlier, only kings and people born into old wealth would hold a puja at their residence, but these days even the puny [and low-born] Teli could be seen bringing the Goddess home. The festival now was quite different from what it used to be.

As time passed the festivities were narrowed down to fewer days. The clay modellers from Krishnanagar could be seen squatting all over Kumartuli and Siddheswaritala. Wigs made of coloured jute, sequin-studded garlands of zari, swords and shields made of brass and tin for the Asur, and drapes for the Goddess, dyed in a variety of colours, were put on display. The tailors hawked caps, chapkaans and cummerbunds from door to door. Peddlers went around crying, 'Want to buy honey?' 'Conch shell bangles, anyone?' Traders out to sell saris from the looms of Dacca and Santipur, perfumes and play tickets, did not mind forfeiting meals and sleep. At the brassware shop, piles of madhuparka bowls,[2] pots and bronze plates were being weighed. More shops selling frankincense, spices and shampoo had mushroomed. Wholesale cloth merchants opened their accounts, making a substantial profit [as they work away] inside the near darkened shops, behind two layers of curtains. Sellers of tiny wicker baskets to hold vermillion, candles, wooden stools and grass mats seized the opportune moment, moving out of the shops on to the road and lining up, flaunting their ware, along the **aqueduct**.[3] The Bangals and men from the country employed in the city bought mirrors, *ghunshis*,[4] gold-washed ornaments and imported pearls indiscriminately. Hundreds of shoes made of rubber, comforters, walking sticks and long-tailed turbans were on display. These and glass bangles, rings made of imported gold, and guard chains made of horsehair were sold to unlikely customers. The shoe shops, which until recently were full of dust and cobwebs, were spruced up like new brides. Multi-coloured papers were stuck on the door using starch. Inside, chairs were laid out, over a piece of torn carpet. All the city shops looked rejuvenated, like crows in winter. As the first day of the festival approached and the shopping got more hectic, Calcutta began to feel the heat. Teachers who ran schools in the country [arrived in the city], scouting for subsidies and annual grants. The roads were crowded with all sorts of visages, personable and otherwise.

Murders, riots and burglaries took place all over the city. A cutpurse had robbed a Brahmin of two *bharis* of gold. Somebody tore a ring off a woman's nose. The guards were on the alert. The police force itself was full of rogues. The thieves had it all going for them in this festive season. They swore by maxims such as: 'Hit or Miss', 'Buy an Elephant, Make a Killing'.[5] Some of them were put behind bars and sent to Bencoolen.[6] The pujas were a time when some had the luck of making gains and some were unlucky and ruined. Gradually, Chaturthi,[7] arrived.

This year Durga Puja was being celebrated with great pomp in the new house of Babu so-and-so.[8] The ritual of giving gifts and money to Brahmin pandits, begun since the first day of the new moon, was in full swing. Brahmins swarmed into the house. The babu, clad in silk, sat on a mattress, one and a half feet high. On his right sat the manager, with bouquets of currency notes—rupees, half-rupee and quarters—and a register. Habiswar Nyayalankar, the pandit who presided over the assembly, sat on the babu's left. He inhaled snuff continuously and kept rubbing the watery phlegm—which had taken on the colour of snuff, and ran down his nose, dropping on the carpet. The jeweller, carrying pouches containing jewel-studded accessories, and a trader with his bundle of saris woven in Dacca had taken their seats. The clerks, sons-in-law and nephews were busy drawing up lists.

Brahmins saddled with Durga idols,[9] book dealers, proprietors of theatres and a few singing mendicants stood in front of the babu, trying to please him by saying things like 'As you please, Sir', and 'Your Lordship, after all, is Justice personified'. Occasionally, the babu would ask someone to sing an *agamani,* a song invoking the Goddess. Somebody tried flattery, small talk and badmouthing other rich men, a prelude to an entertainment programme for the babu. This man's ulterior motive was buried deep under the water in Dwaipayan Lake,[10] and would show up on the surface only at the opportune moment. Those dealing in perfumes, tobacco and horse-feed and moneylenders waiting to claim their dues were hanging around in the verandah. The festivities were halfway through but the bills had not been settled yet.

The presiding pandit makes a public show of striking off the names of the Brahmins linked with the house of Pirali,[11] those known to support the remarriage of widows,[12] and others belonging to rival camps from the list [of beneficiaries] with great flourish. Many of these [unwanted guests] touched his feet and swore that they had nothing to do with the house of Pirali; and that far from attending a widow's marriage ceremony they had lain sick in bed during most of the previous year. But their pleas were swept away, the way fishermen's boats toss and drown in a high tide. The pandit replaced the names that he had struck off with those of his own son-in-law, nephew, grandson-in-law and cousin brothers. The Brahmins who were dropped from the list abused the babu's forefathers and the presiding pandit. They tore apart the sacred thread [worn diagonally across their torsos] and hung it [from the ear, dangling] against their cheeks,[13] cursing as they left in a huff.

The hopefuls who had been steadfastly attending on the babu were dismissed with, 'Not today', 'Come tomorrow', 'No way', 'That's it for now, then', and so on. The babu clearly, employed extraordinary artifice which few noticed, caught up as they were in the pomp and show surrounding the puja.

Chaturthi was over. The morning of Panchami arrived. The confectioners began weighing the sweetmeats and sandesh with protruding tips, made especially for the puja. **Regiments** of he-goats were being **paraded** in the markets. The spice traders were quite exhausted, packing spices and shampoo in small containers all day. It was difficult walking the streets of the city and the porters charged a **premium** for carrying articles. The shops could not offer their customers a place to sit. That was how Panchami passed.

It was Shashthi; the last chance to round off the shopping and for the moneylender to prod his clients, the last occasion to hold onto hope. The babu's house was all decked up. The servants moved around, wearing new uniforms, complete with the household insignia. Pots filled with sacred water and mango leaves tied in a row adorned the door on either side. Drummers played in sync with the hired orchestra and shehnai, intermittently. The son-in-law and nephews, wearing new clothes, were seen strutting their stuff. In one of the drawing rooms, songs invoking the Goddess were being performed. In another a new pack of cards were shuffled. Beggars lined up. Those trying to persuade the babus to buy perfumes had been hanging around for seven days in a row, bottles in hand. But the babus were too busy to check out the perfume samples.

The city's markets and four-point crossings were crowded with drummers and musicians, making it difficult to inch one's way through. The main roads resembled a thick crowd of people. Gardeners sat beside the road, selling lotuses, *chandmala*,[14] leaves of bel and other small flowers from the make-shift shops they had set up. The roads were paved with earthen cups used for serving curd; sweetmeats and remnants of luchi and kachuri, chucked at random. Roving minstrels and folar-eaters like myself were keeping a **memo**. Where did all that food disappear?

On the evening of Shashthi, the idol was installed at the venue. The drums paused for a while. The Night of Shashthi was quite worn out by the spate of 'Bring that', 'Do this' 'What's that now?' bandied across the house in which the puja was being held. The Morning Star rose, riding a light breeze. The birds, seeing that it was dawn, began to leave their nests. At that moment music was heard all around the city. The organizers got busy with the ritual of bathing the Nabapatrika.[15] To the imaginative sort, it seemed that Saptami had arrived wearing a coarse new sari[16] and a smile on her face.

Kalabous from all over the city were on their way to the river for a bath, to the accompaniment of music, playing all the way. The boys of the household walked along, beating on metal plates and bells. The toiletries for the bathing ritual, kept safe in the babu's house, were taken out as well. In front of the procession walked the musicians, playing on drums, big and small, and the shehnai. Behind them came the gatekeepers of the house, wearing new clothes and carrying weapons, followed by the priest, who carried the Kalabou; his assistant, carrying the holy text; the Brahmin, who officiated in household ceremonies, the household guru and the pandit who presided over the babu's court. Behind him walked the babu. A huge umbrella, with a red satin cover hoisted on a silver frame, was held over his head. His nephews and sons-in-law walked alongside. The office-bearers, brothers-in-law living in the same house as the babu, sycophants and hangers-on followed. The gardeners brought up the rear, carrying the offerings, lantern, flower baskets, conch shells, bells, grass mats and other paraphernalia. That was how the babu took the Kalabou for a bath at the bathing ghat of Babu Prasannakumar Tagore. Once there, the babu too, as the Kalabou was being bathed and the rites performed, got a chance to bathe in the holy water of the Ganga and recited prayers. Once again music was played on the way back home.

Readers! A few educated members of the Young Bengal[17] in this city, having turned into slaves of idolatry, were now highly committed to observing the rituals. Instead of feeding the Brahmins, the friends feasted on rice and alcohol—as if it were the *prasad.* Their vivacious **female friends** got invited to the ceremony as well, as part of a **'refined'** new puja trend. In Hindu homes the money offered by invitees as a token of respect to the Goddess would go to the Brahmin priest, but here the host put the money in his own bank account. Imported lard served as fuel for the lamps and the guests were allowed to go up to the podium, where the idol stood, with their shoes still on.[18] The decorations, made to order, were imported from Britain. Mother Durga wore a bonnet instead of a crown and was offered sandwiches. The Kalabou bathed in boiling water poured from the kettle instead of that from the river Ganga. The same water, now made holy by the divine touch, was used to prepare tea and coffee for the host's breakfast.

Gradually all the Kalabous were bathed and returned to their homes. The puja began. The pyramid of offering, topped by a sweetmeat with a raised tip, was piled on a wooden platter and placed at the temple of Durga. A red silk sari, a plate of sugar, a pitcher, a sparkling pot and an iron bangle, coated in gold,[19] would be offered too, depending on what the host could afford. One might as well have replaced sandesh with molasses and the madhuparka bowls with earthen cups to cut down on the expenses.

The puja was done. The devotees, who had fasted all day, showered flower petals on the Goddess as part of the finale. The ladies of the house went inside to break their fast after they have listened to readings from the holy book of Chandi [another name of Durga]. For some people the night was still young.

The puja at the babu's was almost over as well. Preparations were on to hold the ritual sacrifice. The babu and his employees took off their shirts and stood in the courtyard. The blacksmith tightened his belt, picked up the scimitar-like knife, freshly consecrated and worshipped, stuck a blessed flower in the wedge of his ear and stood beside the sacrificial altar. One of the babu's toadies cried from his side, 'Hands off the post![20] Off it, I say!' Holy water was sprinkled over the sacrificial ram, whose head was then pushed inside the stocks and padlocked. One person grabbed its head and another pulled back the rest of its body. 'Hail Mother! Victory to you!' cried the blacksmith as he raised his weapon. The babus joined him in a chorus. 'Hail Mother! Mother dear!' they cried, turning towards the idol.

Chhop! The blade came down. Suddenly drums of all sizes and tambourines began to work up a vigorous crescendo. *Geeza, geeza, geeza, geeza, Nak tup tup tup, Geeza, geeza, geeza, geeza, Nak tup tup tup,* they played. After the blacksmith had collected the blood (and small bits of flesh, as well) in an earthen platter, the mouth of the goat's severed head was pressed shut and the body sent to the courtyard. One of the sycophants covered the earthen platter, carrying it very cautiously and placing it in front of the idol. As if borne by the waves of the loud music, the babus ascended the temple of Durga, clapping all the way. The offerings were in place, the lamps lit and now the *arati* [the worship with lamps] began. The babu himself began fanning the deity with a fine white fly-whisk, as pure as Ganga water. Smoke rising from incense sticks and resin pots had darkened the house. The arati went on for half an hour, until the conch shells were blown. Everybody, including the babu, bowed down, lying prostrate on the ground, and then went across to the living room.

In the courtyard the Brahmins fought over the food that had been offered to the Goddess. Saptami was nearing its end, even as one watched it go by. The rest of the day was spent distributing prasad, giving the beggars their due and serving snacks. In the evening the Chandi singers left, having livened up the party for a while. Jogai, the jeweller, used to be an expert singer of such songs. There had not been another authentic exponent of Chandi since Jogai died, one of the reasons being that it was difficult to get an audience for such songs.

It was six in the evening. The gas-lit chandeliers in the courtyard were ignited and the arati began. A cool evening snack for the Goddess [consisting mostly of fruits], and other paraphernalia were displayed on the courtyard and the raised platform where the idol had been placed. It did not matter whether or not Mother Durga was interested in the menu, as long as the visitors praised the display, the babu would consider his ten rupees well spent. The crowd swelled as the evening wore on. The country-bred types among the shop owners and prostitutes went around in groups to have a look at the idols, as did small boys and middle-aged chaps. The guests arrived, dressed fittingly for the occasion, one offered a coin to the deity: *tonaat!* it dropped on the floor. He bowed to her. At once, the priest put a garland of flowers around the donor's neck, picked up the coin and put it in his purse. The guest departed fast, without any more ado.

This seemed a bizarre trend typical of Calcutta. Just as thieves and blacksmiths rarely met, often neither did the guest and the host. Sometimes the priest would say, 'The babus are upstairs. See the staircase there? Why don't you go up?' But the guest, following the tradition of yore, said, 'No Sir, let it be. I must visit some more houses.' He parted with the money and was back in his carriage the next moment. If there were a chance meeting with the host, the two would nod at each other like geckos and that would be all. The sandesh and sweetmeats were left completely out of the picture and the question of offering paan or tobacco [to the invitee] did not arise. In fact, almost always, a hearty welcome was conspicuously missing. In certain households the host would be seated on a sequinned rug with elaborate patterns, pots of perfume and rosewater sprays displayed in front of him, much like small change piled up in columns at professional moneychangers'. In another, the guest would be too scared to penetrate the tumultuous drunken revelry in the living room, lest the host bit him. In yet another household the doors would be closed, the living room in darkness. The babu could be asleep or might have stepped out of the house. Not a soul was visible on the courtyard of Durga. The guest could not work out whom he might have as witness when he offered the coin to the Goddess or indeed what he ought to be doing. Even the deity would be embarrassed by the host's behaviour.

Nonetheless, there was no stopping these people from inviting guests over. Given the trend, a lot of self-respecting people had stopped attending such 'social' occasions. They would send a nephew or a son with money that was the priest's due or the amount pledged. But since I did not have a son and was unable to go personally, I decided to buy postage stamps and send the money by post. When it came to some of my relatives, I would have it sent by registered post to ensure that the money made a **safe arrival**. The bottom line was that the money must be reached, whatever the means. My puja convenor friends made things a lot easier. Once the puja was over, they took the pains to come personally and collect the money. My relationship with them intensified from the time they sent out invitations till the puja came to an end. In many cases, their coming to collect the money pledged to the Goddess was proof that the puja had indeed been performed.

Let us suppose that this babu of ours belonged to a family

having old wealth. It was his earnest desire to drape himself in a Benaras silk cloth and sit out in the Goddess' courtyard, in front of the raised platform where she was installed, with his fellows after the arati was over. Immediately, the badge-wearing guards unsheathed their swords and started a vigil. The postman, the hookah-attendants, the bearers sent by the babu's mistress and the lackeys stood there with clasped hands (there was no knowing what the babu might want and when). A golden hubble-bubble was placed in front of the babu. There was an emerald-studded flat-based hookah on his right, a diamond-encrusted, covered and tasselled smoking contraption on his left and a spiral tobacco pipe with pearl inlay work. The babu, like a dog in the manger, nuzzled this one and that as he pleased, keeping an eye on the crowd of useless people that had gathered in front of him, eager to find out which among these contraptions got the maximum praise for the craftsmanship that went into its making. The idea was to show off that there was no dearth of artifacts made of silver and gold in the babu's household. In fact, had there been a little more space, he could have displayed two more hubble-bubbles or spiral tobacco pipes. Gradually a lot of people—invited and otherwise—had gathered. The temple of Durga was now full of the dubious sort. The shoe-stealer, despite the presence of guards who moved around with unsheathed swords, managed to pilfer two baskets full of shoes. Like the tortoise which minds its eggs laid on the shore even as it remains in the water, many of the guests as they talked to the babu, sitting on the raised platform, kept an eye on their shoes. But by the time they were ready to go, they found that the pair had vanished like young tortoises breaking out of eggs [and creeping away]. Only a lone, torn sandal remained, like a broken shell.

Gudoom! The guns went off, taking people unawares. It was nine. '*Byom Kali Kolkattawali* (Hail Kali, the presiding deity of Calcutta),' the boys cried out. In view of the dance performance that evening, the host could no longer remain seated in the courtyard. He went to the living room to get dressed. All the gas lamps in the courtyard were ignited for the soirée. The babu's nephews, clad in tasselled caps and cummerbands, went around bossing everyone. Some of the invitees—regulars at such soirées—

had arrived and nautch girls had taken the stage. The babu appeared, dressed in zari, cravat and a myriad of stone-encrusted jewellery—like an Egyptian mummy. He sang with the courtesans to the accompaniment of a sarangi. Everyone in the assembly listened, mesmerized.

Let the invitees watch the dancing as the red-eyed babu cheered lustily, slaying kings and ministers with rhetoric. Dear Readers, please turn your gaze at the city, all decked up. Every house seemed to have its share of fun and revelry. Groups of people went around, checking out the houses where a puja was underway. The roads were overcrowded. Clusters of Marwaris, Biharis, women and yaars filled up the streets. Drivers steering huge lantern flashing vehicles, carrying the invitees to the venue, were raising hell, asking people to give way. They had a hard time steering their way ahead in the crowd. The goddess of sleep had fled from the places where amateur poets were in action, driven out by the drumbeats and the loud music. Every other moment a child sleeping on the mother's lap was jolted awake by the high pitched musical flourish. At panchali readings, wayward young men, pickled to the gills, were taking their turns at spouting rhymes as they indulged in self-congratulatory cheering and clapping. This would go on until the night would almost be over, ending with a fine paid to the cops. Somewhere a play was on. [The actor playing] Mani Gosain,[21] the comic relief, had the kids in splits. The women peered from behind the blinds. A huge torch had been lit. The foul smell of the lamp and that of the farting riff-raff made it difficult to remain in the arena. Even frankincense could not suppress that putrid odour. In certain houses the babus were entertaining themselves. Friends got together in the babu's drawing room where dancing mongooses, jumping frogs, khyamta dancing and a performance of *Vidyasundar*[22] were on the list. Each roar of laughter and jackal-like howl, ignited by the fire of passion, made the Goddess on the raised platform shiver in fear. Instead of attacking the Asur, the lion looked for an escape route, its tail between its legs. Lakshmi and Saraswati were all worked up. Outside, all the city roads were thronging with people, all its houses glittering with lights.

Saptami, Ashtami and Sandhi Puja passed. It was Navami, the

last day of the festivities.[23] The joy that had risen in people's minds like a tidal wave ebbed completely.

A couple of buffaloes—alternatively ninety goats, betel nuts, sugarcane, pumpkin, barbel fish or black pepper—were sacrificed in some of the houses. The host, completely drunk, got his friends to join him in the valedictory singing. They smeared each other with the mishmash of mud and sacrificial blood.[24] Drummers kept the rhythm. The courtyard turned into a sea of people. Women tried to peer [from behind the screens] to catch a view from the second floor. Smoke enveloped the house so completely in certain parts that it was not humanly possible to get in. Let alone beggars, even mosquitoes turned back from the doorway. Then, gradually the sun went down and the puja revelry was almost over for the year. At the hour of dawn, the Bijoya[25] song was sung in many houses, set to the tune of Raga Bhairavi. In the morning it seemed to devotees that Goddess Bhagawati [i.e., Durga], looked pale with grief. And then the celebrations surrounding the immersions began. It was time to submerge the Goddess in the river.

Soon it was ten in the morning. The idol was immersed symbolically[26] after an offering of curds and sweets had been served. Post-arati, the drummers began playing the beats signalling the hour of the immersion. The idols worshipped in Brahmin households were immersed early.[27] Those worshipped by the rich and low-caste people would be immersed with a lot of fanfare, all in keeping with police regulations.

In the meantime, even as one was engaged in this and that, the clock in the church chimed gently. *Tung tang* . . . it went. It was nearly noontime. The mellow heat of the sun sautéed the city lightly. Dust and sand rose in the wind that seemed to blow from all directions, creating a cover of darkness. With nothing to do, dogs lay down beneath the raised platforms in shops, beside the gutter, put out their tongues and panted. Bullocks pulling heavily-loaded carts were frothing at the mouth. The driver screamed abominably, 'These stupid bullocks do not seem to move,' he hollered, twisting their tails and hitting them with a club. But the bullocks could not be persuaded to change their pace. Wheels screeched under the weight of the load that was piled on, causing a lot of excitement on the road as the carts went by. Sparrows and crows sat on the verandah, under awnings and beneath the pipes, eyes closed. Hawkers went home, one by one. Hairdressers and menders of clothes had left a long time ago. 'Want to buy vegetables? Clarified butter, anyone?' the peddlers cried. The tobacco seller [had finished his round and] went back a while ago. 'Want to buy buttermilk, plain butter? Curd made from buffalo milk?' called the cream and curd-sellers who were on their way back home, counting the money they had made. Only hawkers appeared from time to time. 'Want to buy water chestnuts? Here, get cups and saucers, imported toys, utensils exchanged for your old newspapers,' they cried. The riff-raffs had departed. That was not counting the hands employed in houses hosting a puja—people carrying the offerings made to the Goddess on their heads, officiating priests, the *patuas*[28] and the drummers. *Goopus!* The gun went off with a dull thud. It was one in the afternoon. The preparations for the immersion of the Goddess began with due fanfare.

Alas, wasn't it the most auspicious day when idolatry arrived in this country? Having seen and heard so much and known what idolatry entails, we still find it painful and inconvenient to give it up. When we were children we played with dolls, pretended to be man and wife and married off our 'sons and daughters'. Now as grown-ups, we took the very same clay idols to be the ultimate God. Ecstatic when the Goddess came home, there was no end to our sorrow when we had to let her go. And it was not just us. There were quite a number of learned Bengalis who despite being well aware of the philosophy that this world was but temporal and was guided by the Supreme Being, gave in to the entertainment surrounding idol worship, egged on by society or family members. They wept at the time of the immersion, smeared themselves with mud mixed with [the sacrificial] blood and embraced each other. When one enlisted as an atheist and supposedly believed in the 'one and only Supreme Being', it was hardly in the fitness of things to get so excited about idol worship. I would rather such people went and sat in the forest.

Gradually the main roads and four-point crossings began swarming with people. The verandahs of brothels were full of eager candidates. The idols were out on the road, all fashionably attractive and accompanied by English music, flags held aloft, riders dressed as Turkish soldiers trotting on horseback and police sergeants. People were eager to find out who [among the Durga Puja hosts] received the maximum praise: 'Whose idol was the best?', 'Whose costumes were good?' and 'Whose accoutrements were the finest?' [they kept asking]. Unfortunately, nobody was interested in finding out 'Who was the most devoted?' And the puja organizers did not seem to **care** either.

Meanwhile, a big audience of what looked like bhadraloks, small children dressed in new clothes and schoolgoing boys had filled up Babu Prasannakumar Tagore Ghat. Some of the organizers raced their boats, still carrying the idol. Jovial men and young lads danced on the boats, to the beat of the drums. The babus who liked a bit of luxury came out and sat on the open terrace of boats, pinnaces and barges, to be entertained by the khyamta dancers and baijis. Their toadies and hired musicians began singing some of the colouful numbers, to the tune of *kobigaan*.

Fare you well, Ma Bhagawati,
 please do not come again to the city.[29]
Each passing day
 I find Calcutta displays a strange insensitivity,
The judges, honourable men,
 try dealing with utmost impartiality.
The dust on the main roads
 makes it impossible to walk without difficulty.
No crapping on the roads,
No drawing from the watercourse.
Paying licence fee and taxes is mandatory.
No filth to be left overnight in the lavatory.
The health officer, the latrine inspector and
The income tax assessor will be the undoing of everybody.
The governor has his eyes only on the filth,
 his behaviour quite queer.

I can't take it any more, Mother,
  I just can't go on living here.
That's how one has to suffer when alive, Mother,
There's little peace when one's dead.
No ritual setting fire to the funeral pyre,
  the incinerator now a necessity.
That's why poor Hootum is left hovering in the skies,
  having forsaken the city.

Meanwhile, even before one realized it, the sun went down, taking the puja revelry, which was over for the year, with it. Evening, the bride, appeared, wearing a raiment signifying separation. The organizers immersed the idol, released the blue-necked, white-breasted kites[30] in the air and went back home with pots containing holy water, as the music played in sync with the beat that seemed to repeat the words, 'Dear old bro, dear old sis'. At home, they placed the pots in the now empty platform, bowed down before it and had the holy water sprinkled on themselves to ensure peace and order in their lives. Later, they ate raw turmeric, drank the holy water and embraced each other.

The last day of the festival ended with writing the name of the Goddess on a banana leaf and drinking syrup made from hemp. The city wore a deserted look after days of great pomp and splendour. Those who believed in idol worship felt rather sad. For it was difficult to realize the value of good times even as one enjoyed it. It was only when one fell into distress that one could comprehend what a glorious thing happiness was.

Notes

1. Maharaja Krishnachanda Roy popularized Durga Puja festivities by adding grandeur and opulence to it after becoming the raja of Nadia in 1728, pioneering the trend of flaunting one's wealth, which his predecessors hesitated to do as they would have had to pay a bigger tax to the nawab if they did so. Krishnachandra also had a role in simplifying the puja proceedings with the help of the pandits in Nabadwip for the benefit of the huge crowd of spectators who would turn up at the festivities. See Arun Nag, ed., *Sateek Hootum Pyanchar Naksha* (Calcutta: Ananda Publishers, 2008): 281; see also Sketch 2, p. 90, note 33.
2. An oblation of honey, clarified butter, milk, curd and sugar, mixed together. Madhuparka, a small container meant to hold the mixture, also has a figurative sense, meaning anything that's small, fragile and might easily flop. See Sailendra Biswas, *Samsad Bengali-English Dictionary* (Calcutta: Sahitya Samsad, 2008): 834.
3. The aqueduct was a part of the water supply network of the city. 'A steam engine was installed at Chandpal Ghat around 1822 to lift unfiltered water into open masonry aqueducts for watering some important streets. The public tanks were also replenished in the summer in this way'. See P. Thankappan Nair, 'Civic and Public Services in Old Calcutta', in Sukanta Chaudhuri, ed., *Calcutta: The Living City: The Past,* vol. 1 (Calcutta: Oxford University Press, 1990); 225-26.
4. A small metal or stone medallion, worn in a string around the waist of a child.
5. Common Bengali aphorisms suggesting exploiting the opportunities presented by the moment to an optimum, in other words, 'go for the kill'.
6. A British colony on the west coast of Sumatra, under the empire from 1685 to 1824, where deported criminals may have been despatched to serve a term. Gradually the name began to be used as a metaphor, denoting, deportation or prison. Bencoolen was better known as a trade centre. The existence of a prisoners' camp is a possibility that has not been verified; Nag, ed. *Sateek Hootum Pyanchar Naksha:* 281-82.
7. Chaturthi, Panchami, Shashthi, Saptami, Ashtami, Navami and Dashami correspond to the fourth, fifth, sixth, seventh, eighth, ninth and tenth days of Durga Puja. Sandhi Puja marks the passage of the eighth day of the puja to the ninth. Dashami marks the grand finale,

also known as Bijoya, when the Goddess goes back to her heavenly abode.

8. Probably Babu Khelat Chandra Ghosh who had just moved into a huge new property. Ghosh was a leader of the anti-reformists; see Sketch 2, pp. 87-88, notes 13 and 16; Sketch 3, p. 157, note 83.
9. Often mischief-makers would, in the dead of the night, leave a Durga idol on the doorsteps of a Brahmin who was not particularly keen to have a puja at home, for lack of funds or otherwise. But with an idol thrust on him, the duty-bound Brahmin would have to go looking for a rich sponsor. Ibid.
10. See Sketch 1, p. 39, note 44.
11. Orthodox Hindus looked down upon the Brahmin households that were 'corrupted' after Muslim rule was established in Bengal, and mixed marriages (most often Hindu girls abducted from their homes and forced to co-habit with Muslim invaders) began to take place. These de-classed Brahmin families, shunned by the 'pure' Brahmins, were categorized, depending on the degree of corruption. The House of Pirali, to which Rabindranath Tagore's family belonged, was one of these 'adulterated' Brahmin families.
12. Supporters of widow remarriage would often be barred from influential orthodox Hindu households. For more on widow remarriage, see Sketch 3, p. 147, note 34; Sketch 5, p. 195, note 11.
13. Tearing up the sacred thread hung diagonally across a Brahmin's torso is a token of an extreme show of rage, when the wearer feels his high office and superior place in society is not being treated with due respect. One of the most memorable images of the Brahmin's self-righteous anger is in Abanindranath Tagore's illustration of the irascible sage Durbasha who cursed the love-sick Shakuntala who was too preoccupied with thoughts of her beloved Dushyanta to respond to his call. See Abanindranath Tagore, *Shakuntala* (Calcutta: Shishu Sahitya Sangshad).
14. Flowers made of cork, strung together, used to embellish the puja site and also dress up the Goddess.
15. A young banana plant and the leaves of eight other plants are tied together and wrapped in a sari to create the form of a veiled woman. The nine forms of Goddess Durga are represented by the leaves. In other words, Kalabou symbolizes Goddess Durga herself, who is taken out for a ceremonial bath in the river before the five-day puja begins; see also Sketch 2 and note 7 above.
16. Sari made of raw cotton fibre, usually with a red border, the sort

women wear while helping with puja rituals.

17. For Young Bengal, see Sketch 2, p. 95, note 58.
18. Traditionally, it is the norm to take off one's shoes before entering a temple/platform where the idol is kept.
19. Worn by Hindu married women as a mark of their wedded status.
20. It was important that the ritual sacrifice went off smoothly, i.e., the severing of the head from the body must be accomplished with one swipe of the blade. The fellow from the enemy camp who did not want that to happen would be standing in the vicinity, touching a post or a bamboo lath to make his spell work; ibid: 283.
21. See Sketch 2, p. 96, note 63.
22. See Sketch 2, p. 97, note 68; Sketch 6, p. 212, note 6.
23. See note 7 above.
24. In nineteenth-century Bengal, after the animal sacrifice on the ninth day of the Puja, members of the host family would smear themselves with the bloodstained mud and sing obscene numbers. See ibid: 283.
25. See note 7 above.
26. The symbolical immersion, which also indicates the end of the puja rites for a year, is done right on the raised platform where the Goddess is worshipped, to the chanting of valedictory verses by the officiating priest. A small mirror is used to signify the waters, to which the idol would later be consigned.
27. Although by order of the British government the Sovabazar Rajbari idol was to be immersed first, Brahmin households would finish their immersions early in the day. Ibid.
28. Probably refers to the scroll painters of Kalighat, specially commissioned to narrate the story of Goddess Durga's victory over the evil Asura, by singing and describing a hand-drawn image, or a cluster of these, gradually unfolding the story in sequential order. Painted in watercolour, gouache or tempera on canvas and also cheap mill-made unglued paper for economy, the *pats,* which depicted society in Bengal, often came with subtle or pronounced Western elements. Certain stylistic and generic tropes were employed in these two-dimensional images: 'an abstract symbolism, a formalized structure and simplicity in composition. An interior scene was indicated by a stage-like curtain at the top and an outdoor scene by a tree . . . faces were shown frontally or in three-quarters profile.' Beginning with religious or mythological themes, the Kalighat patuas graduated towards contemporary social history, particularly the salacious stuff such as adultery, murder and women dressing up,

getting themselves ready, influenced no doubt by the pulp literature of Battala. See R.P. Gupta, 'Art in Old Calcutta: Indian Style', in Chaudhuri, ed., *Calcutta: The Living City:* 139-40.

29. Arun Nag quotes Mahendranath Vidyanidhi (article *Paridarshak,* in the magazine *Janmabhumi,* Feb-March 1903), according to whom the song was originally written by Bhuvanchandra Mukhopadhyay who would sometimes ghostwrite for Kaliprasanna Sinha. Its theme had to do with certain government orders and civic laws—the pet peeves—introduced at the time. From 1860 onwards anyone earning more than Rs.200 a year had to pay an income tax, which generated strong feelings among the public. Lieutenant Governor Sir Cecil Beaton wanted to shift the two burning ghats—Nimtolla and Kashi Mitra—outside the periphery of the city and beside the Tolly's Nullah. It was proposed that cremations inside the city and throwing of corpses into the river would be banned completely. Sanitary Commission chairman John Strachey wrote in a report filed just two days before the proposal was tabled that more than 5000 dead-bodies were dumped every year into the river from which the people drew water for drinking and cooking purposes. But the proposal to move the Nimtolla burning ghat and introduce incinerators did not materialize. See Nag, ed., *Sateek Hootum Pyanchar Naksha:* 284.
30. A ritual signifying the closure of the puja festivities; the bird set free would carry the message of Durga's arrival back home to her husband, Lord Shiva, before the Goddess reached her abode in Kailash.

9

In the Name of Ram

DURGA PUJA festivities were over. It would be a year before the next one would be held. Having collected their dues from the clients' houses, the drummers now played frivolous beats in front of the liquor shop. The hired chandeliers were carried back to the big houses, suspended from bamboo poles, tinkling as they went. Rice and an assortment of five grains were laid out in the sun.[1] These were collected by the Brahmin from clients' houses, where he performed the rites on a contractual basis. The Brahmin's wife tried to shoo the crows away, stick in hand, a child perched on her hip. The city was dead silent. The tenants were yet to return [from their native villages]. There were a few more days to go before the offices and schools reopened.

The kind of activities, entertainment and business one finds in a culture at a particular time are an index of what the people of that culture might be capable of. It is the temperament of a particular culture that drives it like a **locomotive**, while its [collective] behaviour acts like a **weathercock**. To entertain themselves our ancestors built arenas to hold wrestling matches, watched theatre, encouraged [engagement with] refined music and literature. But nowadays we are satisfied with watching gypsy women dance at a community puja or in our homes and listening to loud music on the theme of 'Cupid Flame'. We cheer at puppet shows, panchali readings and performance of vulgar songs, using the children's request to take them to these programmes as an excuse. We ask jatra performers to present the Chhoku Babu act[2] and *Vidyasundar.* Wrestling matches [of yore] now exist in travestied forms such as bulbul **fights**[3] and a clash of rams. Our ancestors fought each other [face-to-face]. These days we only criticize people behind their backs, ultimately winning this one-sided slanging match. It is a foregone conclusion.

It is no surprise that we are in such a sorry state. As soon as we learn to crawl, we are given rattles, pacifiers and birds made of pith to help us learn the alphabet. A little ahead in life, it is through flying kites, spinning tops, playing hide-and-seek and 'man-and-wife' that one completes the **entrance course** to youth. Only after acquiring expertise in playing cards, dice and learning to checkmate the opponent in a game of chess could one be said to have earned a **degree**. These lessons, learnt when one is young, are what we have to keep revising all through our lives. As one grows older, a few related troubles are added on.

Ramlila was not a festival observed in these parts. It was utterly *khotta*[4] in character. Sometime back the soldiers at Barrackpore[5] began celebrating Ramlila. Initially they would pool in some money to organize a play based on the battle between Lord Ram and Ravan, on the Barrackpore grounds. This went on for a while before being discontinued. Finally, in the year 1757 of Shalibahan, a few rich khottas who had business in Burrabazar took the initiative to re-start the festival. Since then, for the last twelve years, a Ramlila fair had been held here. As this was about the only fair in Calcutta, it drew a lot of visitors. Unemployed babus, khottas from Rajasthan, prostitutes and traders were its mainstay.

Readers, imagine a rich man from your locality—born into old wealth and a leader of his associates—seated on a one-and-a-half feet high mattress, with huge chests and mirrors placed in front of him. He smoked an enormous hookah that thundered like the autumnal cloud as he took each puff. The aroma of Italian tobacco, blended with musk and aloe, seemed to have an intoxicating effect on the household. A little distance away a khotta quack was seated with his range of aphrodisiacs—a paste to spike a drink made from hemp leaves, digestive balls, bed-shatterers[6] and virility-enhancers—tied in a scarf. He was a wealthy jeweller's son from Lucknow, now living in Calcutta, who had probably lost all his assets playing the stocks sometime back and it was therefore imperative that the babu sponsored his upkeep. Imagine that he knew how to prepare a variety of traditional Islamic medicines, and was particularly adept at preparing a paste from hemp leaves. His acquaintance with quite a few nautch girls, Kathak dancers and female singers, besides his own intrepid nature and expertise in other fields, had helped him become the babu's right-hand man in no time.

Next to him sat Bhabani and Haladhar, the head clerk of **Messrs Artful Dodgers**[7]—the lawyers. Bhabani was a local celebrity, drawing a high salary from the court. In addition, he was a closet agent for buying and selling the shares of different companies. He had managed the legal cases of big-time zamindars and often officiated on their behalf with a power of attorney. In fact, a lot of people would agree that Bhabani was more duplicitous than Umesh[8] and a smoother operator than Joykrishna[9] when it came to dealing with money and property. Haladhar, who sat next to him, wasn't too bad either. Don't suppose he was any less skilled than Shubhankar, a mathematical genius, when it came to pushing a particular case taken up by the legal firm that employed him, hatching conspiracies or forging documents. Haladhar wore his moustache like a pair of cones that contained the yet unformed bananas. His paunch reminded one of the roomy leather water containers, tapering towards the bottom. He wore a good-luck charm on his arm, a girdle with an amulet round the waist, a thin diaphanous dhoti with a back pleat tucked inside and a mark of red sandalwood, the size of a coin on his forehead. He also put black powder on his teeth. Haladhar would mostly wear his wrapper in the form of a bundle on his shoulders, smoke non-stop and twist his whiskers, as if to fine-tune his wits.

At this point, Falahari and Rambhadra entered the scene. The babu greeted them most warmly and offered seats. The hookah-attendant served them a smoke. After they had rested, smoked a bit and hedged for a while, the babus said, 'Sir, Ramlila is being celebrated in a big way. The fall of Lakshman[10] will be staged tonight and there will be a fireworks, display as well. On our way here we saw Rambabu's four horse-drawn carriage pass by. Shombhubabu was carting the idol of Goddess Lakshmi in his carriage. There's a huge crowd out there. Aren't you coming, sir?'

Bhabani endorsed the proposal immediately. The babu too said yes. At once there was a huge noise. 'Hey! Who's there? Who's around?' There were echoes of 'Master, my Lord,' and 'What can I do for you?' from all sides. The messenger was told, 'Ask them to have the big Britzschka and the English double horse-drawn carriage readied, fast.'

Imagine the Britzschka being readied. The favoured orderlies, having donned turbans and badges, checked their appearances in the mirror. The babu changed clothes in his **dressing room**. Around five servants had poured over satin shirts, trousers and tasselled caps, tailored in forty-odd **patterns**, to make a selection. Exhausted by the effort of having to think about the dress that might suit him best, the babu wore a shirt, took it off, put on a cap and looked in the mirror, which made him extremely pleased. But when he tried the next one on, that seemed to suit him rather well too. In between, he asked one of the toadies, 'What do you think? Should I put this one on?' The sycophant, careful not to give away anything, said, 'Well, clothes don't look as good on any swine in this city as they do on you.' In the meantime, the babu had put on another cap and asked again, 'How about this?' The sycophant said, 'No one else has anything quite like this,' trying to add to the babu's glory, quoting, sometimes, the couplet, 'Eat to please yourself, dress to please others.' After a great deal of debate and discussions, finally the babu would perhaps wear a weird outfit, put on make-up, **lavender** and perfume, select his ring, **chain** [to hang the pocket watch] and **stick**. He would take two hours to step out of the **dressing room** and be back in the drawing room.

Haladhar, Bhabani, Rambhadra and the others present there perhaps felt it was their duty to praise him. One of them said, 'You are looking so good in this outfit.' Someone else said, 'Did you have this tailored at Gibson's?'[11] Some of the others had unlimited praise for the pocket-watch chain, ring and stick.

The toadies who were not wearing clothes good enough to match the Britzschka and the English carriage, put on some of the outfits discarded by the babu, wedged a cotton dipped in ittar above their ears to improve their looks. They were ecstatic with joy at having worn the babu's hand-me-downs. 'I hope the local grocer from whom I buy stuff on credit, the women and the people I know get to see the kind of clothes I am wearing while I travel with the Master,' each thought. Unfortunately, as a lot of these sycophants often complained, when they went out with the babus in fine clothes and big carriages, nobody saw them; it was when they went out to get the daily groceries, gamccha on the shoulder, that everybody did.

Toong tung, toong tung, struck the McCabe clock. It was five in the afternoon. 'Master, the carriage is waiting,' **proclaimed** the messenger. The babu stepped in, with his satellites. The English carriage took off at the coachman's nod, galloping at top speed. The road shuddered. The carriage left with the babu.

'God, what a relief,' said a servant, rolling on the babu's mat, which had lovely patterns on it. One of them got busy inspecting the babu's gold-coated hookah. A few of them put on the babu's clothes and went out for a stroll. In quite a few rich men's houses in the city, stringent rules were observed in the babu's presence, but as soon as his back was turned, the façade collapsed, and the household was exposed, stark naked.

The Britzschka was now on Chitpore Road. There was quite a crowd of vehicles on the road today. Groups of Marwaris, Biharis and prostitutes drove in tottering hackney coaches. They were off to watch Ramlila too. Those who did not have a vehicle but were unable to resist the goading of desire went on foot. The amazing thing about Calcutta was that everybody—from a wage labourer to a rich man worth hundreds of thousands of rupees—seemed to believe in giving free rein to his or her fancy. If the hugely wealthy people performed a grand and ostentatious last rites' ceremony, a man of modest income would be ready to beg or steal to be able to repeat the feat, even if he had to take extreme pains to do it.

Imagine the fast moving hackney coaches and big carriages, raising dust from the roads, plunging the city in darkness. The Sun, having spent the whole day in the company of the Lotus, and now looking like a spent lover, took refuge in the horizon, as if to rest and shake off the fatigue. Evening, seeking a secret rendezvous with her beloved, followed best friend Dusk and went looking for co-wife, Night. Darkness, holding the key to mysteries, had spent his day in hiding, undisturbed. Now on cue from the signals sent by homing birds, he slowly spread out, enveloping the surroundings to create an unusually lovely place for the Moon to roam in.

By this time the babu's Britzschka had reached the venue where Ramlila would be performed. Raja Bahadur's garden used to be the finest among the others in the city, but now, thanks to the precious sons of the family, had been turned into a veritable zoo garden. Earlier, Ramlila would be held at Raja Baidyanath Bahadur's garden,[12] but since last year it had shifted to the garden of Raja Narasingha Bahadur.[13] Narasingha was very fond of flowers, devoting his life to tending flowering plants. So it was no surprise that his was the best garden in town. In fact, many people agreed that Raja Bahadur's garden was no less picture perfect than the [East India] Company's. But within a month of his father's death, the present owner ruined the garden. The bigger trees were uprooted and sold. Even the shoes worn by the deceased were not spared. All that the heir apparent wanted was to make money at any cost. Finally, the garden—once the city's best—became a Ramlila compound. The monkeys danced, indoors and outside.

It was announced that Ramlila would be held in Raja Narasingha's garden instead of Raja Baidyanath's. This time a fee would be charged for horse-drawn and other vehicles. There was no ticketing system when the fair was held at Raja Baidyanath's. The host himself and other rich men raised generous funds to cover the costs. But when Raja Baidyanath grew old and died two or three years ago, his descendants, the crackerjack princes, claimed individual shares of the garden and raised walls in between to demarcate areas owned by each kin. The rich men [who earlier contributed to the fair] were not so interested any more, which was the reason why tickets had to be sold to raise funds. After all, Calcutta—one might as well say it—is a wonderful city. Many here are quite willing to blow money on low-brow entertainment. In spite of the introduction of ticketing, a huge crowd of carriages, horses and people filled up the fairground.

The Britizschka could not go very far past the crowd. The babu got down from the car with his entourage. He thought it would make better sense to walk. So he ambled along, soaking in the beauty of the garden as he went.

Two rows of shops lined the road from the gate to the stage where the battle of Ramlila would be played out. Ferris wheels rotated in between. Hawkers cried out loud, trying to sell drug-laced paan, toys, spicy fried nuts and groundnuts. The yaars **paraded** around in groups. Seventy-five per cent of the crowd comprised prostitutes, khottas, dubious men and traders. Carriages stood in four or five rows outside the fencing around the arena. In one of these a foppish man was having fun in the company of a few yaars and whores. Inside another were four friends, wearing Chinese coats and chains made of horsehair, with a tart. And in yet another, some boys—the champs among the precocious lot—had sold their textbooks to buy drug-laced paan and cocaine which they enjoyed. Some of the carriages carried only north Indians, Marwaris and idiots, while some were full of well-dressed babus.

Our protagonist, who took in such scenes as he went on his way, was finally led to the gate opening out to the arena, hand-held by a fellow north Indian babu. The crowd was enormous. Around ten to twelve guards used their canes indiscriminately, whacking away. Two sergeants tried to push the crowd back with great force but did not quite succeed. The khottas and [players dressed as] monkey soldiers from inside the arena cried out from time to time, 'Victory to Raja Ramchandra.' Everybody wanted to fulfil their heart's desire by having a glimpse of Lord Ram's pleasing visage, but it was nearly impossible to get anywhere near him.

The master, our protagonist, managed to get past a door in the fence after a lot of effort, mingling with the monkey soldiers. Across the arena from him were the demons. Imagine the actors, dressed up as demons, roaming around and making faces at people in the carriages near the fence. Those who played the monkeys were on a romp, throwing the false arms that had come unstuck and sticks at each other, instead of boulders and trees [like the monkeys in the *Ramayan*]. The babu, mighty glad with the sights he had not seen before, walked along the fence, awestruck. A few more rich traders and vicious babus, born into old wealth, walked in to join him. He also met agents, cotton traders and **influential, reformed** khottas. People greeted him, saying, 'Ram, Ram', 'Adaab' and 'Bandegi',[14] made salutations and welcomed him by handing over a roll of paan. Many of these had come as early as noon and would go back home only after ten at night, when they had had their fill of Ramlila.

When the [estate] manager or an assistant of his saw the babu and a few other **subscriber** rich men's sons wandering around, he ran up to him, offered a pouch filled with rolls of paan and tried explaining the significance of some of the shongs that were on display. He also gave the babu an imaginary **memo** of how many carriages and people had assembled, not forgetting to admire the garb and make-up of each monkey, bear and demon. The babu and his party, in turn, said, 'It is very good this time, was not so good last year', thus pleasing the managers by offering a **compliment.**

Fireworks were lit. Finally, after four-five varieties of indifferent fireworks were burnt, the Ramlila celebrations were over. After ritual offerings were made to Lords Ram and Lakshman and their figures garlanded, the riff-raffs decided that their lives' mission was fulfilled and went home. The horses drawing the hackney coaches broke wind continuously as they took great pains to drag the coaches back home. The babu had great trouble finding his carriage in the crowd before he could board it. And that was how Ramlila came to an end on that day.

Well, I am quite fond of such shows. I too was going to watch Ramlila, perched on the rear seat of a hackney coach. Inside the car was a carpenter, four or five friends of his and two solemn-looking prostitutes. The car had barely covered a distance when an impudent young lad—known for his cheek since the day he was born—cried from the street, 'Coachman, big bum! Coachman, big bum!' The coachman said, 'Take that, you swine,' and cracked his whip, suddenly. The passengers sitting inside cried, 'Who's that? Get down, get down quick.' So my trip that day did not materialize, and the wish remained unfulfilled.

Seeing the autumnal Moon in the company of the stars on the transparent blue sky, Night, his paramour, was miffed and drew her veil over her head. The partridge couple kept coaxing her, to no avail. The Water Lily smiled in the transparent water of the pool, seeing her co-wife's misery. The partridge couple, forever loyal to the Moon but now sorry at the Night's plight, reprimanded him most soundly. Different species of crickets droned loudly, joining them. Nature, the virtuous one, was surprised at the behaviour of this champion of a debauch. It was as if to spare the Night's Beloved any embarrassment that the Wind walked on tiptoe, moving along the big trees and hedges. Drops of tears fell from the eyes of the wounded Night, who pretended this was the dew dropping down on the forests and flowers, as if to crown them.

Meanwhile, the babu's Britzschka and English double horse-drawn carriage trotted ahead. *Thop-thop*, it went, shaking the road on its way until it reached his residence. The babu went inside his **dressing room** to change. The satellites sat in the drawing room, smoking tobacco and regurgitating what they had seen at the Ramlila festival. Certain rich men were pulled up and abused and everybody joined in enthusiastically. A little later, the babu, having changed, came out to join them. *Goodum!* The nine o'clock firing of the gun was heard.

Readers—embodiments of unlimited greatness—would perhaps remember that Rambhadra had accompanied the Master to the Ramlila fairground. Now after some sundry conversation, the babu asked Rambhadra to sing a tappa. Rambhadra was musically inclined, and had a good voice too. Although he was not a professional, he had made quite a name for himself for this special skill in the wealthy people's circuit. Rambhadra was on a high these days. He was making quite a packet from dealing in company shares and bulk purchase of goods, and made it a point to celebrate Dol and Durga Puja at home. Be it a parent's last rites or an offspring's marriage, ten Brahmin pandits would be called to officiate. Almost all the Brahmins in his village were patronized by him. Kayasthas and those belonging to the [low-caste] nine sects too were, mostly, loyal to him. Rambhadra lived mostly in the city, since he had much work there, going home only during festivals and holidays. At his city residence in Badurbagan, he sponsored the upkeep of a number of boys from decent families. A few rich men were extremely fond of him.

Rambhadra was [a living embodiment of] the gold and silver keys[15] that were used to awaken and put to sleep the Rai Bahadur of Simla. He had earned the affection of many other wealthy people. Therefore, at the babu's request, he began playing the tanpura and sang a song of his own composition. Haladhar tuned the tabla and bnaya, and began playing, marking the beat verbally. This is where the sketch of Ramlila ends.

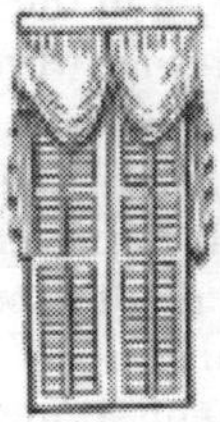

Notes

1. Rice, ground nuts, barley, sesame, pulses.
2. Chhoku Sinha was a zamindar of Tarakeswar, Singur, known for his selfless generosity, which was a theme for lampoon. Skits would have the funny guy Chhoku giving away six-seven layers of clothing till he was stripped to his last loincloth. See Arun Nag, ed., *Sateek Hootum Pyanchar Naksha* (Calcutta: Ananda Publishers, 2008): 285.
3. Favourite pastimes of the nineteenth-century babu. The birds would have blades attached to their legs so there would be maiming and bloodshed.
4. 'Khotta' is an undignified, even pejorative, way of addressing people from Bihar in particular and north India in general; they were looked down upon by the seasoned Calcuttans for their lack of taste and refinement. A little further on in the piece, Marwaris, originally from Rajasthan, are clubbed together with khottas to suggest their rough country manners and supposed lack of sophistication.
5. There were many Biharis among the Company soldiers camping at Barrackpore. Mangal Pandey who led the Sepoy Mutiny was one.
6. An aphrodisiac so powerful that the bed was guaranteed to split under the impact of the intercourse.
7. A reference to the impudent young pickpocket Jack Dawkins who earned himself the sobriquet 'Artful Dodger' in Charles Dickens's *Oliver Twist.*
8. Umesh Chandra Roy alias Motibabu was a con guy and a social climber. He came from a family of toothpick makers and was patronized by Raja Krishnachandra of Nadia who gifted him a 12 per cent ownership of the backward land at Mamjoani. Employed by Dwarkanath Tagore towards the beginning of his career, he rose through the ranks and eventually became the ex-officio ruler of Shantipur. He was notorious for filing lawsuits against people by slapping false charges on them. Justice caught up with him when Justice M. L. Wells condemned him to three years' imprisonment after a false charge brought by him was exposed in 1860. Moti died in jail. Ibid: 286-87.
9. Joykrishna Mukherjee was zamindar of Uttarpara; see Sketch 2, p. 89, note 23 and p. 103, note 96.
10. The episode in *Ramayan* in which Ram's brother Lakshman is locked in a bitter battle with his ace adversary and challenger, the immensely gifted warrior Indrajeet. Lakshman falls to Indrajeet's power-packed

missile, the Shaktisheel, and is revived later when the herb Sanjeevani is administered.

11. Gibson, Wallace and Company was a well-known tailoring house located at 23 Kosaitolla Street in Chitpore area. Ibid: 287.
12. Raja Baidyanath Roy (? – 1859) of Posta was known for his munificence and organizing public events. He set up a zoo and allowed free admission for spectators. The garden at Cossipore was opened to the public at the time of hosting events such as shong displays, races and Ramlila. Baidyanath donated Rs.50,000 to the Hindu College fund and Rs.20,000 to Mrs. Wilson's fund for Ladies Society for Native Female Education. The money from the last was used to fund a Central School for women in 1826, well before the Bethune School—a pioneering institution for women—was opened. Ibid; see also Subodh Chandra Sengupta, ed., *Samsad Bangali Charita-vidhan,* revised 4th edition, Part I (Calcutta: Sishu Sahitya Samsad, 2002): 368.
13. Narasingha Roy (? -1859), the youngest brother of Baidyanath, too, was known for his generosity, having donated more than Rs.104,000 to the Education Committee and also towards building the Native Hospital in Dharamtolla. His garden, across the road from Baidyanath's, was well-known for the extensive collection of flower plants. See Nag, ed., *Sateek Hootum Pyanchar Naksha:* 288
14. The salutations typical of Hindu north Indian, local Muslims and Muslim Urdu-inspired north Indian cultures indicate the kind of inclusive multiculturalism that was generic to Calcutta in the period.
15. This expression has connotations of traditional Bengali fairy tales in which the charmed princess lying in a deep coma would have the gold and silver keys/sticks kept by her bedside. She would wake up at the touch of one and go to sleep at the touch of the other. The use of this metaphor thus indicates that Rambhadra was an advisor who had control over the Rai Bahadur of Simla (the Viceroy).

10

The Railways

A TRAIN service was started from Howrah to Allahabad at the time of the Puja holidays.[1] Posters in English and Bengali, written in red and black, were put up in street corners. Many people went on board to have a joyride. There were several pilgrims as well. Premananda Das Baba[2] of Nimtolla, a heavyweight among those who presided over the biggest monastery of the order of Sreepath, Jorasanko, was determined to visit Benaras during the holiday.

The baba was a wealthy man with a huge following. He was obese, had a big bolster-like belly, his limbs were fleshy, dripping with fat, and his complexion was like the black touchstone, the chalice of a hookah or the polished dark bottom of a pot used to boil paddy. His head was shaven, except for a long tiki, which he usually tied up in a bun. For several years now he had stopped wearing his dhoti with pleats in front. Rather, he wore outfits in different colours, wrapped over his loincloth. His whole body was smeared with the yellow earth[3] from Vrindavan at all times, Premananda wore garlands crafted from beads made from seeds of lotus or tulsi plants. A red silken bag, almost as big as a pillowcase, containing the prayer beads, was suspended from his neck by a brass ring.

Having decided on an auspicious day to start his journey, the baba finished his daily chores early in the morning, had a bit of prasad from what was offered to the household deity for breakfast, and set out, accompanied by two of his disciples who were given the roles of porter and attendant. They stepped out of the monastery and reached Chitpore Road, looking for a carriage.

Dear Readers, try to visualize this: [it was so early in the morning that] schools and offices were yet to open, the last segment of the Ramlila play was still to be performed. So it was a bit difficult to find horse-drawn carriages plying the road. Baba searched high and low and finally located a place where drivers gathered, and after much persuasion managed to hire a carriage. As the vehicle was being readied, the baba waited under the balcony of a brothel.

Gnanananda Baba[4] of the same order from Kumarnagar was a close friend of Premananda. He too was keen to take the train to Benaras. Just a little while back he had dropped by at the monastery, only to be told by the woman who waited on Premananda Baba that the baba was already on his way. Gnanananda was looking around for his mate and here was where the two met.

Gnanananda Baba was very thin. Having suffered from chronic fever and cough-and-cold for ten years, he had shrivelled like a twig. His eyes were sunk deep inside their sockets and there was not a trace of flesh on his body; it was just a bare skeleton. He had a shock of rough, un-oiled hair, a soft woollen wrapper wound twice over around his frame, carried a crooked bamboo stick, and wore a pair of shoes crafted in Orissa. He coughed incessantly and spat out the phlegm, punctuated by intakes of snuff from a case made of seashells. His nostrils, because of the snuff that continuously passed through them, had become so insensate that he did not even feel the dribble of snuff and mucus that ran down his nose at all times. He had developed a nasal accent because of the addiction, and damaged his epiglottis, the reason why he always had his mouth open like a bhetki fish. Premananda was delighted to find Gnanananda. They embraced each other and exchanged pleasantries and then the two friends decided to visit Benaras together, as brothers would.

The carriage, now ready, approached the two. The porter went up on the rooftop with the luggage; the attendant and the driver's assistant, in charge of keeping the whips, sat at the back. The two disciples went inside the coachbox. The babas entered the carriage. The car creaked noisily as soon as Premananda stepped in. Gnanananda took the front seat. The prostitutes standing on the balcony got talking: 'Did you see that carload of Gosains?

The hulk looks like Kumbhakarna,'[5] and so on. The coach driver took his seat, flailed his whip, pulled the reins over and over again, made a clucking sound and rotated the whip over his head, but the horse refused to budge an inch. It kept kicking incessantly. The show reached a climax when the horse started farting intermittently.

Readers will possibly remember that we had already called Calcutta a strange city. Gradually, a crowd accumulated on the road. A flippant young peanut seller called out: 'Hey coachman, you have got a mountain of a man on one side and a skin-and-bone passenger on the other. You got to put similar weight on either side of the scales to make the car move.' The prostitutes cried from the balcony, 'Tie a few stones to the neck of that skinny, that way both sides would be evenly weighted.' Premananda was outraged. He flared up in hatred and anger and then sulked for a while. A little later he lifted his head slightly and told Gnanananda, 'Brother, have you seen how impertinent these city women are?' Finally he yawned and said, 'It's all as you wish, my Lord.' Gnanananda yawned, snapped his fingers twice, consumed another pinch of snuff and said with a distinct nasal accent, 'You are right, brother. They never got lessons in morality from their husbands, they should be taught the *Ramaranjika*.'[6]

Premananda was mighty glad to hear this. 'Who but you could say something that's after my heart, dear brother? There's no text like *Ramaranjika* in the three worlds.[7] It's all your doing, my Lord,' he said. Gnanananda sighed deeply, took a pinch of snuff, remained silent for a long time and then scratched his head and said, 'Brother, I hear the women are reading it!' Premananda was delighted. 'O brother, there's no other text like that in the three worlds. It's only because you willed it, my Lord.'

After a great deal of manoeuvring the carriage began to crawl. The porter, sitting on the rooftop, began kneading opium. And then the autumn clouds brought a spell of heavy rain. The babas shut the door of the carriage and sat stiffly in the darkness, like shongs produced from the baroyaari Durga Puja stockpile. After sitting in silence for a while, Gnanananda looked through a slit in the carriage to check how heavy the shower was, took a pinch of snuff, coughed twice and said, 'Brother, let's have some music in praise of the Lord. Sitting idle like this, as we are, it seems time isn't moving at all.'

Premananda loved music. It did not matter that he could not sing well. He would always sing aloud in private and keep humming unfailingly all through the day. He had even published a book of songs, and, initially, had these sung in soirées at fellow Vaishnavite homes. Thrilled to bits at Gnanananda's suggestion, Premananda began a song in Raga Malhar. Just as schoolboys often make up stuff and insert these into the text when the class captain leads a recitation exercise, Gnanananda too, inspired by Premananda's song, started adding his own version. The coachman pulled up when he heard the combined scream of broken and nasal voices. The porter jumped down from the rooftop and opened the door to find the babas seized by passion and singing away to glory. The guards who had been smoking and dozing off, woke up with a start and dropped their pipes when they heard the caterwauling inside the car, and came running towards it. The shopkeepers craned their necks, trying to get a view. But the babas were so possessed by their devotion for the Lord that they continued to improvize and elaborate on the music. Finally, the sudden halting of the carriage and the commotion raised by the crowd made the singers come to their right senses. The sight of the guards embarrassed them to no end. A porter for hire was passing by with an empty basket at the time. He stopped and swore, 'The f–ers' brothers have started a *kaloati* number inside the car.'[8] Since the guard had had to drop his pipe before he came running at the source of the screams, he too abused the babas to his heart's content before resuming his duty at the shop. A newly anointed city-bred babu had been waiting with his travelling bag in a shop. Stranded in the rain, he was indeed finding it difficult to reach the railway **terminus**. He negotiated the fare with the coachman in the meantime and hurtled inside the car. The coachman started the vehicle, speeding up. The porter ran behind the car for a while and then jumped on at the back.

Now this neophyte babu of ours, you might say, was a famous person, particularly since he had established a centre for the Brahmos in a village not too far away from the city and become its secretary. Besides, he had a highly paid job in that village. The babu was an ace among the 'reformed class' and something like a knave of the Brahmo Samaj. He would offer alcohol to the Supreme Being day and night, and be dead drunk most of the time. On weekends he would pile on more '**cargo**' and get completely knocked out at times. The babu took leave and came to town to buy **furniture** and books for the **library** of the newly established Brahmo Samaj [in the village], but had spent his time in the company of the 'lame' Supreme Being[9] [with the prostitutes of Sonagachhi], as a devout lover of Nature and one who worked towards pleasing her,[10] enjoying the pleasures of Brahmohood in the process. Once inside the carriage, the babu, who was drunk, first swayed and fell on Premananda's paunch. He brushed against Gnanananda's face with the next jerk and landed again on Premananda's belly on the rebound. The babas sat stiffly, looking at each other. But the drunkard, not knowing where to sit, kept shuttling between the two ends of the carriage like Gazi Mian's flag.[11]

Let the babas spend some time with the drunken babu like a hawk and two pigeons shoved inside one cage. Let the carriage, fully loaded, amble on in kingly saunter. Let the porters smoke pot non-stop. In the meantime, the rains have stopped. The city, once again, bubbled with people and noise. Middle-class householders came out to shop. Servants and maids followed them, carrying baskets and bags made of leaves. Chitpore Road often got muddied all over as soon as clouds started to gather. So the pedestrians had a hard time. Some of them walked over the sewer, some along the edge of the canal, clothes hitched up, shoes in hand.

Come buy potatoes and patol [a gourd]. Want some ghee? Molasses, anyone? Whey? The peddlers cried as they went about. Fisherwomen, fish baskets perched on their heads, ran behind them, flailing their hands. Some of them were accompanied by their men, carrying large bhetkis and lobsters that looked like clergymen wearing beards and robes, in huge baskets suspended from their shoulders. The textile shops in Rajabazar and Lalababu's Market[12] were filled to the brim. Goods were being bought and sold. The shopkeepers were a harried lot, [given the] huge crowd of customers.

Declassed Brahmins, the lowly sort, carried icons of Goddess Sitala on a tray and sang in front of the temple, begging for alms. Vaishnavites and shaven-headed devotees were singing too. Four to five people went around, chanting, 'We have been fasting since the last three days. Spare something for this Brahmin who is a stranger to this city, generous souls.' Some were in a state about missing the daily puff of their chosen addiction at the appointed hour as they had not made any money to buy it with and did not see a way out of the crisis. The usual sponsors had refused to lend money. Yesterday, the junkie had managed [to earn a little money] by pawning his shawl. But today he seemed to have nothing left at all.

The sweepers, now done with removing the garbage, came to the watering hole and started drinking rum in large swigs. They began an argument with the undertakers on the relative superiority of their professions. The wine-seller, who acted as the mediator, now tried to please the undertaker by ruling that his vocation was superior to that of the sweeper and now conceded that the sweeper's profession was the greatest. Drummers, funeral-makers, hog-keepers and palanquin-bearers took sides in this great war on the lines of the battle of Kurukshetra.[13] The sudden arrival of a group of dancers, exponents of jhumur or gadai,[14] had the effect of pouring cold water on the heated debate. The liquor shop bubbled with life.

Even the Gods presiding over this city made a fast buck. Goddess Kali and Lord Panchananda[15] had a share in the business of blessed mutton,[16] often run in the courtyard of a bhadralok's residence. Some of these served cooked meat. Seventy-five per cent of the buyers comprised drunken businessmen and prostitutes. These days, since he-goats were rare and exorbitantly priced, sometimes even the female of the species would be sacrificed. The flesh of pet cats and dogs too was cut to pieces and mixed with goat meat. The mouth that did not mind consuming cooked meat sold in the market would surely not let the meat of a dog or a cat go to waste. Only boats among the aquatic, kites among the avian and beds among the quadrupeds seemed inedible.

Now look here, dear Readers! The car carrying Messrs Premananda and Gnanananda has nearly reached the railway terminus. The clock in your drawing room, having struck nine, is still ticking away tirelessly. You chaps tend to get tired when you do more work than usual. The sun and the moon retired in the horizon after completing their course. But time moved on at the same pace, never asking for a moment's rest, respite or relaxation. Alas! Sometimes we waste time that is priceless. Later, with hindsight, the remorse one feels is immeasurable.

Finally, the Brahmo babu flopped himself onto Gnanananda's lap. It almost took the life out of Gnanananda who was crouching against the **panel**. The babu inched forward and stared at Premananda for a while, gave him a brief smile and put his travelling bag down on the footboard. Then he cast a sidelong glance at Gnanananda, pulled out a **phial** bearing the **label** of Presidency Medical Hall,[17] poured the contents into his mouth, made a face, wiped his mouth with a kerchief, took out a betel nut from his purse and started chewing on it. Premananda and Gnanananda had been highly irritated when the babu had piled onto the car. The two sat rigidly, running their eyes all over him. Dressed in a pair of black silk trousers and shirt, on which he wore a blue Chinese coat woven with merino wool, the babu also had on a conical tasselled catechist's cap made of beaver hair and a **comforter** with a red and yellow net pattern around the neck. He carried a bag made of carpet cloth and a short, thick club made from an English oak tree, its knobs prominently visible. Besides, the babu was carrying a **watch**, the proof of which could be seen in the key and the two **seals** hanging from a **guard chain**, made of [horse] hair. He also wore a ring. Gnanananda, after some effort, managed to read the words 'Om Tatsat'[18] engraved on it.

After he had recovered from the heat of the liquor and chucked the **phial** bearing the name of Presidency Hospital on the road, the babu found Premananda and Gnanananda sizing him up from head to toe, holding him in their unflinching gaze. Slightly embarrassed, he smiled a little and asked Gnanananda, 'What's your name, my lord?' Gnanananda became apprehensive the moment the babu turned towards him to talk. Now he took a pinch of snuff for the first time in hours, tapped the shell case a couple of times and then, with great difficulty, said, with a prominently nasal accent, 'You mean me? My name's Sri Gnanananda Das Deb. I'm from Sreepath, Kumarnagar.' The babu, who was drunk, simpered again and asked, 'Where are my lords headed to?' Gnanananda, not knowing what to say in reply, looked at Premananda who obviously was more clever, more seasoned and craftier than he. The worldly wise Premananda said, 'Babu, we are both devout Vaishnavites. We wish to visit Benaras and then travel to Vrindavan. What is your name, babu?' The drunken babu smiled again, took out another betel nut from his pocket, popped it into his mouth and said, 'My name's Kailashmohan. I live around here. Now I'm off to my workplace.' When he heard the name, Premananda tried to look somewhat serious and said, 'That's good. Very good, indeed.'

The babu asked again, 'Is this lord your brother?' 'Yes, you could say so. He is sort of a brother,' said Premananda. 'We believe in the same religion. Besides, he comes from a well-known family. The great venerable Joydeb Goswami[19] is a great grandfather of his.' The drunken babu simpered again and asked, 'So he belongs to Joydeb's family. And which family does your highness belong to? That of the great Lord Sri Chaitanya, I suppose?' This silenced Premananda who sat still, trying to figure out what the words purported. The Brahmo babu was secretly very pleased with himself at being able to annoy the babas thus. Determined to follow up his act, he turned towards Premananda and said, 'Master! You look very well turned out. It seems that there's a play on tonight, and you are attired to take part in it. Your Lordship, why don't you sing a song? The last time you ventured a tune with flourish there was havoc on the roads. Let's see what you can do now. I have heard that your lordship is like the great Tansen.'[20] The more the conversation continued on these lines, the more scared Gnanananda became. He kept looking out of the window to get an idea of how far away they were from the **railway terminus**, hoping to reach there as soon as possible so that they could get rid of the insolent pest.

Premananda too was apprehensive. As a young boy he was scared of and even nursed a racial hatred towards drunks, horses and the English. He had heard several stories about drunkards who might turn abusive. Once, a drunken babu had licked off the holy sandalwood mark on his forehead. And very recently a favourite disciple of his had been kicked to a premature death by a Bhutanese horse. So he said very modestly, 'Babu, we are humble Vaishnavites, what do we know of music? But let's take the name of Radha's lover once more with feeling. As devoted followers of Lord Hari, inspired by his message of love, we can only sing his praise and be at peace with ourselves.'

Gradually, the babu began to feel the power of the liquor that he had sipped only for a moment. His neck swayed, eyes rolled upwards and tongue slurred slightly. After quite a while he said, 'Truly said, Father,' and leaning against the cushions in the car, reclined on one side. He stayed like that for a while, then sat up and started leaning towards Premananda and, finally, holding his hand, said, 'Babaji, we are like friends. My heart is like the sprawling Maidan.[21] Do listen to this number from my repertoire of dhop kirtan.[22] I know the good Lord has females attending on him [and therefore will appreciate the song].' Saying this he laughed loud, tottered and then fell on Gnanananda's face, flailing his arms and screaming:

The mind, forever, wants to worship the idol
Who's full of colour and shine, no wonder the kids like her,
The tinsel that's come by post[23] glitters all over,
And sequins gold and silver reflect the light.
Her two sons on each arm, [while]
  tobacco-loving hubby's back home,
Say how could she run her plaything of a home
  if she stayed on?
How could the old familiar love get shattered?

But she would steal a glance towards the Asura's wig.
He is a brave bloke, only scared stiff of ghosts,
And the mistress at home,
ready with cow dung diluted with Ganga water.[24]

The carriage reached the railway terminus before the song was over. The Brahmo Babu swayed back and forth. He pounced on Premananda's nose and clutching Gnanananda's hair for support, jumped out of the vehicle even before the car had stopped.

The Armenian Ghat looked like a thick forest of people.[25] The melee of vehicles and palanquins matched the boisterous profusion of people. It was very difficult for the babas to get down from the coach in the middle of the crowd. Porters, attendants and disciples took their places in the procession, in keeping with their designated posts in the employment hierarchy, and marched on with their masters in the middle of the line. Gnanananda and Premananda held hands as they walked. It looked as if a cockroach and a tiny green beetle were walking in step.

Tununang ntang, Tununang ntang. . . the bells sounded. It was a signal for the steam-engine-driven ferry run by the railways to set off. There was major pushing and nudging at the third-class booking office. Railway peons cracked the whip, pushing and hitting people, but there was no way the crowd could be controlled. People called out, '[I want one for] Serampore, sir!' 'Bally, [get me] Bally [please]!' 'Burdwan, sir, please give me Burdwan.' The booking clerk, sitting in his wooden enclosure, was trying to sniff out the gullible sort and con them by striking at the precise moment when the stars aligned in his favour. He would issue a ticket worth four annas and return a balance of a couple of two annas against a rupee. If a customer asked for the change, he was advised to keep his mouth shut and get lost. The clerk would make people pay for a ticket to Serampore even when he issued one valid only till Bally. A customer who had paid for his ticket and kept waiting had been crying himself hoarse for ten minutes but no one paid any heed. With a comforter wrapped around his head, the booking clerk kept rattling the machine for printing numbers on tickets, whistling as he pocketed the cut. Most people could not see his face through the minuscule window—the sort one finds in lavatories—which came in the way of their speaking to him directly. They dared not shout to attract his attention for in case they did the guards and constables deployed by the railway police would be at their throats and (eventually) throw them out.

The chaos in the second-class booking counter and goods and luggage departments was similar. The railway **clerks** there were very much like the ones in the third class, only slightly less [offensive]. The first class was meant for the English [passengers]. One didn't hear the slightest sound at those counters. The clerks came empty-handed to sell tickets and went back with no change in their fortunes. They didn't even get a tip to buy paan and tobacco.[26]

The babas, dressed like stage actors, went towards the third-class booking counter when *Tununang ntang, Tununang ntang* . . . the bells rang, and the steamer hissed, releasing steam. Groups of people used the **jetty** to climb on board. 'Hurry! Move! Move!' shouted the railway police staff. The babas managed to squeeze into the crowd with great difficulty and asked for tickets. The booking clerk looked at them and grinned. Then he reached out for the money, collected it and started processing the tickets. In the meantime, the wheels of the steamer turned . . . *jhap, jhap, jhap* . . . and started rotating. 'Fast, give the tickets fast, sir,' Premananda shouted. 'The steamer's leaving.' But the master of the small window was unmoved. He whistled and sang, 'See what the foreigner has done, now Cupid has ignited the flame of desire with double force.' 'Are you listening, sir?' Premananda asked. 'The steamer's leaving. It will be difficult to get another one after this one leaves. What kind of torture is this?' 'Oh, shut up, Thakur,' said the clerk, royally snubbing him. After a long time, he delivered the tickets through the window and promptly shut it to resume his song: 'I feel like submitting my life to his hands, be his maid, the cupid flame.'

'But where's the change? Why did you shut the window?' asked Premananda. There was nobody to heed his plea.

'Constable, clear the crowds. Go away,' cried the clerk from inside the wooden enclosure. The guards pushed the babas with the rest out of the terminus. Premananda was very angry and kept looking back at the booking office. The clerk peeped through the chink in the window, singing the last bits of 'Cupid Flame'.

So the babas, trying to find a way out, left the terminus to look for another boat at another wharf. Fortunately, the steamer in the adjacent wharf had not set off. The babas thanked their respective stars and boarded the steamer with great difficulty. Since there was a huge crowd on board, they got squeezed like **formes** in the hot press and were wrung like bales of jute—the knots tying them together were pressed tight using a contraption with screws.[27] There was a bit of relief once they reached the riverbank where they rested for a little while before going to the station.

Tununang ntang, Tununang ntan . . . the bells sounded. The babas had already suffered the consequences of ignoring the bell, so this time they gathered their bags and baggage and eagerly waited for the train to arrive. Premananda craned his neck to keep an eye on the approaching train. Gnanananda reached for his shell case for a pinch of snuff and found that his purse was missing. At once he started howling, 'Brother, disaster! My purse is missing.' The screams and tears of his mate made Premananda quite miserable as well. He began to create a ruckus, but when the guards and constables appointed by the railway police thundered, 'Shut up! Shut up!', Premananda was scared that he would get thrown out again and decided not to make any more noise but to keep his distress to himself. Gnanananda kept sighing from time to time and took pinches of snuff with the same frequency. The shell case was emptied in no time.

In the meantime, *ghsss, ghsss, ghsss* . . . the train grazed its way in to the terminus. *Tununang ntang, Tununang ntang* . . . the bells sounded again. Passengers raised merry hell as they started climbing in. People were shoved inside third-class compartments with help from a guard and two musketeers. Passengers inside the train were heard screaming: 'Now where do you think you are going?' 'Sahib, there's no room here.' 'Where's my bundle? My bundle, please!' 'That's my child! Hey you, don't sit on his neck.' But the railway staff, bound as they were by regulations, did not pay heed to these. Although each of the third-class compartments had taken the shape of a crab's womb, a couple of stationmasters and guards kept peeping in at a regular interval, to see if there was any breathing space left so that they might push in some more passengers. If only the hapless English who had survived the Black Hole[28] had seen these third-class compartments, perhaps one day they would gather the courage to tell the Company's agents and locomotive superintendents that the pain suffered by third-class passengers was no less than that experienced by the English soldiers trapped in the Black Hole.

Premananda and Gnanananda boarded a train with their followers. *Dhap, dhap* . . . the doors were banged shut [one after the other]. 'Want a copy of the *Harkara,* sir?' '*Daily News*! *Daily News*! Anyone?'[29] Low-caste Muslim boys were hawking the daily papers. 'Want **novels**? Good **novels**!' Chachas[30] wearing coarse red wraps were hawking books. *Tununang ntang, Tununang ntang* . . . the bells sounded again. The stationmaster, a mini white flag in hand and a comforter wrapped around his head, stepped out. 'Is everything **all right**, babu?' asked the guard who walked up to the stationmaster. '**All right.** Good morning, sir,' said the stationmaster, raising the flag. Lifting his hand he signalled the engine to move, took out a small whistle from his pocket and blew on it. *Rat-a-tat swiishh, rat-a-tat swiishh* . . . the train shuffled and hissed as it went on its way out.

The babas, canned like turkeys and rooster imported from Chittagong and Chandernagore in the third-class compartment, had to endure the most inhuman conditions. The waist-long beards sported by two Muslim owners of tax-free land from Pandua dangled quite close to Gnanananda's face. The progeny of poet Joydev found the smell of garlic emitted from these extremely irritating. Sometimes the beard would get swept in the wind and brush against Gnanananda's face like a fly-whisk. Gnanananda found it revolting but there was no way he could turn his face to the other side. Right behind him were two Chinese men, carrying rice for lunch in their handkerchiefs. Premananda had got inside the compartment all right, but had not managed to find a toehold yet. His middle had got caught between a washerman's bundle of laundry and a **panel** inside the train. He remained suspended midair. When the stomach got too stretched for comfort, he tried to keep the balance by putting a hand on somebody's shoulder or head, but was unable to do it easily. A woman carrying a very young child stood beside him. When the baba tried holding on to him for support, the woman cried, 'What are you doing, Babaji. Watch it. That's my child.' The baba was embarrassed to see that all the other passengers were looking at him. Drenched in his own sweat, he gathered his hands together and was eyeing the washerman's bundle and his protruding stomach [as possible places] to put them back on. A theatre group, who had the play *Gangabhakti Tarangini* on their repertoire, was on the train. A frivolous young lad in the group cried out, 'O dear! It looks as if Babaji's paunch will get ripped apart,' and cooed irreverently, imitating the hawk-cuckoo, raising a chorus of laughter across the coach. 'Whatever you wish, my Lord,' sighed Premananda. Gradually, the speed lessened and the train came to a halt. Shouts were heard outside, 'Bally, [it is, we have reached] Bally.'

Bally was a well-known place. Benibabu of Bally, the character created by Tekchand Thakur, was a famous person. Bally was also the town where Motilal in *Alaler Gharer Dulal* received his lessons in good breeding.[31] The Bally Bridge too was quite impressive. The passengers for Bally got down here. The laundrymen and the theatre group got down at Bally, much to Premananda's relief. One of the boys pinched Premananda's belly on the way out. Adjacent to Bally was Uttarpara, these days quite famous, courtesy zamindar Joykrishna Mukherjee. I'm told the Normal School set up by Uttarpara's model zamindar[32] produced a few direct disciples of the guru who turned out to be veritable jacks of all trades.

At each of the stations that the babas went past, the stationmasters, signal-makers, **booking clerks** and **apprentices** displayed a singular character and 'greatness'. Some would, for no reason, cry out for the police all too often, trying to humiliate a decent chap. Some would snatch the bundle containing all the earthly possessions of a poor fellow and put it on the weighing scales. In certain places passengers who looked like country-bred Bangals or those who carried a heavy purse tied in a pouch around the waist would be conned. Robbed of their tickets by a sleight of hand, they would then be urged to produce it, as a cop stood in attendance. At a certain station, the stationmaster wrapping a comforter around his head, put his hands inside [the pocket of] a Chinese coat and strutted around proudly, ordering the porters and apprentices to engage themselves in inconsequential activities. Seeing this sudden **commanding aspect** of his lordship, the people who had assembled might one day start **whispering** among themselves: 'But who is he?' In fact, we might as well give it to him; he is **the Stationmaster**, no less.

Those great souls, who in their young age tried to push the sale of their goods at Calcutta's China Bazaar by shouting all day, '**Come Sir! Good shop Sir! Take take, no take, no take.** But do have a **see** at least once, Sir,' the great ones who hired carriages from sailors and light-skinned men to take their clients to liquor shops, **empty houses,**[33] the seven tanks and Dum Dum, and tried reaching inside their client's pockets, depending on the kind of state they were in, had suddenly turned into '**The Stationmaster**', as cockroaches would turn into a green beetle. A bhadralok who had boarded the train at least once, and came in contact with these great human beings, would complain about these formidable members of the railway staff. Civility was scared of coming near these '**policemen**'. Words like 'courtesy' and 'simplicity' were unheard of. All that these men were concerned with were red, white and **green** signals. **The station, tickets** and torture were the only things they always found worth worshipping. When it came to humiliating people from one's own community, these people were hardly ever lacking in the requisite skills.

Notes

1. The first train to be flagged off from Howrah Station was run experimentally on 28 June 1854. It travelled till Pandua, although the line was sanctioned to Raniganj, with the idea of transporting coal. From 15 August 1854, the East Indian Railway ran a regular service, morning and evening, between Howrah and Hooghly with stops at Bally, Serampore and Chandernagore. The fare ranged from Rs.3 by first class to 7 annas by third class. See Sukanta Chaudhuri, 'The Railway Comes to Calcutta', in Sukanta Chaudhuri, ed., *Calcutta: The Living City: The Past.* vol. 1 (Calcutta: Oxford University Press, 1990): 238.
2. 'Railways' is a parody of the novel *Yatkinchit* (Just a Little Bit, 1865), written by Peary Chand Mitra (1818-1883) who was also the author of the second Bengali novel, *Alaler Gharer Dulal* (1858). Premananda Das is modelled after Peary Chand Mitra, a public figure since his student days at Hindu College, and a prominent member of Young Bengal, led by Henry Louis Vivian Derozio. Mitra was also a member of the Calcutta University Senate, Society for Prevention of Cruelty to Animals, Bethune Society and British India Society, and a Justice of Peace. Later, he was the Deputy Librarian of Calcutta Public Library, a successful businessman and a nationalist. He was a member of the Brahmo Samaj. Conversant in Bengali, Persian and English, Mitra wrote both in Bengali and English. He contributed regularly to *The Englishman, Indian Field, Calcutta Review, The Hindoo Patriot, Friend of India*, and so on. See Subodh Chandra Sengupta, ed., *Samsad Bangali Charitavidhan,* rev. 4th ed., Part 1 (Calcutta: Sishu Sahitya Samsad, 2002): 292.
3. A variety of clay supposedly collected from the site where a young Lord Krishna would cavort with the milkmaids, used by the Vaishnavites to draw patterns on their forehead and body, as a mark of devotion.
4. Shibchandra Deb (1811-1890), the model for Gnanananda Das, was a close friend of Peary Chand Mitra and part of Young Bengal. Later, the two were related through a marriage between the two families. Deb dabbled in higher mathematics and worked as a Survey Department computer, before becoming a deputy collector in several districts of Bengal and Orissa. After retirement he played a role in the general development of his native town Konnagar, and founded the Konnagar Brahmo Samaj. A women's education enthusiast, Deb sent his daughters to Bethune School and founded a girls' school in

his house, besides founding English and 'vernacular' schools in Konnagar. See ibid: 221.

5. The second brother of Ravan in the *Ramayan*, his size like a mountain, famed for his enormous appetite for food and sleep.
6. A guidebook with a view to creating model women, written by Peary Chand Mitra (1860).
7. Heaven, earth and hell.
8. Hindustani classical music, dhrupad, kheyal, and so on.
9. A popular euphemism for red-light districts, specifically Sonagachhi. See Arun Nag, ed., *Sateek Hootum Pyanchar Naksha* (Calcutta: Ananda Publishers, 2008): 290.
10. One of the basic tenets of the Brahmo Samaj is to 'worship Him by loving Him and doing what pleases Him'. Here of course the author is talking of a different kind of love made to a different sort of people. Ibid.
11. Huge flags tied to longish poles, part of Muslim religious processions. Often, when the poles are too long, they sway madly from side to side. Ibid: 291.
12. The former was owned by the zamindars of Sovabazar and is now called Sovabazar Market. The latter was located to the south of New Market, owned by Lalababu of the Sinha family of Paikpara. Ibid.
13. Before the decisive battle between the warring cousins in the *Mahabharat*, it was decided that the generals and family friends would be split between the rival groups. By a clever move employed by Krishna, the Kauravs got to keep all the highly skilled warriors, while the Pandavs had only Krishna, the champion strategist, manipulator and an incarnation of God.
14. Dance forms. While jhumur, a romantic song-and-dance passage, is still traceable in the districts of West Bengal, Gadai seems to be unknown.
15. A black God, who causes diseases in children and hence has to be kept in good humour; see also Sketch 3, p. 145, note 25).
16. Respectable Hindus were not supposed to eat meat unless it had been offered to a God first during puja. But the taste for meat was catching on. So meat shops began mushrooming in Kali temples. Later, when the shops moved out of the temples, the practice was to keep an idol of Kali or Panchananda, perfunctorily, in them. The rampant adulteration of meat led to a ban on these shops in 1884. It became mandatory to slaughter animals only in the government-run abattoir. Ibid: 291.

17. A well-known medicine shop owned by Dr. B.N. Bundoo on Cornwallis Street, with a branch in Lower Chitpore Road. It was quite regular to have medicine shops running a liquor business under cover. Ibid: 292.
18. He is the One—a Brahmo aphorism.
19. The twelfth-century poet Joydev of Kenduli, Birbhum, the author of *Gitagovinda* and *Padmavati,* also the court poet of Lakshman Sen. *Gitagovinda* is admired by devout Vaishnavites and the literary audience, and is often sung in temples. See Sengupta, ed., *Samsad Bangali Charitavidha:* 170.
20. Legendary musician in Emperor Akbar's court.
21. The Maidan is the biggest patch of sprawling greens in central Calcutta; it remains almost the same unspoilt verdant patch after over 160 years of Hootum's writing.
22. Light, slightly lewd songs, meant to be sung by women.
23. The tinsel to deck up the Durga idol which used to come by post from Britain.
24. The purifying mixture with which the wife, who obviously disapproves of the husband's wayward tendencies, will bathe him once he returns home after spending time with his mistress.
25. A railway booking counter was opened at the Armenian Ghat on the Calcutta bank in 1854. This was the pre-Howrah Bridge days when the railways used to run a ferry service taking people across the Ganga from where they boarded the train. The fare covered the feeder service offered by the ferry. See Chaudhuri, 'The Railway Comes to Calcutta': 238.
26. Euphemism for small bribes, the precursor of today's *chaai paani* (tea or a drink).
27. A machine used to press and bind bales of jute, tying them together in secure knots.
28. In 1756, after Sirajuddaula defeated the East India Company's forces and captured Fort William, according to magistrate-collector J. Z. Holwell's account, Siraj made 146 English captives spend the night in a room in the fort. It was a narrow and tall structure about 18 feet high and 14 feet wide, and 123 people were supposed to have died. Other versions say it was the soldiers wounded in the fight who were imprisoned and some of whom died and that the numbers have been magnified in Holwell's version. In fact, Siraj may not have had a hand in meting out the punishment. But the event left a permanent scar on the minds of East India Company chiefs and by extension, the

English collective memory, so much so that the expression 'Black Hole of Calcutta' suggesting unmitigated chaos became a part of the English lexicon. See R. C. Majumdar et al, *An Advanced History of India* (Madras: Macmillan, 1981): 649-50.

29. *The Daily News* replaced *The Morning Chronicle* in 1857, and ran for two weeks. *The Indian Daily News* was published in 1866. It's noteworthy that only English newspapers were being hawked at the railway station. Train travel was seen as attracting the educated men with progressive ideas and the Europeans. See Nag, ed., *Sateek Hootum Pyanchar Naksha:* 294.
30. Ibid; hawkers selling books was a common sight, although there was no dearth of bookshops. There was a heavy demand for books among travellers. The hawkers were mostly Muslims and hence addressed as 'chacha' i.e., uncle.
31. Benibabu and Motilal are the two major characters in the book. Motilal is the protagonist, a spoilt brat who embraces a life of unmitigated hedonism, wallowing in the vices of babudom. Beni, a knowledgeable man, yet modest to the core, offers the checks in Moti's wayward life. Beni, a Bally resident, takes on the role of Motilal's mentor. Bally is where Motilal arrives at and kicks up a rumpus at the outset of the story, before his onward journey to Calcutta for schooling. See Brajendranath Bandyopadhyay and Sajanikanta Das, eds., *Alaler Gharer Dulal* by Tekchand Thakur (Calcutta: Bangiya Sahitya Parishad, 1941/1999).
32. See Sketch 2, p. 103, note 96.
33. Houses rented out for sex trade. The call girls, Armenian, Jewish and English, would be brought in by palanquin bearers who doubled as touts. See Nag, ed., *Sateek Hootum Pyanchar Naksha:* 295.

A Note on the Bengali Calendar

THE BENGALI calendar or Bangla Shan (BS) is a traditional solar calendar formulated by Fatehullah Shirazi on the basis of the lunar Hijri and the solar Bengali calendars. Introduced in 1584, it was dated from the Emperor Akbar's accession to the throne in 1556. The Bengali year is always 593 years less than the year in the Gregorian calendar.

The Bengali months are as follows:

Baisakh (mid-April to mid-May)
Jaistha (mid-May to mid-June)
Asharh (mid-June to mid-July)
Shraban (mid July to mid-August)
Bhadra (mid-August to mid-September)
Ashwin (mid-September to mid-October)
Kartik (mid-October to mid-November)
Agrahayan (mid-November to mid-December)
Paush (mid-December to mid-January)
Magh (mid-January to mid-February)
Phalgun (mid-February to mid-March)
Chaitra (mid-March to mid-April)

Glossary

adda a free-flowing, often impromptu, discussion held usually between friends, ranging from the highly intellectual to pure gossip; a way of life in Hootum's Calcutta, held any time and anywhere, from a rich man's drawing room to, typically, on the red, cemented porch of households in more plebeian areas.

aatchala a stage/room with an 8-thatched roof (and not the more common single roof or *ekchala*), indicating the relative prosperity of the owner.

adya shraddha the last day of a fortnight-long period of mourning, when the mourners have their nails cut to signify the end of a period of abstinence.

akhrai a competitive musical form started in late seventeenth century, sung by groups of musicians; the songs had a substantial lewd component, which was later refined by the famous tappa singer Ramnidhi Gupta.

alpana beautiful patterns of rice paste made on the floor and on the low, wooden wedding seats for bride and groom.

amani a light alcoholic drink made by fermenting stale rice in water.

anandalahari one-stringed musical instrument played by bauls, wandering minstrels.

Asur the evil demon, depicted as half-bull-half-man, slain by the Goddess Durga, his demise symbolizes the victory of good over evil.

babu in the modern context, a suffix to a man's first name; a polite form of address, comparable to 'sir'. In mid-nineteenth century, it denoted a class of English-educated, cash-rich, decadent people who imitated what they thought were western ways: heavy drinking and womanizing, with wasteful expenditure and were derided by Kipling and by Bankimchandra Chatterjee in *Kamalakanter Daptar* (Kamalakanto's Office, serialized in *Bangadarshan,* 1872-73). Depicted in several literary works that were contemporaries of Hootum's *Sketches:* Peary Chand Mitra's *Alaler Gharer Dulal* (The Son of the House of Alal, 1858), Michael Madhusudan Dutt's play *Ekei Ki Bole Sabhyata* (Is This Civilisation?) and Dinabandhu Mitra's *Sadhabar Ekadashi* (When the Wife Keeps a Fast, Like the Widow, 1866).

baiji a courtesan who would sing and dance at private functions for the rich babu.

Bangals people who originally came from the eastern parts of rural Bengal, looked down upon by the supposedly more sophisticated and urbanized Kolkata babu.

bhadralok people belonging to a genteel society, often full of hypocrisy and affectation, the ideal subjects of Hootum's own Comedy of Manners. In middle-class Bengali society, great value would be ascribed to a *bhadra* upbringing, which denoted education, good deportment, a degree of status and position in society, as different from that of the riff-raffs or people in blue-collar jobs.

bhajan a devotional song in praise of the deity.

bhari unit by which gold is measured, weighing a little more than 11 gm.

bhouliya a medium-size barge meant for family trips.

bigha measure of land in Bengal, approximately one-third of an acre.

bnaya a component of the pair of drums in a *tabla* set, played with the left hand.

bori little dry balls of lentil paste, added to vegetable and fish dishes.

Brahmo a follower of the Brahmo faith, a member of the Brahmo Samaj, started by Rammohan Roy, espousing monotheistic worship, abjuring idol worship and traditional rituals.

chalchitra painted frame fixed behind the idols of Gods and Goddesses as a backdrop; traditionally, idols of Goddess Durga and family would be built on a combined frame and made to stand against a single backdrop; later Durga's sons and daughters began to be placed separately.

Chandi Goddess Durga; also known as Bhagwati, Jagadhatri in her other incarnations; also a series of verses in praise of the Goddess, sung around the time of Durga Puja.

Chandimandap a raised platform in a rich man's household/village centre on which Goddess Durga is worshipped. In a village it doubles as the meeting place for elders; in the rich man's city residence, its use is restricted to holding the puja and performing related rituals.

chapkaan a high-necked long, loose shirt.

cowrie the smallest unit of currency.

dohar the band of singers who support the vocal lead, by repeating the refrain, like a chorus.

Doljatra the festival of colours, used here in the Bengali cultural context; celebrated all across India as Holi.

durba grass three blades of grass rising from a single stem, needed in rituals.

Durgapradip a large lamp used by goldsmiths for soldering.

esraj stringed instrument, played with a bow, often as an accompaniment.

firinghi literally, a man with Caucasian looks. This is the term the natives would use to refer to an Anglo-Indian, a European or anyone with light skin.

folar a purely vegetarian meal comprising fruits, yoghurt and sweetmeats, alternatively luchi (fried bread) and vegetables, associated popularly as food impoverished Brahmins craved.

gamccha a multi-purpose piece of coarse cotton cloth, most commonly used to dry oneself after bathing, also worn by the poor: around the waist like a sash, hung loosely from one's neck like a scarf or wrapped round the head like a turban.

Garuda the eagle-beaked sacred bird in Hindu mythology, carrier of Lord Vishnu.

ghat wharf, quay, a place in a river where boats are moored, also metalled/cemented/stone steps leading to a river or a pond, meant for bathers

gosain a spiritual guide or saintly man, mainly a worshipper of Lord

Krishna, patronymic of a family of the followers of Gouranga (one of the best-known disciples of Lord Krishna).

haat makeshift marketplace, meant mainly for selling fish and vegetables, at the appointed hour of the day, or on particular days of the week.

half-akhrai variation of *akhrai*, also known as *kobir lorai*, i.e. war of the poets who would sing impromptu compositions and ask the opponent to respond.

jatra precursor of theatre in Bengal, usually held in the open, in a circular playing area surrounded by spectators. The themes were usually mythological and the performance melodramatic, a form still quite popular in rural Bengal.

jhumur songs of this genre probably have their origin in plays based on the life of Lord Krishna; by the nineteenth century regarded as low-brow entertainment.

judi gadi fancy cars drawn by a pair of horses, state carriages are more improved, grander versions of the same, drawn by four horses.

kanchpoka bright green insect whose skin would be used to make *teep* (a little decorative spot) worn by women on their forehead.

khyamta popular form of dance to the accompaniment of a lewd song, suggestive and full of sexual innuendos.

kirtan songs in praise of the iconic lovers in Hindu mythology, Radha and Krishna.

kobigaan light entertaining songs sung in the form of a repartee between poets; usually, one would begin with a philosophical/spiritual theme and ask the other to respond.

koonch fruits red seeds of a small shrub used as a weight by goldsmiths.

kothiwallah salaried worker employed with a merchant house (*kothi*), a predecessor of today's boxwallah or corporate man.

lopeta slippers a variety of the fashionable *nagrai* shoes, with elongated and tasseled toe-ends, often came with heavy embroidery, involving gold thread and precious stones.

Mother Shashthi Goddess responsible for the birth and well-being of small children.

naatmandir the portico of a temple, from where devotees worship or observe the puja, sometimes used as a stage to hold performances

nawabi practising the extravagant way of life of *nawabs,* ie, Muslim aristocrats.

panta bhaat leftover rice is soaked overnight in water to be had the following day with pickles, fried fish; breakfast of the poor.

panchali song sung in praise of a particular deity, often containing a mythical story; metaphorically, a lengthy and boring spiel.

prasad food offered to the Gods and thus blessed by them is distributed to people.

pandit a Brahmin, traditionally teachers and priests, interpreters of the Sanskrit scriptures, placed on the highest rung of the social ladder, thus commanding the highest respect. Hootum's pandits are either small-time school masters, looking for a free meal or thoroughly corrupted sharks, living off a rich man's patronage.

Rakhi Purnima a full moon night in August when sisters tie a band around their brothers' wrists, affirming the bond between siblings and wishing brothers a long life.

rudraksha dry fruits from the rudraksha tree are used as beads with healing properties. Strung together to make necklaces, used as prayer beads by Hindu/Vaishnav devotees.

sanyasi generally a saint or mendicant, but a Gajan sanyasi is a performer who inflicts pains on himself to reaffirm his devotion to Lord Shiva.

sarangi a bowed musical instrument with three main strings.

Shakabda the era of Shalibahan, beginning 78-79 AD.

shehnai a double-reed conical oboe, originally from north India with a two-octave range.

shong a clown, a mannequin or an impersonator; the latter in a pageant, or hired for a show. The characters were familiar to the audience, drawn from history, mythology or topical; in the spirit of lampoon or satire. Metaphorically, it denotes a funny or bizarre sort of guy.

slokas verses from Vedas, *Puranas,* or even worship manuals dedicated to different Gods and Goddesses.

sutoshon an iron tool to pierce the Charak performer's body.

Shakti cult worship of Shakti (Goddess Kali), a female personification of divine energy and power.

tappa a light song of love, which involves long-drawn movements across the notes, the most famous exponent of this style being Ramnidhi Gupta.

thakur depending on the context, God, an idol, a cook, a priest or a holy man.

tilak sandal-paste mark on one's forehead and/or the bridge of the nose as a symbol of one's allegiance to a religious sect, Hindu or Vaishnav

ustadji a master musical exponent, a teacher; suffix' ji' denotes respect.

Vaishnav/Vaishnavite follower or worshipper of Lord Vishnu (Krishna), believers in the cult of renunciation, non-violence and universal brotherhood.

yaar a friend to hang out and have fun with; with connotations of flippancy, rather than deep, ever-lasting friendship. In *Hootum* the *yaars* frequent the dens of vice, associate with questionable people and generally indulge in a profligate life.

zamindar also known as a raja, appointed by the British rulers by the Permanent Settlement of 1798 to collect land revenue on their behalf. Historically zamindars, with a few exceptions, were ruthless and corrupt tyrants.

Selected Bibliography

Primary Texts

Nag, Arun, ed., *Sateek Hootum Pyanchar Naksha,* Kolkata: Ananda Publishers, 2008.

—, *Sateek Hootum Pyanchar Naksha,* Calcutta: Subarnarekha, 1986.

Bandyopadhyay, Brojendranath, and Sajanikanta Das, eds., *Hootum Pyanchar Naksha, O Anyanyo Samaj Chitra,* Calcutta: Bangiya Sahitya Parishad, 1967.

Secondary Texts

Ahmed, A. F. Salahuddin, *Social Ideas and Social Change in Bengal, 1818-1835, Leiden: Brill,* 1965.

Bandyopadhyay, Brajendranath, *Kaliprasanna Sinha,* Calcutta: Bangiya Sahitya Parishad, 1940/2007.

Bandyopadhyay, Brajendranath and Sajanikanta Das, eds., *Alaler Gharer Dulal* by Tekchand Thakur, Calcutta: Bangiya Sahitya Parishad, 1941/1999.

Bandyopadhyay, Sibaji, *Gopal-Rakhal Dvandasamas: Upanibeshbad O Bangla Shishusahitya,* Calcutta: Papyrus, 2006, p.142.

Banerjee, Sumanta, *The Parlour and the Street: Elite and Popular Culture in Nineteenth-Century Calcutta,* Calcutta: Seagull Books, 1998.

Blackburn, Stuart, and Vasudha Dalmia, *India's Literary History: Essays on the Nineteenth Century,* Delhi: Permanent Black, 2004.

Chatterjee, Sria, and Jennie Renton, eds., *Kolkata, Book City: Readings, Fragments, Images,* Edinburgh: Textualities; Kolkata: Council, 2009.

Chaudhuri, Amit, ed., *Memory's Gold: Writings on Calcutta,* Delhi:

Penguin/Viking, 2008.

Chaudhuri, Sukanta, ed., *Calcutta: The Living City: The Past,* vol 1, Calcutta: Oxford University Press, 1990.

Dalrymple, William, *The Last Mughal: The Fall of a Dynasty, Delhi, 1857,* Delhi: Penguin/Viking, 2006.

Das, Soumitra, *A Jaywalker's Guide to Calcutta,* Mumbai: Eminence Designs, 2007.

Ghosh, Anindita, *Power in Print: Popular Publishing and the Politics of Language and Culture in a Colonial Society,* Delhi: Oxford University Press, 2006.

Ghosh, Manmathanath, *Mahatma Kaliprasanna Singha* [1915], Calcutta: Parul Prakashani, 2008.

—. *Memoirs of Kali Prassunno Singh,* Calcutta: Barendra Library, Calcutta, 1920.

Harvey, Paul, ed., *The Oxford Companion to English Literature,* London: Clarendon Press, 1960.

Hibbert, Christopher, *The Great Mutiny: India 1857,* London: Allen Lane, 1978.

Joardar, Biswanath, *Anya Kolkata,* Calcutta: Ananda Publishers, 2003.

Losty, J. B., *Calcutta: City of Palaces,* London: British Library with Arnold Publishers, 1990.

Majumdar, R.C. H.C. Raychaudhuri, and Kalikinkar Datta, *An Advanced History of India,* Madras: Macmillan, 1981.

Mitra, Subal Chandra, *Isvar Chandra Vidyasagar: Story of His Life and Work,* Calcutta: Parul Prakashani, 2008.

Oddie, Geoffrey, *Missionaries, Rebellion and Proto-Nationalism: James Long of Bengal, 1814-87;* London: Routledge-Curzon, 1999.

Paul, Ashit, ed., *Woodcut Prints of Nineteenth Century Calcutta,* Calcutta: Seagull Books, 1983.

Sangari, Kumkum, and Sudesh Vaid, *Recasting Women: Essays in Colonial History,* Delhi: Kali for Women, 1993.

Sen, Sukumar, *Bangala Sahityer Itihaas,* vol. 3, 1801-1880, Calcutta: Ananda Publishers, 1944/2008.

—. *Battalar Chhapa O Chhobi,* Calcutta: Ananda Publishers, 1984/2008.

Sengupta, Subodh Chandra, ed., *Samsad Bangali Charitavidhan,*

rev 4th ed., Part 1, Calcutta: Sishu Sahitya Samsad, 2002.
Sripantha, *Battala*, Calcutta: Ananda Publishers, 1997.
Sterne, Laurence, *The Life and Opinions of Tristram Shandy, Gent*, vol. 4 [1761], London: Penguin, 2003.
Wild, Antony, *The East India Company: Trade and Conquest from 1600*, London: HarperCollins, 1999.
Winchester, Simon, and Rupert Winchester, *Simon Winchester's Calcutta*, Footscray, Victoria: Lonely Planet Publications, 2004.
Yule, Henry, and A. C. Burnell, *Hobson-Jobson* [1886], Delhi: Rupa, 2007.

Web page

King's College, London, Information Services and Systems, http://www.kcl.ac.uk/depsta/iss/library/speccoll/littre/hhwrds.html
Norton Anthology of English Literature, http://www.norton.com/nael

Acknowledgements

THIS BOOK IS the culmination of a rather long journey that began quite casually. This was in 2002. I was looking for a suitable article to run in *The Statesman's* Sunday supplement, which in those days would carry a four-page broadsheet 'Literary' section. Quite a few of my articles and short fiction published in those pages were written just an hour or two before we went into print, under extreme duress, only after I had exhausted all options, knocking on the doors of all the prospective writers in town, and outside of it.

It was around the time of the Bengali New Year and Hootum's *Charak* seemed an apposite answer. I translated a few selected passages and ran a piece. Sumitro Basak did a lovely illustration, dressing up a nineteenth-century woodcut by adding his own quirky acknowledgement of the present-day manifestations of *Hootum-i* fashion, showing a Pepsi banner in the background of Charak performers in a whirl, for instance. Sumitro has always been a *Hootum Pyanchar Naksha* enthusiast, and would goad me to translate the entire text from time to time. I'm delighted that he could come on board as the illustrator of this book.

Amit Chaudhuri, who had at that point of time begun work on editing a compilation of writings on Calcutta for Penguin, read my translation in the paper and commissioned me to do more. I translated five rather long extracts from *Hootum Pyanchar Naksha* for him that would not be published until December 2008 in *Memory's Gold: Writings on Calcutta* (Viking/Penguin). In between Amit kept insisting that Hootum's *Sketches* deserved a far wider audience than it has had so far, being a milestone work in the lead-up to the arrival of modernism in Indian literature. The text had been in existence for nearly one hundred and fifty years, but the general feeling among some of the prospective publishers and magazine editors we talked to was that *Hootum* was 'untranslatable'. It is, primarily, and ultimately, to Amit's unwavering faith in Hootum's overriding significance as a pioneer of modern Bengali prose who deserved a go at translation, even if it were just for the record, that I owe this book. I hope I have, at least to an extent, been able to live up to the very generous attributes he has conferred on this translation in his remarkable Foreword.

Thanks are due to Mandira Sen of Stree-Samya for taking on this project that is both daring and daunting. I thank her colleague Madhuparna Banerjee for her meticulous work on the text. I am grateful to Anusua Mukherjee for her discerning comments and suggestions that have brought greater clarity to the translation. I thank Soumitra Das whose books on Calcutta were consulted by me and Chandrima Bhattacharya who kindly lent me her copies of books on Calcutta.

I would also like to thank Penguin for kindly allowing me to use the extracts published in *Memory's Gold* in this edition, albeit with several changes and updates.

Thanks to Naveen Kishore of Seagull for very generously lending some of their publications, most notably Sumanta Banerjee's *The Parlour and the Street,* as reference material.

I would also like to acknowledge the contribution of Arun Nag—whom I've never met—in producing the most complete annotated edition of *Hootum Pyanchar Naksha* (Subarnarekha/ Ananda), which served as my primary source text. Without his work to refer to, it would have been an even more arduous journey, negotiating the bends in Hootum's labyrinth.

My parents, Mitra and Bikas Basu, had a role in the making of this book, and not just because they introduced me to the treasures that lay embedded in printed words, which they did well before I could actually read. Even after several readings of Hootum over months, probably years, there were still a few things in the text whose meaning I was not sure of. In the time-honoured tradition of Bengali parents who would happily hold the hands of their children in a moment of crisis—even if the child in question was well past adolescence—my parents gave me an afternoon when we sat together, trying to get as close as possible to the intended meanings of some of the most confounding words in the text. My mother's familiarity with Sanskrit and my father's sustained curiosity about etymology and the backstage drama that often informs the theatre of the evolution of a language came in handy.

My friend Rinku Chatterjee is probably the first person to read my introduction to this book in its draft stage and rather ruthlessly tore it apart—quite deservedly so. I am extremely lucky to have her continued support and affection.

Arunava Sinha, who gave me my first commission as a translator for the now-defunct *Calcutta Skyline,* also exposed me to the tantalizing pull of the texts that resist translation and the joy of being able to connect with and convey these, the most obstinate words, in a different cultural context. Thanks are due to him for acquainting me with the challenges and thrills of this war without violence.

Besides the people I have mentioned, several others—friends, acquaintances, readers of the published extracts—have at different points in time shown eagerness and, in some cases, concern over this project which has been a little too long in the making. I am extremely touched by the range of emotions this book has generated even before getting published.

Index